MICROSOFT

FrontPage 2000

Complete Concepts and Techniques

Gary B. Shelly
Thomas J. Cashman
Michael L. Mick

COURSE TECHNOLOGY
ONE MAIN STREET
CAMBRIDGE MA 02142

Thomson Learning™

SHELLY
CASHMAN
SERIES®

Australia • Canada • Denmark • Japan • Mexico • New Zealand • Philippines
Puerto Rico • Singapore • South Africa • Spain • United Kingdom • United States

"Microsoft and the Microsoft Office User Specialist Logo are registered trademarks of Microsoft Corporation in the United States and other countries. Course Technology is an independent entity from Microsoft Corporation, and not affiliated with Microsoft Corporation in any manner. This textbook may be used in assisting students to prepare for a Microsoft Office User Specialist Exam. Neither Microsoft Corporation, its designated review company, nor Course Technology warrants that use of this textbook will ensure passing the relevant Exam.

"Use of the Microsoft Office User Specialist Approved Courseware Logo on this product signifies that it has been independently reviewed and approved in complying with the following standards: 'Acceptable coverage of all content related to the Microsoft Office Exam entitled "Microsoft FrontPage 2000 Core Exam," and sufficient performance-based exercises that relate closely to all required content, based on sampling of text."

PHOTO CREDITS: *Project 1, pages FP 1.4-5* Fountain pen, eye glasses, www text, man and woman at computer, Courtesy of PhotoDisc, Inc.; Alex Haley, Courtesy of Christian Vioujard/The Gamma Liaison Network; Allen Ginsberg, Courtesy of UPI/ Corbis-Bettman; Ernest Hemingway, Courtesy of Archive Photos; *Project 2, pages FP 2.2-3* Robert Schumann, Courtesy of North Wind Picture Archives; Bedrich Smetana, Courtesy of Culver Pictures; pen, crumpled paper, Courtesy of KPT Metatools; parchment, conductor, musical notes, Courtesy of PhotoDisc, Inc.; small photo images, Courtesy of Expert Software; *Project 3, pages FP 3.2-3* Woman with laptop, Courtesy of PhotoDisc Inc.; camel, cloud button, Courtesy of Corel Professional Photos CD-ROM Image usage, calculator, disks, Courtesy of KPT Metatools; Tim Berners-Lee, World Wide Web Consortium Web site, © 1999 W3C © (MIT, INRIA, Keio) All Rights Reserved, used with permission; *Project 4, pages 4.4-5* Personal photos, Courtesy of Course Technology employees; *Project 5, pages 5.4-5* Globe, Courtesy of Map Art by Cartesia Software.

ISBN 0-7895-5613-8

5 6 7 8 9 10   BC   04 03 02 01

MICROSOFT

FrontPage 2000

Complete Concepts and Techniques

C O N T E N T S

Preface

The Shelly Cashman Series® offers the finest textbooks in computer education. We are proud of the fact that our Internet-related textbooks have been the most widely used in education. Each edition of our Internet-related textbooks have included innovations, many based on comments made by the instructors and students who use our books. The *Microsoft FrontPage 2000* books continue with the innovation, quality, and reliability that you have come to expect from the Shelly Cashman Series.

In our *Microsoft FrontPage 2000* books, you will find an educationally sound and easy-to-follow pedagogy that combines a step-by-step approach with corresponding screens. All projects and exercises in this book are designed to take full advantage of the FrontPage 2000 enhancements. The popular Other Ways and More About features offer in-depth knowledge of FrontPage 2000. The project openers provide a fascinating perspective of the subject covered in the project. The project material is developed carefully to ensure that students will see the importance of learning FrontPage 2000 for future course work.

Objectives of This Textbook

Microsoft FrontPage 2000: Complete Concepts and Techniques is intended for a two- or three-unit course that presents Microsoft FrontPage 2000. Neither World Wide Web nor Internet experience is necessary. Specific objectives of this book are as follows:

- To teach students how to use Microsoft FrontPage 2000
- To expose students to proper Web page design techniques
- To provide an introduction to managing collections of related Web pages
- To expose students to common Web page formats and functions
- To encourage curiosity and independent exploration of World Wide Web resources
- To develop an exercise-oriented approach that allows students to learn by example
- To encourage independent study and help those who are learning about the Internet on their own in a distance education environment

Approved by Microsoft as Courseware for the Microsoft Office User Specialist Program – Core Level

This book has been approved by Microsoft as courseware for the Microsoft Office User Specialist (MOUS) program. After completing the projects and exercises in this book, students will be prepared to take the Core-level Microsoft Office User Specialist Exam for Microsoft FrontPage 2000. By passing the certification exam for a Microsoft software application, students demonstrate their proficiency in that application to employers. This exam is offered at participating centers, participating corporations, and participating employment agencies.

The Shelly Cashman Series Microsoft Office User Specialist Center Web page at www.scsite.com/off2000/cert.htm has more than fifteen links to Web pages you can visit to obtain additional information on the MOUS certification program, or visit the Web site at www.mous.net. The Shelly Cashman Series Microsoft Office User Specialist Center Web page includes links to general information on certification, choosing an application for certification, preparing for the certification exam, and taking and passing the certification exam. You also can click the FrontPage 2000 Skill Sets link to obtain a list of the skill sets and page numbers in the book where you can learn about each skill.

The Shelly Cashman Approach

- Project Orientation, Step-by-Step Approach: Practical problems with complete solutions. Tasks are presented with a resulting full-color screen after each step.
- Thoroughly Tested Projects: Every screen in the book is correct because it is produced by the author only after performing a step.
- Other Ways Boxes: The steps and the Other Ways box make a comprehensive reference unit.
- More About Feature: These marginal annotations provide background information that complements the topics covered, adding depth and perspective.
- Integration of the World Wide Web: (1) More Abouts that send students to Web sites for up-to-date information and alternative approaches to tasks; (2) a MOUS information Web page (www.scsite.com/off2000/cert.htm) and a MOUS map Web page; (3) a FrontPage 2000 Quick Reference Summary Web page; and (4) project reinforcement Web pages with student activities.

Other **Ways**

1. On Frames menu click Frame Properties, type new size values
2. Right-click frame, click Frame Properties on shortcut menu, type new size values
3. Press ALT+R, P, type new size values

More *About* 2000

Positioning Form Fields

As you insert form fields in a form, it is best to preview the page in a browser to determine form field positioning. This is especially true for wide text fields that cannot be wrapped. They may display on a different line when editing, yet display on the same line in the browser.

Organization of This Textbook

Microsoft FrontPage 2000: Complete Concepts and Techniques is comprised of five projects and an appendix that introduces students to creating and publishing Web pages. The projects are organized as follows:

Project 1 – Creating a FrontPage Web Using a Template   In Project 1, students are introduced to HTML and the FrontPage environment, and learn how to use FrontPage templates. Students create a simple three-page web consisting of a Home page, an Interests page, and a Favorites page. Topics include basic Web page editing and customization techniques; changing the templates; and saving, printing, publishing the Web pages to an available Web server, using a browser to view the Web pages.

Project 2 – Creating a New FrontPage Web   In Project 2, students learn how to create a new FrontPage web. Topics include basic Web page design criteria; setting up the page background; inserting tables and images; adding, replacing, and applying special formatting features to text; and adding linked targets to the page.

Project 3 – Using Images, Hotspots, Bookmarks, and Excel to Create Web Pages   In Project 3, students are introduced to techniques for using graphics and images in Web pages. Topics include opening an existing FrontPage web; displaying and using the Pictures toolbar to apply formatting to images; setting up a tiled background image; assigning a hyperlink to an image; creating an image map and assigning URLs to the image map hotspots; highlighting hotspots on an image map; copying and pasting objects from another Web page; displaying the hyperlinks in a FrontPage web; inserting bookmarks and using bookmarks as targets of a link; previewing a FrontPage web in a browser; and using an Excel worksheet in a Web page.

Project 4 – Creating and Using Interactive Forms on the Web   In Project 4, students are introduced to interactive forms. After learning the basics of forms, form handlers, and form data formats, students create a Web page with a form consisting of the most-used form fields. Topics include inserting a form in a Web page; inserting a table in a form; inserting a form in a table; creating a nested table; inserting radio buttons, drop-down menus, text boxes and check boxes in a form; adjusting form field properties; assigning text as a form field label; and choosing a form handler. Students also learn to manage files in Folders view and modify HTML code in FrontPage.

Project 5 – Using Frames in Web Pages In Project 5, students are introduced to frames Web pages. Topics include how frames work; using a frames template; saving frames Web pages; creating an initial Web page for a frame; adjusting the size of frames; modifying properties of a frame and of a frames page; creating hyperlinks to pages in frames; using an existing Web page as the initial page in a frame; opening the target of a hyperlink in a different frame; printing Web pages in frames; and displaying the No Frames view. Students learn how to use Find and Replace across a Web site; use the reporting features of FrontPage; and verify hyperlinks in a Web. Students create a thumbnail image from a larger image; add a bevel effect to an image; use a Word document as a URL; and import Web resources into an existing FrontPage web.

Appendix A Microsoft FrontPage 2000 Help System Appendix A presents a detailed step-by-step introduction to the Microsoft FrontPage Help system. Students learn how to use the Contents, Answer Wizard, and Index sheets in the FrontPage Help window. The Appendix includes Use Help exercises to help students gain confidence.

End-of-Project Activities

A notable strength of the Shelly Cashman Series *Microsoft FrontPage 2000* books is the extensive student activities at the end of each project. Well-structured student activities can make the difference between students merely participating in a class and students retaining the information they learn. The activities include the following.

- **What You Should Know** A listing of the tasks completed within a project together with the pages where the step-by-step, screen-by-screen explanations appear. This section provides a perfect study review for students.

- **Project Reinforcement on the Web** Every project has a Web page (www.scsite.com/off2000/reinforce.htm). The Web page includes true/false, multiple choice, and short answer questions, and additional project-related reinforcement activities that will help students gain confidence in their FrontPage 2000 abilities.

- **Apply Your Knowledge** This exercise requires students to open and manipulate a file on the Data Disk. To obtain a copy of the Data Disk, follow the instructions on the inside back cover of this book.

- **In the Lab** Three in-depth assignments per project require students to apply the knowledge gained in the project to solve problems on a computer.

- **Cases and Places** Up to seven unique case studies that require students to apply their knowledge to real-world situations.

Shelly Cashman Series Teaching Tools

A comprehensive set of Teaching Tools accompanies this textbook in the form of a CD-ROM. The CD-ROM includes an Instructor's Manual and teaching and testing aids. The CD-ROM (ISBN 0-7895-5628-6) is available through your Course Technology representative or by calling one of the following telephone numbers: Colleges and Universities, 1-800-648-7450; High Schools, 1-800-824-5179; Career Colleges, 1-800-477-3692; Canada, 1-800-268-2222; and Corporations and Government Agencies, 1-800-340-7450.

- **Instructor's Manual** The Instructor's Manual is made up of Microsoft Word files that include lecture notes, solutions to laboratory assignments, and a large test bank. The files allow you to modify the lecture notes or generate quizzes and exams. The Instructor's Manual includes project objectives and overview; detailed lesson plans with page number references; teacher notes and activities;

answers to the end-of-project exercises; test bank of 110 questions for every project (25 multiple-choice, 50 true/false, and 35 fill-in-the-blank) with page number references; and transparency references. The test bank questions are numbered the same as in Course Test Manager. Print a copy of the project test bank and use the printout to select your questions in Course Test Manager.

- **Figures in the Book** Illustrations for every screen and table in the textbook are available in JPEG format. Use this ancillary to create a slide show from the illustrations for lecture or to print transparencies for use in lecture.

- **Course Test Manager** Course Test Manager is a powerful testing and assessment package that enables instructors to create and print tests from the large test bank. Instructors with access to a networked computer lab (LAN) can administer, grade, and track tests online.

- **Course Syllabus** Any instructor who has been assigned a course at the last minute knows how difficult it is to come up with a course syllabus. For this reason, sample syllabi are included for each of the FrontPage 2000 products that can be customized easily to a course.

- **Lecture Success System** Lecture Success System files are for use with the application software, a personal computer, and projection device to explain and illustrate the step-by-step, screen-by-screen development of a project in the textbook without entering large amounts of data.

- **Instructor's Lab Solutions** Solutions and required files for all the In the Lab assignments at the end of each project are available.

- **Project Reinforcement** True/false, multiple choice, and short answer questions, and additional project-related reinforcement activities for each project.

- **Student Files** All the files that are required by students to complete the Apply Your Knowledge exercises are included.

- **Interactive Labs** Eighteen interactive hands-on labs that take students from ten to fifteen minutes each to step through help solidify and reinforce mouse and keyboard usage and computer concepts. Student assessment is available.

- **WebCT Content** This ancillary includes book-related content that can be uploaded to your institution's WebCT site. The content includes a sample syllabus, practice tests, a bank of test questions, a list of book-related links.

Acknowledgments

The Shelly Cashman Series would not be the leading computer education series without the contributions of outstanding publishing professionals. First, and foremost, among them is Becky Herrington, director of production and designer. She is the heart and soul of the Shelly Cashman Series, and it is only through her leadership, dedication, and tireless efforts that superior products are made possible. Becky created and produced the award-winning Windows series of books.

Under Becky's direction, the following individuals made significant contributions to these books: Doug Cowley, production manager; Ginny Harvey, series specialist and developmental editor; Ken Russo, senior Web designer; Mike Bodnar, associate production manager; Stephanie Nance, graphic artist and cover designer; Mark Norton, Web designer; Meena Mohtadi, production editor; Chris Schneider, Hector Arvizu, and Kathy Mayers, graphic artists; Jeanne Black and Betty Hopkins, Quark experts; Lyn Markowicz, copyeditor; Kim Kosmatka and Pat Hadden proofreaders; Cristina Haley, indexer; and Susan Sebok and Ginny Harvey, contributing writers.

Special thanks go to Richard Keaveny, managing editor; Jim Quasney, series consulting editor; Lora Wade, product manager; Erin Bennett, associate product manager; Francis Schurgot, Web product manager; Marc Ouellette, associate Web product manager; Rajika Gupta, marketing manager; and Erin Runyon, editorial assistant.

Gary B. Shelly
Thomas J. Cashman
Michael L. Mick

MICROSOFT
FrontPage 2000

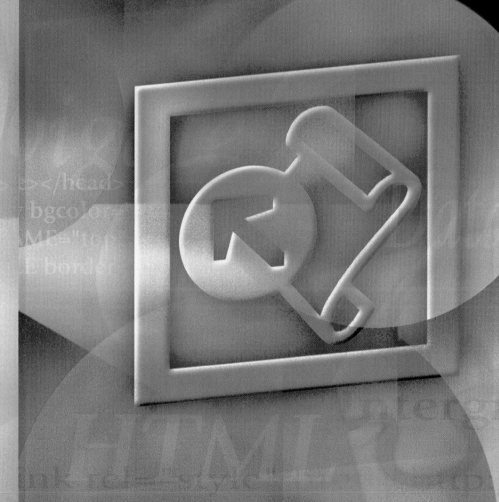

Microsoft **FrontPage 2000**

Microsoft FrontPage 2000

PROJECT 1

Creating a FrontPage Web Using a Template

Web Authors
Create Award-Winning Sites

Initially, these three best-selling authors, Allen Ginsberg, American poet known as the spokesman for the Beat Generation; Ernest Hemingway, American novelist and short-story writer whose style is characterized by crispness, concise dialog, and emotional understatement; and Alex Haley, American author who helped popularize the study of black history and genealogy, appear to have little in common with each other or with authoring Web pages as you will do in this project. The three authors wrote unique works for distinct audiences at historical literary moments. Yet, despite these apparent differences, each author was highly regarded for his literary contribution. These authors shared a common trait: editors had the final say in the design of their books.

As an author of Web pages, you have the opportunity to make your contribution in Web publishing circles. As well as providing appeal and interest for Web page visitors, you can offer functionality and purpose for sites you develop. You are an author of a unique work in the online age of Web publishing. In your case, you are the writer and the editor of your own work.

In traditional publishing, an author writes a manuscript and an editor suggests content changes and marks up the pages with instructions for layout. The designer, in conjunction with the markups, lays out the pages accordingly. Adjustments are made by the editor and author, and the designer revises the layout until it is complete.

In traditional Web page publishing, the author writes a text file and marks up the words with special HTML (hypertext markup language) character sequences, called tags, to indicate the various formatting features. HTML tags begin and end with brackets (< and >) and usually come in pairs to indicate the beginning and end of a formatting feature such as headings, bulleted lists, placement of inline images, hyperlinks to other pages, and more. HTML is a coding scheme that can be interpreted by a Web browser, such as Internet Explorer. Creating Web pages by writing HTML can be tedious and confusing, but a basic understanding of the process is valuable.

As an HTML document stored on an Internet server, a Web page can be retrieved and displayed on a computer with a Web browser. The HTML tags specify how the Web page displays and indicates links to other documents. These links to other documents are called hyperlinks. Hyperlinks can be text, graphics, sound, or other media. Text links are known as hypertext.

The Web page creation capabilities of Microsoft FrontPage 2000 are designed for both experienced and beginning Web site developers with a simple yet powerful tool for designing and building great-looking, easy-to-navigate World Wide Web sites.

With FrontPage, Web pages are constructed in an environment similar to word processing that requires no programming knowledge. For example, formatting attributes such as fonts, borders, and bulleted lists look very close to the way they display in your browser, and many features and options are available using familiar elements such as toolbars, dialog boxes, and templates.

This project illustrates using a template to create a FrontPage web. Web site design is a complex process. You are required to make decisions related to the structure and theme of the Web site and the appearance and content of each Web page. Templates help organize and format the Web pages in a site using a consistent framework.

Authors interact with their audience through their characters and stories. As an aspiring Web page author, you can use your Web page to interact with your audience by including hyperlinks and e-mail capabilities. Everything you need and more to develop an award-winning site is available to you in FrontPage 2000, with the added advantage of being the author, editor, designer, and publisher.

Microsoft FrontPage 2000

Microsoft FrontPage 2000

Creating a FrontPage Web Using a Template

PROJECT 1

CASE PERSPECTIVE

For the past month, you have worked as a buyer at The First Draft, a busy art and drafting supplies store. The three-year old company is growing rapidly, and the recent launch of its Web site has fueled additional sales.

The First Draft's CEO, Sean Christopher, is delighted with the company's growth, and he wants the company to maintain its startup culture, in which employees are encouraged to be innovative and challenge tradition. To encourage the staff's creativity, Sean established a section on The First Draft's Web site where staff members can publish personal Web pages. He then outlined basic content and format guidelines to help ensure consistency across the Web site. The guidelines specify that personal Web pages should include at least three pages: a Home page introducing the developer; an Interests page listing outside interests; and a Favorites page including links to favorite Web sites. The guidelines also request that employees format the Web pages using FrontPage's Blueprint theme.

Yesterday, Sean sent you an e-mail message, encouraging you to develop and publish your personal Web pages.

What Is Microsoft FrontPage 2000?

Microsoft FrontPage 2000 is a Web page authoring and site management program that allows you to create and manage professional quality Web sites without programming. Microsoft FrontPage offers two key types of functionality, including:

▶ **Web page creation**   Microsoft FrontPage allows you to create and edit Web pages without needing to know HTML or other programming languages. FrontPage includes many features that make Web page creation easy, such as templates, graphics, and more.

▶ **Web site management**   Microsoft FrontPage allows you to view Web pages, publish them to the World Wide Web, and manage existing Web sites. Using FrontPage, you can test and repair hyperlinks on a Web page, view all of the files and folders on a site, import and export files, and more.

Project One — Personal Web Pages

From your discussion with Sean and your review of the staff's existing personal Web pages, you determined the following needs, formatting requirements, and content requirements.

Needs: A group of related Web pages, referred to as a **web** in Microsoft FrontPage, that includes three Web pages: a Home page, an Interests page, and a Favorites page. The Home page introduces you to site visitors (Figure 1-1a); the Interests page outlines your hobbies and interests (Figure 1-1b); and the Favorites page includes links to three Web sites, including your favorite art site (Figure 1-1c). The Home page includes links to the other two pages in the FrontPage web. Once complete, you will publish the web to make it available for viewing on the World Wide Web.

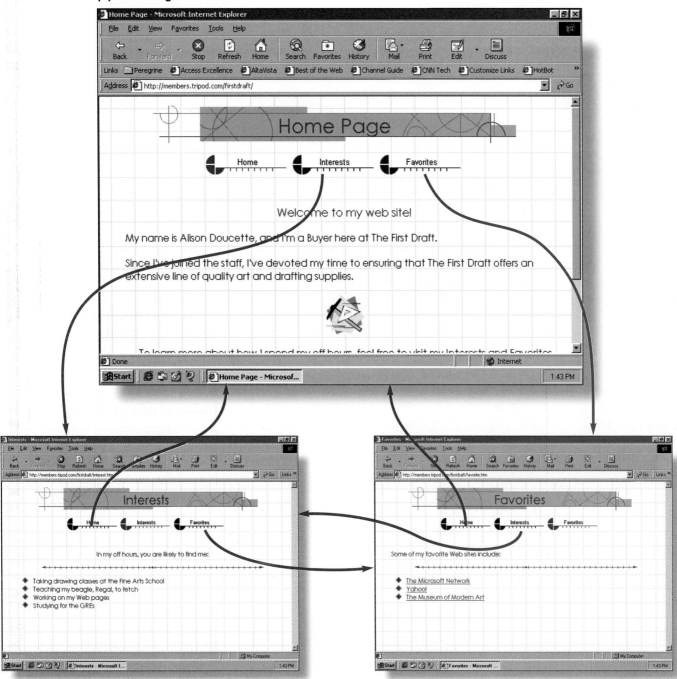

(a) Home Page

(b) Interests Page

(c) Favorites Page

FIGURE 1-1

Formatting Requirements: To create the Web pages, you will use the Personal Web template included in FrontPage. The Web pages then should be formatted using the Blueprint theme included in FrontPage. The Home page should include at least one inline image, which is a separate graphic file that is merged into the page as it displays.

Content Requirements: The Home page lists your name, your position at The First Draft, and provides an e-mail address so customers can contact you. The Interests page includes a minimum of four activities that you pursue outside of work. The Favorites page includes links to at least three Web sites, one of which is an art-related site.

More *About*

World Wide Web Basics

To learn general techniques related to authoring Web pages, visit the Shelly Cashman Series Web Design Techniques Web page at www.scsite.com/web/ SCWebDes.htm and then click Authoring, Programming, Graphics, and more.

World Wide Web Basics

The **World Wide Web** (**WWW**), often simply referred to as the **Web**, consists of a worldwide collection of electronic documents that have built-in links to other related documents. Each of these electronic documents on the Web is called a **Web page**; a Web page can contain text, graphics, sound, and video, as well as connections to other documents. These connections to other documents, called **hyperlinks,** or **links**, allow you to move quickly from one document to another, regardless of whether the documents are located on the same computer or on different computers in different countries.

A collection of related Web pages that you can access electronically is called a **Web site**. Most Web sites have a starting point, called a **home page**, which is similar to a book cover or table of contents for the site and provides information about the site's purpose and content. In a Personal web, for example, the home page will list your name, your position at The First Draft, and your e-mail address.

Hypertext Markup Language (HTML)

A Web page is a file that contains both text and hypertext markup language (HTML). **Hypertext markup language (HTML)** is a formatting language that tells the browser how to display text and images; how to set up list boxes, hyperlinks, and other elements; and how to include graphics, sound, video, and other multimedia on a Web page.

HTML uses a set of special instructions called **tags** to define the characteristics of items such as formatted text, images, hyperlinks, lists, and forms. HTML tags are used throughout the text document to indicate (or mark) how these items should display and function when viewed as a Web page in a browser. Browsers are discussed in the next section. HTML thus is considered a **markup language**, because the HTML tags mark elements in the text file.

Although HTML includes hundreds of tags, most Web developers use only a small subset of these tags when building a Web page. Table 1-1 lists some commonly used HTML tags and an explanation of their functions.

Table 1-1 Common HTML Tags

HTML TAG	FUNCTION
<HTML> </HTML>	Indicates the beginning and end of a Web document.
<HEAD> </HEAD>	Indicates the beginning and end of the header section of a Web document (used for the title and other document header information).
<TITLE> </TITLE>	Indicates the beginning and end of the Web page title. The title displays on the title bar of the browser, not in the body of the Web page itself.
<BODY> </BODY>	Indicates the beginning and end of the main section (body) of the Web page.
<Hn> </Hn>	Indicates the beginning and end of a section of text called a heading, which uses a larger font than normal text. In the tag, <Hn>, n indicates the size of the heading font; sizes range from <H1> through <H6>.
<P></P>	Indicates the beginning of a new paragraph; inserts a blank line above the new paragraph. The end tag </P> is optional. It will insert a blank line below the new paragraph, unless followed by a new paragraph.
<B> </B>	Indicates the beginning and end of a section of bold text.
<I> </I>	Indicates the beginning and end of a section of italic text.
<U> </U>	Indicates the beginning and end of a section of underlined text.
<UL> </UL>	Indicates the beginning and end of an unordered (bulleted) list.
<OL></OL>	Indicates the beginning and end of an ordered (numbered) list.
<LI> </LI>	Indicates that the item in the tag is an item within a list.
<HR>	Inserts a horizontal rule.
<A> </A>	Indicates the beginning and end of a hyperlink.
HREF="URL"	Indicates a hyperlink to a file in the location specified by the URL in quotation marks.
<IMG SRC="URL">	Inserts an inline image in the page. The URL in quotation marks specifies the location of the image.
<CENTER> </CENTER>	Indicates that the text, graphic, or other elements between the tags should display centered on the Web page.
<LEFT> </LEFT>	Indicates that the text, graphic, or other elements between the tags should display left aligned on the Web page.
<RIGHT> </RIGHT>	Indicates that the text, graphic, or other elements between the tags should display right aligned on the Web page.

Defining the type and layout of an element on a Web page requires one or more HTML tags. As shown in Table 1-1, HTML tags begin with the less than sign (<) and end with the greater than sign (>). Tags may be entered as either uppercase or lowercase. Tags often are used in pairs to indicate the beginning and end of an element or format. The end tag contains a forward slash (/). The tag, <B>, for example, indicates the beginning of a section of bold text, and </B> indicates the end of a section of bold text. To display the text, World Wide Web, as bold text, you would type the tags as follows:

```
<B>World Wide Web</B>
```

You also can use tags in combination to apply multiple formatting features to text or other Web page elements. The tag

```
<CENTER><B>World Wide Web</B></CENTER>
```

for example, would center the words on the page. If you use HTML tags in combination, as in the example above, be sure to place the end tags in an order opposite that of the beginning tags.

HTML tags can contain keywords that further define the appearance of the element created by the tag. Keywords take the form

```
keyword=value
```

where keyword is an HTML tag describing a characteristic of a Web page element and value is one of a range of numbers or words describing that characteristic. Instead of using the CENTER tag to center text on the page, for instance, you can use the keyword, ALIGN, and the value, CENTER. The tag, which you can use within another tag, might display as

```
<B ALIGN=CENTER>My Favorite Web Sites</B>
```

The tag tells the browser to display the text in bold and center the text on the page.

All of these elements are defined using HTML tags. The HTML used to create a Web page is called the **HTML source**, or **source code**. Figure 1-2 on the next page shows the HTML source for the Web page displayed in Figure 1-1c on page FP 1-7.

More About

HTML

To learn HTML basics, visit the Shelly Cashman Series Web Design Techniques Web page at www.scsite.com/web/SCWebDes.htm and then click HTML Basics.

Microsoft **FrontPage 2000**

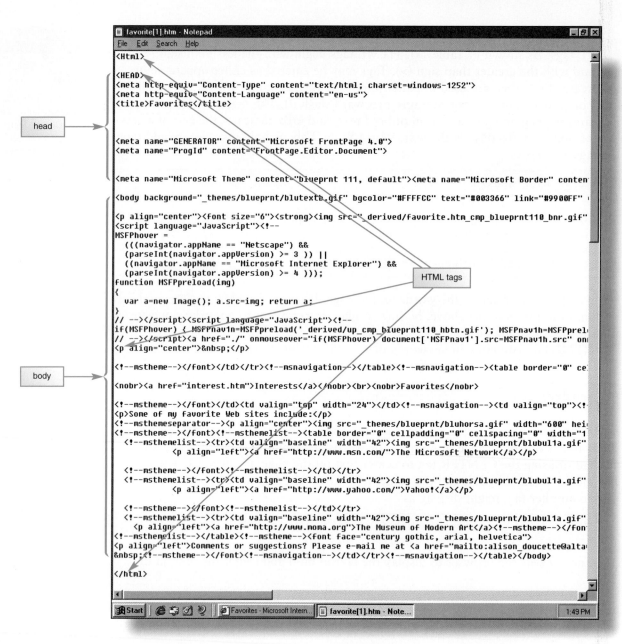

FIGURE 1-2

Most Web browsers allow you to view the HTML source for the Web page currently displayed in the browser window. If you are using Internet Explorer, for example, you can click the **Source command** on the View menu to display the HTML source.

Many HTML tags exist to help you design a Web page exactly as you want. When using FrontPage to develop Web pages, you do not need to know every HTML tag. Instead, you simply determine the best way to convey the information and then make those changes on the Web page using FrontPage commands. FrontPage inserts the appropriate HTML code for you.

Web Browsers

You access and view Web pages using a software program called a Web browser. A **Web browser**, also simply called a **browser**, is a software program that requests a Web page, interprets the HTML codes and text used to create the page, and then displays the Web page on your computer screen. Today, the two more popular browsers are **Microsoft Internet Explorer** and **Netscape Navigator** (Figure 1-3a and 1-3b). Browsers have special buttons and other features to help you navigate through Web sites.

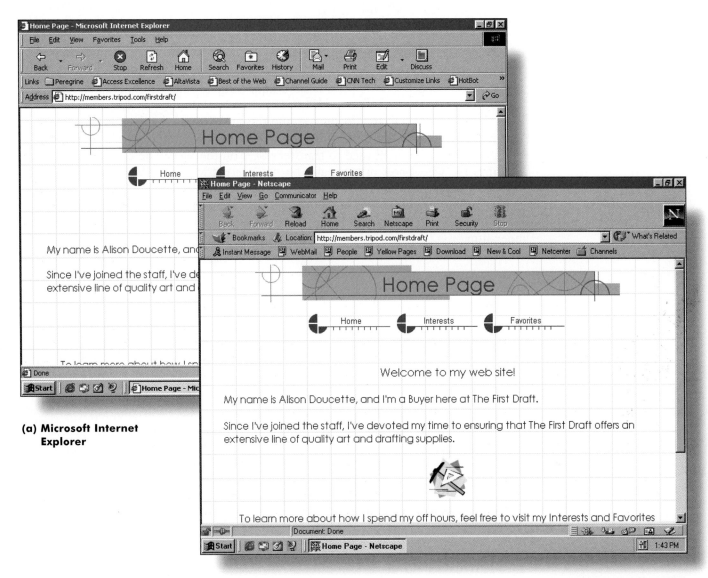

(a) Microsoft Internet Explorer

(b) Netscape Navigator

FIGURE 1-3

Different browsers will display the same Web page with slight variations. Netscape Navigator, for example, may display fonts, hyperlinks, tables, and other Web page elements in a manner different from Microsoft Internet Explorer. When developing a Web site, you should test the Web pages using Netscape Navigator, Microsoft Internet Explorer, and any other browsers your audience might use to ensure that the Web pages display correctly in the various browsers.

The Web pages that comprise a Web site are stored on a server, called a Web server. A **Web server**, or **host**, is a computer that delivers (serves) requested Web pages. Every Web site is stored on and runs from one or more Web servers; a Web server can have thousands of Web pages available for viewing. Multiple Web sites also can be stored on the same Web server. For example, many Internet service providers grant their subscribers storage space on a Web server for their personal or company Web sites. Each Web page on the Web site is comprised of one or more files that are stored on the hard disk of the Web server or other computer.

Testing Pages in Browsers

When testing Web pages in various browsers, you may want to test the pages in several versions of the same browser (usually the two most recent versions). You might, for example, test your Web pages in Netscape Navigator 4.5 and 5 and Microsoft Internet Explorer 4 and 5. You should consider if you need to test the pages on PC and Macintosh platforms.

A Web server runs **Web server software** that allows it to receive the requests for Web pages and sends the pages over the Internet to your browser, so you can view them on your computer. For example, when you enter a Web page address in your browser, your browser sends a request to the server; the server then uses the Web server software to fetch the Web page and send it to your browser.

Uniform Resource Locators (URLs)

Each Web page on a Web site has a unique address called a **Uniform Resource Locator** (**URL**). As shown in Figure 1-4, a URL consists of a protocol, a domain name, the path to a specific document, and the file name of the document. Most Web page URLs begin with **http://**, which stands for **hypertext transfer protocol**, the communications protocol used to transfer pages on the Web. The **domain name** identifies the Web server or computer on the Internet where the Web document is located. The **path** and **file name** indicate where the Web document is stored on the computer. In the URL shown in Figure 1-4, for example, the domain name is www.nationalgeographic.com, the path to the file is /ngm/, and the file name is index.htm.

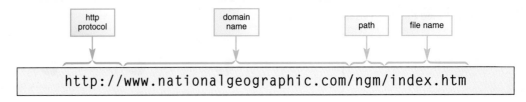

FIGURE 1-4

Each hyperlink on a Web page is associated with a URL, thus making it possible for you to navigate the Web using hyperlinks. When you click a hyperlink on a Web page, you are issuing a request to display the Web document specified by the URL. If, for example, you click a hyperlink associated with the URL, http://www.scsite.com/index.htm, your browser sends a request to the server whose domain name is www.scsite.com. The server then fetches the page named index.htm and sends it to your computer, where the browser displays it on your screen.

Elements of a Web Page

Although Web pages can be as distinctive and unique as the individuals who create them, almost every Web page has several basic features, or **elements**. Web page elements include basic features such as the background, text, hyperlinks, and images; and more advanced features such as forms and frames. As you begin to view Web pages through the eyes of a Web page developer, you will notice that most Web pages use variations on one or more of the elements identified in Figures 1-5a and 1-5b.

Window Elements

The **title** of a Web page is the text that displays on the title bar of the browser window when the Web page displays. The **background** of a Web page is either a solid color or a small graphic image that provides a backdrop against which the other elements display. Like the wallpaper in Windows, a background color or graphic can be **tiled**, or repeated, across the entire page.

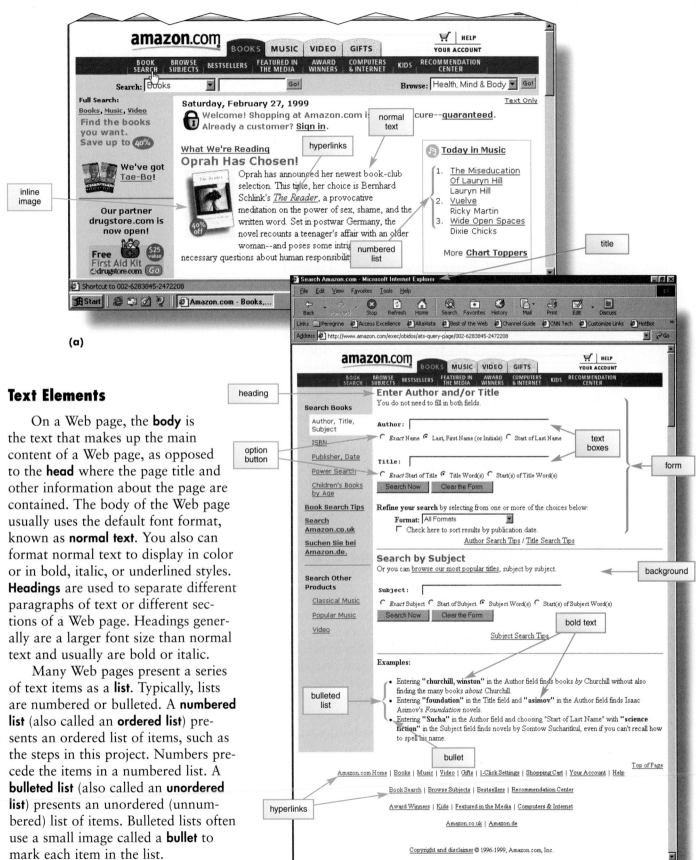

(a)

(b)

FIGURE 1-5

Text Elements

On a Web page, the **body** is the text that makes up the main content of a Web page, as opposed to the **head** where the page title and other information about the page are contained. The body of the Web page usually uses the default font format, known as **normal text**. You also can format normal text to display in color or in bold, italic, or underlined styles. **Headings** are used to separate different paragraphs of text or different sections of a Web page. Headings generally are a larger font size than normal text and usually are bold or italic.

Many Web pages present a series of text items as a **list**. Typically, lists are numbered or bulleted. A **numbered list** (also called an **ordered list**) presents an ordered list of items, such as the steps in this project. Numbers precede the items in a numbered list. A **bulleted list** (also called an **unordered list**) presents an unordered (unnumbered) list of items. Bulleted lists often use a small image called a **bullet** to mark each item in the list.

Hyperlink Elements

A **hyperlink**, or **link**, is an area of the page that you click to instruct the browser to go to a location in a file or to request a file from a Web server. On the World Wide Web, hyperlinks are the primary way to navigate between pages and among Web sites. Links not only point to Web pages, but also to graphics, sound, multimedia, e-mail addresses, program files, and other parts of the same Web page. Text hyperlinks are the most commonly used hyperlinks. When text is used to identify a hyperlink, it usually displays as underlined text, in a color different from the regular text.

Image Elements

Web pages typically use several different types of graphics, or images. An **image** is a graphic file that can be inserted on a Web page and displayed in a Web browser. An **inline image** is an image or graphic file that is not part of the page's HTML file itself. Rather, an inline image is a separate graphic file that is merged into the page as it displays. The HTML file contains an <IMG SRC> tag that tells the browser which graphic file to request from the server, where to insert it on the page, and how to display it. Some inline images are animated, meaning they include motion and change in appearance. Inline images often are used to identify hyperlinks.

An **image map** is a special type of inline image that is divided into sections, with a hyperlink associated with each section. Clicking one of the sections, called a **hotspot**, instructs the browser to link to a Web page, graphic, sound, e-mail address, or other file.

As just described, the background of a Web page is the solid color, image, or pattern that serves as the backdrop on which text, images, hyperlinks, and other elements display on the Web page. If you use an image for the background, the image is repeated across and down the page.

Horizontal rules are lines that display across the page to separate different sections of the page. Although the appearance of a horizontal rule varies, many Web pages use an inline image as a horizontal rule.

Form, Table, and Frame Elements

A **form** is an area of a Web page that allows the viewer to enter data and information to be sent back to the Web server. Input elements within the form, such as **option buttons**, which allow for a single choice among several choices, or **text boxes**, which provide an area for the user to enter text, instruct the individual what items to enter, and how to send them to the server.

A **table** is used to present text and graphics in rows or columns. The intersection of a row and a column is called a **cell**. The text or graphic within a cell often is used as a hyperlink. The border width of the table determines the width of the grid lines surrounding the cells. When the border width is greater than zero, grid lines surround the cells. When the border width is set to zero, grid lines do not display.

A **frame** allows you to divide the display area of the browser into sections, so the browser can display a different Web page in each frame. Web pages with frames have many possible applications. You can display a table of contents for your Web site in a smaller frame, for example, while displaying different content pages in a separate main frame. Users can click hyperlinks in the smaller table of contents frame and display the linked page in the main frame.

FrontPage Webs

As previously defined, a collection of related Web pages that you can access electronically is called a Web site. A typical Web site contains one to several thousand Web pages, often with links to other pages in the same Web site and pages on separate Web sites.

In FrontPage, a group of related pages is called a **web**. A **FrontPage web** consists of the Web pages, images, and other files, folders, and programs that make up the related content that will comprise the Web site. The Web pages in a FrontPage web usually are related by topic or purpose; most webs use a series of hyperlinks to connect the related pages. A Web site may consist of one or more FrontPage webs.

When working with a web in FrontPage, the web that currently is open is called the **current web**. Once created, a FrontPage web can be stored on the computer on which FrontPage is installed or on a Web server anywhere on the World Wide Web. Using FrontPage, you can upload and download a complete web to and from your computer and a Web server. **Publishing** involves sending, or uploading, copies of Web pages, image files, and other files, folders, and programs to a server where they then are made available on the World Wide Web. To publish a FrontPage web, you must have access to a Web server to which you are allowed to upload files. As you complete this project, you will use FrontPage to develop and publish your own web to the World Wide Web.

Starting FrontPage

To learn how to develop a Web site, you will start FrontPage and then use a template to create a Personal web that introduces an individual, describes the person's hobbies and interests, and lists several favorite Web sites. To start FrontPage, Windows must be running. Perform the following steps to start FrontPage.

 To Start FrontPage

1 **Click the Start button on the taskbar and then point to Programs. Point to Microsoft FrontPage on the Programs submenu.**

The Start menu and Programs submenu display. The Microsoft FrontPage command is highlighted on the Programs submenu (Figure 1-6).

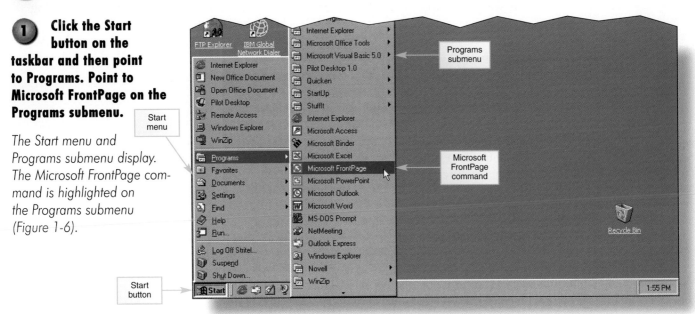

FIGURE 1-6

2 **Click Microsoft FrontPage. If necessary, click the Page icon on the Views bar.**

The Microsoft FrontPage window displays in Page view (Figure 1-7). When you first create a new web, an empty page is displayed.

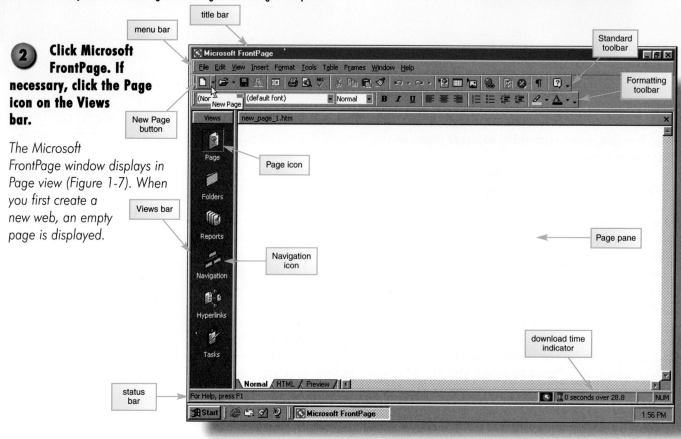

FIGURE 1-7

When you first create a new web, FrontPage displays in Page view. A **view** provides a different way of looking at the information in a web, so you can effectively manage a Web site. The selected view determines how the FrontPage window displays. For example, **Navigation view** displays a graphical representation of the web's **structure**, which is the set of relationships among the pages in a FrontPage web. A web's structure defines the overall site organization and navigation, determining which pages are linked, how many levels of pages exist, and so on. The structure of one Web site, for example, might be linear, with few levels; another site might use a hierarchical structure, with several levels of pages.

The FrontPage Window

The **FrontPage window** consists of a variety of features to help you work efficiently. It contains a title bar, status bar, menu bar, toolbars, Views bar, and a pane that displays different content, depending on the current view.

Title Bar

The **title bar** (Figure 1-7) displays the application name, Microsoft FrontPage, and the location of the current FrontPage web. If you open a web saved in the webpages folder on drive A, for example, the title bar will display the title, Microsoft FrontPage – A:\webpages.

Status Bar

The **status bar**, which is located at the bottom of the FrontPage window, consists of a message area and a download time indicator (Figure 1-7). As you are developing a page or web, the message area on the left side of the status bar displays information on file location, file name, hyperlinks, and more. The **download time indicator** displays the number of seconds it will take the page to download on the Web, based on a certain connection speed.

Menu Bar

The **menu bar** displays the FrontPage menu names (Figure 1-7). Each name represents a menu of commands that allows you to create, retrieve, edit, save, print, and publish a FrontPage web. To display a menu, such as the Format menu, click the Format menu name on the menu bar. If you point to a command with an arrow on the right, a submenu displays, from which you can choose a command.

When you click a menu name on the menu bar, a **short menu** displays listing only basic or the most recently used commands (Figure 1-8a). If you wait a few seconds or click the arrows at the bottom of the short menu (Figure 1-8a), the full menu displays. The **full menu** lists all of the commands associated with a menu (Figure 1-8b). You also can display a full menu immediately by double-clicking the menu name on the menu bar. In this book, when you display a menu, you should always display the full menu using one of the following techniques.

1. Click the menu name on the menu bar and then wait a few seconds.
2. Click the menu name and then click the arrows at the bottom of the short menu.
3. Click the menu name and then point to the arrows at the bottom of the short menu.
4. Double-click the menu name on the menu bar.

More About

Short Menus

FrontPage allows you to turn off short menus and display all of the commands on each menu all of the time on a full menu. Click Customize on the Tools menu, click the Options tab, and then clear the Menus show recently used commands first check box.

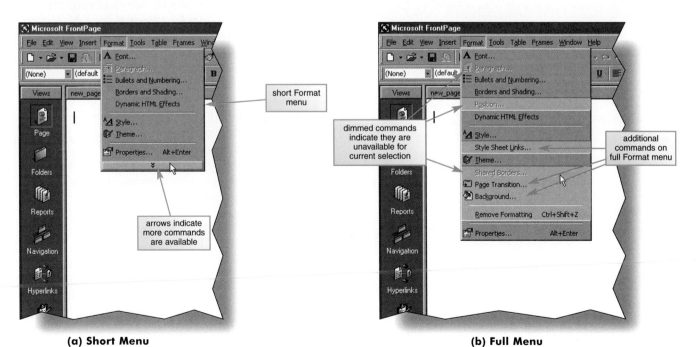

short Format menu

arrows indicate more commands are available

dimmed commands indicate they are unavailable for current selection

additional commands on full Format menu

(a) Short Menu

(b) Full Menu

FIGURE 1-8

When a full menu displays, some of the commands are recessed into a shaded gray background and others are dimmed. A recessed command is called a **hidden command** because it does not display on the short menu. As you use FrontPage, it automatically personalizes the short menus for you based on how often you use commands. That is, as you use hidden commands, FrontPage will unhide them and place them on the short menu. A **dimmed command** displays in a faint type, which indicates it is not available for the current selection.

Toolbars

A **toolbar** consists of buttons that allow you to perform tasks more quickly than when using the menu bar. To save a Web page, for example, you can click the Save button on a toolbar, instead of clicking File on the menu bar and then clicking Save on the File menu. Each button uses a graphical representation to help identify the button's function.

When you first start FrontPage, many of the buttons on the toolbars are dimmed (or grayed) to indicate that the toolbar buttons are inactive. When a button or command is **inactive**, the function performed by that button or command is not available. Once you have opened a Web page or a web, the buttons on the FrontPage toolbars are **active**, meaning you can use them to perform tasks in FrontPage. Figure 1-9a and Figure 1-9b show the buttons on each of the two toolbars that display when you open a Web page or web using FrontPage: the Standard toolbar and the Formatting toolbar. The text explains each button in detail when it is used.

More About 2000

Toolbars

FrontPage allows you to customize the toolbars so you can add the toolbar buttons you use most often and remove those you rarely use. To customize a toolbar, click the More Buttons button arrow at the end of toolbar and then select a button from the More Buttons menu. If the button you want does not display on the More Buttons menu, click the Add or Remove Buttons button and then select the check box next to the button you want to add.

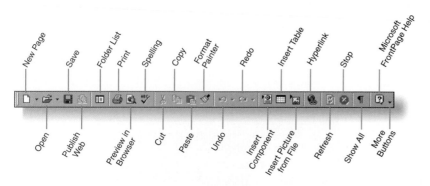

FIGURE 1-9a Standard Toolbar

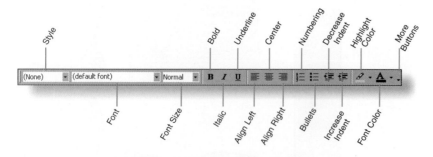

FIGURE 1-9b Formatting Toolbar

STANDARD TOOLBAR The **Standard toolbar** (Figure 1-9a) contains buttons that execute commonly used commands such as Open, Print, Save, Cut, Copy, Paste, and many more. The Standard toolbar also contains a Microsoft FrontPage Help button that you can click to start **FrontPage Help,** which is a collection of reference materials, tips, and other assistance you can access at any time while using FrontPage.

FORMATTING TOOLBAR The **Formatting toolbar** (Figure 1-9b) contains buttons used to execute commonly used formatting commands that allow you quickly to change font, font size, and alignment. It also contains buttons, such as Bold, Italic, and Underline, which allow you to change text formats and create lists.

FrontPage has several other toolbars to help you perform your work. You can display a toolbar by right-clicking any toolbar to display a shortcut menu that lists the available toolbars and then clicking the name of the toolbar you want to display. A **shortcut menu** contains a list of commands that are related to the items to which you are pointing when you right-click.

Views Bar

The **Views bar**, which is located at the left of the FrontPage window, contains icons that allow you to switch to different views of your web (Figure 1-7 on page FP 1.16). The icon indicating the selected view displays recessed on the Views bar. As previously described, a view provides a different way of looking at the information in your web so you can effectively manage your Web site. Table 1-2 identifies the icons on the Views bar and provides a description of each view.

Table 1-2	Views Bar Icons	
ICON	**VIEW**	**DESCRIPTION**
[Page]	Page	Used for creating, editing, and previewing Web pages. Page view displays Web pages as they will display in a Web browser.
[Folders]	Folders	Displays a view of a web that shows how the content of the web is organized. Similar to Windows Explorer, you can create, delete, copy, and move folders in Folders view.
[Reports]	Reports	Allows you to analyze a web's contents. You can calculate the total size of the files in your web, show which files are not linked to any other files, identify slow or outdated pages, group files by the task or person to whom the files are assigned, and so on.
[Navigation]	Navigation	Used to create, display, print, and change a web's structure and navigation. Navigation view also allows you to drag and drop pages into the web structure.
[Hyperlinks]	Hyperlinks	Displays a list showing the status of the hyperlinks in the web. The list includes both internal and external hyperlinks, and graphically indicates whether the hyperlinks have been verified or whether they are broken.
[Tasks]	Tasks	Displays a list of the tasks required to complete or maintain a web.

Using a Template to Create a FrontPage Web

Designing a Web site is a complex process that requires you to make decisions concerning the structure of the Web site and the appearance and content of each Web page within the site. When developing a web composed of several pages, for example, you should use a consistent layout and design on each page. In addition, you should be sure to link appropriate pages using a navigation that is easy to understand. To help simplify this process, FrontPage 2000 includes several wizards and preformatted webs that will help you create a set of pages for a Web site. These preformatted webs are called templates.

A FrontPage **template** is a series of Web pages that are organized and formatted with a basic framework of content upon which you can base new pages and new FrontPage webs. Each template consists of linked Web pages that already include basic elements such as headings, formatted text, images, and hyperlinks.

When you create a new web, you can choose to:

▶ Create an empty web or a web with one page
▶ Import a web from a Web server or your personal computer
▶ Create a web using a template or wizard

Table 1-3 outlines the options from which you can choose when creating a FrontPage web.

Table 1-3	FrontPage Web Options	
OPTION	*TYPE*	*DESCRIPTION*
One Page Web		Creates a FrontPage web with a single page (a home page). Used to create a FrontPage web from scratch with no suggested content.
Corporate Presence Web	Template	Creates a FrontPage web with pages tailored to an organization's Web site.
Customer Support Web	Template	Creates a FrontPage web to help organizations improve a company's online customer support, particularly for software companies.
Discussion Web Wizard	Wizard	Helps you create a discussion group with threads, a table of contents, and full-text searching.
Empty Web		Creates a FrontPage web with nothing in it. Used to create a FrontPage web from scratch with no suggested content.
Import Web Wizard	Wizard	Imports an existing web into a new FrontPage web. Starts the Import Web Wizard, which guides you through the process of importing an existing Web site.
Personal Web	Template	Creates a FrontPage web with Web pages about an individual's interests, photos, and favorite Web sites.
Project Web	Template	Creates a FrontPage web designed to support a project. The web includes pages for a list of members, a schedule, status, archive, and discussions.

After you create a page or web using a template, you can customize the page or web. To reduce the editing work required to finish your Web site, you should choose the template closest to your desired site design and structure. The following steps show how to use a template to create a FrontPage web.

 Steps ## To Use a Template to Create a FrontPage Web

1 **Click the New Page button arrow on the Standard toolbar. Point to Web on the New Page button menu.**

The New Page button menu displays with the Web command selected (Figure 1-10).

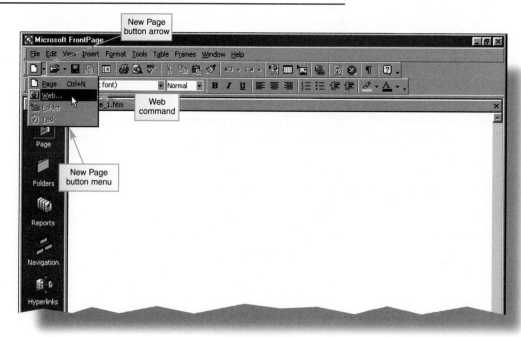

FIGURE 1-10

2 Click Web. When the New dialog box displays, click the Personal Web icon.

The New dialog box displays, prompting you for information needed to create a new FrontPage web. The Personal Web icon is highlighted; the Description area describes the web the Personal Web template creates. The Specify the location of the new web text box indicates the location where FrontPage will store the new web (Figure 1-11).

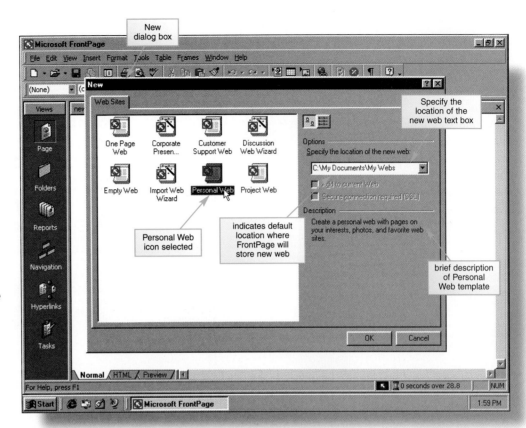

FIGURE 1-11

3 Click the Specify the location of the new web text box to highlight the default location text. Insert a floppy disk in drive A. Type a:\webpages in the text box. Point to the OK button.

The new location displays in the text box. FrontPage will save the new web in the webpages folder on the floppy disk in drive A (Figure 1-12).

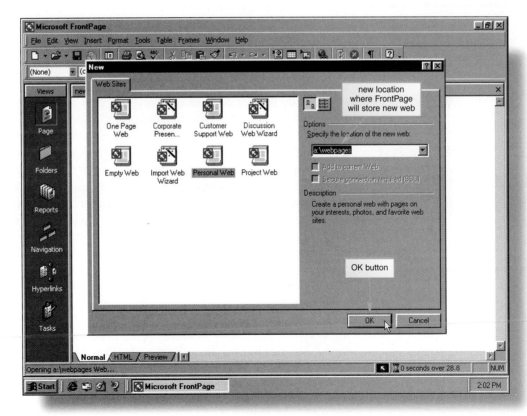

FIGURE 1-12

4 **Click the OK button.**

FrontPage begins creating a set of folders and making copies of the Web pages in the Personal Web template for you to customize. When finished, the FrontPage window displays in Page view (Figure 1-13).

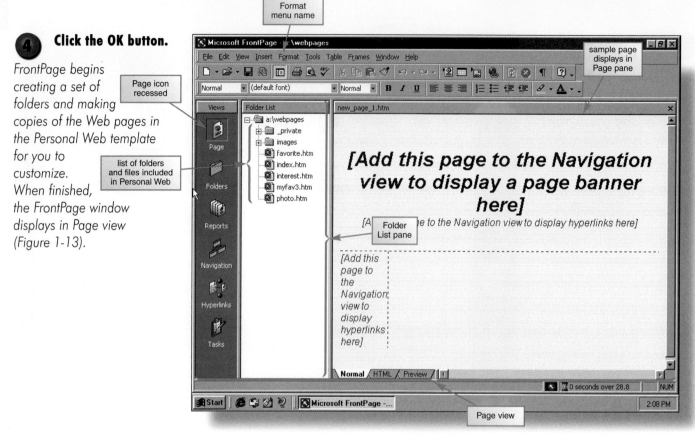

FIGURE 1-13

While FrontPage is copying the Personal Web template pages, FrontPage displays a **Create New Web dialog box** indicating that FrontPage is creating the new web in the folder, webpages, on drive A and the status of the copying process.

After making a copy of the Personal Web template pages, the FrontPage window displays in **Page view**. The Page icon on the Views bar is recessed to indicate that Page view is selected. When a web is open, Page view includes two panes: the Page pane and the Folder List pane. The **Page pane** displays the active page; the title of the active page, new_page_1.htm, displays on the title bar at the top of the Page pane. The page being edited in Page view is referred to as the **active page** or **current page**.

When you create a new web, FrontPage automatically creates certain files and folders and displays them in the Folder List pane. The **Folder List pane** lists the file names of all of the files and folders in the current FrontPage web. When you first start FrontPage, the Folder List pane lists no folders; once you open a page or web, the Folder List pane will display the file name of the Web pages, images, and other files in the web.

As shown in Figure 1-13, the Folder List pane displays the pages and folders in the current web. When you first create a new Personal web, it contains two folders: images and _private — included in the Personal web. The **images folder** holds any image files used in the FrontPage web. The **_private folder** holds files that you can use on the Web pages in the current web, but do not want people who are browsing your web to access individually. If you store a logo image in the _private folder, for example, you can use this on your Web pages, but others browsing your web cannot access the logo image. FrontPage also automatically creates a file named **index.htm** (or **default.htm**, depending on your server), which serves as the home page for your Web.

Applying a Theme to a FrontPage Web

When developing a web that consists of many pages, you should maintain a consistent, professional layout and design throughout all of the pages. The pages in a web, for example, should use similar features such as background color, margins, buttons, and headings. To help you create pages with a cohesive and professional appearance, FrontPage includes a gallery of more than 50 preset themes. A **theme** is a unified set of design elements and color schemes for bullets, fonts, graphics, navigation bars, and other page elements.

When applied to a web, a theme formats the Web page elements (images, backgrounds, text, and so on) so they share a consistent layout and design. You also have the option of applying themes to individual pages. The theme affects all aspects of a page's appearance, including text, color, and images, as follows:

▶ **Text:** A theme uses a unique set of fonts for the body text and headings.

▶ **Colors:** A theme uses a color scheme to set the color of body text, headings, hyperlinks, table borders, page background, and more.

▶ **Images:** A theme uses images (graphics) for several page elements, such as the background, bullets, horizontal rules, and more.

When you insert new elements on a page that uses a theme, FrontPage automatically formats those elements to match the theme. FrontPage also automatically applies the theme to any new pages you create in the web.

Each FrontPage template uses a default theme. When you selected the Personal Web template in the previous set of steps, FrontPage automatically applied a theme to the web. The following steps show how to preview the default theme used for the web, apply a new theme to the web, and then preview the new theme applied to your web.

Web Design Tips

Many Web design guidelines are available on the Internet. Visit the Shelly Cashman Series Web Design Techniques Web page at www.scsite.com/web/SCWebDes.htm and then click Web Design Tips.

 To Apply a Theme to a FrontPage Web

1 Click Format on the menu bar and then point to Theme (Figure 1-14)

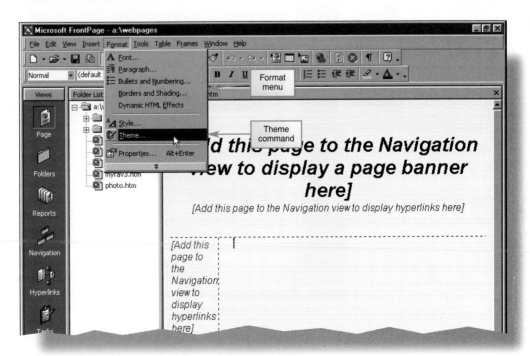

FIGURE 1-14

2 Click Theme. Point to Blueprint.

The Themes dialog box displays. The *Sample of Theme area* allows you to preview a sample page using the currently selected theme. The *Themes list box* lists all of the themes provided with FrontPage (Figure 1-15).

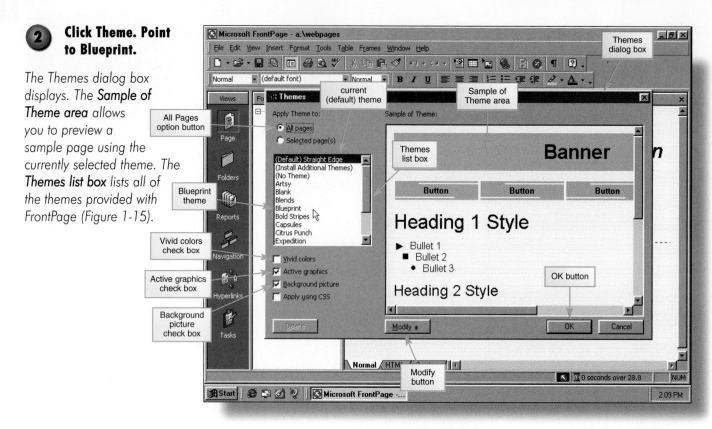

FIGURE 1-15

3 Click Blueprint in the Themes list. If necessary, click All pages. Click Vivid colors. Point to the OK button.

The *All pages option button* and the *Vivid colors check box* are selected. FrontPage displays a sample page in the Sample of Theme area of the Themes dialog box to show how the Blueprint theme will apply a color scheme, background image, and headings to a Web page (Figure 1-16).

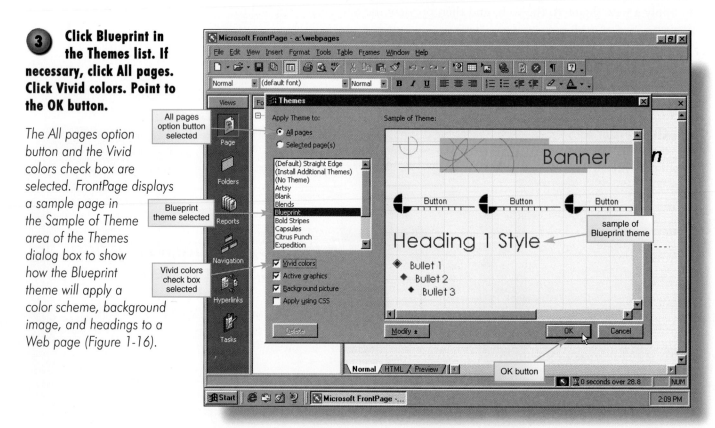

FIGURE 1-16

Click the OK button.

FrontPage displays a message on the status bar indicating that FrontPage is applying the new theme to all of the pages in the web. When finished, FrontPage displays in Page view. The active page, new_page_1.htm, displays in the Page pane with the Blueprint theme background (Figure 1-17).

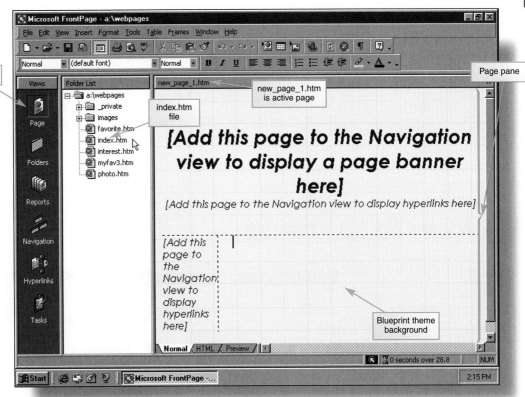

FIGURE 1-17

Other Ways

1. Right-click page in Page pane, click Theme on shortcut menu
2. Press ALT+F, T

The **Themes dialog box** contains options you can select to control how the current web uses themes. As you saw in Step 3, clicking the **All pages option button** instructs FrontPage to apply the theme to every page in the current web. Selecting the **Vivid colors check box** changes the theme's normal set of colors to a brighter color scheme. Selecting the **Active graphics check box** animates certain graphic elements. Selecting the **Background picture check box** applies a textured background image to the pages in the current web. Clicking the **Modify button** allows you to modify the color, graphics, and text of the selected theme.

While applying a theme to a web, FrontPage displays information about the operation in progress on the status bar. Depending on the number of pages in the web, this process can take anywhere from a few seconds to a few minutes. When FrontPage has applied the theme to every page in the current web, FrontPage displays in Page view. Once the theme is applied, FrontPage changes the background, fonts, and graphics used in the web. Applying the Blueprint theme, for example, adds a blue grid pattern to the white background.

If you want to add your own graphics or color sets to a preset theme, you can change and customize the theme. You can change a theme's background picture or heading font, for example, to create a new theme that displays the company logo on every page.

Opening and Modifying a Web Page in Page View

FrontPage allows you to open and modify text, images, tables, and other elements on each individual page in the current web. If the page is in the current web in any view, you can open the page by double-clicking the page's icon or file name. To open a Web page in Page view, for example, you simply double-click the file name of the page in the Folder List pane. After FrontPage displays the page in the Page pane, you can edit the page by selecting text, images, and other elements. The following step shows how to open a Web page in Page view.

To Open a Web Page in Page View

1 **Double-click the file name, index.htm, in the Folder List pane.**

The Home Page displays in the Page pane (Figure 1-18). The page contains placeholder text that you can edit to display your own message. A small pencil icon in the Folder List pane indicates that the Home Page file, named index.htm, is open. The Normal tab at the bottom of the Page pane indicates that you can edit the page.

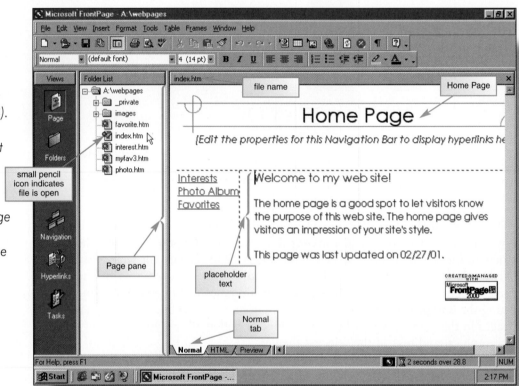

FIGURE 1-18

1. Click page name in Folder List pane, press ENTER
2. Right-click page name in Folder List pane, click Open on shortcut menu

When you open a page in Page view, the page displays on the Normal tab in the Page pane. The **Normal tab**, which is the default tab in Page view, is a **WYSIWYG (What You See Is What You Get)** design tool that displays a page as it will appear in a Web browser. As you create or modify a Web page using the Normal tab, FrontPage displays the page as it will display on the Web, while generating the needed HTML code for you. If you insert a image on a page, for example, FrontPage automatically enters the proper HTML code (in this case, the <IMG> tag). Using FrontPage, you can insert text, images, hyperlinks, and other elements without having to type any HTML code.

Editing Text on a Web Page

As you have learned, a FrontPage template is a series of linked Web pages that are organized and formatted with a basic framework of content upon which you can base new pages and new FrontPage webs. To help you design your own Web page, the template Web pages include placeholders for basic page elements such as headings, formatted text, images, and hyperlinks.

Adding your own content to the page involves editing one or more placeholders to convey the desired information – or deleting them altogether. On the home page of your Personal web, for example, you will want to edit the text to introduce yourself, delete any unneeded text, and add new text to complete the page. Perform the following steps to edit text on a Web page.

 To Edit Text on a Web Page

1 Point to the beginning of the second paragraph, which begins with the text, The home page is a good spot... (Figure 1-19).

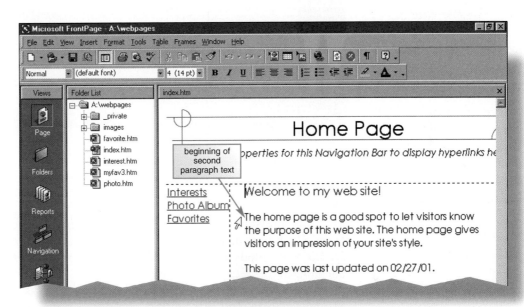

FIGURE 1-19

2 Drag through the second paragraph of the text to select it.

The text is selected (Figure 1-20).

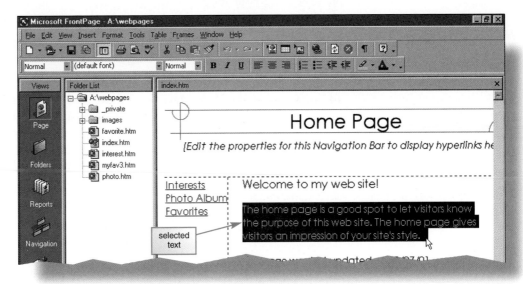

FIGURE 1-20

3 **Type** My name is Alison Doucette, and I'm a Buyer here at The First Draft. **as the second paragraph. (You may substitute your personal information here.)**

The new text replaces the selected text (Figure 1-21).

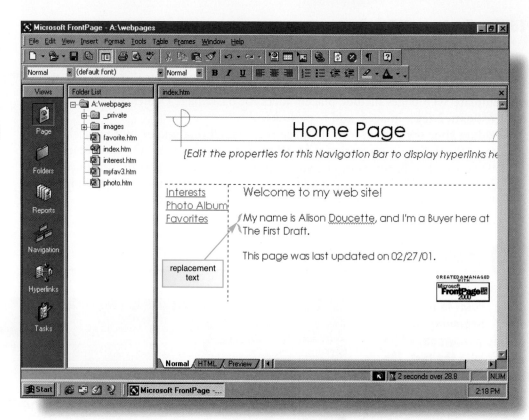

FIGURE 1-21

In the previous steps, you edited most of the placeholder text on the template page, which now displays your desired information. The last line, which FrontPage automatically updates to reflect the date the page was last updated, remains unchanged.

Using FrontPage, you can edit and add text just as you would with word processing software. To begin editing, you position the insertion point where you want to make a change and then perform the desired action. You even can move around the text using your mouse or the arrow keys. If you make a mistake typing, you can use the BACKSPACE key or the DELETE key to correct the mistake.

Adding New Text to a Web Page

If you want to include more text than that contained in the template, you can add new text to the Web page. Just as you add new text to a word processing document, you add new text to a Web page by positioning the insertion point where you want the text to display and then typing the text. The following steps show you how to add text to a Web page.

To Add New Text to a Web Page

1 **Press the ENTER key to start a new paragraph below the second paragraph.**

The insertion point displays at the beginning of the new paragraph (Figure 1-22)

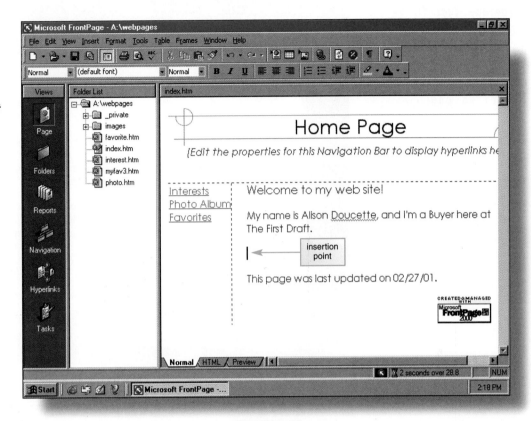

FIGURE 1-22

2 **Type** Since I've joined the staff, I've devoted my time to ensuring that The First Draft offers an extensive line of quality art and drafting supplies.

The new text displays as the third paragraph (Figure 1-23). The inserted text automatically wraps to the next line as you type.

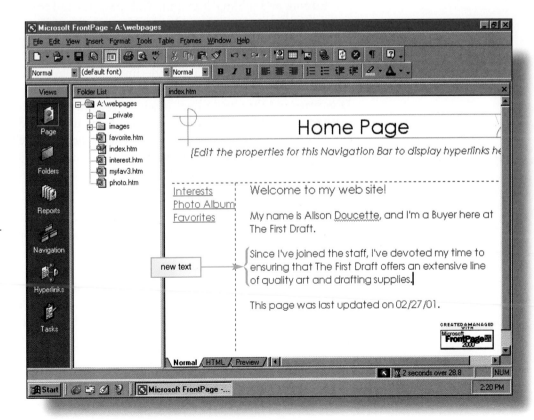

FIGURE 1-23

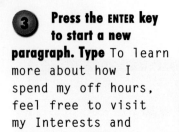

Press the ENTER key to start a new paragraph. Type To learn more about how I spend my off hours, feel free to visit my Interests and Favorites pages.

The new text displays as the fourth paragraph on the Web page (Figure 1-24).

FIGURE 1-24

Editing and adding text on a Web page using FrontPage is similar to editing a word processing document. On the Normal tab of Page view, you can insert, delete, cut, copy, and paste text, just as you would with word processing software.

As with many word processing applications, FrontPage automatically checks your spelling as you type and underlines misspelled words with a red wavy line. In the Home Page, for example, the spell checker does not recognize the word, Doucette, and thus underlines it with a red wavy line. To add an unrecognized word to the spell checker dictionary, right-click the underlined word and then click Add on the shortcut menu. To correct a misspelled word, right-click the underlined word and then click the correct spelling on the shortcut menu.

Editing a Bulleted List

In the previous steps, you edited the file, index.htm, which FrontPage created as the default home page. To complete the web, you need to edit the other pages in the web. The template for the Interest page, for example, includes a bulleted list of interests for you to customize.

Recall that a bulleted list is an unordered list of items that usually uses small icons called bullets to indicate each item in the list. In Page view, you can edit the bulleted list on the Interests page, changing, adding, and deleting items as needed to customize it to your interests. Complete the following steps to edit the bulleted list.

Steps **To Edit a Bulleted List**

1 **Double-click the file name, interest.htm, in the Folder List pane.**

The Interests page displays on the Normal tab in the Page pane (Figure 1-25). The template page for the Interests page includes a bulleted list of items; a bullet image precedes each item in the list. In the Folder List, a small pencil displays on the icon next to the file name, interest.htm, to indicate that the file is open.

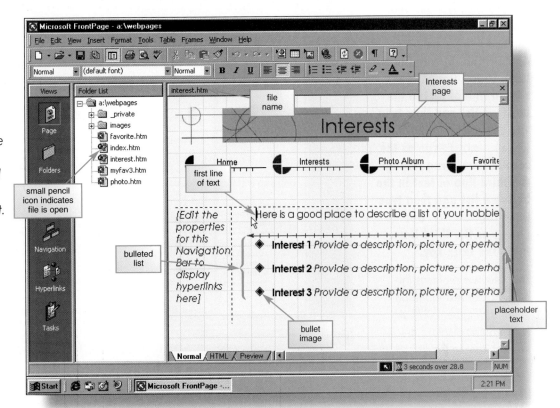

FIGURE 1-25

2 **Drag through the first line of text that begins, Here is a good place, to select it. Type** In my off hours, you are likely to find me: **as the new text.**

The new text replaces the selected text (Figure 1-26).

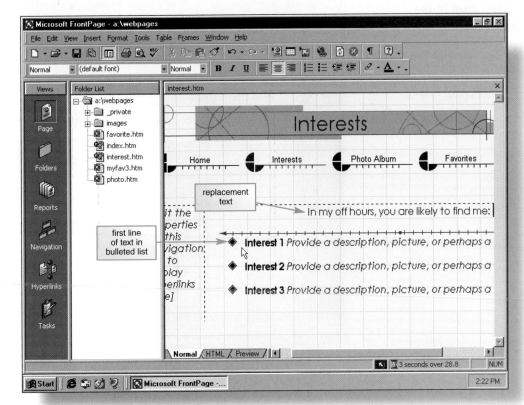

FIGURE 1-26

3 Drag through the first line of text in the bulleted list and then type Taking drawing classes at the Fine Arts School **as the first item. Drag through the second line of text in the bulleted list and then type** Teaching my beagle, Regal, to fetch **as the second item. Drag through the third line of text in the bulleted list and then type** Working on my Web pages **as the third item. Press the ENTER key.**

The new text replaces the placeholder text in the bulleted list (Figure 1-27). A fourth bullet displays below the last item in the list.

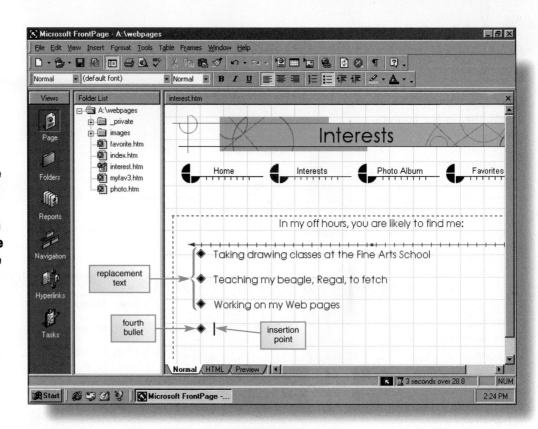

FIGURE 1-27

4 Type Studying for the GREs **as the last item in the bulleted list.**

The new text displays next to the bullet as the last item in the bulleted list (Figure 1-28).

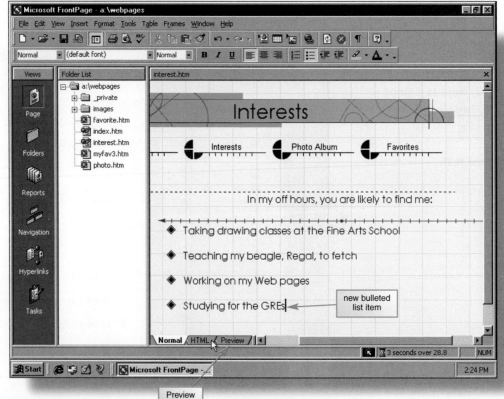

FIGURE 1-28

You have edited the items in a bulleted list successfully and added an item to the list. As you add text and make edits to a Web page, FrontPage automatically generates HTML source code that defines how the Web page will display on the Web. To see how your changes will display on the Web, you can click the Preview tab to preview the Web page. Before previewing the page, however, you should save your work to retain any changes.

Saving a Web Page

FrontPage allows you to save a Web page to many different locations, including the current web, a different Web, or a location on a network. To save a Web page to the current web, use the Save button on the Standard toolbar. Complete the following step to save the Web page to the current web.

Steps **To Save a Web Page**

1 **Click the Save button on the Standard toolbar (Figure 1-29).**

The Web page is saved in the webpages folder on the floppy disk in drive A using the file name, interest.htm.

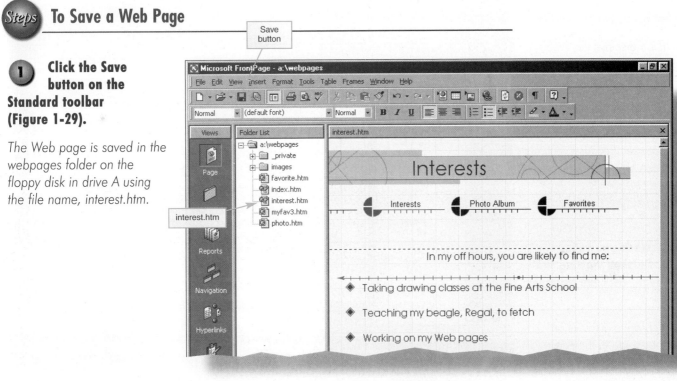

FIGURE 1-29

Clicking the **Save button** on the Standard toolbar saves the active page in HTML format, using the default file name, interest.htm. Because the Web page was opened from the current web, FrontPage saves the page without prompting you for a file name or file location. If you save a new Web page, clicking the Save button will cause FrontPage to display a Save As dialog box that prompts you to enter a file name. When you save a Web page, FrontPage also will prompt you to save any new images, sound files, or other objects to the same location as the page.

Once you have saved a Web page, you can preview how the page will display when viewed on the World Wide Web.

More About

The Preview Tab

The Preview tab in Page view exists only if you have installed Microsoft Internet Explorer version 3.0 or later on your computer. If you have not installed Microsoft Internet Explorer version 3.0 or later on your computer, FrontPage will not display a Preview tab.

Previewing a Web Page Using the Preview Tab

Clicking the **Preview tab** allows you to preview your page as it will display when viewed by a site visitor. To preview the page, you may click the Preview tab in Page view. FrontPage will not display a Preview tab if you have not installed Microsoft Internet Explorer version 3.0 or later on your computer. In such a case, you can click **Preview in Browser** on the File menu. The following steps show how to preview the page using the Preview tab.

 To Preview a Web Page Using the Preview Tab

1 **In Page view, click the Preview tab at the bottom of the Page pane.**

FrontPage displays the Web page on the Preview tab in the Page pane (Figure 1-30). The Preview tab displays how the page will display on the Web when viewed with a Web browser. Because you edited the HTML source, the first line of text may display left-aligned on the page.

2 **When you have finished viewing the Web page, click the Normal tab.**

The Web page displays on the Normal tab in the Page pane. With FrontPage, most Web page development and design takes place on the Normal tab in Page view.

Other Ways

1. On Normal tab in Page view, press CTRL+PAGE UP
2. On HTML tab in Page view, press CTRL+PAGE DOWN

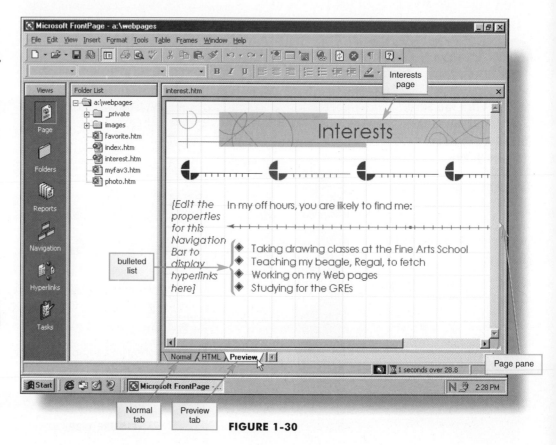

FIGURE 1-30

When you display a page using the Preview tab, a comment at the top of the Page pane indicates that the page contains some elements that may need to be saved or published to preview correctly. Some elements, such as navigation bars, may not display properly until viewed on the Web. While it does not offer perfect viewing, using the Preview tab does eliminate the need to save a partially completed Web page continuously, preview it in your Web browser to test it, switch to the editor to make changes, and so on.

Before you publish your web, you may want to add other elements to the page, such as a set of hyperlinks to the other pages in the web. In FrontPage, you can add a set of hyperlinks using a built-in FrontPage object, called a component.

Modifying Components

An active element, called a **component**, is a dynamic, built-in FrontPage object that is evaluated and executed when you save the page or, in some cases, when you display the page in a Web browser. Most components generate HTML automatically using the text, image files, and other items you supply. Examples of FrontPage components include a **Hit counter component** that keeps track of the number of visitors to a Web site and a **Search form component** that creates a form that provides full text-searching capability in a web.

When working on a web, you can identify a component by positioning the mouse pointer on the component. The mouse pointer changes to a **component cursor**, which looks like a hand holding a written list.

A commonly used component is a navigation bar. In FrontPage, a **navigation bar** is a collection of graphical or textual buttons each containing a link to related Web pages in the current FrontPage web. The Blueprint theme you applied to the web includes two navigation bars – one on the top and one on the left-hand side of the page. The **horizontal navigation bar** on the top of the page is used for **parent-child navigation**, which allows you to move between the Home Page (the parent) and the Interests page or Favorites page (the children). The **vertical navigation bar** on the left-hand side of the page is used for **same-level navigation**, which allows you to move back and forth between the Interests and Favorites pages. The following steps show you how to modify the navigation bars in the current web.

 To Modify a Navigation Bar Component

1 **Click the vertical navigation bar to select it.**

FrontPage highlights the vertical navigation bar (Figure 1-31). The mouse pointer changes to the component cursor, thus indicating that the selected item is a component.

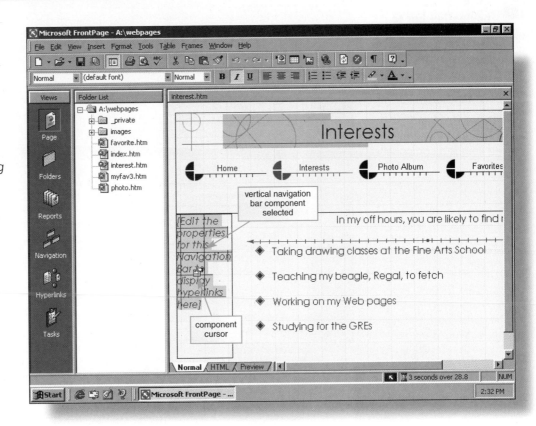

FIGURE 1-31

2 **Press the DELETE key.**

The Interests page displays with the vertical navigation bar deleted (Figure 1-32). FrontPage automatically changes the navigation bar on all pages in the current web.

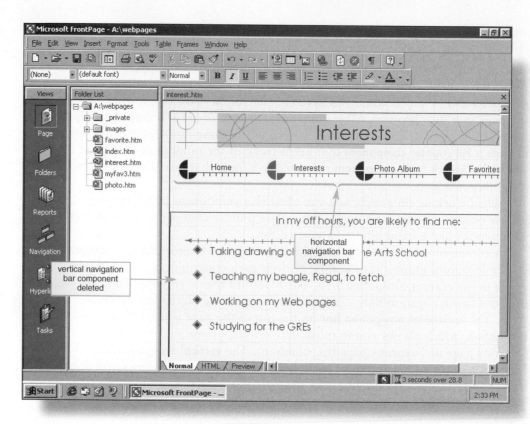

FIGURE 1-32

3 **Click the horizontal navigation bar to select it.**

FrontPage highlights the horizontal navigation bar (Figure 1-33). The mouse pointer changes to the component cursor, thus indicating that the selected item is a component.

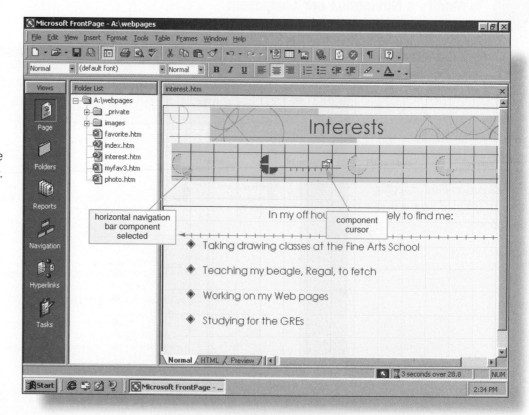

FIGURE 1-33

4 Double-click the horizontal navigation bar. Point to Child pages under Home.

The Navigation Bar Properties dialog box displays (Figure 1-34). The dialog box contains options that control the organization and appearance of the navigation bar. A graphical diagram indicates the pages that display on the horizontal navigation bar.

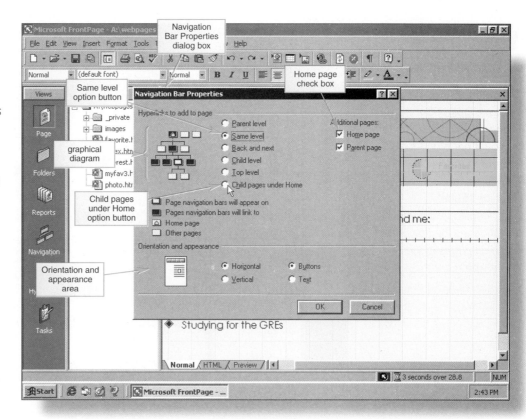

FIGURE 1-34

5 Click Child pages under Home and then point to the OK button.

The Child pages under Home option button is selected (Figure 1-35). Selecting the Child pages under Home option button modifies the navigation bar to link to the first level of pages below the Home page, which is at the parent level. The graphical diagram changes to indicate this modification to the navigation bar and to the relationship of the pages in the web.

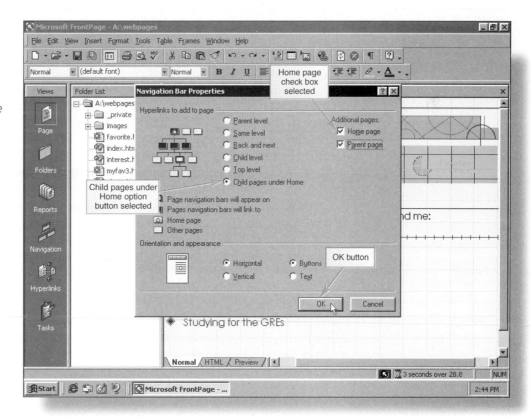

FIGURE 1-35

6 **Click the OK button.**

The Interests page and the horizontal navigation bar display (Figure 1-36). The horizontal navigation bar now includes buttons that link to the Home page and the three pages at the first hierarchical level under the Home page. FrontPage automatically changes the navigation bar on all pages in the current web.

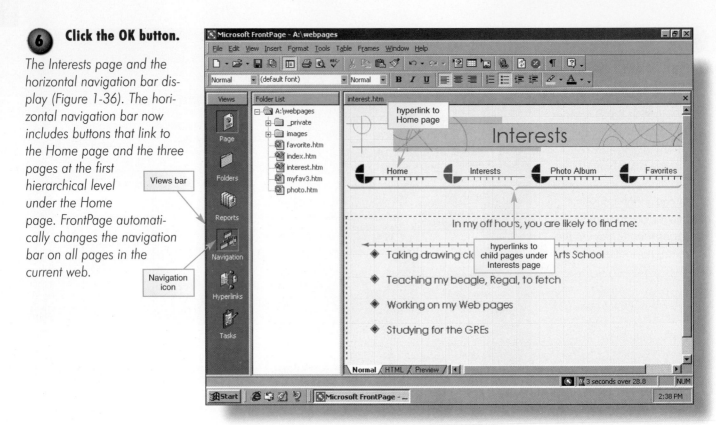

FIGURE 1-36

You have changed the properties of a FrontPage component – in this case, a navigation bar. In the example, when you changed the properties of the navigation bar, the appearance did not change. This is because the child pages under the Home page — the Interests, Favorites, and Photo Album pages – already are included in the navigation bar. Setting the navigation bar properties to display only the child pages under the Home page ensures that the buttons on the navigation bar will not change if you add pages below the first hierarchical level. If you added a Hobbies page under the Interests page, for example, the navigation bar on the Interests page would not display a Hobbies button. This allows you to add many pages, while retaining a navigation that directs users back to one of three main sections – Interests, Favorites, or the Photo Album – or to the Home page.

Different FrontPage components have different properties. The options that display in the component Properties dialog boxes vary, based on the properties of each specific component. Most FrontPage components change automatically in response to changes you make in the FrontPage web. The horizontal navigation bar you just changed, for example, links to three child pages in the web – the Interests page, the Photo Album page, and the Favorites page. If you delete one of these pages from the current web, the horizontal navigation bar component automatically removes links to the deleted page from the navigation bars on all pages in the current web.

Deleting a Web Page from a Web

FrontPage provides several ways to delete pages from a current web. You can delete a page in Page view, for example, by selecting in the Folder List pane the file name of the page to delete and then pressing the DELETE key. You also can delete pages in Navigation view by clicking the page icon and then clicking Delete on the shortcut menu. In this project, you will delete the Photo Album page in Navigation view to create a web with three pages: a Home page, an Interests page, and a Favorites page.

In FrontPage, **Navigation view** allows you to create, change, display, and print a web's structure and navigation. As previously discussed, a web's structure is the set of relationships among the pages in a FrontPage web; Navigation view includes a **Navigation pane** that displays a graphical diagram similar to an organization chart that indicates the current web's structure. The Home page displays at the top (parent) level of the chart and linked pages display at the lower (child) levels. As with Page view, Navigation view includes a Folder List pane and a Navigation pane.

Making changes to the web's structure in Navigation view, such as deleting a page, allows you to see immediately how the change affects the structure. Complete the following steps to delete the Photo Album page from the current web.

Steps **To Delete a Web Page from a Web**

Click the Navigation icon on the Views bar. If necessary, click the Close button on the Navigation toolbar.

The current web displays in Navigation view, showing a graphical diagram of the web structure of the current web. A rectangular page icon represents each page in the web (Figure 1-37).

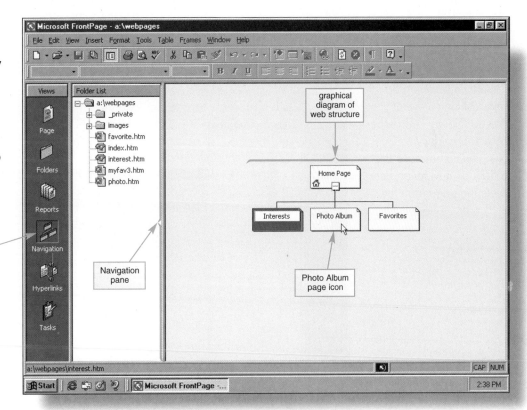

FIGURE 1-37

2) **Right-click the Photo Album page icon. Point to Delete on the shortcut menu.**

A shortcut menu displays (Figure 1-38). The shortcut menu contains commands to manage individual pages within a FrontPage web.

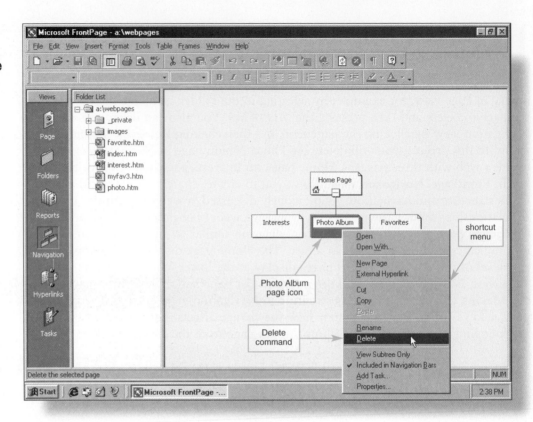

FIGURE 1-38

3) **Click Delete.**

The Delete Page dialog box displays, asking you what you want to do (Figure 1-39). The dialog box provides two options: you can remove this page from all navigation bars or delete the page from the web.

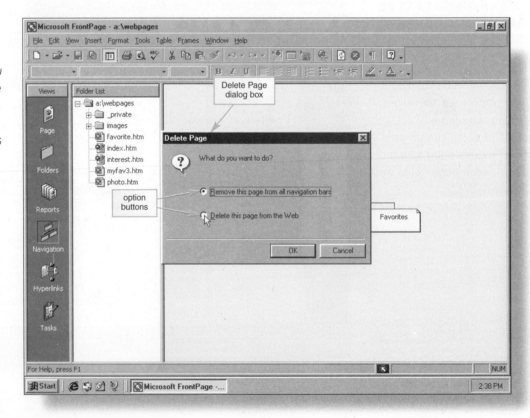

FIGURE 1-39

4 **Click Delete this page from the Web and then point to the OK button.**

The Delete Page dialog box displays with the Delete this page from the Web option button selected (Figure 1-40).

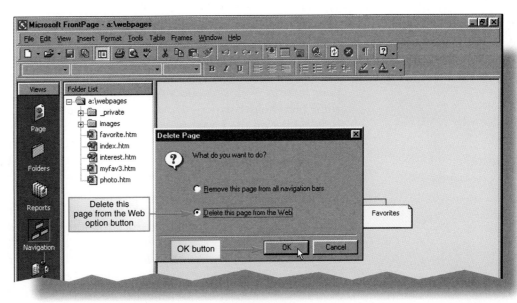

FIGURE 1-40

5 **Click the OK button.**

After a few moments, the web displays in Navigation view. The file (named photo.htm) is removed from the Folder List pane and the Photo Album page icon is removed from the graphical diagram of the web structure (Figure 1-41).

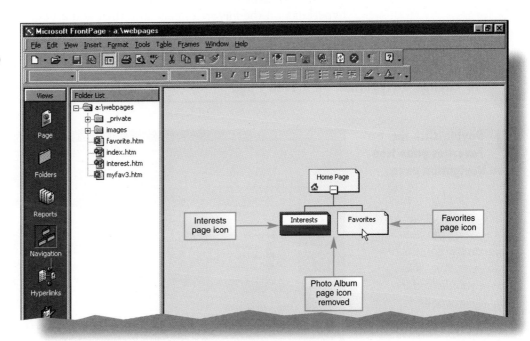

FIGURE 1-41

If you choose to remove the Web page from all navigation bars, the Web page still exists on disk and can be linked to other pages. If you choose to delete a page from the web, as you did in the previous steps, the Web page is deleted from disk and removed from all navigation bars.

When you make changes to your web's navigation structure in Navigation view; for example, adding or deleting a page from the structure, or creating a new page, those changes are saved automatically when you switch to another view, such as Page view. You also can open files from Navigation view by double-clicking the page icon. Double-clicking the Favorites page icon, for example, will open the Favorites page so you can edit the final page in the current web.

Managing Hyperlinks on a Web Page

The final page to edit is the Favorites page, which contains hyperlinks to some of your favorite Web sites. Because you are using a template, the page already includes some placeholder hyperlinks. You can edit the links much like you edited the bulleted list on the Interests page.

Recall that a hyperlink, or link, is an area of the page that you click to instruct the browser to go to a location in a file or to request a file from a server. Often, a hyperlink consists of text or a picture that is associated with a URL that points to a page on the World Wide Web. Using FrontPage, you can create text or image links on your Web page. Adding a hyperlink to a Web page involves inserting text or an image on a Web page and then associating the text or image with a URL.

FrontPage provides several ways to associate a URL with the text or image on a Web page. You can type the URL, select a file within the current web or on your computer, or specify an e-mail link. You also can browse the Web to display the page to which you want to link; FrontPage automatically displays the URL in the appropriate text box.

To learn how to manage hyperlinks on a Web page, you will edit the existing hyperlinks on the Favorites page and then add a new hyperlink. Complete the following steps to change an existing hyperlink on a Web page.

 Steps

To Change a Hyperlink on a Web Page

1 **Double-click the Favorites page icon in the Navigation pane.**

FrontPage displays the Favorites page in Page view (Figure 1-42). The horizontal navigation bar consists of only three buttons links, because you deleted the Photo Album page.

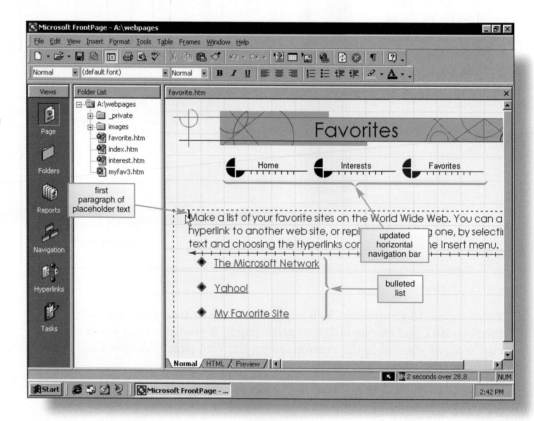

FIGURE 1-42

2 **Drag through the first paragraph of text, which begins with, Make a list of your favorite sites, to select it. Type** Some of my favorite Web sites include: **as the replacement text.**

The new text replaces the placeholder text (Figure 1-43). The list entries are underlined, which identifies them as hyperlinks.

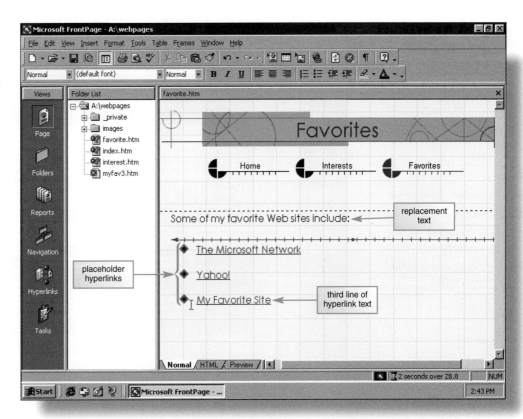

FIGURE 1-43

3 **Drag through the third line of hyperlink text, which reads, My Favorite Site, to select it. Type** The Museum of Modern Art **as the replacement hyperlink text.**

The new hyperlink text replaces the placeholder hyperlink text (Figure 1-44). While you have changed the text that identifies the hyperlink, you still must edit the URL behind the hyperlink.

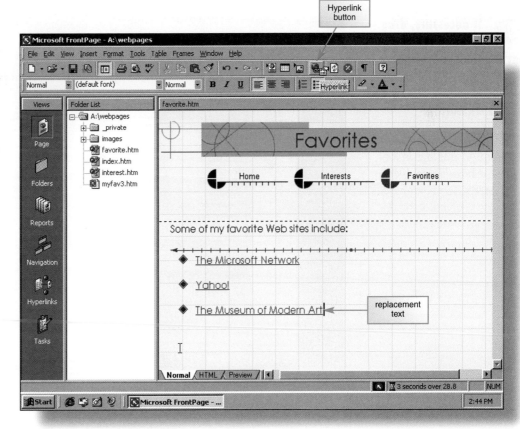

FIGURE 1-44

4 **Click the Hyperlink button on the Standard toolbar.**

The Edit Hyperlink dialog box displays, with the current URL, myfav3.htm, selected (Figure 1-45). The current URL, myfav3.htm, links to a page in the current web. The **Edit Hyperlink dialog box** *contains options that allow you to change the current URL and specify the URL of the Web resource to which you want to link.*

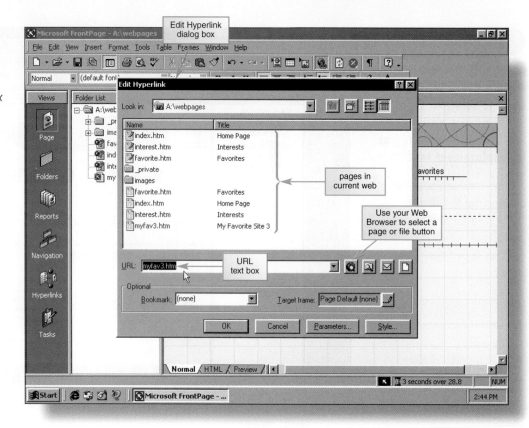

FIGURE 1-45

5 **If necessary, drag through the text, myfav3.htm, to select it. Type** http://www.moma.org **as the new URL. Point to the OK button.**

The URL for The Museum of Modern Art displays in the URL text box (Figure 1-46).

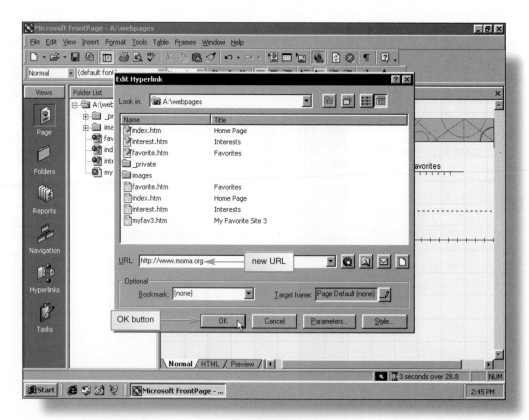

FIGURE 1-46

6 **Click the OK button. Position the mouse pointer on The Museum of Modern Art hyperlink.**

The Museum of Modern Art hyperlink displays as the third item in the Favorites list. The URL for The Museum of Modern Art Web page displays on the status bar (Figure 1-47). A ScreenTip prompts you to press Ctrl+Click to follow a hyperlink.

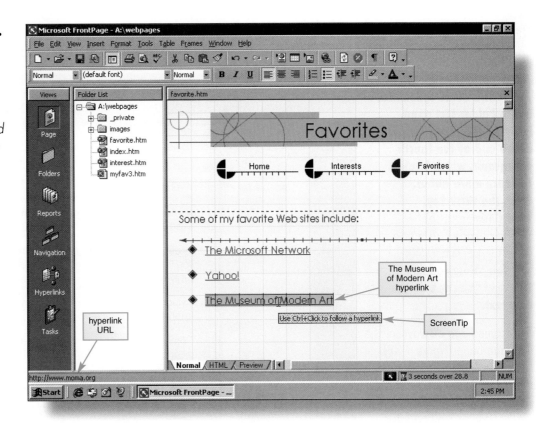

FIGURE 1-47

You also can edit a URL by clicking the Use your Web Browser to select a page or file button in the Edit Hyperlink dialog box and then browsing the Web to locate the Web resource to which you want to link. Once the desired page is displayed in the browser (Internet Explorer) window, you can return to FrontPage and the browser automatically will return the URL of the current page to the URL list box.

Adding an E-Mail Hyperlink to a Web Page

Using the Edit Hyperlink dialog box, you also can create e-mail hyperlinks in a Web page. When a user clicks an **e-mail hyperlink** on your Web page, the Web browser will start the designated e-mail program, such as Microsoft Outlook Express, and prompt the user to enter a message. The message automatically is addressed to the e-mail address specified in the e-mail hyperlink. Many Web pages include e-mail hyperlinks to allow visitors to send questions, comments, or requests via e-mail, simply by clicking the e-mail hyperlink.

E-mail hyperlinks use the **mailto protocol**, which is an Internet protocol used to send electronic mail. Because not all Web browsers and e-mail programs support the mailto protocol, you should specify the e-mail address somewhere on the Web page. The easiest way to do this is to use the e-mail address as the hyperlink text for the e-mail hyperlink. Complete the steps on the next page to add an e-mail hyperlink to a Web page.

Other Ways

1. Click hyperlink to select it, press CTRL+K

Steps To Add an E-Mail Hyperlink to a Web Page

1 **Double-click the file name index.htm in the Folder List pane. Position the insertion point at the end of the fourth paragraph, which begins, To learn more about. Press the ENTER key. Type** Comments or suggestions? Please e-mail me at alison_doucette @altavista.net **as the new text.**

The Home Page displays in the Page pane (Figure 1-48). Using the e-mail address as the e-mail hyperlink text provides a quick way for users to identify your e-mail address

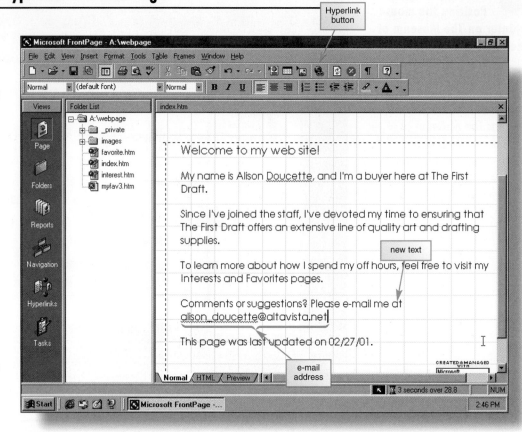

FIGURE 1-48

2 **Drag through the text, alison_ doucette@altavista.net, to select it. Click the Hyperlink button on the Standard toolbar.**

The Create Hyperlink dialog box displays (Figure 1-49). A small envelope icon identifies the Make a hyperlink that sends E-mail button.

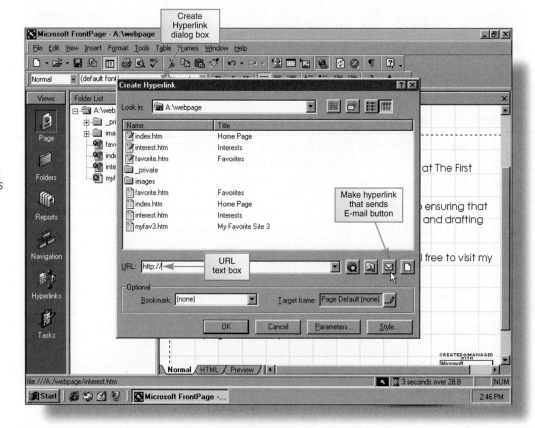

FIGURE 1-49

3 **Click the Make a hyperlink that sends E-mail button.**

The Create E-mail Hyperlink dialog box displays (Figure 1-50).

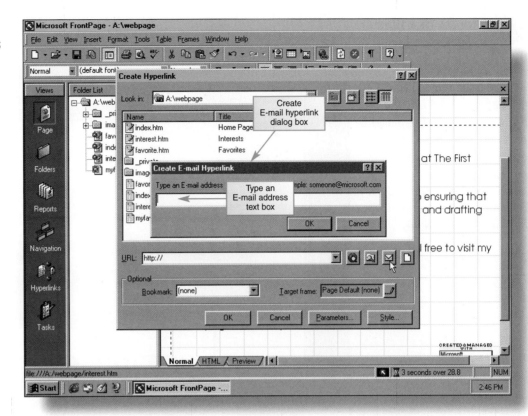

FIGURE 1-50

4 **Type** alison_ doucette@ altavista.net **in the Type an E-mail address text box.**

The e-mail address displays in the text box (Figure 1-51).

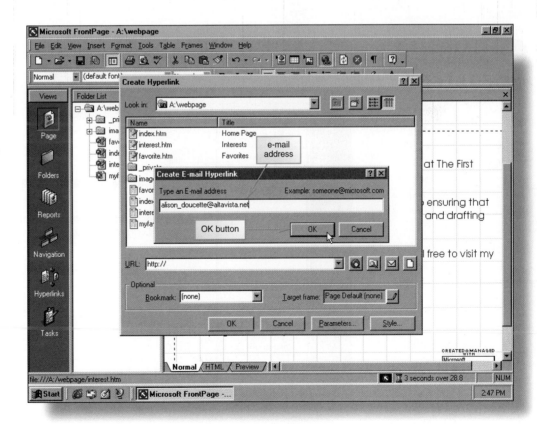

FIGURE 1-51

5 **Click the OK button in the Create E-mail Hyperlink dialog box.**

*The complete e-mail hyperlink displays in the URL text box (Figure 1-52). The **mailto protocol** before the e-mail address instructs the Web browser to start the designated e-mail program and address the message to the indicated e-mail address.*

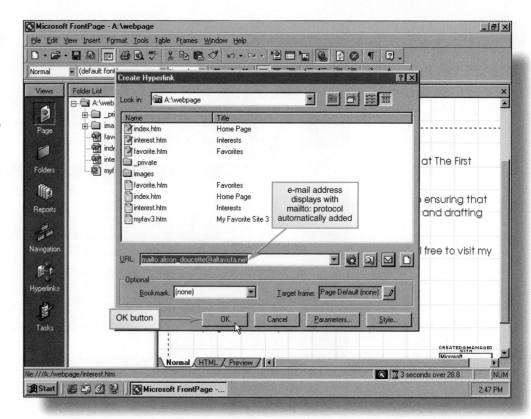

FIGURE 1-52

6 **Click the OK button. Position the mouse pointer on the e-mail hyperlink.**

The e-mail hyperlink displays on the Home Page. The URL for the e-mail hyperlink displays in the status bar, using the mailto protocol before the e-mail address, alison_doucette@ altavista.net (Figure 1-53). A ScreenTip prompts you to press Ctrl+Click to follow a hyperlink.

7 **Click the Save button on the Standard toolbar.**

The Home Page is saved on disk as part of the current web.

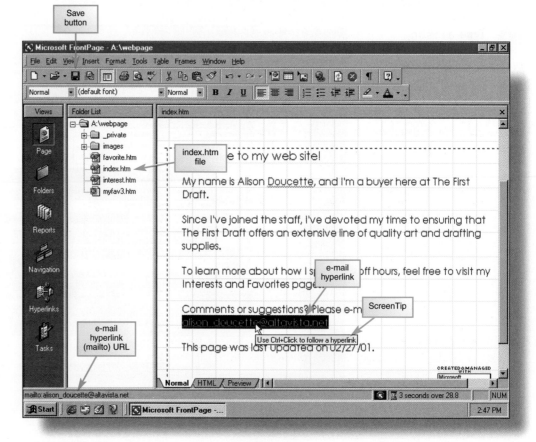

FIGURE 1-53

You now have included two new text hyperlinks: a hyperlink to a Web page on the Favorites page and an e-mail hyperlink on the Home page.

Inserting an Image on a Web Page

FrontPage allows you to insert an image on a Web page in several ways. Recall that an image – which FrontPage refers to as a picture – is a graphics file that can be inserted on a Web page and displayed in a Web browser. The first time you save the page with the image, FrontPage automatically saves the image as a file as part of the current web.

The Web supports several different file formats for graphics, but JPEG and GIF are the two more common file formats for graphic images on the Web. A graphic image saved as a **GIF** (pronounced jiff or giff) is saved using compression techniques to make it smaller for download on the Web. GIF files are limited to only 256 colors, so the images are not as complex. Developers sometimes use GIF files for computer-generated artwork. A graphics images saved as a **JPEG** (pronounced JAY-peg) also is saved using compression techniques to make it smaller for download on the Web. Unlike GIF files, JPEG files can contain millions of colors and thus often are used for photographs and more complex images. The **PNG** (pronounced ping) format also is a compressed file format that supports millions of colors. Table 1-4 provides more information about each of these image file formats.

More *About*

Images

To learn more about images that are available on the Web, visit the Shelly Cashman Series Web Design Techniques Web page at www.scsite.com/web/ SCWebDes.htm and then click Andy's Art Attack.

Table 1-4 Image File Formats		
FILE FORMAT	**DESCRIPTION**	**FILE EXTENSION(S)**
GIF (Graphics Interchange Format)	• Supports up to 256 colors. • Used for line art, grayscale images, and simple graphics. • A popular graphics format used by CompuServe and other online services. • The technique used to compress GIF files (called LZW compression) is patented; companies making products that use the GIF format thus must obtain a license (developers of nonprofit or personal home pages do not require a license).	.gif
JPEG (Joint Photographic Expert Group)	• Supports up to 16.7 million colors. • Used for true-color photographic images scanned or digitized from films.	.jpg, .jpeg, .jpe
PNG (Portable Network Graphics)	• Supports up to 16.7 million colors. • Patent-free replacement for the GIF. • Not yet widely used.	.png, .ping

FrontPage lets you import graphics in a variety of formats; the imported graphics are converted to GIF format (for graphics containing up to 256 colors) or JPEG format (for graphics containing more than 256 colors) when the page is saved to the current web.

In this project, you will insert a GIF file on the Home Page of your Personal web to enhance the design of the page and draw the visitor's attention. Complete the steps on the next page to insert an image on a Web page.

To Insert an Image on a Web Page

1 **Position the insertion point at the beginning of the fourth paragraph, which begins, To learn more about.**

The Home Page displays in the Page pane (Figure 1-54).The insertion point displays at the beginning of the fourth paragraph.

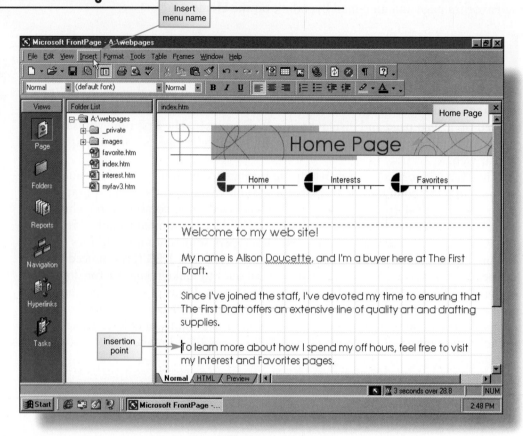

FIGURE 1-54

2 **Click Insert on the menu bar. Point to Picture and then point to From File on the Picture submenu.**

*The Insert menu and Picture submenu display (Figure 1-55). The **Picture submenu** consists of commands that allow you to insert a clip art picture, a picture from a file, or a video.*

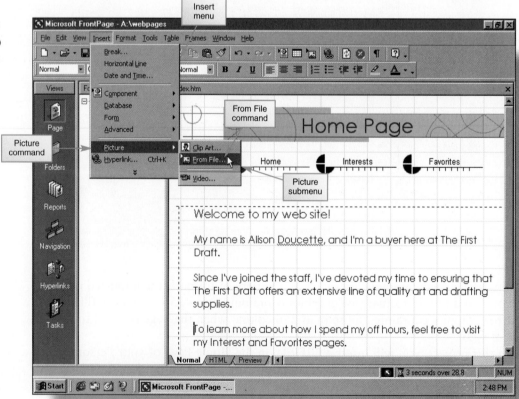

FIGURE 1-55

3 Click From File on the Picture submenu. Point to the Use your Web Browser to select a page or file button.

The Picture dialog box displays (Figure 1-56). The dialog box contains options that allow you to select an image file saved on your computer or to browse the World Wide Web to select a file.

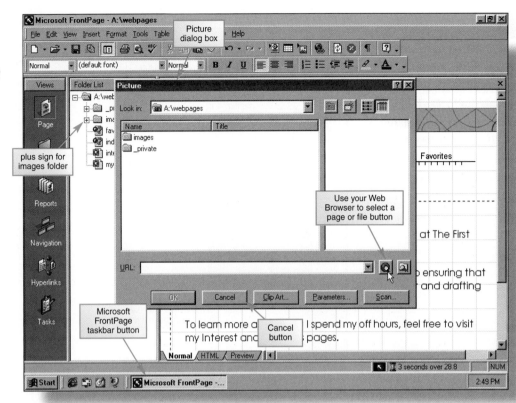

FIGURE 1-56

4 Click the Use your Web Browser to select a page or file button.

The browser (Internet Explorer) window opens and displays a message indicating that you should browse to the page containing the desired image file and then return to FrontPage to continue (Figure 1-57).

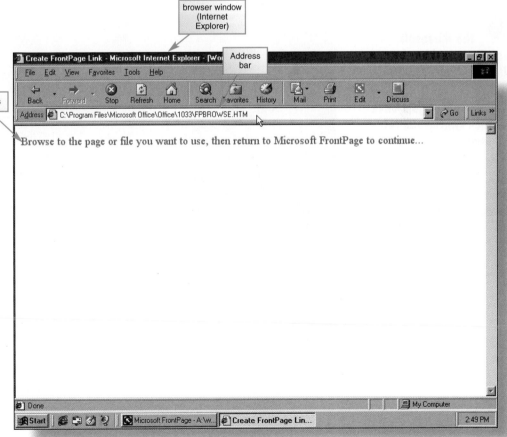

FIGURE 1-57

Click the Address bar in the browser window (Internet Explorer). Type http://www.scsite.com/fp2000/pr1/draft.gif **and then press the ENTER key. Right-click the image, draft.gif. Point to Copy on the shortcut menu.**

A Web page is displayed with the image, draft.gif, and a shortcut menu displays (Figure 1-58).

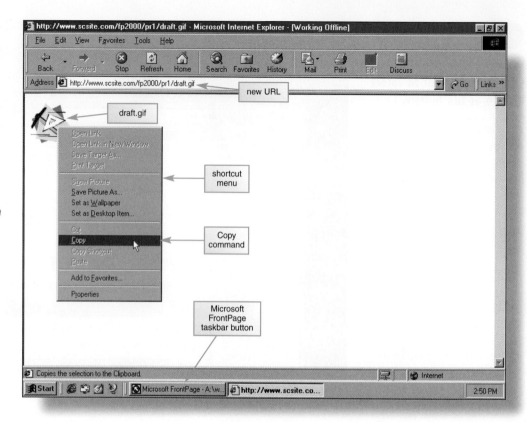

FIGURE 1-58

Click Copy. Click the Microsoft FrontPage taskbar button. Click the Cancel button (shown in Figure 1-56 on the previous page). Click the plus sign to the left of the images folder in the Folder List pane. Right-click the images folder. Point to Paste on the shortcut menu.

The shortcut menu displays (Figure 1-59). The images folder is expanded. A copy of the image, draft.gif, is placed on the Clipboard.

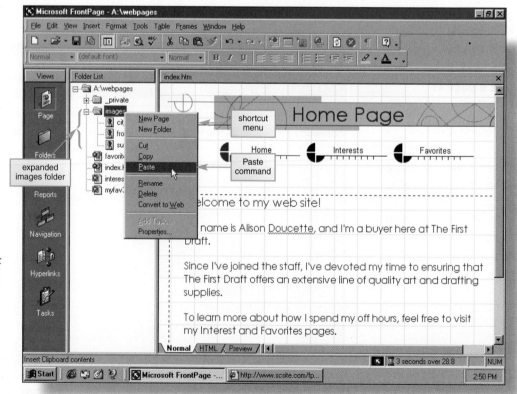

FIGURE 1-59

7 Click Paste. Drag the file draft[1].gif from the Images folder to the insertion point as shown in Figure 1-60. Point to the Center button on the Formatting toolbar.

The Home Page displays with the image inserted (Figure 1-60).

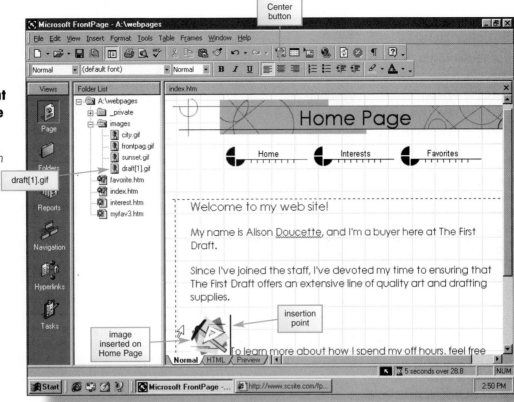

FIGURE 1-60

8 Click the Center button and then press the ENTER key.

The image is centered on the Home Page between the third and fourth paragraphs (Figure 1-61).

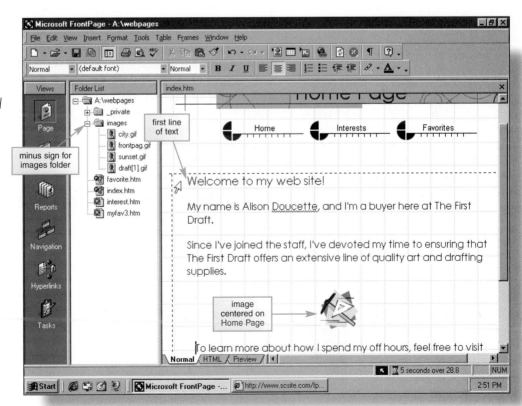

FIGURE 1-61

9 Click the minus sign to the left of the images folder in the Folder List pane to collapse the folder. Position the insertion point at the beginning of the first line of text, which reads, Welcome to my web site! Click the Center button on the Formatting toolbar. Point to the Save button on the Standard toolbar.

The first line of text is centered on the Home Page (Figure 1-62).

10 Click the Save button.

FrontPage saves the Home Page on the floppy disk in drive A.

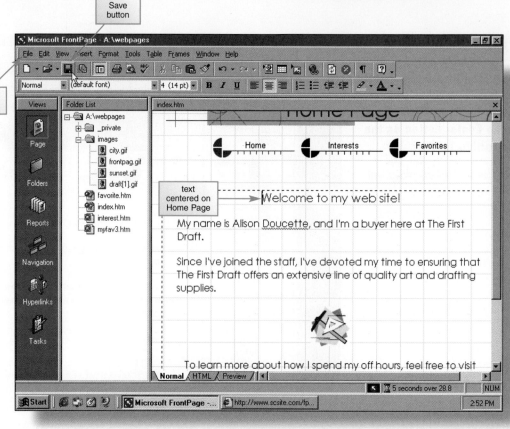

FIGURE 1-62

When you insert an image on a Web page, FrontPage automatically generates HTML instructions to include the image file in the page, using the **<IMG SRC> tag**. While the page includes a reference to the file name of the image, you copied the image to the images folder and used that copy so the image would be saved to the current web. Saving the image files to the current web ensures that the image files will be available when you publish the FrontPage web to a Web server.

Printing a Web Page Using FrontPage

Once you have created a Web page and saved it on disk, you may want to print the page. A printed version of a document — in this case, a Web page — is called a **hardcopy** or **printout**.

You can print a Web page in Navigation view or Page view. In Navigation view, you must select the page icon in the Navigation pane and then click the Print button on the Standard toolbar. To print a page in Page view, you open the Web page so it displays in the Page pane and then click the Print button on the Standard toolbar. After you print the first page, you can open additional pages to print the remaining pages in the web. To print the Home Page of your Personal web, complete the following steps.

Steps **To Print a Web Page**

1 Ready the printer. If necessary, double-click the file name, index.htm, in the Folder List pane to display the Home Page in the Page pane. Click File on the menu bar and then point to Print.

The File menu displays (Figure 1-63). Positioning the mouse pointer on the File menu for a few seconds causes the full menu to display with additional commands.

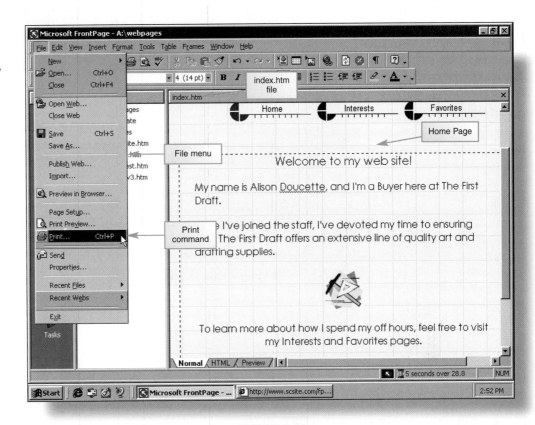

FIGURE 1-63

2 Click Print.

The Print dialog box displays (Figure 1-64). The All option button in the Print Range area is selected, indicating that the entire document will print, regardless of its length.

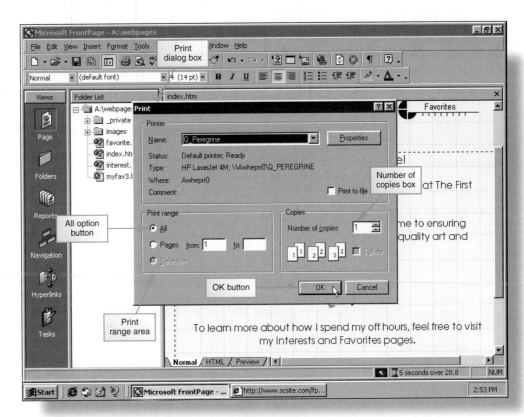

FIGURE 1-64

Click the OK button.

The FrontPage message box displays, showing the status of the print process. The Home Page prints (Figure 1-65). FrontPage prints hyperlinks and images on the Web page as they display on the Normal tab in Page view.

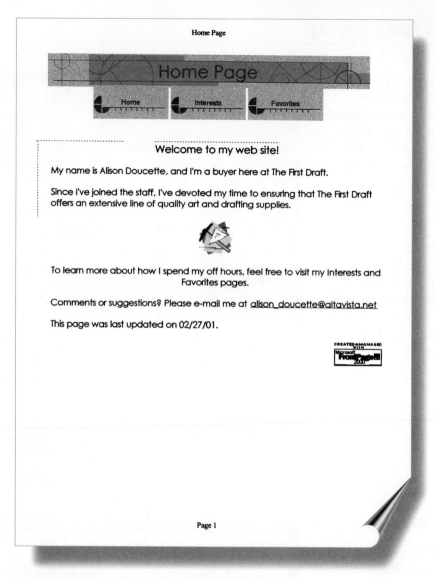

FIGURE 1-65

1. Click Print button on Standard toolbar
2. Right-click page, click Print on shortcut menu
3. Press CTRL+P, click OK button

The **Print dialog box** in Figure 1-64 on the previous page provides many printing options. In the **Print range area**, the **All option button** instructs FrontPage to print the entire document. The **Pages option button** lets you print selected pages of a multiple-page document. The **Number of Copies box** allow you to specify the number of copies you want to print.

To print the Web page as shown in Figure 1-65, the Web page must display on the Normal tab in Page view. FrontPage also allows you to print the HTML source for a home page. To print the HTML source for a home page, click the HTML tab to display the Web page on the HTML tab and then print the page. You cannot, however, print a Web page on the Preview tab in Page view. When the page displays on the Preview tab, FrontPage disables the printing function.

Publishing a FrontPage Web

If you have access to a Web server, FrontPage provides an easy way to publish your Web pages to the World Wide Web. As previously mentioned, **publishing a Web page** is the process of sending copies of Web pages, image files, multimedia files, and any folders to a Web server. Once saved on the Web server, the Web pages and files are available on the World Wide Web. With FrontPage, you can publish your Web using a series of dialog boxes that walk you step by step through the process.

Many schools and companies provide a small amount of space on their Web servers for students and employees to publish personal Web pages and related files. For a modest fee, most Internet service providers (ISPs) also will provide space for publishing personal Web pages. An **Internet service provider (ISP)** is an organization that has a permanent connection to the Internet and provides temporary connections to individuals and companies for a fee, usually about $20 per month. Some other Web-based services, such as Tripod, provide space on their Web servers for individuals to publish personal Web pages. To pay for the cost of maintaining these servers, these companies place advertisements at the top or bottom of your personal Web pages.

FrontPage 2000 comes with a program that allows your Windows-based computer to act as a Web server. You can install this program, called **Personal Web Server**, when you install FrontPage 2000. You then can publish your personal Web pages to your computer using the Personal Web Server.

Because your web currently resides on drive A, you must use an Internet utility called a **File Transfer Program**, or **FTP**, to copy the files in your FrontPage web to a Web server. FTP is a method of transferring files over the Internet.

The following steps show how to publish your FrontPage web to a Web server. These steps work only if you have an account that gives you publishing rights on a Web server. To ensure that you publish your Personal web successfully, be sure to substitute the URL of your own Web server when you see the URL, http://members.tripod.com/firstdraft/, in the following steps. If you do not know which URL to use, see your instructor for more information.

More About

ISPs

To publish a personal Web page, you need space on a school, company, or personal Web server. Contact your local Internet service provider (ISP) for more information about obtaining space on a Web server to publish your personal Web pages.

More About

Publishing a Web

Clicking the Options button in the Publish Web dialog box allows you to choose from options that permit you to publish changed pages only or publish all pages, overwriting any pages already on the Web page server.

 Steps To Publish the FrontPage Web

1 Point to the Publish Web button on the Standard toolbar (Figure 1-66).

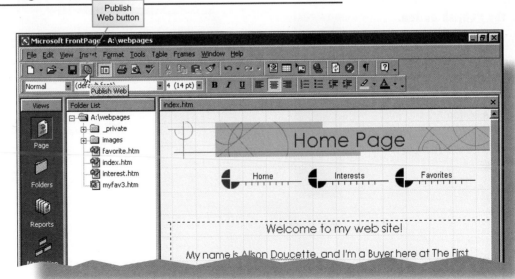

FIGURE 1-66

Click the Publish Web button.

The Publish Web dialog box displays (Figure 1-67). The Specify the location to publish your Web to text box displays the URL of the location where FrontPage will publish the Home Page of the current web. FrontPage will publish all other files in the same directory or folders within that directory.

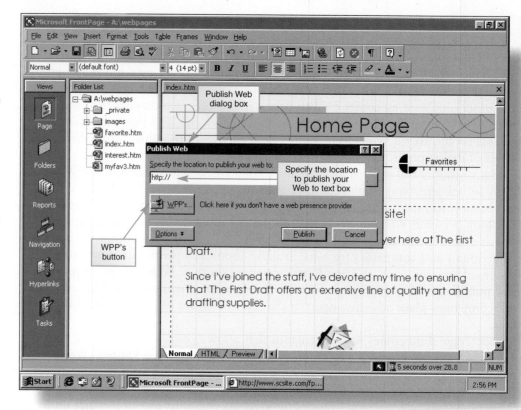

FIGURE 1-67

3 **Type** http:// members.tripod. com/firstdraft/ **in the Specify the location to publish your Web to text box. Be sure to substitute your own URL when you see the URL, http://members. tripod.com/firstdraft/. Point to the Publish button.**

The destination URL displays in the Specify the location to publish your Web to text box (Figure 1-68). Clicking the WWP's button links to information on ISPs and other Web Presence Providers (WWPs).

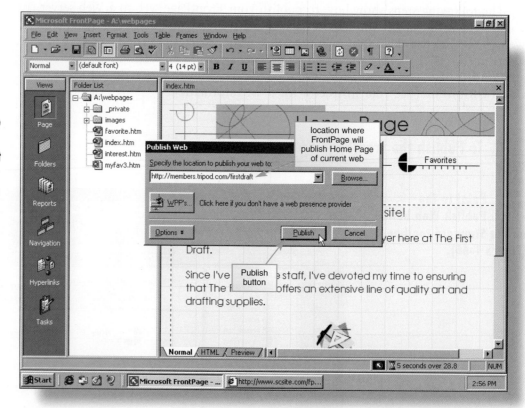

FIGURE 1-68

4 **Click the Publish button.**

The Name and Password Required dialog box displays, requesting authorization information to allow you to publish your web to the server entered in the Specify the location to publish your Web to text box (Figure 1-69).

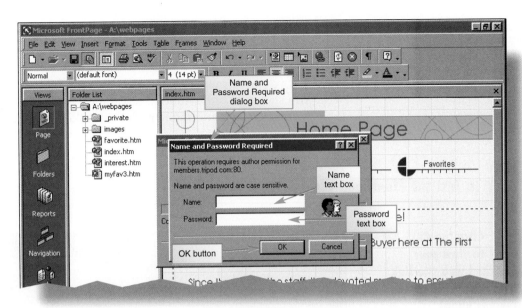

FIGURE 1-69

5 **Type your name in the Name text box and then type your password in the Password text box. Click the OK button. Do not click the Done button at this time.**

The Microsoft FrontPage dialog box displays a status bar indicating the progress of the file transfer. When FrontPage has finished publishing the web, the Microsoft FrontPage dialog box displays the message, Web site published successfully! and provides a link you can click to view your published Web site (Figure 1-70).

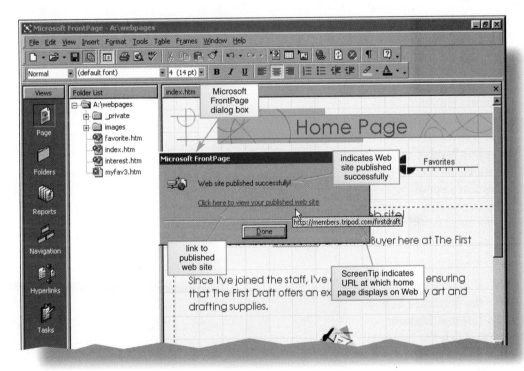

FIGURE 1-70

Of the many files FrontPage will transfer, most of them contain elements in the Blueprint theme selected for the web. The publishing process may take a few minutes, depending on the number of files in the web.

FrontPage remembers the location to which you published the current web, so the next time you click the Publish Web button on the Standard toolbar, FrontPage automatically lists the location of the current web in the Specify the location to publish your Web to text box. To publish to a new location, you can change the URL listed in the text box.

Testing the FrontPage Web

Now that you have published the web, it is available to anyone on the World Wide Web. You should take the time to test the newly published web to ensure the pages look as you expected and the hyperlinks work. Complete the following steps to test your Personal web.

 To Test the FrontPage Web

1 **Click the Click here to view your published web site link (see Figure 1-70 on the previous page).**

The Internet Explorer window opens and displays the Home Page of your web in the browser window (Figure 1-71). Because you deleted the vertical navigation bar, your Web pages include only a horizontal navigation bar. Because you changed the navigation bar to show Child pages under Home, all pages at all levels have the same horizontal navigation bar.

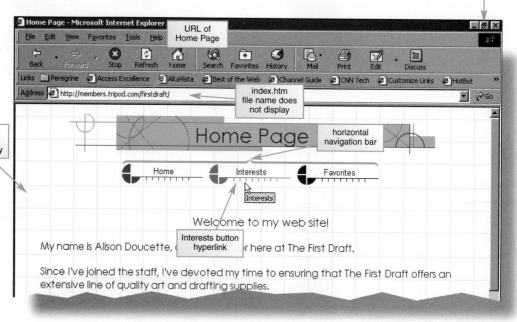

FIGURE 1-71

2 **If necessary, click the Maximize button on the Internet Explorer title bar. Click the Interests button on the horizontal navigation bar.**

The Interests page displays (Figure 1-72). The horizontal navigation bar displays a button hyperlink to the Favorites page, which is located at the same level as the Interests page. The horizontal navigation bar also includes a button hyperlink to the Home page, which is located at the parent level.

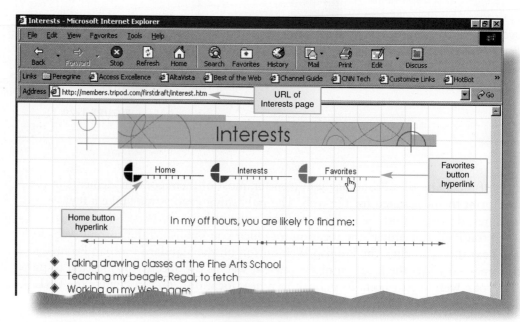

FIGURE 1-72

3 **Click the Favorites hyperlink in the horizontal navigation bar.**

The Favorites page displays (Figure 1-73). The horizontal navigation bar displays the button hyperlink to the Favorites page in a different color than that of the button hyperlinks to the Home page and to the Interests page. This is done to indicate that it links to the currently displayed page.

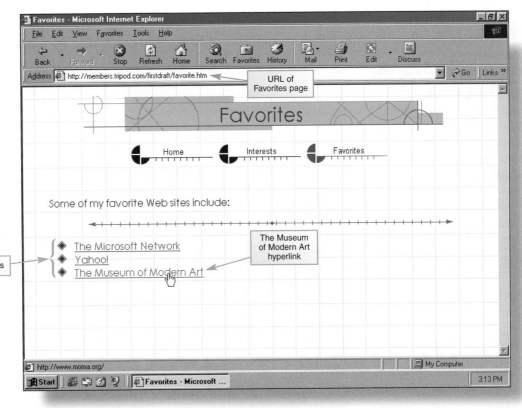

FIGURE 1-73

4 **Click The Museum of Modern Art hyperlink.**

The Museum of Modern Art home page displays in the Internet Explorer window (Figure 1-74).

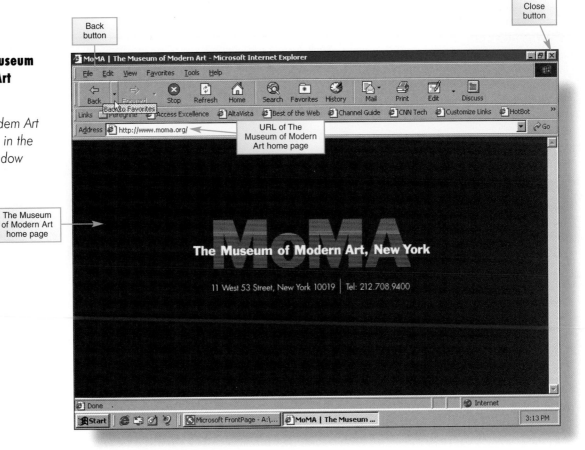

FIGURE 1-74

5 Click the Back button to return the Favorites page. After viewing the remaining Web page for accuracy and ensuring the hyperlinks function properly, click the Close button on the Internet Explorer title bar to close the browser.

The Internet Explorer window closes. FrontPage displays the Home Page in Page view (Figure 1-75). The Microsoft FrontPage dialog box still displays.

6 Click the Done button in the Microsoft FrontPage dialog box.

The dialog box closes and FrontPage displays the Home Page in Page view.

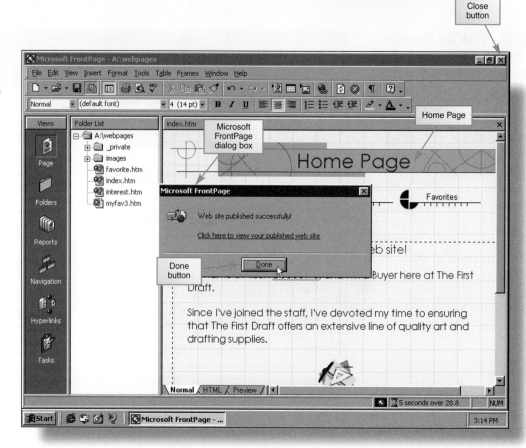

FIGURE 1-75

When you first link to your published site, the Web server displays a default Web page, called index.htm, in the URL in the Address bar. In your Personal web, the Home Page uses the file name, index.htm, and thus displays as the default page.

More *About* 2000

Web Site Testing

Nothing is more frustrating for a Web page visitor than to have difficulties navigating a Web site. Take time to ensure your Web pages serve the purpose you planned, and the hyperlinks take visitors to the intended locations. For more information on testing, visit the Shelly Cashman Series Web Design Techniques Web page at www.scsite.com/web/SCWebDes.htm and then click Web Site Testing/Marketing.

FrontPage Help System

Reference materials and other forms of assistance are available using the **FrontPage Help system**. You can display these materials, print them, or copy them to other Windows applications. Table 1-5 summarizes the categories of online Help available to you. For additional information on using FrontPage Help, see Appendix A.

Table 1-5   FrontPage Help System

TYPE	DESCRIPTION	HOW TO ACTIVATE
Answer Wizard sheet	Displays a list of topics that pertain to a natural language question or phrase that you type in the text box. From that point, you can select the topics you want to display.	Click the Microsoft FrontPage Help button on the Standard toolbar. If necessary, maximize the Help window by double-clicking its title bar. Click the Answer Wizard tab.
Contents sheet	Groups Help topics by general categories. Use when you know only the general category of the topic in question.	Click the Microsoft FrontPage Help button on the Standard toolbar. If necessary, maximize the Help window by double-clicking its title bar. Click the Contents tab.
Detect and Repair command	Automatically finds and fixes errors in the application.	Click Detect and Repair on the Help menu.
Index sheet	Similar to an index in a book. Use when you know exactly what you want.	Click the Microsoft FrontPage Help button on the Standard toolbar. If necessary, maximize the Help window by double-clicking its title bar. Click the Index tab.
Office on the Web command	Use to access technical resources and download free product enhancements on the Web.	Click Office on the Web on the Help menu.
Question Mark button and What's This? command	Identify unfamiliar items on the screen.	In a dialog box, click the Question Mark button and then click an element in the dialog box. Click What's This? on the Help menu, and then click an item on the screen.

Quitting FrontPage

Once you have finished the steps in the project and developed and published your Personal web, you can quit FrontPage. Complete the following steps to quit FrontPage.

TO QUIT FRONTPAGE

 Click the Close button on the FrontPage title bar.

 If necessary, click the Close button on the Internet Explorer title bar to quit Internet Explorer.

The Windows desktop displays.

More About

Quick Reference

For a table that lists how to complete the tasks covered in this book, visit the Office 2000 Web page (www.scsite.com/off2000/qr.htm), and then click Microsoft FrontPage 2000.

CASE PERSPECTIVE SUMMARY

Sean visited your new Web pages and found the results to be quite attractive. He indicated that your pages exemplify what he would like all employees to do: be innovative, show creativity, and be enthusiastic. Consequently, he wants to feature your personal Web page as the Employee Personal Web Page of the Month. He thinks that introducing some friendly competition will encourage employees to put forth their best efforts. If you are willing, Sean wants you to lead a training session for employees who want to develop their first Web pages. Sean also asks you to consider developing other Web pages for The First Draft's corporate Web site.

Project Summary

Having completed Project 1, you developed your Personal web and posted the pages to The First Draft's Web site. In this project, you learned the basic World Wide Web concepts, including HTML and the elements of a Web page. You learned how to create a FrontPage web using a template, to apply a theme, and to edit the place-holder text on a template page. You also learned how to modify a bulleted list, modify a FrontPage component, edit and add hyperlinks on a Web page, and insert an image on a Web page. You gained an understanding of how to use the tabs in Page view to edit page layout and to preview a Web page. Finally, you learned how to print Web pages, publish a web to the World Wide Web, and use FrontPage Help.

What You Should Know

Having completed this project, you now should be able to perform the following tasks.

▶ Add an E-Mail Hyperlink to a Web Page (*FP 1.46*)
▶ Add New Text to a Web Page (*FP 1.29*)
▶ Apply a Theme to a FrontPage Web (*FP 1.23*)
▶ Change a Hyperlink on a Web Page (*FP 1.42*)
▶ Delete a Web Page from a Web (*FP 1.39*)
▶ Edit a Bulleted List (*FP 1.31*)
▶ Edit Text on a Web Page (*FP 1.27*)
▶ Insert an Image on a Web Page (*FP 1.50*)
▶ Modify a Navigation Bar Component (*FP 1.35*)
▶ Open a Web Page in Page View (*FP 1.26*)

▶ Preview a Web Page Using the Preview Tab (*FP 1.34*)
▶ Print a Web Page (*FP 1.55*)
▶ Publish the FrontPage Web (*FP 1.66*)
▶ Quit FrontPage (*FP 1.63*)
▶ Save a Web Page (*FP 1.33*)
▶ Start FrontPage (*FP 1.15*)
▶ Test the FrontPage Web (*FP 1.60*)
▶ Use a Template to Create a FrontPage Web (*FP 1.20*)

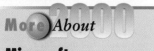

More About

Microsoft Certification

The Microsoft Office User Specialist (MOUS) Certification program provides an opportunity for you to obtain a valuable industry credential — proof that you have the FrontPage 2000 skills required by employers. For more information, visit the Shelly Cashman Series MOUS Web page at www.scsite.com/off2000/cert.htm.

Apply Your Knowledge

1 Modifying a Corporate Presence Web

Instructions: Start FrontPage. Open the file, index.htm, from the Project 1/magnorth folder on the FrontPage Data Disk. See the inside back cover for instructions for downloading the FrontPage Data Disk or see your instructor for information on accessing the files required for this book.

1. If necessary, click the Page icon on the Views bar to display the Magnetic North Trading Company home page (Figure 1-76).

2. Click the third item in the bulleted list to select it and then type `To actively promote environmental awareness` as the new text.

3. Select the fourth item in the bulleted list and then delete it.

4. Select the heading, Contact Information, and then type `Reaching Magnetic North` as the new text.

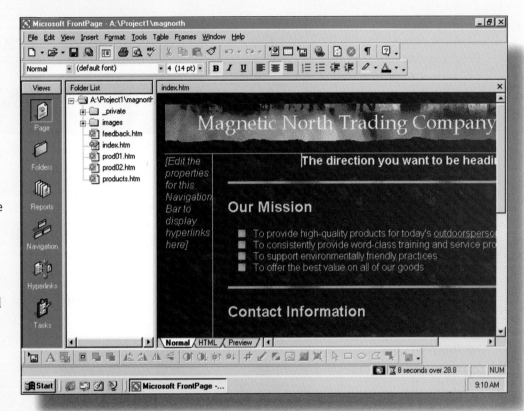

FIGURE 1-76

5. Position the insertion point after the word, Sales:, and then type `sales@magnorth.com` as the e-mail hyperlink text. Create an e-mail hyperlink that sends e-mail to sales@magnorth.com.

6. Click the Preview tab to preview the Web page. When you have finished, click the Normal tab.

7. Print and then save the Web page.

8. Click the Navigation icon on the Views bar. Delete the Feedback Web page from the Web.

9. Double-click the Products button to open the Products Web page.

10. Double-click the vertical navigation bar component. Edit the properties to include hyperlinks at the child level. Deselect the Home Page check box. In the Orientation and appearance area, select the Buttons option button to display the hyperlinks as buttons.

11. Double-click the Products Page Banner component. Edit the page banner text by typing `New Products` as the new text.

12. Print and save the Web page and then close FrontPage. Hand in the printouts to your instructor.

In the Lab

1 Creating and Modifying a Corporate Presence Web

Problem: As the manager for Platter Records, you want to develop a Web site that will provide customers with information about your newest in-stock CDs and updates on the recording industry.

Instructions: Perform the following tasks.

1. Insert a formatted floppy disk in drive A.
2. Create a new web using the Corporate Presence template. In the New dialog box, click the Corporate Presence icon and then type `a:\Project 1\records` in the Specify the location of the new web text box. Click the OK button.
3. When the Corporate Web Wizard displays, click the Next button. When prompted for information about the company, use the information in Table 1-6 to fill in the fields and choose which pages to include in your web. Choose Citrus Punch as the web theme. If necessary, click the Vivid colors, Active graphics, and Background picture check boxes. When you have finished, click the Finish button.
4. When FrontPage is finished copying the template pages, click the Navigation icon on the Views bar to display the web in Navigation view. Open the Home page.
5. Click the first paragraph to select it, click the Center button on the Formatting toolbar, and then type `Welcome to Platter Records!` as the new text. Press the ENTER key.
6. Delete the header, Our Mission. Select the second paragraph. Type `Searching for a new musical style? Adding to your focused collection of CDs? Let our Web site streamline your musical search. From alternative to zydeco, classical to New Age, we can guide you to the recordings that will satisfy your musical taste.` as the new text (Figure 1-77).

Table 1-6 Corporate Presence Web Field Information	
FIELD	*INFORMATION*
Main pages to include in Web	Products/Services
Home page information	Mission statement Contact information
Products/Services information	2 Products 0 Services
Additional information	Pricing information
What should appear at the top of each page	Page title Links to your main web pages
What should appear at the bottom of each page	E-mail address of your webmaster Date page was last modified
Under Construction icon	No
Full name of company	Platter Records
One-word version of name	Platter
Company's street address	421 Wilshire Way Los Angeles, CA 90621
Telephone and fax numbers	641.555.7528
E-mail address of your webmaster	luis@platter.com
E-mail address for general information	toshi@platter.com
Choose Web theme	Citrus Punch, with Active graphics
Show Tasks view after Web is uploaded	Yes

7. Scroll down and select the third paragraph under the header, Contact Information. Press the DELETE key twice to delete the text from the page.
8. Print and then save the Web page.
9. Click the HTML tab. View and then print the HTML source code for the Home page. Click the Normal tab.
10. Click the Navigation icon on the Views bar.
11. Open the Products page by double-clicking the Products page icon.

In the Lab

12. Select the horizontal navigation bar below the Products banner, click the Center button on the Formatting toolbar, and then edit the properties to include hyperlinks at the child level. Make sure the Home page check box is selected. In the Orientation and appearance area, select the Text check box.

13. Select the vertical navigation bar and then edit the properties to include hyperlinks at the same level.

14. Select all of the text on the page. Type
    `Join us for this month's Grammy Celebration Sale!` and then press the ENTER key. Type `All CDs from Grammy-winning artists are up to 40% off through the end of the month. Click the links to browse through our collection.` as the new text.

15. Print and save the Web page, and then close FrontPage. Hand in the printouts to your instructor.

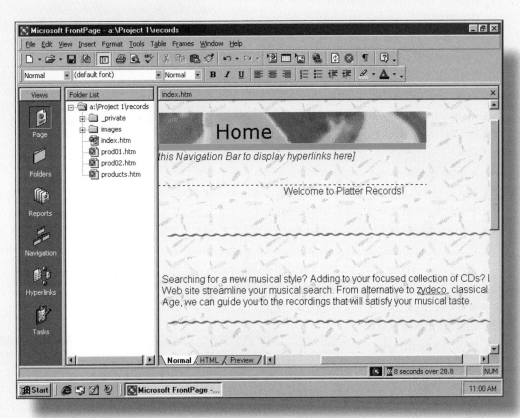

FIGURE 1-77

2 Creating and Modifying a One-Page Web

Problem: As part of your American Studies course, your instructor asks you to develop a one-page web with information on your final project. The page should include a description of your topic, one or more photos, and your contact information.

Instructions: Perform the following tasks.

1. Insert a formatted floppy disk in drive A.
2. Create a new web using the One Page Web template. In the New dialog box, click the One Page Web icon and then type `a:\Project 1\amstudies` in the Specify the location of the new web text box. Click the OK button.
3. Double-click the file name, index.htm, in the Folder List pane to open the Home Page.
4. Apply the Expedition theme to the web. Select Background picture.

(continued)

In the Lab

Creating and Modifying a One-Page Web *(continued)*

5. When FrontPage has finished applying the theme, type the text in Table 1-7 to describe the American Studies project. When you have finished typing the text, press the ENTER key.

6. Type David Reamy, University of Wakefield for the contact information (You can substitute your name and school for the text shown here.) Press the ENTER key.

7. Type Please e-mail comments and questions to davidr@wakefield.edu. as the last line of text.

8. Drag through the e-mail address text to select it.

9. Create an e-mail hyperlink to the e-mail address, davidr@wakefield.edu.

10. Position the insertion point at the end of the first paragraph of text. Click Picture on the Insert menu and then click From File on the Picture submenu.

11. Click the Use your Web Browser to select a page or file button. Browse to www.scsite.com/fp2000/pr1/glenn.jpg.

12. Click the Microsoft FrontPage taskbar button and then insert the picture on the Home Page (Figure 1-78).

13. Save and print the Web page. Write your name on the page, and hand it in to your instructor.

14. Close Internet Explorer and FrontPage.

Table 1-7 American Studies Final Project
THEME: THE TURBULENT SIXTIES (1961-1968)
The 1960s were a time of change — a decade marked equally by progress and defeat. The new style of President John F. Kennedy, John Glenn's earth orbit, President Johnson's innovative domestic policies, and the civil rights and women's movements infused America with life. By contrast, events such as the shocking assassinations of JFK, Martin Luther King, and Bobby Kennedy; riots; and the stalemate of the Vietnam War overshadowed the buoyant mood, breeding frustration and anger.

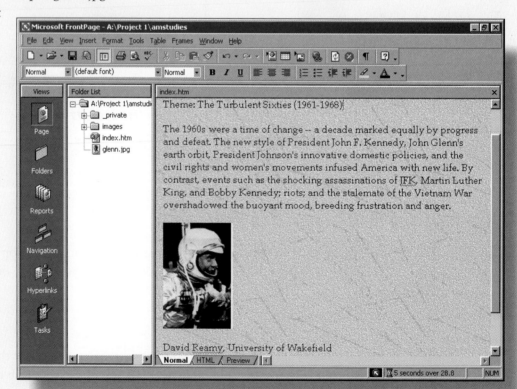

FIGURE 1-78

In the Lab

3 Creating and Modifying a Personal Web

Problem: You have decided to develop a Personal web with your exclusive information about buying cars online. In addition to an introductory Home Page, you plan to include a page of links to online car dealers, references, and other relevant Web sites.

Instructions: Perform the following tasks.

1. Insert a formatted floppy disk in drive A.
2. Create a new web using the Personal Web template. In the New dialog box, click the Personal Web icon and then type `a:\Project 1\cars` in the Specify the location of the new web text box. Click the OK button.
3. Click the Navigation icon on the Views bar. Delete the Interests and Photo Album pages from the web.
4. Double-click the Home Page page icon in the Navigation pane to open the Home Page.
5. If necessary, apply the Straight Edge theme to the web.
6. Select the vertical navigation bar and then edit the properties to include hyperlinks at the Same level.
7. Select the horizontal navigation bar and then edit the properties to include hyperlinks to Child pages under Home. Deselect the Home Page check box.
8. Select the placeholder text in the second paragraph and then type `Planning to buy a new car? Or simply want to trade in your old one? Browse through my collection of favorite car links to learn how to get the best deals and information on the Web.`
9. Delete the third paragraph of placeholder text and then save the Web page.
10. Open the Favorites page.
11. Select the first paragraph of placeholder text and then type `An alphabetical listing of some of the best car sites on the Web.`
12. Edit the bulleted list of hyperlinks to include the sites and URLs listed in Table 1-8.

Table 1-8 Bulleted List Hyperlinks	
HYPERLINK TEXT	*URL*
Autobytel.com	http://www.autobytel.com
AutoSite	http://www.autosite.com
Edmund's Automobile Buyer's Guide	http://www.edmunds.com
Kelly Blue Book	http://www.kellybluebook.com/
Microsoft CarPoint	http://www.carpoint.com/

(continued)

In the Lab

Creating and Modifying a Personal Web *(continued)*

13. Save the Web page (Figure 1-79).
14. Print the Home page and the Favorites page, write your name on the pages, and hand them in to your instructor.
15. If you have access to a Web server, publish the web. Once you have tested the Web pages in your browser, close your browser and then quit FrontPage.

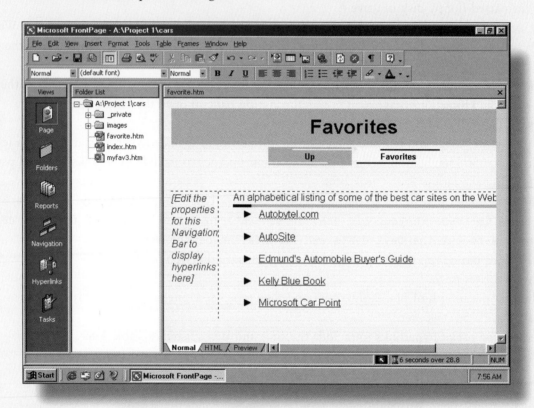

FIGURE 1-79

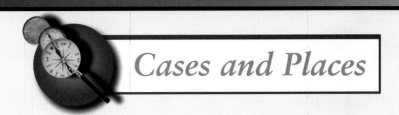

Cases and Places

The difficulty of these case studies varies:
❿ are the least difficult; ❿❿ are more difficult; and ❿❿❿ are the most difficult.

1 ❿ Your instructor wants his course syllabus available on the Web. Using the One Page Web template, create a text-only course Home page that includes information from the course syllabus. Apply the theme of your choice to the web. Include an e-mail hyperlink to the instructor's e-mail address.

2 ❿ Each month, your manager at the BookBytes online bookstore asks you to publish a one-page review of a newly released book. Using the One Page Web template, develop a Web page that includes the following information about a book of your choice: title, author, copyright year, publisher, BookBytes price, and a brief review. Obtain a graphic from the Web at the URL, http://www.scsite.com/fp2000/pr1/book.gif, and then insert the graphic on the Home page. Include an e-mail hyperlink to your Web address at the bottom of the page.

3 ❿ You are a paralegal at the prestigious law firm, Ludwig, Johnson, and McCallister. One of the partners informs you that the firm has space on its Web site for you to publish a Personal web. Using the Personal Web template, develop a Web site that includes a Home page, an Interests page, and a Favorites page. Edit the horizontal navigation bar properties to include Child level pages; edit the vertical navigation bar properties to include Same level pages. Edit the placeholder text to include your own replacement text. The Home page should include an e-mail hyperlink to your Web address; the Favorites page should include at least one hyperlink to the firm's site at http://www.ljim-law.com.

4 ❿❿ As captain of your Recreation League basketball team, you have decided to develop a Web page that lists upcoming games, scores of recent games, and current league standings. Using the One Page Web template, develop a Web page that lists the information shown in Table 1-9 and Table 1-10. The Web page should include an e-mail hyperlink to your Web address and a hyperlink to the Recreation League's main site at http://www.recleagueball.com.

Table 1-9   Games and Scores

GAME/SCORE	DATES/TIMES/RESULTS
Upcoming Games	JumpShots vs. Dunks (Home) Tuesday, 7 PM
	JumpShots vs. AirBalls (Home) Thursday, 6 PM
	JumpShots vs. Dribblers (Away) Saturday, 2 PM
Recent Scores	JumpShots vs. Hoopsters, 66-48
	JumpShots vs. AllNets, 56-62
	JumpShots vs. Dunks, 82-72

Table 1-10   Current League Standings

TEAM	WON	LOST
JumpShots	5	1
Dunks	5	1
Hoopsters	4	2
AllNets	3	3
Dribblers	3	3
AirBalls	2	4

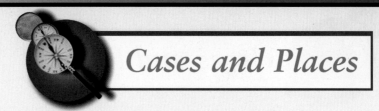

Cases and Places

5 ▶▶▶ As a columnist for the Arts section of the local newspaper, you have a Movie Review Web site, which you use to publish updates to your latest columns. Using the Corporate Web Presence template, develop a Web site that includes at least a Home page and two pages for movie reviews (use Product pages for each movie review page). Edit the placeholder text on each page to include information about your movie Review Web site. Obtain a graphic from the Web at the URL, http://www.scsite.com/fp2000/pr1/movie.jpg, and then insert the graphic on the Home Page.

Microsoft **FrontPage 2000**

Microsoft FrontPage 2000

P R O J E C T

Creating a New FrontPage Web

O B J E C T I V E S

You will have mastered the material in this project when you can:

- List Web page design criteria
- Create a new one-page web
- Change the title of a Web page
- Change the page label of a Web page
- Set the Web page background color
- Insert a table in a Web page
- Undo and redo actions in FrontPage
- Insert an image in a Web page
- Change an image in a Web page
- Copy and paste items on a Web page
- Align items on a Web page
- Change table border properties
- Add a heading to a Web page
- Add horizontal rules
- Add normal text
- Create hyperlinks
- Import a Web page
- Preview a Web page

Web Designers Among the Great Composers

Composers in a new era are changing the way people view the World Wide Web. The early limitations placed on Web designers are becoming a thing of the past; due in large part to the upsurge in capabilities of many of the Web browsers, increased modem speeds, and a multitude of browser plug-ins available for enhancing site content.

The objective of an accomplished Web page designer is to create high-quality, noteworthy Web pages that are admired by colleagues, win awards, and are models of exceptional style.

This appreciation does not come from verbose, complex, overanimated designs, but from thoughtful planning, sensitivity to viewers, and focus on detail. Among the skills required are a thorough understanding of the diverse community of potential viewers and the goal to be achieved by the Web page.

The Internet is rich with examples of exemplary sites utilizing content and graphics

that draw thousands of visitors and keep their attention as they offer their wares and services, provide information, educate, and entertain.

Literature abounds with examples of authors who pursue very similar objectives as they prepare a first draft and continue to rewrite as they struggle to get the words right. In his book, *On Writing Well*, respected Yale University English professor William Zinsser states, "Writing improves in direct ratio to the things we can keep out of it that shouldn't be there."

In the world of musical arrangements, celebrated composers exhibit the struggles they experience as they toil to score their greatest pieces in scrupulous detail and thought. Some are eccentric; others are driven to seclusion to write the ultimate concerto or symphony. Two such great virtuosos are composers of the nineteenth century. Schumann and Smetana composed masterpieces in unusual circumstances. Each experienced comparable fame and both suffered progressive deafness.

Robert Schumann, whose beautiful musical compositions still grace the world, had to spend the final years of his life in a mental institution, where many of the hundreds of his compositions were composed. In his diary, Schumann wrote that his hallucinations drove him to write, "glorious music with instruments sounding more wonderful than one ever hears on earth." Some of his best works, such as *Kreisleriana*, the *Spring* symphony, and the *Manfred Overture*, were written at the urging of inner voices coming from "angels who hovered over me." As his deafness progressed, he would hear complete original scores in his mind, with the final chord ringing continuously until he forced himself either to write out the entire piece or go on to another composition.

One of Schumann's many famous musical contemporaries, Czechoslovakian composer Bedrich Smetana, also began to lose his hearing at the height of his fame. A continuous high-pitched E note from a violin — a condition now known as tinnitus — sounded inside his ear, driving him to madness. Yet, he continued to compose some of his more beautiful pieces. Today, Czechs consider this gifted composer of hundreds of works, including *The Bartered Bride*, *Ma Vlast* (My Country), and the lovely *Die Moldau*, to be their supreme national composer.

To join the company of eminent composers, your finished product must leave a unique and lasting impression on those who will visit your Web page. With the perpetual growth of the World Wide Web and an international audience, using FrontPage 2000 can provide you with the tools you need to produce superior Web sites. In this project, you will learn proper design techniques to ensure an attractive and tasteful work as you create a new FrontPage web for the Bits 'n' Bytes computer club of Hilltop Community College.

Always consider the purpose of your page and intended audience to help you shape information and content and select consistent components. Structure your information so the casual reader can grasp your concept. Group topics onto a single page. Decide on and test the hyperlinks so browsers can navigate with ease. Animation and graphics can contribute to the purpose of your page, but remember that the more complex your page, the more time required to create it and download it.

With simplicity in mind, you may find yourself among the great Web composers of the new millennium.

Microsoft FrontPage 2000

Microsoft FrontPage 2000

Creating a New FrontPage Web

P R O J E C T

2

C A S E   P E R S P E C T I V E

Your cousin, Paul, is a member of Bits 'n' Bytes, the computer club at Hilltop Community College. The club has been offered space on the school's Web server to promote its activities. To take advantage of this offer, the club must create its own Web pages. Unfortunately, no one in the club has experience creating Web pages, and something must be completed by tomorrow. Because Paul is familiar with your work, he showed your personal Web site to club members. They agreed to ask if you would develop a Web site for the club.

Because this will be the first Web site ever for the club, and there is little time for a more complex design, club officers decided that a simple, single-page Web site is sufficient for now. They want links in place for a page on club officers, a sign-up page for potential members, and a page for listing current discount pricing deals the club has negotiated. While these Web pages will be developed later, the links will be inserted now.

Introduction

Every Web page designer wants to build a high-quality Web page that is attractive, gets the attention of new visitors, is admired by colleagues, and may even be imitated. This appreciation does not come from complicated or over-animated designs, but from thoughtful planning, sensitivity to viewers, and careful attention to detail. You must have a thorough understanding of the diverse community of potential viewers and the goal to be accomplished by the Web page.

Web page development consists of two phases: design and implementation. **Design** consists of understanding the audience, determining the purpose of the Web page, then selecting and organizing the individual elements that, together, will achieve that purpose. **Implementation** consists of writing the HTML statements and organizing files and folders to give substance to the design. Sometimes the design and implementation tasks are separated, with a design group rendering the designs and another group responsible for the implementation.

Designing a Web page is an iterative process. Typically, you would perform some analysis concerning the requirements of the Web page, then call upon your creativity to arrive at a design that satisfies those requirements in its functionality, and is also attractive.

Once a page is designed, it is a simple matter to create it using an HTML editor, such as Microsoft FrontPage. Microsoft FrontPage has many rich features that will assist you in implementing Web page designs, from the simple to the complex. In this project, you will learn some of the criteria used to arrive at well-designed Web pages and then implement the design for the Bits 'n' Bytes Home page shown in Figure 2-1.

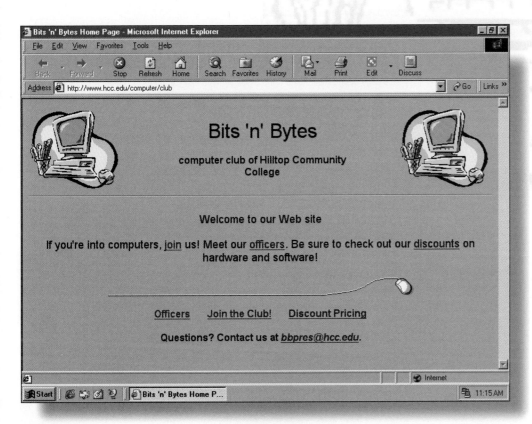

FIGURE 2-1

Web Page Design Criteria

If you ask several experienced Web page designers what the criteria are for a good Web page design, you will get as many different answers. Each designer will emphasize different elements that he or she thinks are important. A basic set of common criteria exists, however, on which all developers can agree.

When a Web page is well designed, the mechanics of the page almost disappear, enabling the users to concentrate on their research, exploration, or pleasure. Table 2-1 on the next page lists several important criteria with their associated guidelines for designing and developing Web pages. The list is by no means exhaustive.

More About 2000

Web Page Design

Discover tips, tricks, and techniques for designing Web pages by perusing the numerous formal and informal Best of the Web sites. These sites contain links to outstanding Web pages. Use a search engine to find Best of the Web sites or visit the FrontPage 2000 More About Web page (www.scsite.com/fp2000/more.htm) and click Web Page Design.

Table 2-1

CRITERIA	GUIDELINES
Authentication	• Announce who is responsible for the existence of the Web page. • Name the sponsoring organization and author of the Web page. • Use clear, concise titles that identify or announce the purpose of the page. • List appropriate dates, such as the date written or the date the page was last changed. • List the sources for information or other data used on the Web page.
Aesthetics	• Ensure the Web page looks good and is easy to navigate. • Provide functionality and clear organization. • Select good metaphors to represent your concepts and ideas. • Use complementary color schemes. • Eliminate the use of too many animated graphics on a single page. • Avoid long paragraphs of plain text.
Performance	• Keep the pages relatively short. Long pages take time to display. • Web page design should be a compromise between many graphics vs. speed of display. • Use the 10 second response rule when possible: A user will wonder if something is wrong after waiting about 10 seconds without a response.
Consistency	• Use the same colors, locations, and navigation techniques for all related pages. • Maintain a uniform look and feel for all related pages. • Utilize themes and templates to ensure consistency.
Validity	• As with any paper, story, or other literary piece, proofread the text for accuracy. • Verify all the hyperlinks to ensure they are valid. • Check the image, sound, or movie files used in the Web pages. • View the Web page using different browsers. Not every neat HTML trick or every file format is supported in all browsers.
Images	• Use alternate text in your Web page to provide support for text-only browsers. • Note the size of a large image next to a hyperlink so viewers can decide whether or not to download it. • Use thumbnail images to provide a preview of larger images. • Use universally recognized images for items such as Forward and Back buttons. Remember that you have a global audience.
Hyperlinks	• Ensure that each Web page stands on its own; users can come in from anywhere. • Provide hyperlinks to resources mentioned in the page. • Use clear navigation hyperlinks such as Next, Back, and Home. • At a minimum, always have a hyperlink to the site's Home page. • Limit the number of hyperlinks. • Avoid click here hyperlinks.
External Files	• Note the type of file, such as avi for compressed video files, or jpg for image files. • Include a notation of the size of the file next to the hyperlink.

More About 2000

Viewing HTML Code

In addition to using the HTML tab, you can click Reveal Tags on the View menu. This will display (or hide) HTML tags on the Normal tab in Page view. Position the mouse pointer on any tag and the details of the tag will display in a ScreenTip.

Each individual Web page should have one purpose or present one concept. Avoid splitting one concept into two parts simply to reduce the size of a page. Likewise, refrain from combining two unrelated ideas just to make a Web page larger.

To help you learn new tips and techniques, examine a number of well-designed pages. View the HTML source to see how other developers created the effects that interest you.

Many HTML style guides are accessible on the Web. Style guides can contain rules, guidelines, tips, and templates that assist you in creating Web pages. Use any Web search engine and search for the keywords, html style guide. Your school or local library also may have an HTML style guide available.

Web Page Components

A typical Web page is composed of three common sections: the header, the body, and the footer (Figure 2-2). The **header** can contain text or images that identify the sponsoring site, the author, or the purpose of the page. Many business Web sites will place an advertisement in the header area, because this is the first part of the Web page that shows in the browser's display area. The header also can contain hyperlinks to related pages at the Web site. The header is an important part of the Web page. Viewers evaluate your site from their first impression of the header information. An appealing header will pique their interest, so they will want to see what else is on the page.

The **body** of the Web page contains information and other materials that initially bring visitors to the Web page. The information will be conveyed with combinations of text, images, animation, and hyperlinks.

The **footer** of the Web page provides contact information and navigation controls. You would expect to find the name and perhaps the e-mail address of the author of the Web page or other official contact person responsible for the Web site. Hyperlinks to other resources at the Web site, such as the Home page or Help information also will be included in this section.

It is useful, when designing a Web page, to divide the page into these three logical sections to ease the design process. You can focus your attention on completing one of the three sections, test it, and then move on to the next one.

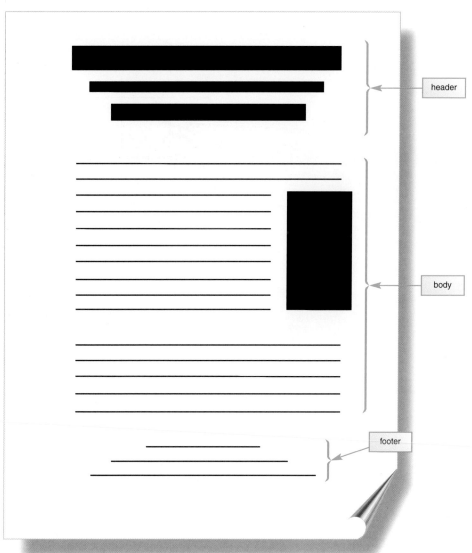

FIGURE 2-2

Designing the Web Page

Ideally, you would create several Web page design alternatives and then discuss with other designers the merits and shortcomings of each. The leading contenders then are refined, until a final design is agreed upon. In practice, usually you will work alone and thus be responsible for these tasks yourself.

Several techniques, including brainstorming and word association, are available for use during the creative process. As with any artistic endeavor, form follows function. If something appears on the Web page, then it serves some purpose. If something serves no purpose, then it should not be on the Web page.

After receiving input from the Bits 'n' Bytes president, you design a Home page. In a second session with the club officers, the design shown in Figure 2-3 is approved. Notice the page is divided easily into the header, body, and footer sections.

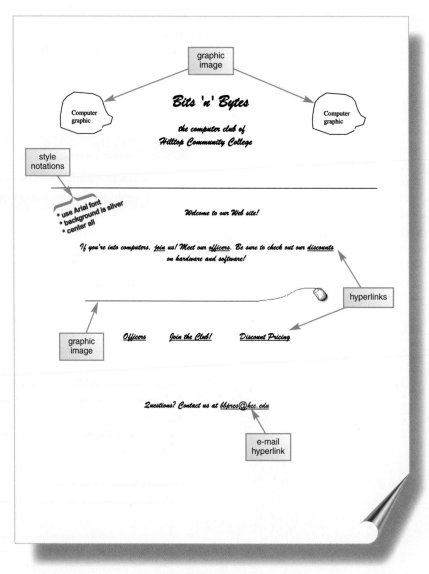

FIGURE 2-3

The header contains two images and a heading that identifies the club. The body of the page contains descriptive information and hyperlinks to other Web pages in the Bits 'n' Bytes web. The footer contains navigation hyperlinks and contact information in the form of an e-mail hyperlink.

Notice the **notations** on the design document indicating special formatting requirements such as color, text size, and alignment. With the design of the page completed, you now can implement the design using Microsoft FrontPage 2000.

Starting Microsoft FrontPage and Creating a New FrontPage Web

In Project 1 you learned that you can create a new FrontPage web in several ways. You can import an existing Web from a Web server. You can use a template or wizard. Finally, you can create a simple, one-page web. Before using any of these options, however, you must start Microsoft FrontPage. The following steps summarize how to start Microsoft FrontPage.

TO START FRONTPAGE 2000

 Click the Start button on the taskbar. Point to Programs on the Start menu.

Click Microsoft FrontPage on the Programs submenu.

The FrontPage window opens and an empty page displays.

Creating a One-page Web

Templates and wizards, such as the one used in Project 1, are great work-saving devices. Sometimes, however, the requirements necessitate the design of Web pages that do not fall neatly into any of the more complex template categories. In this case, you can create a one-page Web and add new pages as necessary. Adding pages to an existing FrontPage web is discussed in Project 3. The following steps demonstrate how to create a new FrontPage web consisting of a single page. Because FrontPage creates many files for a web, and because you use files from the Data Disk in this project, it is advisable to create the project using the computer's hard drive (typically drive C:) rather than the floppy drive (A:).

Perform the following steps to create a new one-page web.

 To Create a New One-page Web

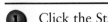 **Click the New Page button arrow on the Standard toolbar. Point to Web on the New Page button menu.**

The New Page button menu displays with the Web command selected (Figure 2-4).

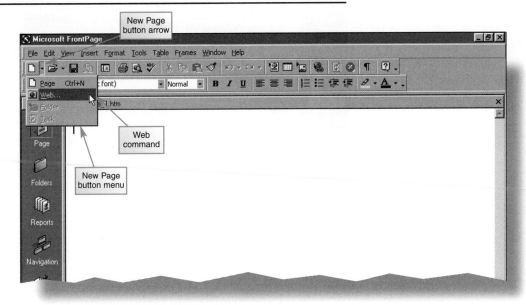

FIGURE 2-4

2 **Click Web. When the New dialog box displays, if necessary, click the One Page Web icon to select it.**

The New dialog box displays with the One Page Web icon selected (Figure 2-5).

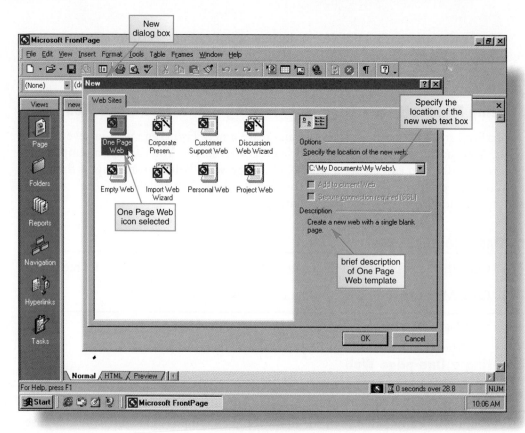

FIGURE 2-5

3 **Click the Specify the location of the new web text box to highlight the default location text. Type** C:\My Documents\My Webs\Club **in the text box. Point to the OK button.**

The new location displays in the text box (Figure 2-6). Use the drive and location that is appropriate for your environment.

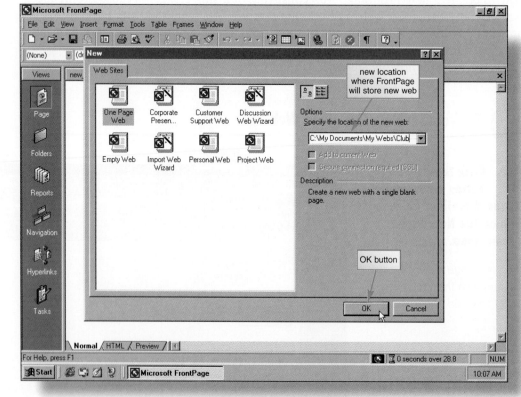

FIGURE 2-6

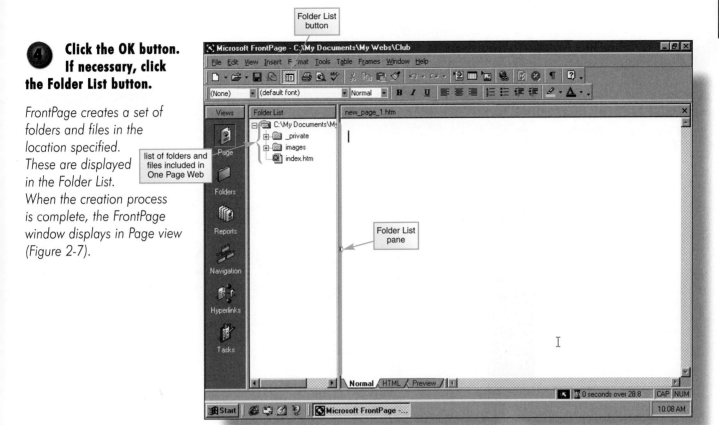

4 Click the OK button. If necessary, click the Folder List button.

FrontPage creates a set of folders and files in the location specified. These are displayed in the Folder List. When the creation process is complete, the FrontPage window displays in Page view (Figure 2-7).

FIGURE 2-7

In Project 1, you learned that FrontPage creates several folders and files that together compose a FrontPage web. Once FrontPage has created the files and folders, you can begin to customize the Web page.

Changing the Title of a Web Page

The title of a Web page displays in the title bar of most browsers and in any bookmarks or favorites for that page. This is not the same as the page label, which displays in page banners and navigation bars created by Microsoft FrontPage. Each file, or page, in a web has its own title. The default title for the file named index.htm is Home Page. The title of a file can be changed without modifying its file name. Titles should reflect the name of the organization or purpose of the Web page.

The steps on the next page change the title of the Bits 'n' Bytes Home page to the name of the organization so that it will be placed on the title bar of browsers and in favorites or bookmark lists.

Steps | To Change the Title of a Web Page

1 **Click the Navigation icon on the Views bar. If necessary, click the Close button on the Navigation toolbar.**

FrontPage displays in Navigation view (Figure 2-8).

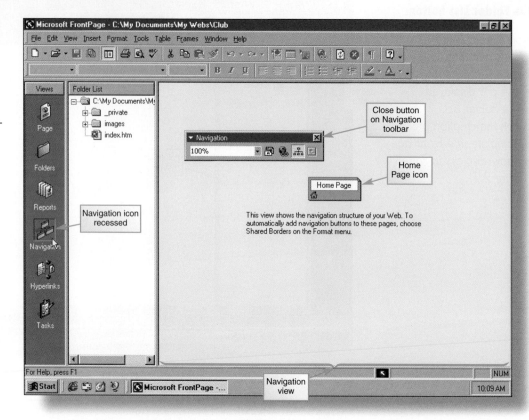

FIGURE 2-8

2 **Right-click the Home Page page icon. Point to Properties on the shortcut menu.**

A shortcut menu displays (Figure 2-9).

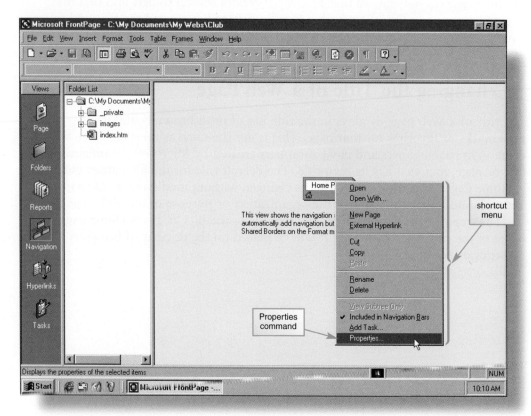

FIGURE 2-9

③ Click Properties. Click the General tab, if necessary.

The Properties dialog box displays and the default title is highlighted (Figure 2-10).

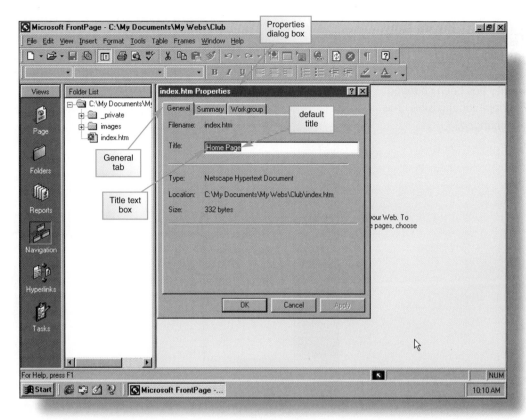

FIGURE 2-10

④ Type Bits 'n' Bytes Home Page **in the Title text box. Point to the OK button.**

The new text replaces the old text (Figure 2-11).

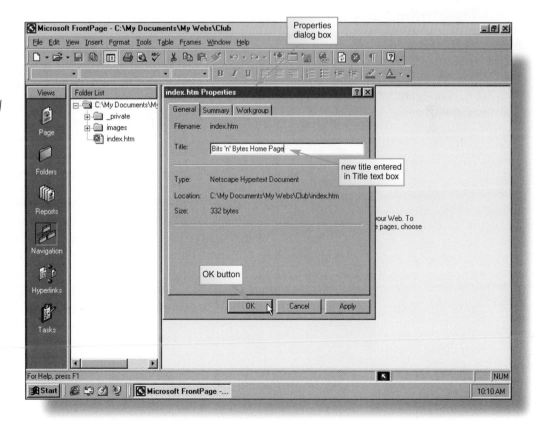

FIGURE 2-11

5 **Click the OK button.**

The Properties dialog box closes. Although the title (not visible) has been changed, the page label (visible) has not changed.

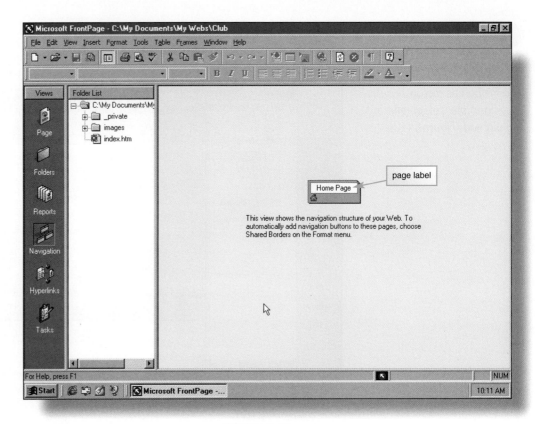

FIGURE 2-12

***Other* Ways**

1. Right-click file name in Folder List pane, click Properties on shortcut menu, enter new title in Title text box on General tab of Properties dialog box

You can change the titles of other new or existing Web pages using the same techniques. Although FrontPage allows you to enter very long titles, browser title bars display approximately 80 to 90 characters, so keep this limitation in mind when entering the title. Once you have changed the title, you can start the FrontPage Editor and begin to edit the Web page.

Changing the Page Label of a Web Page

As you have seen, changing the title of a Web page did not affect the page label. FrontPage uses the page labels displayed in Navigation view as the labels for navigation bars. If you change a page title, you also may want the labels on corresponding navigation bars to match. You can change the text that is displayed on a navigation bar by changing the page labels in Navigation view.

The following steps change the page label of the Bits 'n' Bytes Home page to include the name of the organization so it will be placed in the labels of navigation bars.

To Change the Page Label of a Web Page

1 **Right-click the Home Page page icon in the Navigation pane. Point to the Rename command.**

The shortcut menu displays (Figure 2-13).

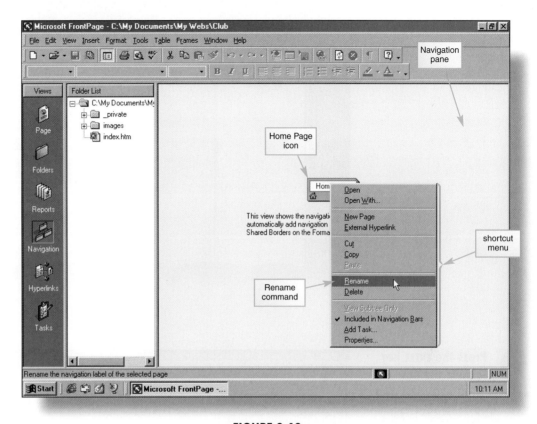

FIGURE 2-13

2 **Click Rename on the shortcut menu.**

An edit text box displays around the default label and the label is highlighted (Figure 2-14).

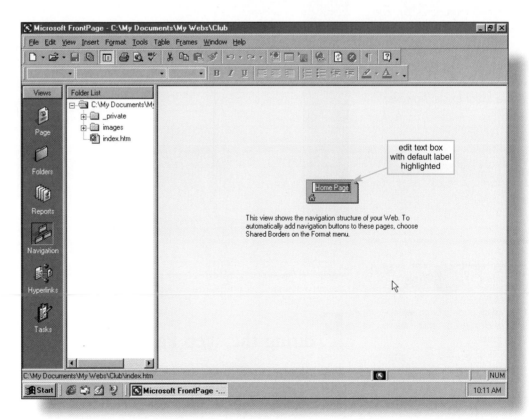

FIGURE 2-14

③ Type Bits 'n' Bytes Home Page **in the edit text box.**

The new text replaces the old text (Figure 2-15).

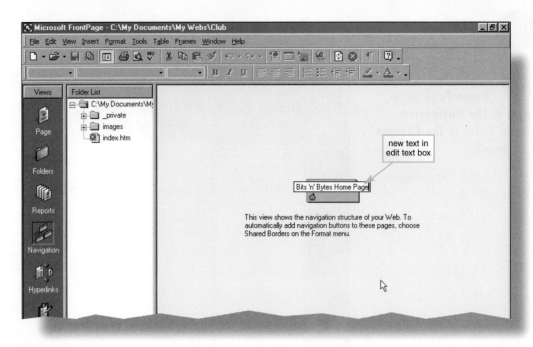

FIGURE 2-15

④ Press the ENTER key to save the new label.

The edit box closes and the new label displays in the page icon (Figure 2-16). The new label does not display in its entirety because it is longer than the room available in the page icon. The entire label exists, however.

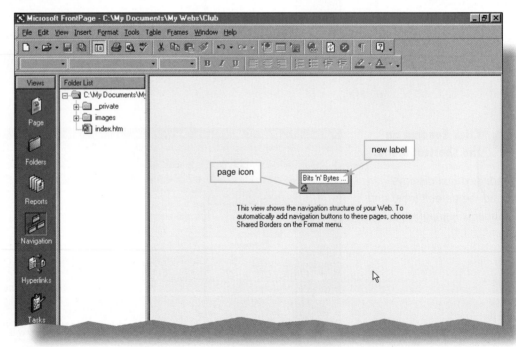

FIGURE 2-16

Other **Ways**

1. Click page icon to select, click text box, type new label

Editing the Web Page

The tasks required to create the Bits 'n' Bytes Web page consist of selecting the page background; inserting headings, images, and text; establishing hyperlinks; and testing the page. In FrontPage 2000, Web pages are edited in Page view. Perform the following steps to edit the Bits 'n' Bytes Home page.

To Edit the Web Page

1 **Double-click the Bits 'n' Bytes page icon in the Navigation pane.**

The file index.htm opens in Page view (Figure 2-17). The display area is empty.

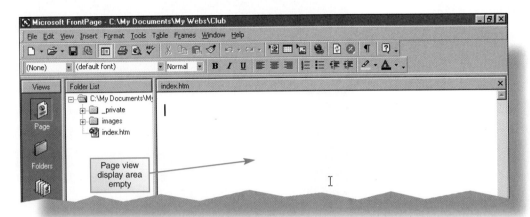

FIGURE 2-17

Other Ways

1. Double-click index.htm file name in Folder List pane
2. Select page icon, click Page view icon

With the page open in Page view, you can start customizing the Web page to implement the design shown in Figure 2-3 on page FP 2.8. The first step is to change the background color.

Changing the Background Color of a Web Page

The **background** of a Web page can be a solid color, an image, or a pattern that is repeated across and down the page. You can select a color from within FrontPage, select an image or pattern stored on your local computer, or copy an image or pattern from any Web page on the World Wide Web.

Currently, the page displays in the default background color white. According to the design, you are to use the color silver for the background. Perform the following steps to change the background color of the Web page to silver.

To Change the Background Color

1 **Click Format on the menu bar and then point to Background.**

The Format menu displays (Figure 2-18). The Format menu contains commands to manage Web page formatting items such as themes, style sheets, and backgrounds.

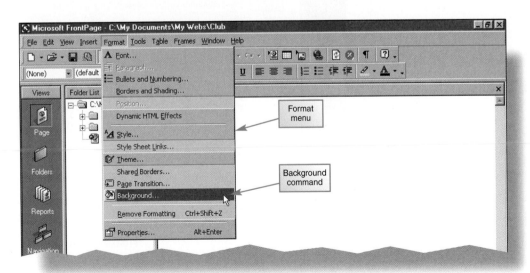

FIGURE 2-18

2 Click Background. If necessary, click the Background tab.

The Page Properties dialog box displays (Figure 2-19). The **Background sheet** contains settings to control the background image or color.

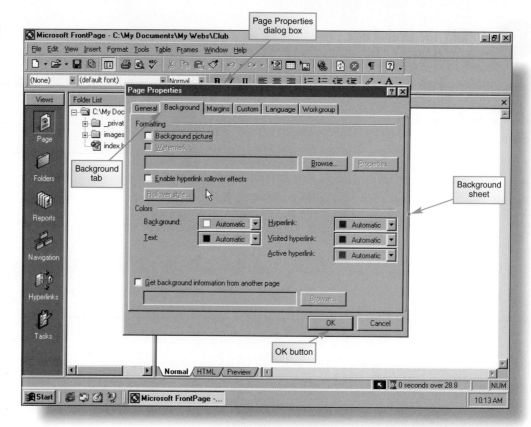

FIGURE 2-19

3 In the Colors area, click the Background box arrow. Point to Silver on the color palette.

A palette of available background colors displays and the color Silver is highlighted (Figure 2-20).

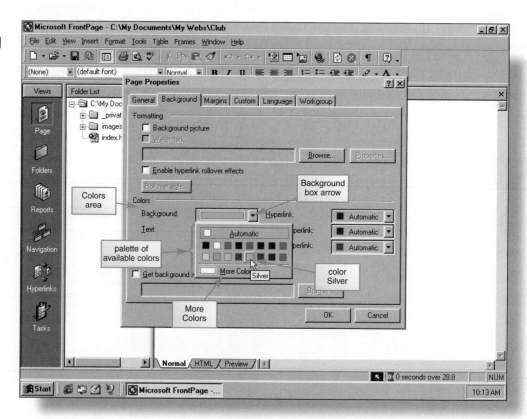

FIGURE 2-20

Click Silver. Point to the OK button.

Silver is selected as the background color in the Background box (Figure 2-21).

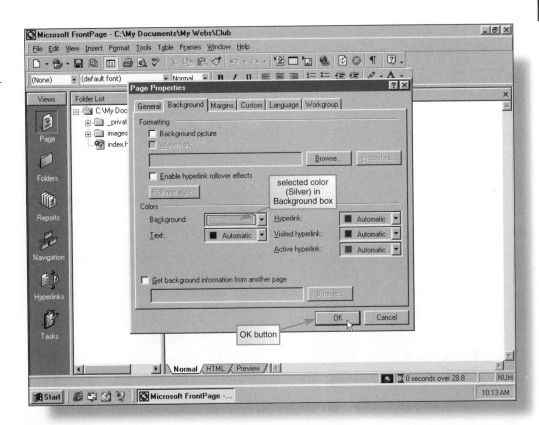

FIGURE 2-21

 Click the OK button.

The Page pane displays with the Silver background color (Figure 2-22).

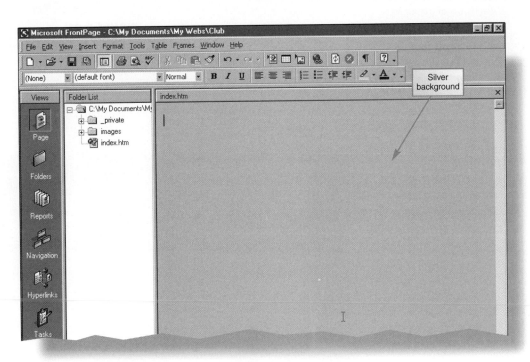

FIGURE 2-22

When you click the Background box arrow, the color palette displays and allows you to select the color of your choice. If you happen to prefer another color, simply click the Background box arrow and select the desired color.

Selecting **More Colors** on the color palette displays a More Colors dialog box (Figure 2-23) with additional predefined colors available. For even more colors, select Custom to display a Color dialog box (Figure 2-24) in which you can mix your own color, save it as a custom color, and then use it as the background color.

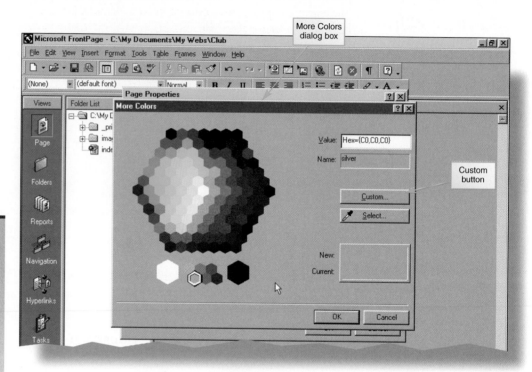

FIGURE 2-23

Web Page Colors

FrontPage uses hue, saturation, and luminosity to specify colors. Hue represents a gradation of color, such as red or blue. Saturation is the amount of color in a hue. Luminosity is the brightness of a hue. Many sites have help on selecting appropriate colors for Web pages. Visit the FrontPage 2000 More About Web page (www.scsite.com/fp2000/more.htm) and click Web Page Colors.

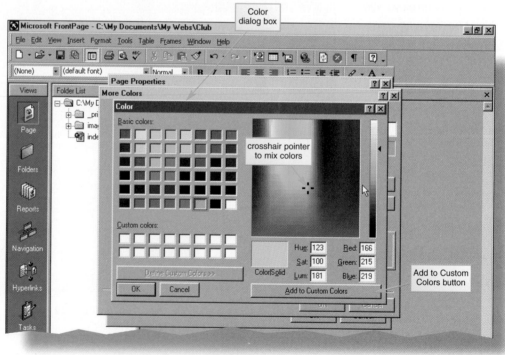

FIGURE 2-24

Other Ways

1. Right-click Page pane, click Page Properties on shortcut menu, click Background tab
2. Press ALT+O, K

Using Tables on a Web Page

Tables are used frequently in applications to present information in a clear, concise format. Disciplines such as mathematics, engineering, and chemistry all take advantage of tables. A computer spreadsheet is laid out in the form of a table with rows and columns. Many different applications exist for which tables are an ideal solution.

As noted earlier, an HTML table consists of one or more rows containing one or more columns. The intersection of a row and column is called a **cell**. Any Web page component, such as text or an image, can be placed in a cell.

Normally, you would use tables on a Web page to display any type of information that looks best in rows and columns, such as a list of products and their corresponding prices. In Web pages, tables also can be used to accomplish special design effects.

You can create a table and insert your entire Web page in the cells. Using tables, you can define headings, sidebars, and captions and use other creative design techniques.

In the Bits 'n' Bytes Web page, you will use a table with one row and three columns to control the horizontal spacing between the two outside images and the club name in the header at the top of the page (Figure 2-1 on page FP 2.5). Perform the following steps to insert a table in a Web page.

More About

Tables

Tables on a Web page can contain different background colors and images than the rest of the Web page. The Table Properties dialog box contains options that allow you to select a different background color or an image file.

 Steps **To Insert a Table in a Web Page**

1 **Click the Insert Table button on the Standard toolbar.**

The Insert Table box displays (Figure 2-25). You can indicate how many rows and columns the table will have by dragging through the cell matrix.

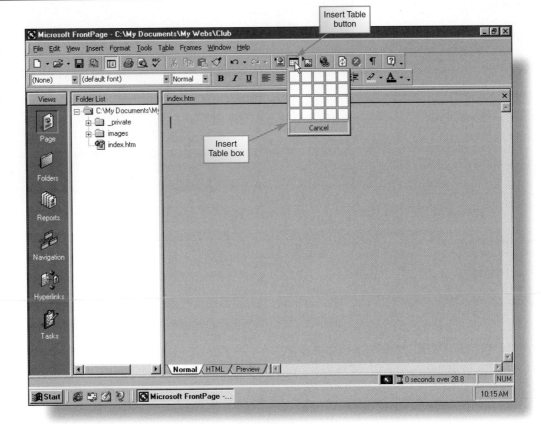

FIGURE 2-25

Point to the third square from the left to highlight three squares in the cell matrix.

The three squares become highlighted (Figure 2-26). This indicates you want a one-row table with three columns, for a total of three cells.

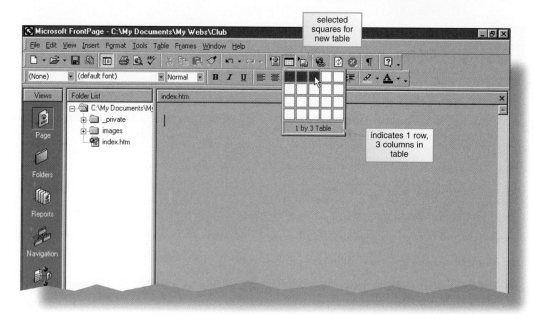

FIGURE 2-26

 Click the mouse button.

A table displays in the Web page with one row and three columns (Figure 2-27). The table extends across the width of the Web page. Each cell is the same size.

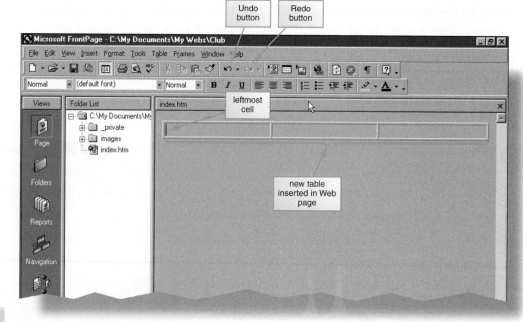

FIGURE 2-27

Other Ways

1. On Table menu point to Insert, click Table
2. Press ALT+A, I, T

The Insert Table box opens with only four rows and five columns. You can add more rows or columns simply by continuing to drag through the cell matrix. Front-Page will add more rows and columns automatically.

Extra rows can be added to the bottom of the table on the Web page by positioning the insertion point in the last column of the last row and then pressing the TAB key. You also can insert rows anywhere in the table by positioning the insertion point on the row above the desired new row and then clicking Insert Rows or Columns on the Table menu. Extra columns can be inserted in a similar fashion.

Undoing the Last Action

Although you will take great care when creating your Web pages, you may make mistakes or you may want to make an immediate change. FrontPage provides facilities to help you undo errors with the **Undo button** on the Standard toolbar (Figure 2-27) or the **Undo command** on the Edit menu. Thus, if you make a change or a mistake, undo it using either the Undo button or the Undo command. FrontPage will reverse your action up to 30 consecutive actions.

Also available for quick reversal of errors and changes are the **Redo button** on the Standard toolbar and the **Redo command** on the Edit menu. Redo reverses the effect of the last Undo command. If you decide the undo is incorrect, you can click the Redo button or Redo command to restore the last change you made. Redo is available for 30 consecutive actions.

Both the Undo button and the Redo button have arrows that allow you to see the most recent undo or redo commands, respectively. This allows you to see what actions you would be undoing or redoing before actually selecting them, and to select more than one consecutive action to undo or redo.

As you work with FrontPage, you will find that using the Undo and Redo buttons facilitates the creative process. You can add and rearrange items to see if they work, knowing you can return to a previous starting point with little effort.

Inserting an Image in a Web Page

Regardless of how impressive your written message, people always will respond to images. The viewer's eye is drawn naturally to a picture before reading any text. The choice and quality of images you use largely will determine whether someone will take the time to read your Web page or pass it by.

Much of the Web's success is due to its capability of presenting graphics. Because of the impact of images on the Web, it is important to master the graphic options necessary to include pictures on your Web pages.

Along with the company heading, the Bits 'n' Bytes Home page has two images in the header. The table you inserted in earlier steps will be used to control the amount of horizontal spacing between the images and the club name. The image on the left will be left-aligned in the left cell of the table. The image on the right will be right-aligned in the right cell of the table. The club name, which is inserted later in the project, will be centered in the middle cell.

The goal of the images at the top of the page is to reflect the concept that the Bits 'n' Bytes computer club is for computer users in an academic environment who use computers for both work and recreation and who enjoy various aspects of computing, including details beyond casual use. Therefore, a graphic with an inviting cartoon caricature of a computer, along with some work tools next to it is appropriate. Refer to Table 2-1 on page FP 2.6 for criteria on the appropriate use of metaphors in your Web designs.

FrontPage includes a library of ready-to-use images, called **clip art** and a selection of photographs you can insert into your Web pages. You also can use graphics from many different sources outside of FrontPage. You will use both clip art from the FrontPage library and from the Student Data Disk to select an image for the Bits 'n' Bytes Web page.

To insert an image, you first position the insertion point at the desired location, and then select the image. Perform the steps on the next page to insert an image in the Web page.

More About

Clip Art

One way to reorganize clip art is to open more than one Clip Art Gallery window. On the Categories sheet, right-click the category you want opened, and then click Open in New Window on the shortcut menu. Locate and size both Clip Art Gallery windows on your screen so you can view them concurrently. Then, drag clips from the category in one window and drop them into the desired categories in the second window.

To Insert a Clip Art Image in a Web Page

1 If necessary, click in the leftmost cell of the table to position the insertion point and then click the Insert Picture from File button on the Standard toolbar.

The Picture dialog box displays (Figure 2-28). You can select an image file or clip art file from your local computer, or select an image from any Web page on the World Wide Web.

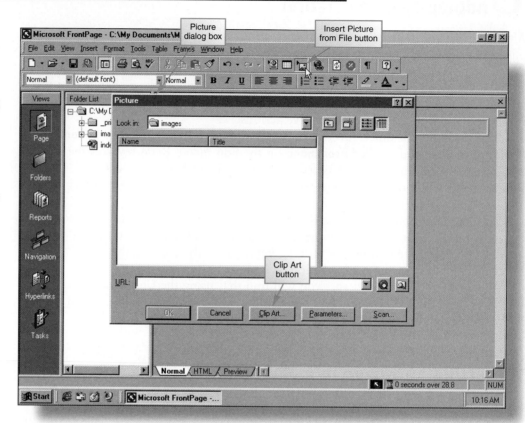

FIGURE 2-28

2 Click the Clip Art button.

The Clip Art Gallery window displays (Figure 2-29). It contains one sheet containing clip art images and photographs that have been transferred into a computer-readable format using a scanner. The Pictures sheet contains a list of clip art categories with small sample images for each category. Your preview of pictures may be different.

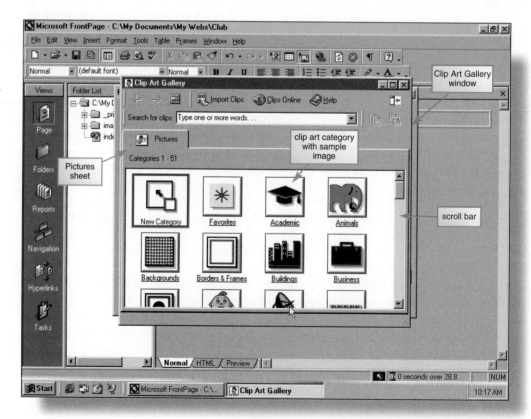

FIGURE 2-29

3 Scroll down the categories list box until the Science and Technology category displays. Click the Science and Technology category.

Clip art images relating to science and technology display (Figure 2-30).

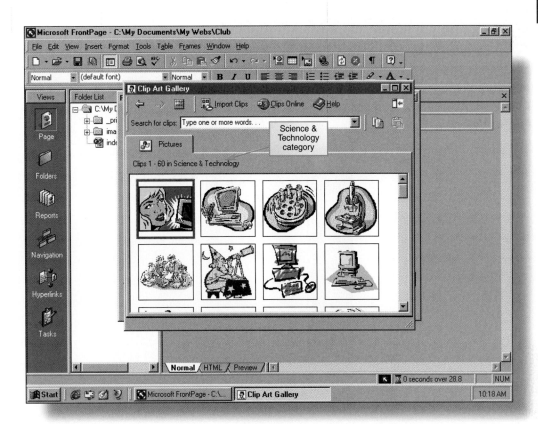

FIGURE 2-30

4 If necessary, scroll down the preview list box until the image of a cartoon computer displays, or another image of your choice. Click the image to select it, then point to the Insert clip button on the Pop-up menu.

The clip art image of a cartoon displays along with a Pop-up menu containing four graphic buttons (Figure 2-31). A selected image contains a blue border, as the image does in Figure 2-31.

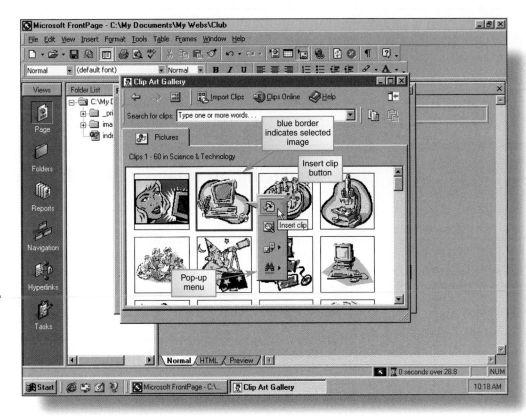

FIGURE 2-31

5 **Click the Insert clip button. If necessary, click the image to select it and drag the handles to obtain an appropriately-sized image.**

The clip art image is inserted into the leftmost cell of the table (Figure 2-32). A selected image has eight small boxes, called **handles,** *surrounding it.*

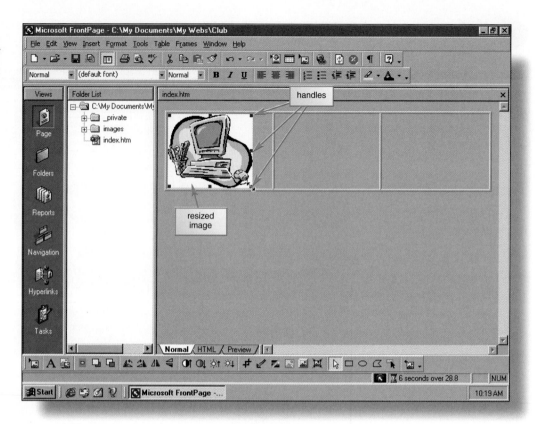

FIGURE 2-32

As you can see in Figures 2-29 and 2-30 on the previous pages, many categories of clip art are available. Each category has a varying number of images. Some of the same clip art images appear in several categories. For example, the computer image you inserted in the left table cell on the Web page also can be found in the Office category.

Replacing an Image in a Web Page

Once an image has been inserted into the Web page, you may decide that it is not as appealing as originally thought. While there may be many reasons to change an image, replacing an image in a Web page is as easy as inserting the original image.

Many images used on a Web page may appear to be irregular in shape when in fact they are rectangular. When the background color of the image is not the same as that of the Web page, the rectangular shape of the image becomes very obvious. To hide this rectangular shape, we can use images that have the same background color as our Web page, or we can use images that have a **transparent** background. Using images with a transparent background allows the color or graphic used in a Web page background to show through the background of the image, thus hiding the rectangular shape of the image.

Perform the following steps to replace the graphic just inserted with a similar one that has a transparent background.

To Replace a Clip Art Image in a Web Page

1 **Right-click the image to be replaced. Point to Picture Properties on the shortcut menu.**

A shortcut menu displays and handles display around the selected image (Figure 2-33).

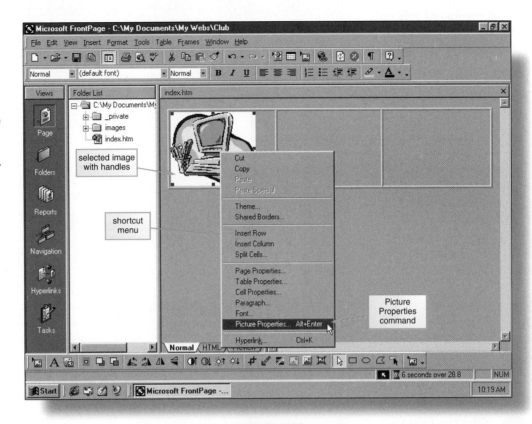

FIGURE 2-33

2 **Click Picture Properties. Point to the Browse button in the Picture source area.**

The Picture Properties dialog box displays. The name and location of the current image file is selected in the Picture source text box (Figure 2-34).

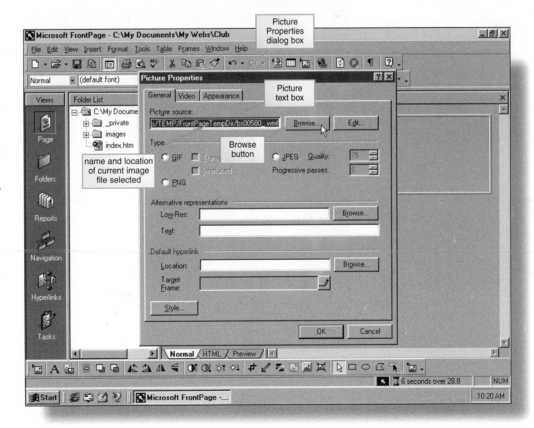

FIGURE 2-34

3 **Click the Browse button. When the Picture dialog box displays, point to the Select a file on your computer button.**

The Picture dialog box displays (Figure 2-35).

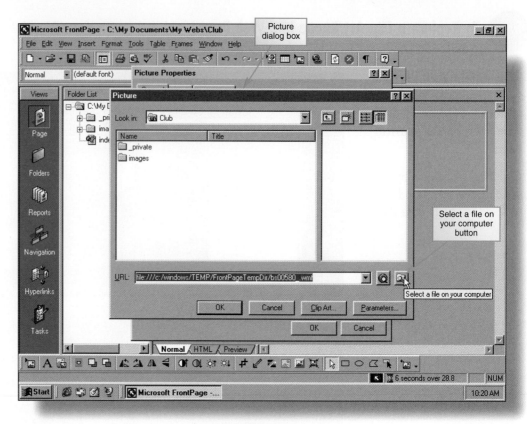

FIGURE 2-35

4 **Click the Select a file on your computer button. Insert the Data Disk in drive A and select the computer02.gif file in the Project2 folder. Point to the OK button.**

The Select File dialog box displays (Figure 2-36).

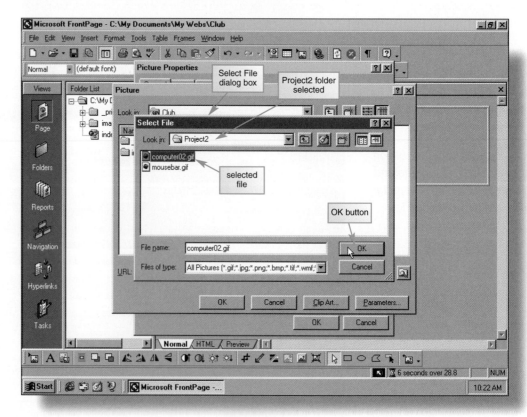

FIGURE 2-36

5 Click the OK button in each dialog box until all dialog boxes are closed. If necessary, resize the replacement image.

Handles display around the selected image (Figure 2-37). The mouse pointer changes to a double-headed arrow to resize image.

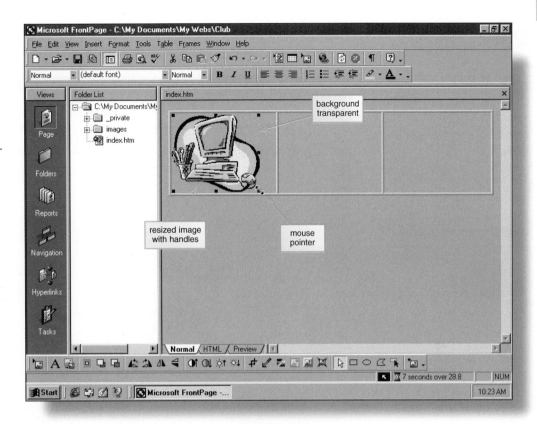

FIGURE 2-37

Copying and Pasting an Image on a Web Page

One of the features of Windows applications is the capability of copying information from one Windows application and inserting it in another Windows application. You can cut or copy portions of a Web page to a temporary storage area in computer memory, called the **Clipboard**, and then paste the contents of the Clipboard to other areas of the Web page. **Copy** and **cut and paste** are useful when you want to move an item to another location or have the same item appearing several times in various places throughout the Web page. The computer clip art image you just inserted is to be inserted again, this time in the rightmost cell of the table.

You can, of course, insert the clip art image using the steps you performed previously for inserting an image. You also can copy the image to the Clipboard and then paste the image from the Clipboard to the Web page at the location of the insertion point. In this instance, the copy and paste operation would be more efficient, because you would have to maneuver through several windows to get the image from the Microsoft Clip Gallery or from an image on disk. Perform the steps on the next page to copy and then paste the computer image to another location on the Web page.

More About

Images

The more images, or pictures, in your Web, the longer it takes to download your pages. To get a count of the total number of pictures in your Web, on the View menu, point to Reports, and then click Site Summary. In the Pictures row, the Count column lists the number of pictures in your web. Pictures located in hidden folders normally are not included in this report.

Steps **To Copy and Paste an Image on a Web Page**

1 **If necessary, click the clip art image to select it. Click Edit on the menu bar and then point to Copy.**

The image is selected and the Edit menu displays (Figure 2-38). The **Copy** *command copies a selected item to the Clipboard.*

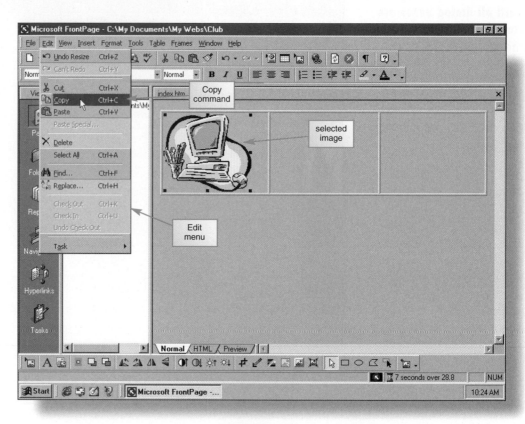

FIGURE 2-38

2 **Click Copy and then click the rightmost cell of the table to position the insertion point. Click Edit on the menu bar and then point to Paste.**

The Edit menu displays (Figure 2-39). The image is copied to the Clipboard. The **Paste command** *inserts the contents of the Clipboard at the location of the insertion point.*

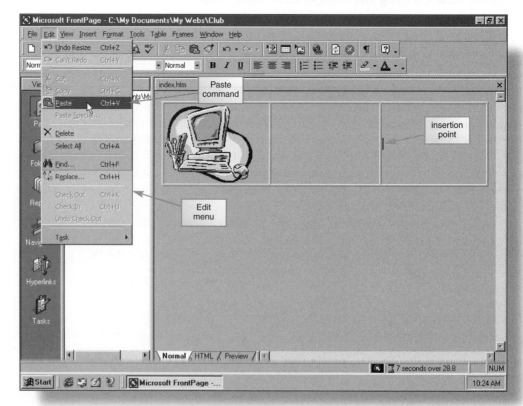

FIGURE 2-39

Click Paste.

The image on the Clipboard is copied to the rightmost table cell (Figure 2-40).

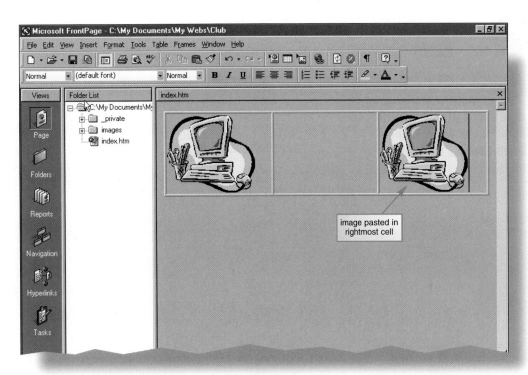

image pasted in rightmost cell

FIGURE 2-40

You can copy text or an entire table and then paste it in a similar fashion. Although the contents of the Clipboard can be inserted into other Windows applications, some objects will not display as you would expect. Because other Windows applications do not understand HTML, they will not make an accurate copy of the one row, three column table if you were to try pasting it. You can, however, copy or cut and paste the clip art images and any text into other Windows applications. You will lose any special formatting applied to the text, however. This, again, is because of the problem with translating HTML.

Using Tables to Control Spacing on a Web Page

One advantage of using tables is that they allow you to control the arrangement of items on the Web page. You can arrange, or **align**, the current text or image to the left within a table cell, to the right within a table cell, or centered in the table cell. The default alignment for newly inserted items is left-aligned.

FrontPage provides three alignment buttons on the Formatting toolbar. The **Align Left button** aligns an item at the left margin of the page or table cell. The **Align Right button** aligns items at the right margin of the page or table cell. The **Center button** centers items on the page or in a table cell. You simply select the paragraph or graphic by clicking it, and then click the appropriate alignment button on the Formatting toolbar.

To demonstrate how to align items on a Web page, you will select the clip art image you inserted in the rightmost cell and right-align it in the cell, which results in the clip art image aligning at the right margin of the Web page. This alignment allows more room for the club name, which will be entered in the center cell. Perform the following steps to align an item on a Web page.

Other Ways

1. Press ALT+E, C to copy, press ALT+E, P to paste
2. Press CTRL+C to copy, press CTRL+P to paste

More About

Table Borders

You can adjust the width, style, and color of table borders, giving the table a three-dimensional look. You also can specify a color for individual cell borders that is different from that of the rest of the table.

To Align Items on a Web Page

① **Click the clip art image in the rightmost cell to select it. Point to the Align Right button on the Formatting toolbar.**

The clip art image is selected, as indicated by the handles surrounding it (Figure 2-41).

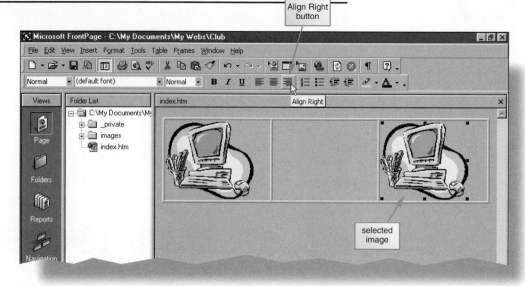

FIGURE 2-41

② **Click the Align Right button.**

The clip art image is aligned to the right margin of the table cell (Figure 2-42). The Align Right button on the Formatting toolbar is recessed to denote that the image has been aligned to the right.

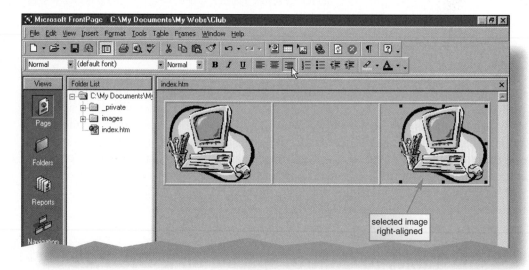

FIGURE 2-42

The image is right-aligned in the rightmost table cell on the Web page. In later steps you use the Center button to center headings, text, and other items on the Web page.

Adjusting Table Borders

Another useful feature of tables is the capability of moving the outside borders of a table and the borders between individual cells, thus providing added flexibility in controlling spacing on the Web page.

You can adjust the borders of the table to control vertical and horizontal spacing. The bottom border can be dragged up or down to control vertical spacing. The left border can be dragged right or left to control horizontal spacing. The borders between cells also can be moved to control spacing within the table.

As shown in Figure 2-42, the clip art images do not consume all the space in their respective cells. You can adjust the borders between the cells to reduce the space in the two outside cells and increase the space in the center cell, thus providing more room for the company name. Perform the following steps to adjust the borders of table cells.

 Steps **To Adjust Table Cell Borders**

1 **Point to the cell border between the second and third cell.**

The mouse pointer changes to a double-headed arrow (Figure 2-43).

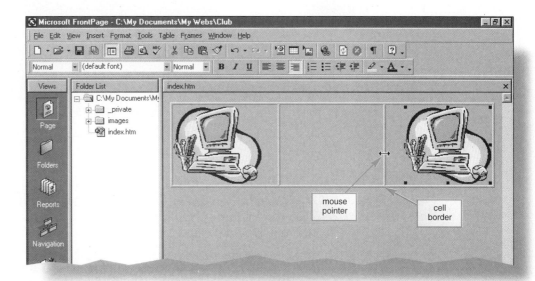

mouse pointer

cell border

FIGURE 2-43

2 **Drag the cell border right, to the left edge of the clip art image.**

The cell border moves to the right (Figure 2-44).

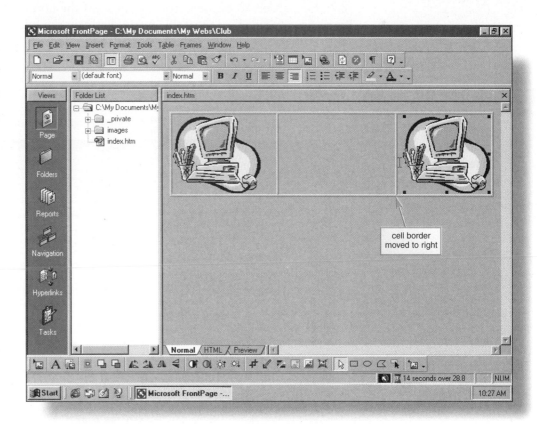

cell border moved to right

FIGURE 2-44

③ Point to the cell border between the first and second cell. Drag the cell border left, to the right edge of the clip art image.

The cell border moves to the left (Figure 2-45).

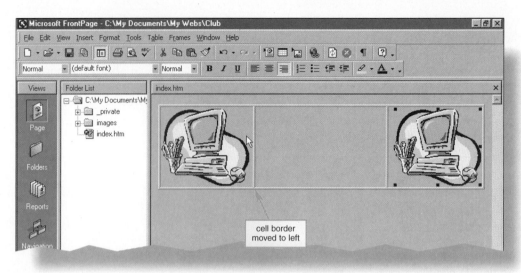

cell border
moved to left

FIGURE 2-45

Other Ways

1. Right-click cell, click Cell Properties on shortcut menu, enter width

Moving the cell to occupy the minimum width for the images allows more space in the center cell for the Bits 'n' Bytes club name. You should insert the images in the table cells before adjusting the cell borders so that you can see how much space is available. Adjusting table and cell borders is a powerful way of controlling spacing on a Web page.

Tables and the individual cells are surrounded by a default table border. You can adjust the properties of the border, such as the width, color, and use of a 3-D shadow. When using a table for spacing purposes, you most likely will not want the table borders to be seen. You can turn off the border display using the **Table Properties command** on the Table menu. Perform the following steps to turn off the table border.

 To Turn Off the Table Border

① If necessary, click in one of the three cells of the table. Click Table on the menu bar and then point to Properties.

*The Table menu and Properties submenu display (Figure 2-46). The **Table menu** contains commands to manage tables. The **Properties command** allows you to specify table border information.*

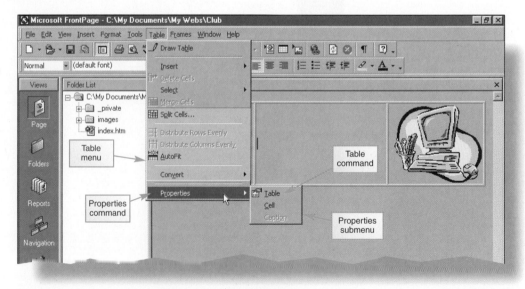

Table
menu

Properties
command

Table
command

Properties
submenu

FIGURE 2-46

2 **Click Table on the Properties submenu.**

The Table Properties dialog box displays (Figure 2-47). Options in this dialog box allow you to control various aspects of the table border and table background. The Size box in the Borders area allows you to control how wide the table border will be in pixels. A pixel, short for picture element, is the smallest addressable element on your computer screen. The default border size is one pixel.

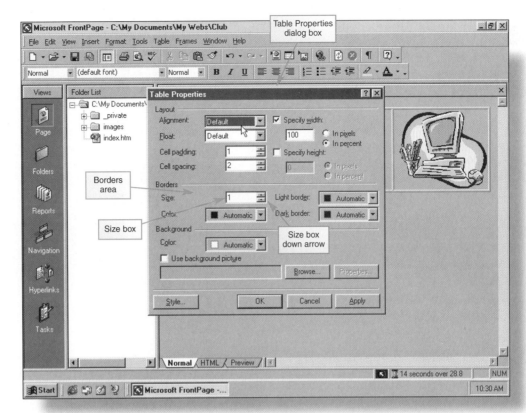

FIGURE 2-47

3 **In the Borders area, click the Size box down arrow until zero (0) displays in the box. Point to the OK button.**

Zero (0) displays in the Size box indicating that no visible border will appear around the table cells (Figure 2-48).

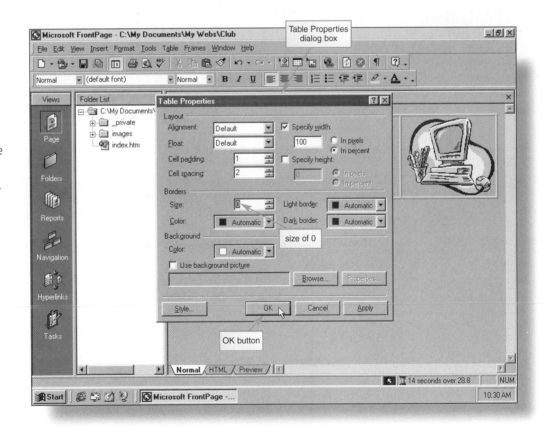

FIGURE 2-48

4 **Click the OK button.**

The table border is replaced with dashed lines (Figure 2-49). These lines show you where the cell borders are and also indicate that no visible border will appear when the Web page displays in a browser.

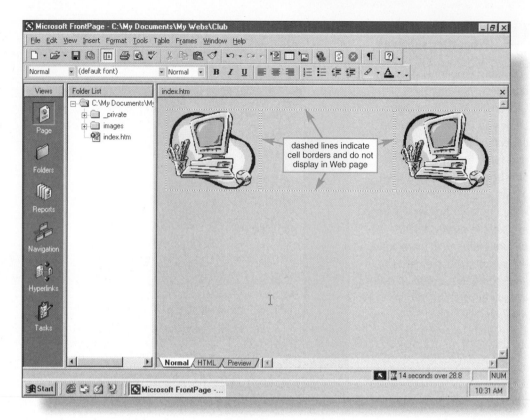

FIGURE 2-49

Other **Ways**

1. Right-click table, click Table Properties on shortcut menu
2. Press ALT+A, R, T

Fonts

You can choose to display each font name as a sample of the font in the list of fonts in the Font box. On the Tools menu, click Customize. In the Customize dialog box, click the Options tab. Click List font names in their font to select it. Changing this setting affects all Microsoft Office programs.

You have adjusted the borders around table cells and turned off the display of the table border. Now that the size of the center cell has been adjusted, you can insert the heading for the Web page.

Inserting a Heading in a Web Page

Text on a Web page can take many forms, such as a heading, ordered and unordered lists, menus, and normal text. To this text, you can apply special formatting such as different fonts, colors, and sizes. You use the Formatting toolbar for the more frequently used formatting options.

The process of entering text using FrontPage has several steps. You might skip one or more of the steps, depending on the current settings. The first step is to select a text style. The **Style box** on the Formatting toolbar contains styles such as lists, menu items, headings, and normal text.

After selecting a style, you will select a font type for the text. A **font** is another name for character set. Some commonly used fonts are Courier, Helvetica, and Arial. You change the font using the **Font box** on the Formatting toolbar.

Next, you select a color for the text. The default color is black. A text color that complements the background color or image you have chosen is preferred so your text does not fade in and out as it moves across a background image or pattern. You do not want your page to be difficult to read because of poor color selection. To change the color of text, use the **Font Color button arrow** on the Formatting toolbar. You can choose from a set of standard colors, from a set that matches a theme if a theme is applied, or mix your own custom colors.

The Formatting toolbar contains many text formatting options. The **Font size box** allows you to increase or decrease the size of the characters in your text. Using the **Bold**, **Italic**, and **Underline** buttons, you can format certain text in bold, italic, or underline.

The Bits 'n' Bytes club name, which will be placed in the center table cell, consists of Normal as its style, Arial as its font, and black (default) for the font color. Two different font sizes are used. The heading also is centered in the cell. Perform the following steps to set the style, font type, size and color, and then insert the club name in the center cell.

More About

Text Formatting

If the text formatting in Front-Page does not give the effect you desire, try creating an image of the formatted text using a graphics program and then insert the image into the Web page.

 Steps | To Add a Heading to a Web Page

1 If necessary, click the center table cell to position the insertion point.

The insertion point displays in the center table cell (Figure 2-50).

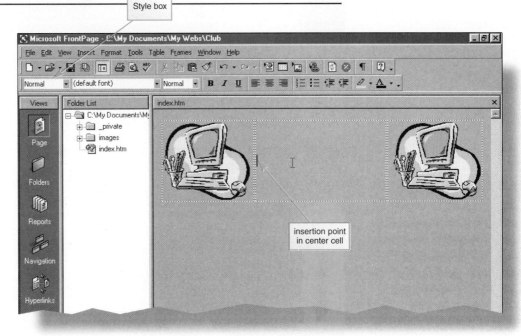

FIGURE 2-50

2 If necessary, click Normal in the Style box. Click the Font box arrow. If necessary, scroll down, then point to Arial in the font list.

The Font list displays (Figure 2-51). It contains a list of fonts available for use when developing Web pages. Your list of fonts may be different.

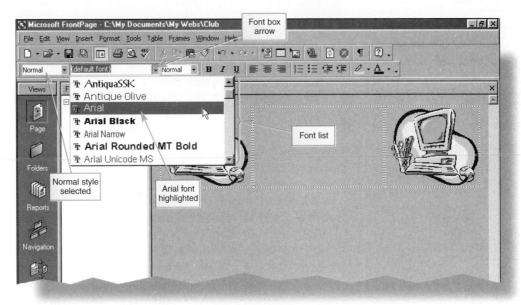

FIGURE 2-51

③ **Click Arial. Click the Font Size box arrow. Point to 6 (24 pt).**

Arial becomes the text font and the Font Size list displays (Figure 2-52).

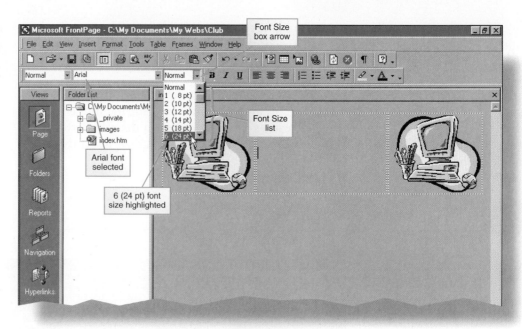

FIGURE 2-52

④ **Click 6 (24 pt). Type** Bits 'n' Bytes **to enter the club name. Click the Center button on the Formatting toolbar. Press the ENTER key. Click 3 (12 pt). Click the Bold button on the Formatting toolbar. Type** computer club of Hilltop Community College **to enter the remainder of the club name.**

The text displays centered in the middle table cell with a style of Normal, in Arial font, in the default color, and in two font sizes (Figure 2-53).

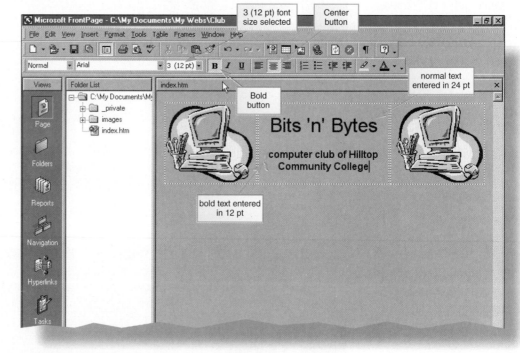

FIGURE 2-53

 Other Ways

1. Highlight text, right-click text, click Font on shortcut menu
2. Highlight text, press ALT+ENTER

Because it is the part of the page that first-time viewers initially see in their browsers, it is important to format the header of the Web page so it is appealing and draws further interest. The body of the Web page keeps the viewer's attention when it is verbalized and formatted appropriately. It is customary to separate logical sections of Web pages, such as the header and body, using dividing elements called horizontal rules.

Inserting a Horizontal Rule

The use of elements such as a horizontal rule can add a special look to your pages, as well as provide the viewer with visual clues concerning the location of information on the Web page. Horizontal rules are used to break up the page into sections, and to separate elements on the page. A **horizontal rule** is a small, thin line that goes across the entire Web page.

You will use a horizontal rule to separate the header section of the Web page from the body. Perform the following steps to insert a horizontal rule below the table containing the clip art images and club name.

More About

Horizontal Rules

After adding a horizontal line, or rule, you can modify its appearance. Double-click the line, and in the Horizontal Line dialog box, change the alignment, width, height, and color properties. If your page uses a theme, the horizontal line uses a graphic to match the theme, and you can change only the alignment of the line.

 To Add a Horizontal Rule to a Web Page

1 **Click below the table to position the insertion point, click Insert on the menu bar, and then point to Horizontal Line.**

The Insert menu displays and the Horizontal Line command is highlighted (Figure 2-54). The Insert menu contains commands to insert various elements in the current Web page.

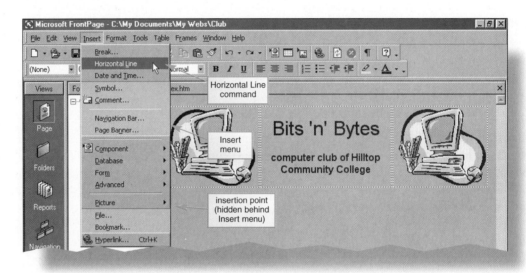

FIGURE 2-54

2 **Click Horizontal Line.**

The horizontal rule displays below the table (Figure 2-55).

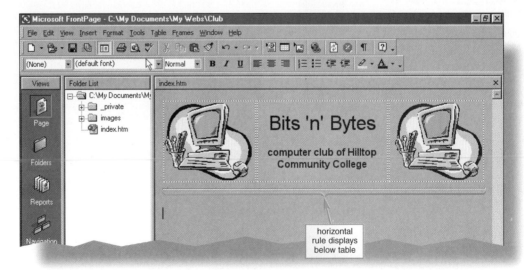

FIGURE 2-55

Other Ways

1. Press ALT+I, L

You can adjust the properties of the horizontal rule, such as the thickness and length, by right-clicking the horizontal rule and then clicking Horizontal Line properties on the shortcut menu. The alignment of the horizontal rule also can be controlled using the Align Left, Center, and Align Right buttons on the Formatting toolbar.

Adding Normal Text to a Web Page

Notice in Figure 2-55 that the style and font reverted to the default values. This occurs whenever you move the insertion point with the mouse or arrow keys. You need to set the style, font, and color again in preparation for entering more text.

The steps for adding normal text are similar to the steps you used previously to add the heading: set the style, set the font, and set the font size. Follow these steps to add all the normal text that will display on the Web page.

To Add Normal Text to a Web Page

① Click anywhere below the horizontal rule to position the insertion point. Click the Style box arrow. If necessary, click Normal in the Style list. Click the Font box arrow and then click Arial. Click the Font Size box arrow and then click 4 (14 pt).

The Style box indicates Normal style, the Font box indicates Arial, and the Font Size box indicates 4 (14 pt) (Figure 2-56). The new text entered from this point on will reflect these formatting attributes.

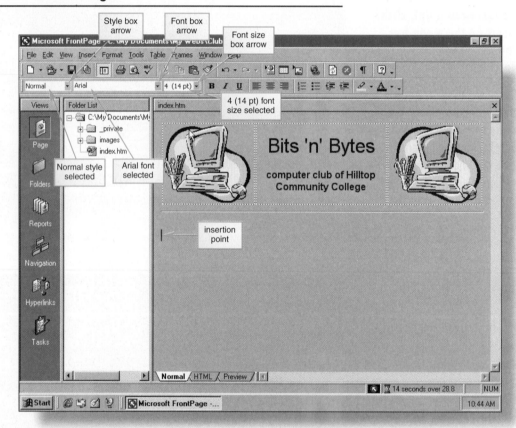

FIGURE 2-56

2 **Type** Welcome to our Web site **as the first line of text. Click the Center button on the Formatting toolbar.**

The text displays centered on the Web page in the Arial font (Figure 2-57).

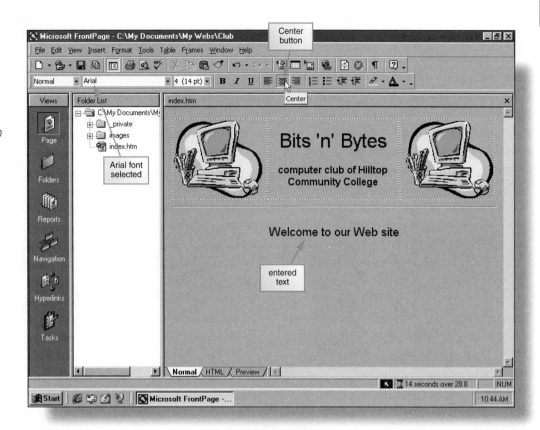

FIGURE 2-57

3 **Press the ENTER key to insert a new paragraph and then type** If you're into computers, join us! Meet our officers. Be sure to check out our discounts on hardware and software! **to enter more text.**

The text displays centered on the Web page (Figure 2-58). Notice the style, font, font size, and alignment settings are preserved. This is because you have not repositioned the insertion point using the mouse or arrow keys. Your text may wrap differently.

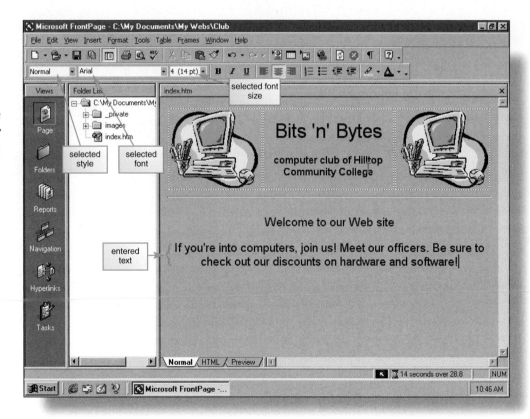

FIGURE 2-58

4 Press the ENTER key. Click the Style box arrow. Click Heading 3. Click the Font Size box arrow and then click 3 (12 pt). Type Officers and then press the SPACEBAR seven times. Type Join the Club! and then press the SPACEBAR seven times. Type Discount Pricing to enter the final text for this line.

The text displays centered with a style of Heading 3 and a font size of 12 pt (Figure 2-59).

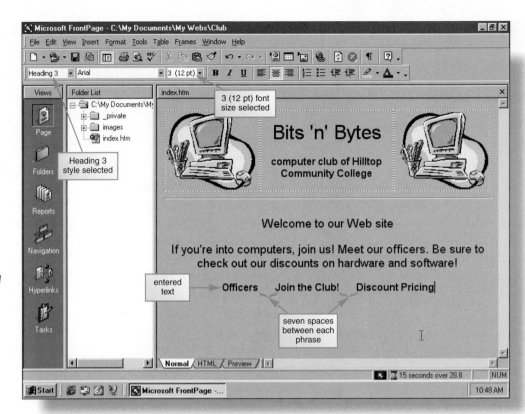

FIGURE 2-59

5 Press the ENTER key. Click the Font box arrow and then click Arial. Click the Font Size box arrow and then click 3 (12 pt). Click the Bold button, and then type Questions? Contact us at bbpres@hcc.edu. as the new text.

The text displays as bold and centered with a style of Normal and a font size of 12 pt (Figure 2-60). Because the previous line used a Heading style, pressing the ENTER key caused the style, font, and font size to change to the default values.

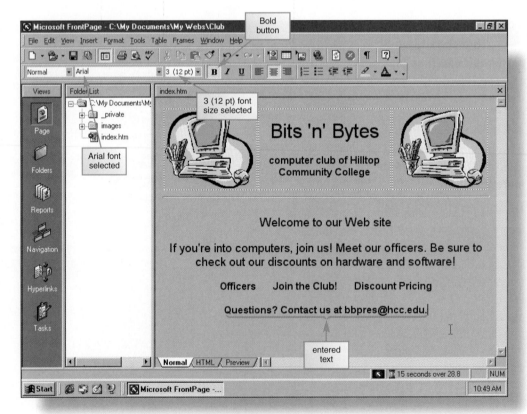

FIGURE 2-60

6 **Drag through the bbpres@hcc.edu. text to select it.**

The selected text is highlighted (Figure 2-61). This text is underlined in red to indicate a possible misspelling.

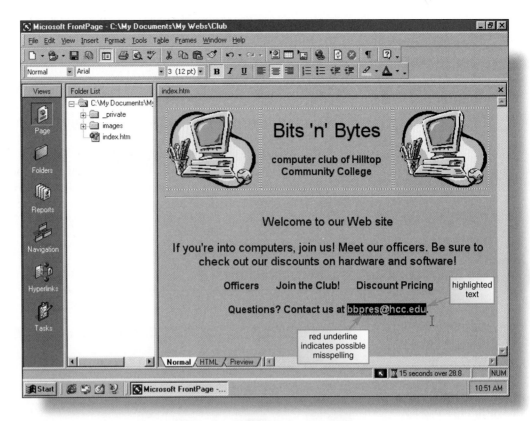

FIGURE 2-61

7 **Click the Italic button on the Formatting toolbar.**

The selected text is changed to italic (Figure 2-62). It is customary to display e-mail addresses formatted in italic text to further differentiate them from the rest of the text.

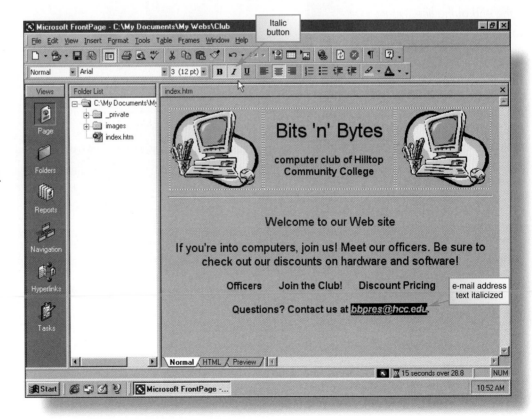

FIGURE 2-62

You can see from the previous steps that the Formatting toolbar is very useful when entering text. You can change styles, fonts, size, and other properties very quickly as you move through the body of the Web page.

Using an Image as a Horizontal Rule

With the insertion of the e-mail contact information, you actually have entered both the body and the footer of the Web page. The footer of the page begins with the, Officers Join the Club! Discount Pricing, line. Another horizontal rule is appropriate between the body and the footer to distinguish the two sections.

Instead of inserting the ordinary horizontal rule, however, you will use an inline image as a divider. Perform the following steps to insert a clip art image as a horizontal rule.

To Insert an Image as a Horizontal Rule

1 **Click the end of the line that begins, check out our discounts, to position the insertion point at the end of that line, as shown in Figure 2-63.**

The insertion point displays at the end of the line (Figure 2-63).

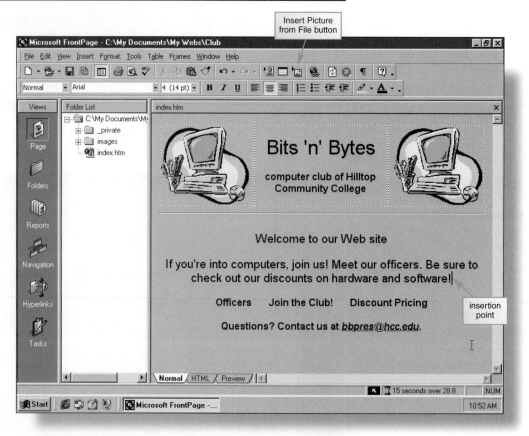

FIGURE 2-63

2 Press the ENTER key to insert a new paragraph. Click the Insert Picture from File button on the Standard toolbar. Point to the Select a file on your computer button.

The Picture dialog box displays (Figure 2-64).

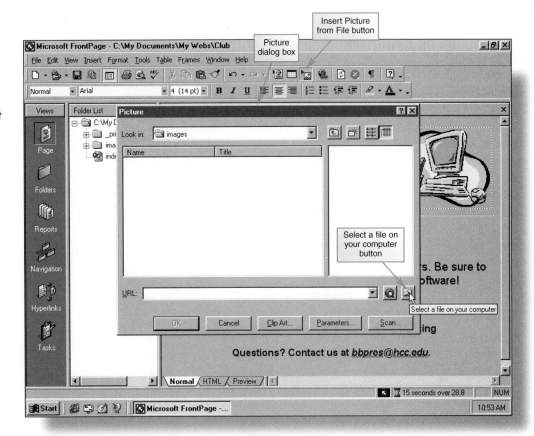

FIGURE 2-64

3 Click the Select a file on your computer button. Select the file mousebar.gif from the Project2 folder on the Data Disk. Point to the OK button.

The Select File dialog box displays (Figure 2-65).

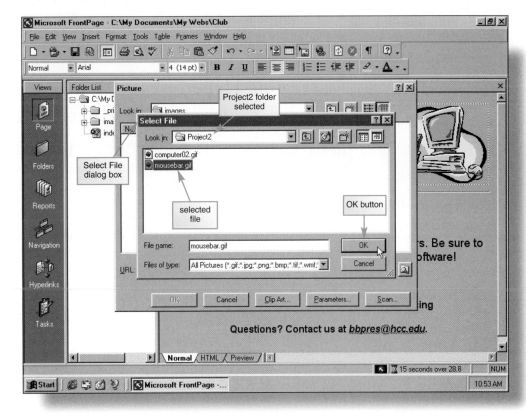

FIGURE 2-65

Click the OK button.

The divider image displays in the Web page at the location of the insertion point below the line of text, If you're into computers (Figure 2-66).

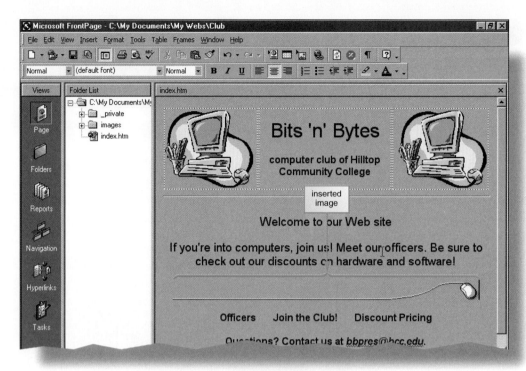

FIGURE 2-66

FrontPage comes complete with a wide selection of colorful dividers, buttons and other images designed specifically for use on Web pages. It is worthwhile to spend some time browsing through the clip art selections to see what is available.

Creating Hyperlinks

The World Wide Web consists of millions of diverse documents. All of these documents are brought together through the use of **hyperlinks**. You navigate the Web by clicking hyperlinks on the Web page. Hyperlinks are crucial for Web page development – the Web would not exist without them. Good Web sites have useful hyperlinks to local pages within the site, and hyperlinks to other related sites on the World Wide Web.

A well-designed Web page has multiple hyperlinks written in such a way as to produce an easy-to-use, easy-to-read Web document. The Web page should be designed keeping in mind the choice and placement of hyperlinks. Referring to the guidelines in Table 2-1 on page FP 2.6, avoid using the click here notation, unless no other way to create the hyperlink exists.

Use appropriately worded hyperlink text to produce a natural association within the topic. For example, if you were creating a series of Web pages on whales and wanted to include a hyperlink to a page about whale flippers, you might include a sentence on the Web page that reads, Whales maneuver using their flippers to steer through the water. The word, flippers, would be set up as the hyperlink to the flippers Web page. Avoid this type of wording, To see information about whale flippers, click here.

The first step in creating a hyperlink is to select the text or image that the viewer will click as the hyperlink on the Web page. The next step is to provide the URL of the resource to be retrieved when the hyperlink is clicked. Several hyperlinks appear on the Bits 'n' Bytes Home page: one e-mail hyperlink and three hyperlinks to other Web pages, which are to be added later, in the FrontPage web. Perform the following steps to add hyperlinks to the Bits 'n' Bytes Home page.

 Steps ## To Insert a Hyperlink in a Web Page

1 **Drag through the bbpres@hcc.edu e-mail address to select it. Point to the Hyperlink button on the Standard toolbar (Figure 2-67).**

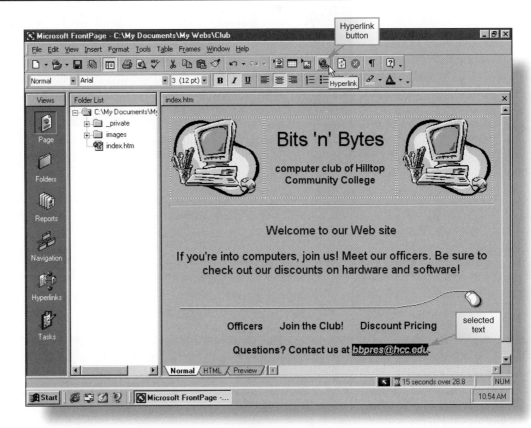

FIGURE 2-67

2 **Click the Hyperlink button. Point to the Make a Hyperlink that sends E-mail button.**

The Create Hyperlink dialog box displays (Figure 2-68).

FIGURE 2-68

3 **Click the Make a Hyperlink that sends E-mail button.**

The Create E-mail Hyperlink dialog box displays (Figure 2-69).

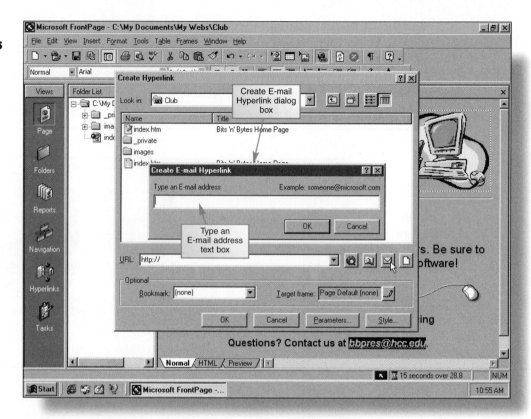

FIGURE 2-69

4 **Type bbpres@hcc.edu in the Type an E-mail address text box.**

The text displays in the text box (Figure 2-70).

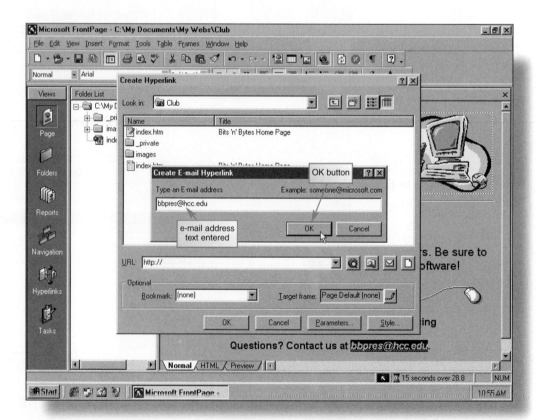

FIGURE 2-70

5 Click the OK button in the Create E-mail Hyperlink dialog box. When the Create Hyperlink dialog box is again visible, point to the OK button.

The Create E-mail Hyperlink dialog box closes. The Create Hyperlink dialog box displays the e-mail URL in the URL text box using the mailto protocol (Figure 2-71).

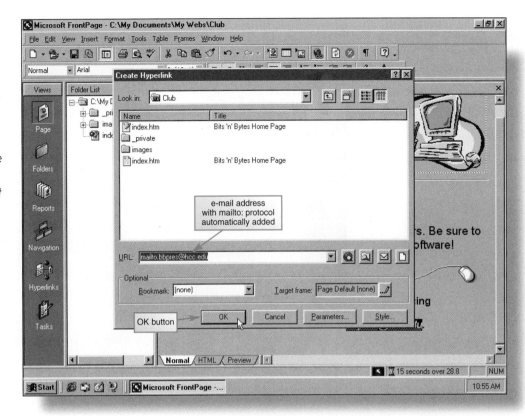

FIGURE 2-71

6 Click the OK button. Position the mouse pointer on the e-mail hyperlink.

The e-mail URL displays on the status bar at the bottom of the screen when the mouse pointer is positioned over the e-mail hyperlink (Figure 2-72).

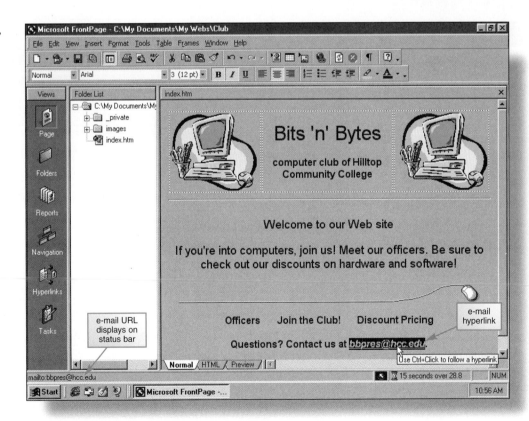

FIGURE 2-72

7 **Drag through the word, Officers, below the divider and then click the Hyperlink button on the Standard toolbar.**

The Create Hyperlink dialog box displays (Figure 2-73).

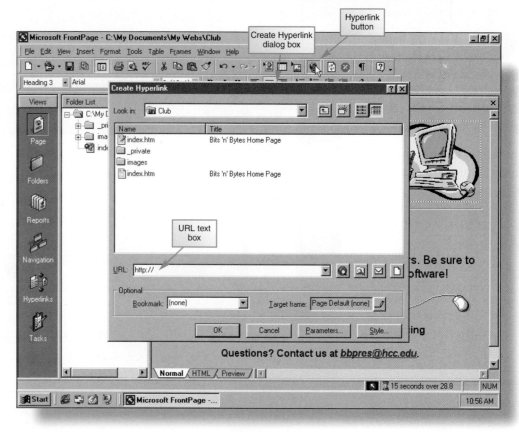

FIGURE 2-73

8 **Double-click the URL text box and then type** officers.htm **in the text box. Point to the OK button.**

The officers.htm text replaces the http:// text (Figure 2-74).

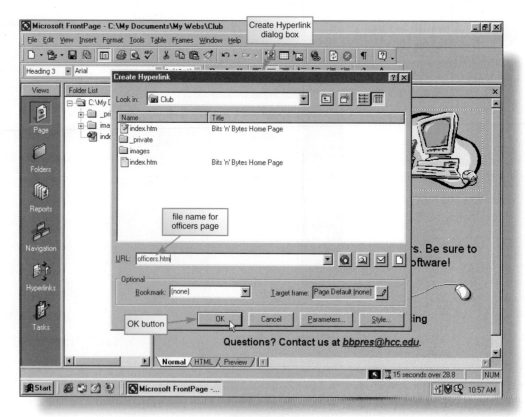

FIGURE 2-74

9 **Click the OK button. Position the mouse pointer on the Officers hyperlink text.**

The officers.htm URL displays on the status bar when the mouse pointer is positioned on the Officers hyperlink text (Figure 2-75).

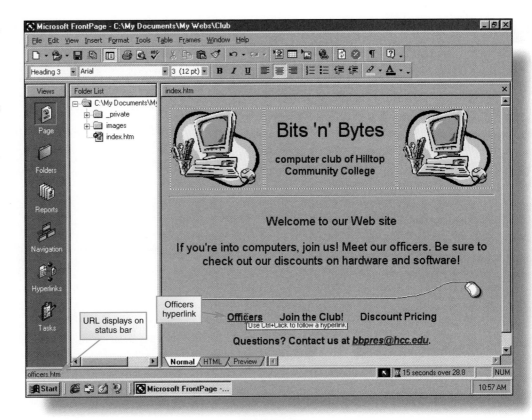

FIGURE 2-75

10 **Drag through the words, Join the Club!, click the Hyperlink button on the Standard toolbar, double-click the URL text box, type** join.htm **in the text box, click the OK button, and then position the mouse pointer on the Join the Club! hyperlink.**

The join.htm URL displays on the status bar when the mouse pointer is positioned over the Join the Club! hyperlink text (Figure 2-76).

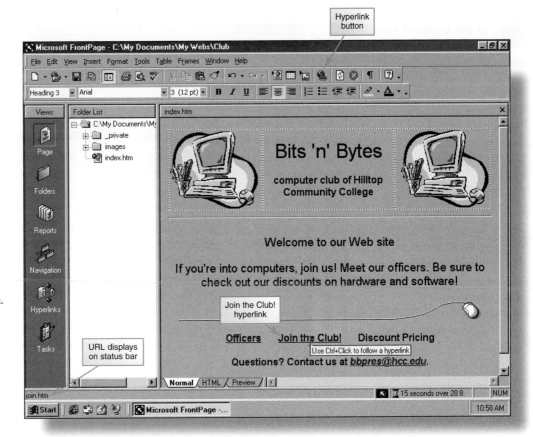

FIGURE 2-76

11 **Drag through the words, Discount Pricing, click the Hyperlink button on the Standard toolbar, double-click the URL text box, type** `discount.htm` **in the text box, click the OK button, and then position the mouse pointer on the Discount Pricing hyperlink.**

The discount.htm URL displays on the status bar when the mouse pointer is positioned over the Discount Pricing hyperlink text (Figure 2-77).

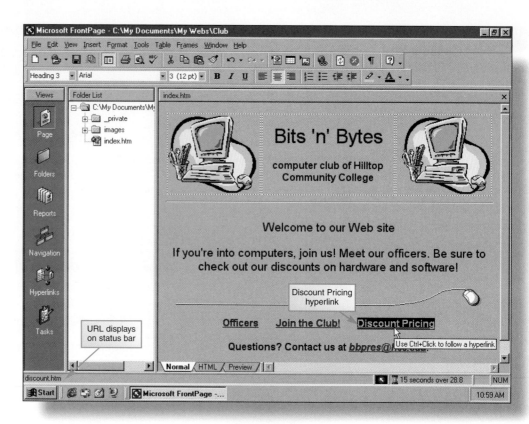

FIGURE 2-77

12 **In the sentence that begins, If you're into computers, drag through the word, join, click the Hyperlink button on the Standard toolbar, double-click the URL text box, type** `join.htm` **in the text box, click the OK button, and then position the mouse pointer on the word, join.**

The join.htm URL displays on the status bar when the mouse pointer is positioned on the join hyperlink text (Figure 2-78).

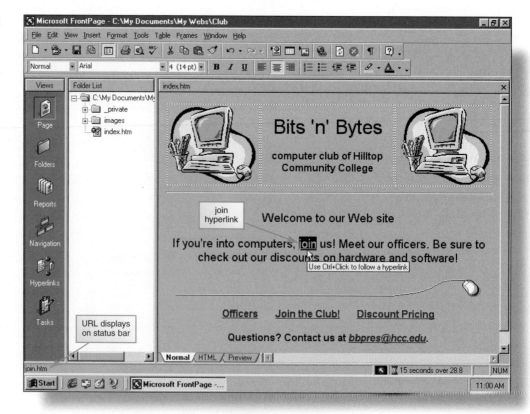

FIGURE 2-78

13 In the sentence, Meet our officers, drag through the word, officers, click the Hyperlink button on the Standard toolbar, double-click the URL text box, type `officers.htm` in the text box, click the OK button, and then position the mouse pointer on the word, officers.

The officers.htm URL displays on the status bar when the mouse pointer is positioned on the officers hyperlink text (Figure 2-79).

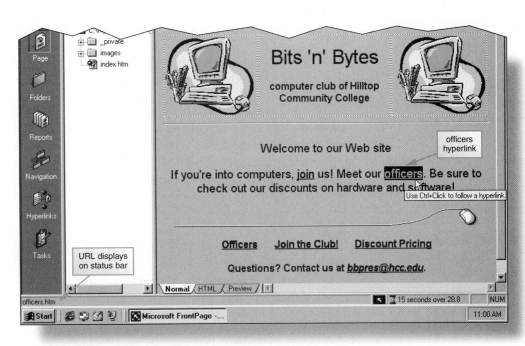

FIGURE 2-79

14 In the sentence that begins, Be sure to check, drag through the word, discounts, click the Hyperlink button on the Standard toolbar, double-click the URL text box, type `discount.htm` in the text box, click the OK button, and then position the mouse pointer on the word, discounts.

The discount.htm URL displays on the status bar when the mouse pointer is positioned over the discounts hyperlink text (Figure 2-80).

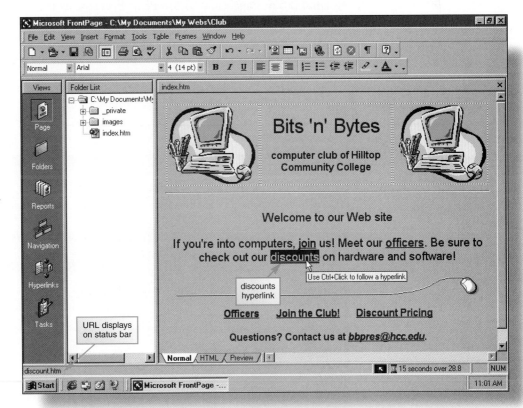

FIGURE 2-80

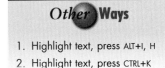

Other **Ways**

1. Highlight text, press ALT+I, H
2. Highlight text, press CTRL+K

Font Effects on Hyperlinks

If the page does not use a theme, you can add font effects to a hyperlink so that when the mouse pointer is positioned on the hyperlink, the hyperlink changes font. On the Background tab of the Page Properties dialog box (see Figure 2-19), in the Formatting area, click Enable hyperlink rollover effects to select it. Click the Rollover style button. Set the font properties for hyperlinks on the current page. These effects are set for the entire page, rather than for individual hyperlinks. Not all Web browsers support this feature.

Two sets of hyperlinks were created for each linked page: officers.htm, join.htm, and discount.htm. The set of hyperlinks in the footer at the bottom of the page allow repeat visitors quick access to all the important hyperlinks in this web. Knowledge-able viewers will not have to search through all the items on the Web page to find the desired hyperlink.

The hyperlinks embedded within the text in the body of the Web page were chosen carefully from the available wording to avoid using the click here types of labels and allow the transparent flow from one document to the next. These elements are important to preserve good design on the Web page. The content of the linked resource is explained within the context of the sentence. First-time viewers can access an interesting hyperlink as soon as they encounter it.

Previewing and Printing a Web Page

In Project 1, you printed the Web page without previewing it on the screen. By previewing the Web page, you can see how it will look when printed without generating a printout, or hard copy. Previewing a Web page using the Print Preview command on the File menu can save time, paper, and the frustration of waiting for a printout only to discover it is not what you want. Additionally, you can preview how the Web page will look in a browser by clicking the Preview tab. You must be using the Normal tab in Page view to use Print Preview, as this command is not accessible when using the Preview tab.

You also can print the Web page while in Print Preview. Perform the following steps to preview and then print the Bits 'n' Bytes Web page.

Steps To Preview a Web Page

1 Ready the printer according to the printer instructions. Verify that the Normal tab is selected. Click File on the menu bar and then point to Print Preview (Figure 2-81).

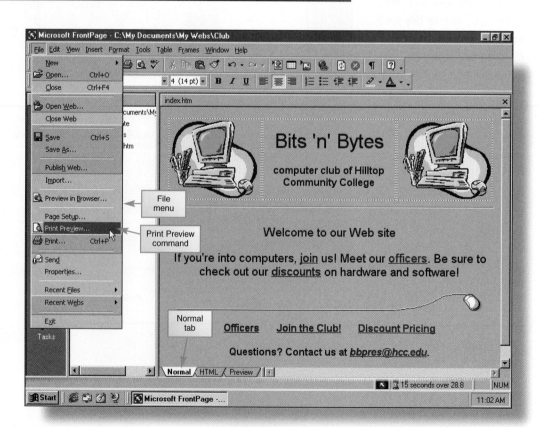

FIGURE 2-81

Click Print Preview.

FrontPage displays a preview of the Web page in the preview pane and the mouse pointer changes to a magnifying glass (Figure 2-82).

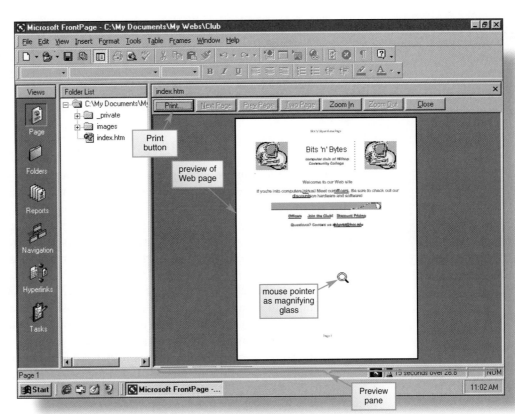

FIGURE 2-82

Click the Print button on the Print Preview toolbar. Click the OK button in the Print dialog box.

The preview pane closes and the Web page prints. When the printing operation is complete, retrieve the printout (Figure 2-83).

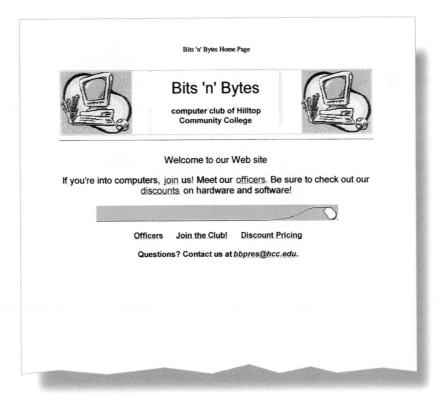

FIGURE 2-83

Other Ways

1. Press ALT+F, V

The Print Preview toolbar contains buttons to scroll through a multipage print-out, to zoom in and out of the Web page, and to close the preview pane. You can use Print Preview to determine the page number of a particular page in a multipage printout, and then print only that page. This allows you to print only that section of a long Web page you are working on, thus saving time and paper.

Saving the Web Page

Once you have finished editing the Web page you should save it on disk. With the Bits 'n' Bytes Home page, the save operation consists of saving the HTML and the clip art images for the Web page. The clip art images you inserted in earlier steps were not physically inserted in the Home page. FrontPage placed HTML instructions to include the clip art image files using an <img src=> tag. This tag has a reference to the file name containing the clip art image, but it still must be saved with the Web page.

When the Web page is saved, it contains only the HTML tags referencing the file. FrontPage will save the image files in the web folders as well. As a default, FrontPage will save the image files to the current folder. However, you may want to have all images used in your Web page stored in a folder separate from the actual Web page. Because FrontPage created an images folder when this new web was created, it makes sense to place the images in that folder. Perform the following steps to save the Bits 'n' Bytes Home page, along with the embedded image files.

To Save a Web Page

1 **Click the Save button on the Standard toolbar.**

The Save Embedded Files dialog box displays (Figure 2-84). This dialog box shows the file names of the clip art images you inserted in the Web page.

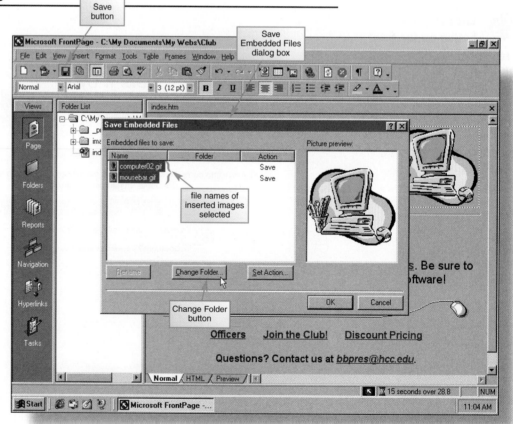

FIGURE 2-84

2 Click the Change Folder button. Click the images folder.

The Change Folder dialog box displays (Figure 2-85). The images folder is selected.

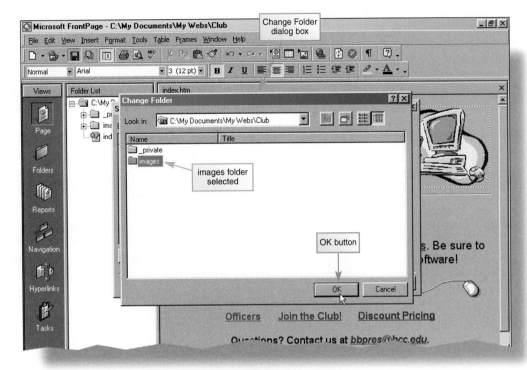

FIGURE 2-85

3 Click the OK button in the Change Folders dialog box.

The Save Embedded Files dialog box indicates that the images folder will be used to store the images selected (Figure 2-86).

4 Click the OK button in the Save Embedded Files dialog box.

The Bits 'n' Bytes Home page and the clip art image files are saved.

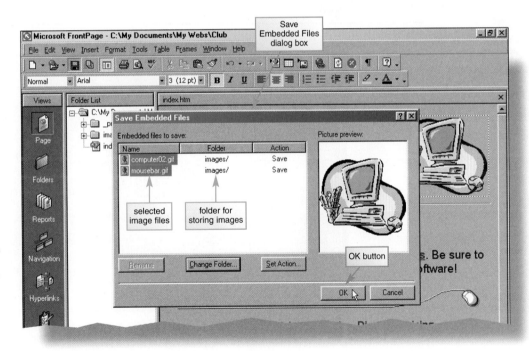

FIGURE 2-86

It is important that the clip art images are saved as part of the FrontPage Web. These image files must be available when publishing the FrontPage web to a Web server. If you do not save them and then publish the FrontPage web, those <img src=> tags will be broken because the files referenced by the tags will not be on the Web server. Thus, the Web page will not display properly.

More About

Publishing

If you are given a specific folder on your Web server to publish your web, create sub-folders below the top-level folder. Publishing individual webs in their own folders eases management of the files and folders that comprise each web.

Publishing the Web Page

Publishing a Web page is the process of sending copies of Web pages, image files, multimedia files, and any other files and folders to a Web server where they then become available to the World Wide Web. With FrontPage, you can publish your web by clicking a single button.

You can publish the Bits 'n' Bytes Home page using the steps listed on page FP 2.61. The Officers, Join the Club!, and Discount Pricing Web pages in the Bits 'n' Bytes FrontPage web do not yet exist, however, and those are indicated as hyperlinks on the Home page to other Web pages.

If you publish the Home page, individuals viewing the Home page will encounter errors if they click any hyperlink except the e-mail hyperlink. This might cause viewers to get a bad impression of the club. Therefore, it is best to wait until all the other pages in the web on which you are working are completed before publishing the Web. If you need to publish the web before completing the other pages, however, you should provide a temporary page, or pages, that indicate the incomplete pages are being developed; that is, that they are under construction. Several temporary under construction pages for this project are supplied on the Data Disk. These pages can be imported into the web as shown in the following steps.

 To Import Existing Pages

1 **Insert the Data Disk in drive A. Click File on the menu bar and then point to Import.**

The File menu displays (Figure 2-87).

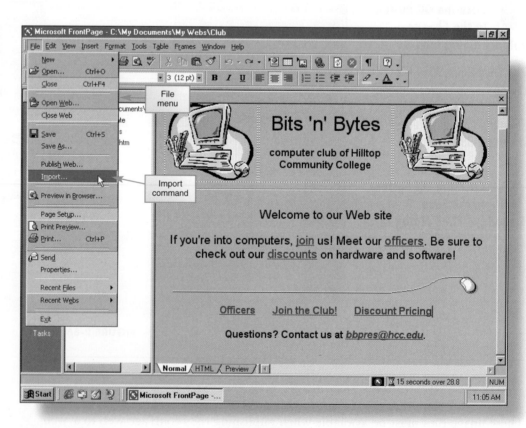

FIGURE 2-87

2 **Click Import. When the Import dialog box displays, point to the Add File button.**

The Import dialog box displays (Figure 2-88). Buttons are available for importing pages from files on the local machine, for importing an entire folder, or for importing pages from the Web.

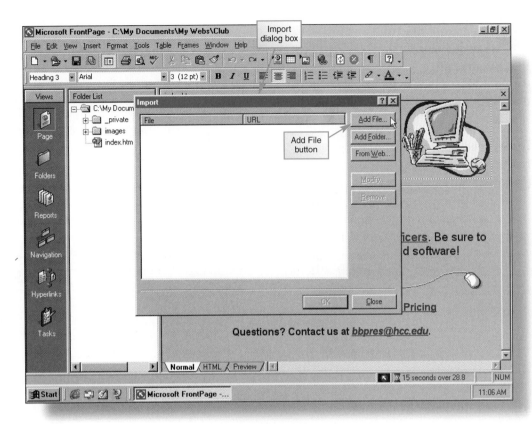

FIGURE 2-88

3 **Click the Add File button. If necessary, click the Look in box arrow and then click 3½ Floppy (A:) in the Look in box. If necessary, double-click the Project2 folder.**

The Add File to Import List dialog box displays (Figure 2-89). The Project2 folder displays in the Look in box and the files on the on the floppy disk in drive A display. Your list may be different.

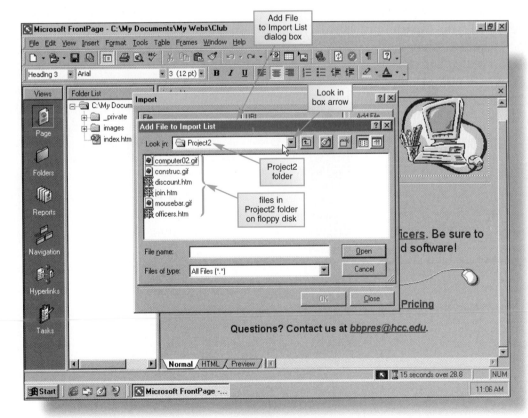

FIGURE 2-89

④ Hold down the CTRL key and select the files construc.gif, discount.htm, join.htm, and officers.htm. Point to the Open button.

The selected files are highlighted in the Project2 folder (Figure 2-90).

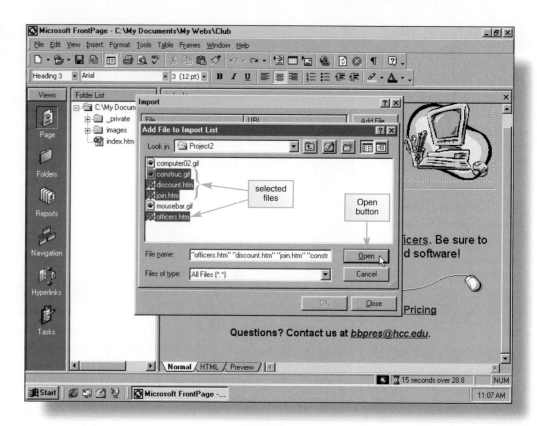

FIGURE 2-90

⑤ Click the Open button. When the Import dialog box displays, point to the OK button.

The Import dialog box shows the selected files to import (Figure 2-91).

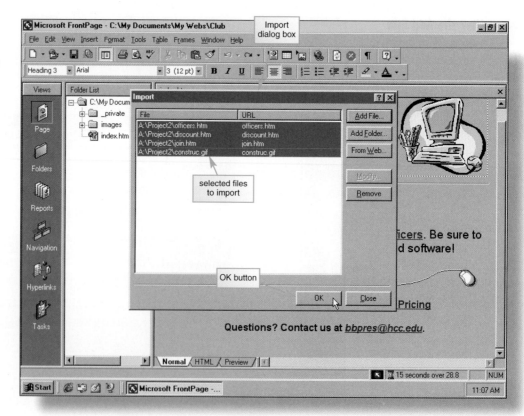

FIGURE 2-91

6 **Click the OK button. Click the Save button on the Standard toolbar to save these changes to your web before publishing it.**

The Import dialog box closes and the imported files are listed in the Folder List pane (Figure 2-92).

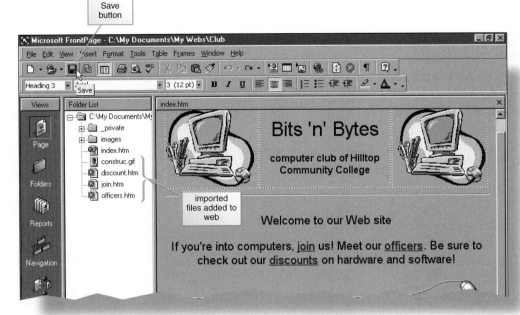

FIGURE 2-92

Once all of the page links in the current web point to an existing page, even if such pages simply state that their contents are under construction, the web can be published. The following steps summarize how to publish the Bits 'n' Bytes web. Be sure to substitute your own URL, or an error will occur. If you do not know what URL to use, ask your instructor.

 To Publish the FrontPage Web

1 **Click the Publish Web button on the Standard toolbar.**

The Publish Web dialog box displays (Figure 2-93).

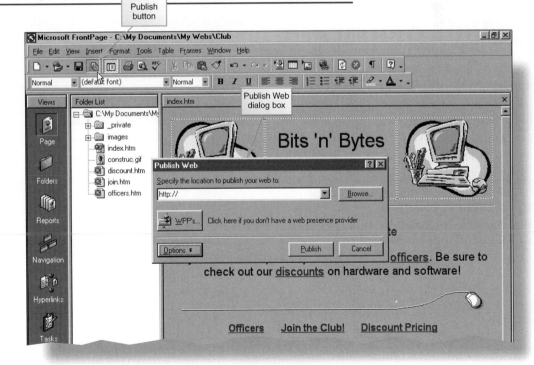

FIGURE 2-93

2 Type your FTP server name and file location (e.g., ftp:// www.hcc.edu/computer/ club) in the Specify the location to publish your web to text box. Point to the Publish button.

The FTP server name and folder name are entered in the text box (Figure 2-94). You must use a valid server and file location or an error will occur.

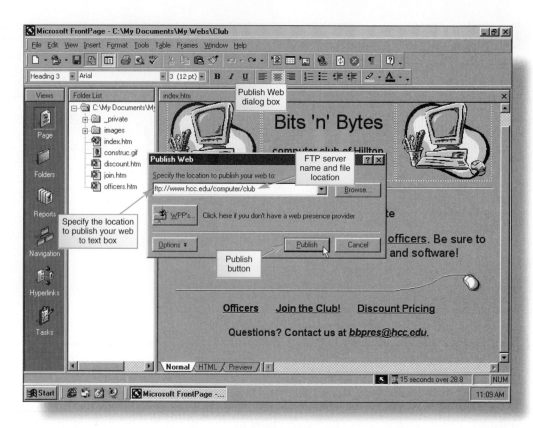

FIGURE 2-94

3 Click the Publish button. Type your FTP user name and password in the text boxes and then point to the OK button.

The Name and Password Required dialog box displays (Figure 2-95). If your server has Microsoft FrontPage extensions installed, you may use the http protocol to publish your web rather than the FTP protocol. The user name and password display in the text boxes. The password displays as asterisks.

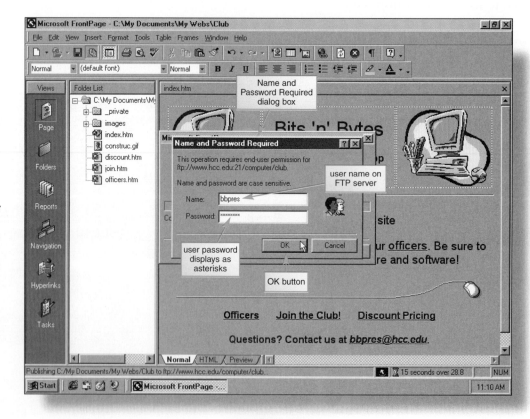

FIGURE 2-95

Publishing the Web Page • FP 2.63

 Click the OK button.

The Microsoft FrontPage dialog box displays indicating the status of the transfer (Figure 2-96). When the transfer is complete, the message in the dialog box indicates that the Web site published successfully (Figure 2-97).

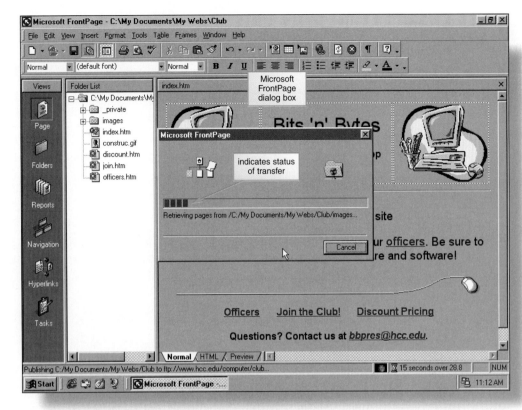

FIGURE 2-96

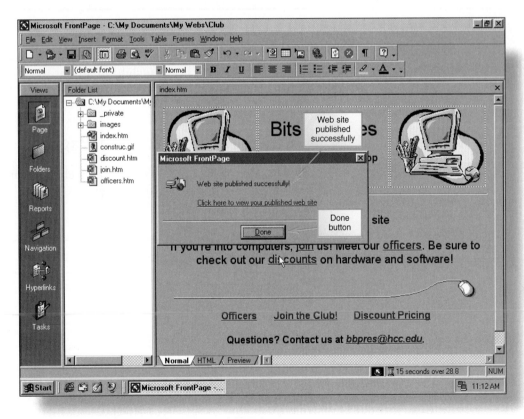

FIGURE 2-97

⑤ Click the Done button.

The dialog box closes and the FrontPage window redisplays (Figure 2-98).

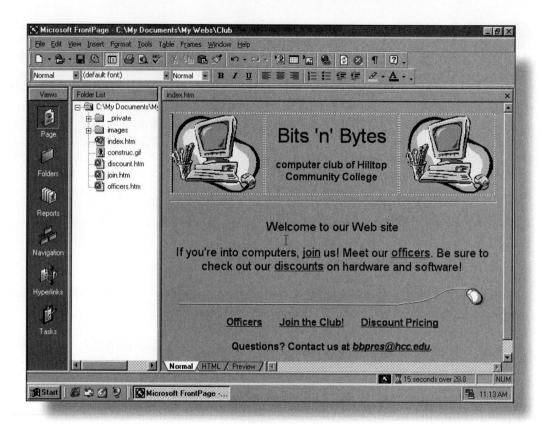

FIGURE 2-98

You now can view the Bits 'n' Bytes Home page by typing your Web page location (e.g., http://www.hcc.edu/club) in any browser and then pressing the ENTER key.

Quick Reference

For a table that lists how to complete the tasks covered in this book, visit the Office 2000 Web page (www.scsite.com/off2000/qr.htm), and then click Microsoft FrontPage 2000.

Quitting Microsoft FrontPage

When you have published the Bits 'n' Bytes web, you can quit Microsoft FrontPage. The step for quitting is summarized below.

TO QUIT MICROSOFT FRONTPAGE

① Click the Close button on the FrontPage title bar.

The FrontPage window closes and the Windows desktop displays.

CASE PERSPECTIVE SUMMARY

Paul thinks the Web page you developed looks great. He arranges a meeting with the officers of the Bits 'n' Bytes computer club to review your work. All of the officers are pleased with your development and are eager to have you complete the additional pages necessary to have a working site. They agree to provide details for the discount pricing and officers pages, as well as the information required from those seeking membership. These materials will be provided at your next meeting, where design details for those pages will be completed.

Project Summary

In creating the Home page, you gained knowledge of HTML basics and Microsoft FrontPage. Project 2 introduced you to essential Web page development. You learned about good design criteria. With these tools, you created a new, one-page web providing your own original content, then you changed the background of the Web page. You inserted a table and adjusted the table properties. Using appropriate images, you inserted clip art to enhance the appearance of the Web page and replaced the clip art with a more suitable image. Then, you added text and learned how to change formats such as style, font, font size, and alignment. Next, you inserted horizontal rules. You learned how to select items carefully for use as hyperlinks, and then you previewed your Web page before printing. Finally, you saved a Web page along with the embedded image files.

What You Should Know

Having completed this project, you now should be able to perform the following tasks:

▶ Add a Heading to a Web Page *(FP 2.37)*
▶ Add a Horizontal Rule to a Web Page *(FP 2.39)*
▶ Add Normal Text to a Web Page *(FP 2.40)*
▶ Adjust Table Cell Borders *(FP 2.33)*
▶ Align Items on a Web Page *(FP 2.32)*
▶ Change the Background Color *(FP 2.17)*
▶ Change the Page Label of a Web Page *(FP 2.15)*
▶ Change the Title of a Web Page *(FP 2.12)*
▶ Copy and Paste an Image on a Web Page *(FP 2.30)*
▶ Create a New One-page Web *(FP 2.9)*
▶ Edit the Web Page *(FP 2.17)*
▶ Import existing Web pages into a Web *(FP 2.58)*

▶ Insert a Clip Art Image in a Web Page *(FP 2.24)*
▶ Insert a Hyperlink in a Web Page *(FP 2.47)*
▶ Insert a Table in a Web Page *(FP 2.21)*
▶ Insert an Image as a Horizontal Rule *(FP 2.44)*
▶ Preview a Web Page *(FP 2.54)*
▶ Publish the FrontPage Web *(FP 2.61)*
▶ Quit Microsoft FrontPage *(FP 2.64)*
▶ Replace a Clip Art Image in a Web Page *(FP 2.27)*
▶ Save a Web Page *(FP 2.56)*
▶ Start FrontPage 2000 *(FP 2.9)*
▶ Turn Off the Table Border *(FP 2.34)*

More About

Microsoft Certification

The Microsoft Office User Specialist (MOUS) Certification program provides an opportunity for you to obtain a valuable industry credential — proof that you have the FrontPage 2000 skills required by employers. For more information, visit the Shelly Cashman Series MOUS Web page at www.scsite.com/off2000/cert.htm.

Apply Your Knowledge

➕ Project Reinforcement at www.scsite.com/off2000/reinforce.htm

1 Creating a Table

Instructions: Start FrontPage 2000 and perform the following steps with a computer.

1. Open the one-page web, RegSales, on the Data Disk. Edit the Home page (index.htm).
2. Insert a six-row, six-column table in the Web page below the horizontal rule.
3. Using the following data, populate the table cells with the proper text and alignment. Use bold and 14 pt font size for column and row headings.

	EASTERN REGION	CENTRAL REGION	WESTERN REGION
January	2345.44	1120.33	1436.33
February	5400.00	1923.23	1212.33
March	2343.22	1232.10	1124.54
April	2345.60	1750.50	1656.35
May	5453.33	1654.90	1910.50

4. Right-align all numeric data and right-align column headings.
5. Adjust the borders to align cells appropriately (leave the first and last cell columns of the table empty to help align other table elements), and then center the table in the Web page. (*Hint*: Use the Table Properties dialog box.)
6. The completed lab is shown in Figure 2-99. Print the Web page, write your name on it, and hand it in to your instructor.

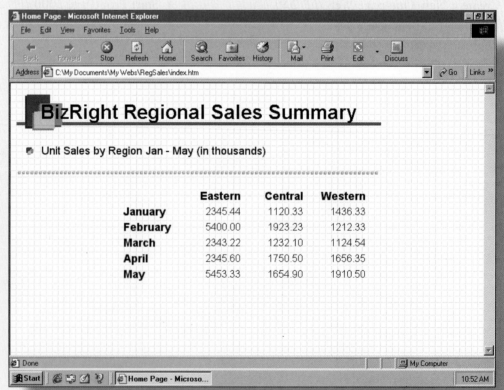

FIGURE 2-99

In the Lab

1 Creating a Web Page

Problem: As the manager of an automobile parts mail-order business, you want to enhance sales by offering parts via the World Wide Web and have decided to develop a home page for the company.

Instructions: The Parts 'n' Parcel Home page is shown in Figure 2-100 as it would appear in a Web browser. Perform the following activities to create the Parts 'n' Parcel Home page.

1. Start FrontPage and create a new one-page web.
2. Change the title of the Home page to Parts 'n' Parcel Home Page.
3. Insert a one row, two column table in the Web page.
4. Insert a clip art image with an appropriate automotive or repair theme into the left table cell.
5. Adjust the table properties so the table border does not show and the middle border is adjacent to the right side of the clip art image inserted in step 4.
6. Align the image at the right of its table cell. Align the text in the table at the left of the cell.
7. Insert the text, and apply the appropriate formatting so the text looks similar to Figure 2-100. Select appropriate horizontal rules to separate the header and footer from the body of the Web page.
8. Create the e-mail hyperlink using mastermechanic@ parts.com as the e-mail address.
9. Create the parts hyperlink using parts.htm for the URL. Create the delivery hyperlink using delivery.htm as the URL. Create the about us hyperlink using about.htm as the URL.
10. Save the Web page. Print the Web page, write your name on it, and hand it in to your instructor.

FIGURE 2-100

In the Lab

2 Using Tables and Images in a Web Page

Problem: The local Little League baseball team for which you volunteer would like to have a Web site to publish game schedules, news about the team, and to help raise funds for equipment. They have asked you to develop a home page for the Westchester Little League team.

Instructions: Start FrontPage 2000 and perform the following steps with a computer.

1. Create a new one-page web.
2. Insert a one row, three column table in the Web page.
3. Click the left cell of the table. Using a font similar to that in Figure 2-101, or one of your choice, set the font size to 24 pt. and click the bold button. Type `Westchester Little League`.
4. Click the center table cell. Click the Italics button. Using normal font size and the default font, type `… for the love of the game.`

FIGURE 2-101

5. Insert a clip art image with an appropriate baseball picture into the right table cell.

6. Adjust the table properties so the table border does not show and the text in the left cell wraps appropriately.

7. Insert the graphic batBar01.gif from the Data Disk as a horizontal line after the table.

8. Insert a one row, eight column table below the horizontal line graphic. In the odd-numbered cells, insert a small baseball clip art image. Adjust the cell widths to remove extra space around the graphics.

9. In the second cell, create the our game schedule hyperlink using schedule.htm for the URL. In the fourth cell, create the our sponsors hyperlink using sponsors.htm for the URL. In the sixth cell, create the our team roster hyperlink using roster.htm for the URL. In the eighth cell, create the our field hyperlink using field.htm for the URL. Adjust cell widths to evenly space the hyperlinks.

10. Insert a one row, three column table at the bottom of the Web page. In the first cell, insert a clip art image representing baseball equipment. Create the Equipment Fund Drive hyperlink using fund.htm for the URL. In the third cell, insert a clip art photo (JPEG) image representing a baseball game. Create the Our trip to the pros! hyperlink using trip.htm for the URL.

11. In the second cell, insert a baseball clip art image and appropriately size it. Click the graphic. Click the text tool on the Picture toolbar. Type Ask the coach at. Below the graphic, create the e-mail hyperlink using coach@league.org as the e-mail address.

12. Save the Web page. Print the Web page, write your name on it, and hand it in to your instructor.

3 Formatting and Aligning Text

Problem: For years, you have used the same travel agency to help with business trips and vacations. They want a Web site and have asked you to develop a home page according to their initial design.

Instructions: Start FrontPage 2000 and perform the following steps with a computer.

1. Create a new one-page web and use tables to position text and appropriate images from the Clip Art Gallery as indicated in Figure 2-102 on the next page. Use font colors as shown.

2. Insert a one row, three column table in the Web page.

3. Click the left cell of the table. Search the Clip Art Gallery to find a travel image and insert it in this cell. Copy the image and paste it into the third, or rightmost, cell.

4. Click the center table cell. Type WorldWide Travel in the default font with a style of Heading 1. Center the text with the Center button on the Formatting toolbar.

5. Insert a one row, three column table below the first table. In the center cell, insert a beach vacation image from the Clip Art Gallery. Center the image with the Center button on the Formatting toolbar.

6. In the left cell, type Plan Your Own, Book a Flight, Find Flight Info, Reserve a Room, and Rent a Car. After each phrase except the last, hold down the shift key and press the ENTER key to avoid a paragraph break. Press ENTER after the last phrase. Highlight the first phrase, Plan Your Own, and change the formatting to bold, with a font color of red.

7. For each of the remaining phrases, highlight each in turn and make it a hyperlink, linking to BookFlight.htm, FindFlight.htm, ReserveRoom.htm, and RentCar.htm, respectively.

(continued)

In the Lab

Formatting and Aligning Text *(continued)*

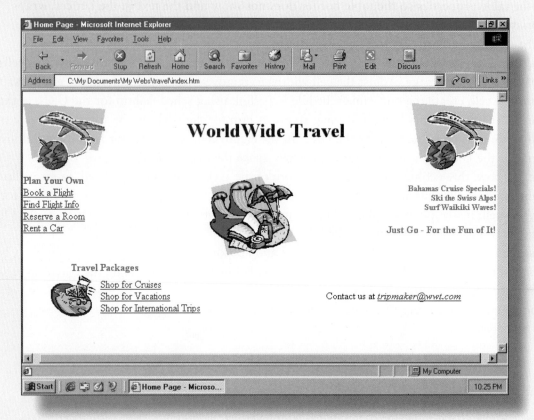

FIGURE 2-102

8. In the right cell, type `Bahamas Cruise Specials!`, `Ski the Swiss Alps!`, and `Surf the Waikiki Waves!`, again avoiding a paragraph break between phrases. After the last phrase, press the ENTER key and then type the phrase `Just Go - For the Fun of It!`, and do not press the ENTER key.

9. Change the font color of all four phrases to red. Highlight the first three phrases and change the style to Heading 5. Highlight the last phrase and change the style to Heading 4.

10. Insert a two row, three column table below the last table. In the top, left cell, type `Travel`. Bold and right-align the text. Change the font color to red. In the top, middle cell, type `Packages`. Make the font color red, then bold and left-align the text.

11. In the left cell of the second row, insert an image from the Clip Art Gallery that indicates shopping.

12. In the middle cell of the second row, create the Shop for Cruises hyperlink using ShopCruise.htm for the URL. Avoiding paragraph breaks, create the Shop for Vacations hyperlink using ShopVacation.htm for the URL and the Shop for International Trips hyperlink using ShopTrip.htm for the URL.

13. In the right cell of the second row, create the e-mail hyperlink, using tripmaker@wwt.com as the e-mail address.

14. Save the Web page. Print the Web page, write your name on it, and hand it in to your instructor.

Cases and Places

The difficulty of these case studies varies:
▷ are the least difficult; ▷▷ are more difficult; and ▷▷▷ are the most difficult.

1 ▷ You want to create your own personal Web page of clip art images, arranged in a table. Use one of the Web search engines to find sources of free Web page clip art. Copy and paste at least nine clip art images onto your own page. Add a header and footer to the page. Publish the page if you have access to a Web server.

2 ▷ Many companies that offer Web-related products and services sponsor awards programs for the best Web pages. Search for one of these award-winning pages or Best of the Web sites. Print one of the best pages. On the back of the printout, list the good design criteria that you think won it the award.

3 ▷ Many companies that offer Web-related products and services sponsor awards programs for the worst Web pages. Search for one of these Worst of the Web sites. Print one of the worst pages. On the back of the printout, write a list of the good design criteria that you think would improve the page.

4 ▷▷ Many sites on the World Wide Web offer libraries of images such as buttons, dividers, and background patterns for use with Web pages. Using the Web search engine of your choice, search for four or five sites that have such libraries of images. Create your own personal Web page that has links to at least four of these libraries of images. Use appropriate names for the links, indicating the type of images available for each library. Add a header and footer to your library directory page. Publish the page if you have access to a Web server.

5 ▷▷ Many times, the information that will be placed in a table on a Web page already exists in some type of electronic format – a text document or a spreadsheet. FrontPage has facilities for loading data into a table on a Web page. Using FrontPage Help, find out how to convert existing text into a table.

6 ▷▷▷ You are starting a business and want to create a Home page introducing your business and its services. Create a Home page for your business that incorporates tables, clip art images, background, and text, without violating any of the good design criteria. Publish the page if you have access to a Web server.

7 ▷▷▷ Find a local business or organization that does not have a Web page. Collect information about that organization. Build a Home page for that organization, incorporating tables, clip art images, background, and text, without violating any of the good design criteria.

Microsoft FrontPage 2000

P R O J E C T

Using Images, Hotspots, Bookmarks, and Excel to Create Web Pages

You will have mastered the material in this project when you can:

O B J E C T I V E S

- Open an existing FrontPage web
- Display the Pictures toolbar
- Apply a background image to a Web page
- Wash out an image
- Apply a new theme to a FrontPage web
- Insert a page banner
- Copy and paste from another Web page
- Insert bookmarks into a Web page
- Create a transparent image
- Create an image map
- Add a hotspot to an image map
- Highlight hotspots
- Specify targets of an image map hotspot
- Use a graphic image as a hyperlink
- Use an Excel spreadsheet in a Web page
- Display the hyperlinks in a FrontPage web
- Test a Web page by previewing it in a browser

Online Silk Road

Linking Web Travelers Worldwide

In today's online world, every Web site leads to countless new ones, all brimming with the riches of information, ideas, knowledge, and news. The journey from one exciting page to the next can make you feel like a merchant-explorer in an electronic world. Attractive and appealing Web sites market goods and services, entertain, and educate.

Connecting a global population, the World Wide Web has made it possible for organizations, corporations, educational institutions, individuals, and special interest groups to travel a worldwide route of communication, commerce, and learning.

Long before the birth of the Web, the Silk Road connected the world. For 2,000 years, this road — a tenuous thread of communication and

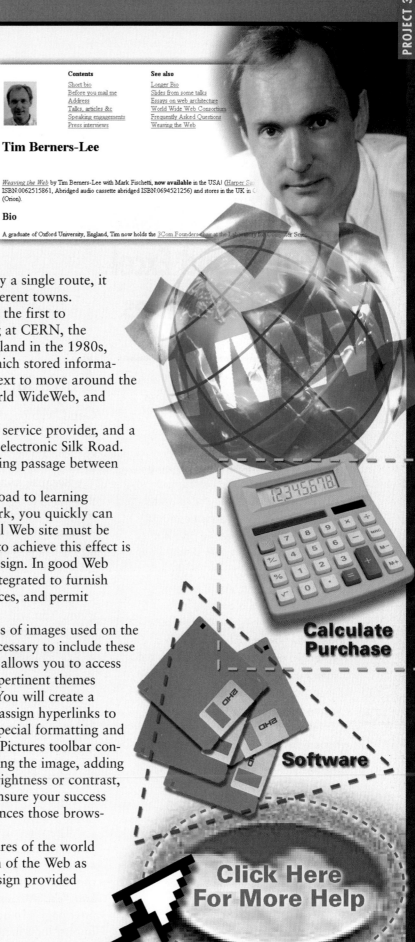

Tim Berners-Lee

Weaving the Web by Tim Berners-Lee with Mark Fischetti, **now available** in the USA! (Harper S
ISBN:0062515861, Abridged audio cassette abridged ISBN:0694521256) and stores in the UK in (
(Orion).

Bio

A graduate of Oxford University, England, Tim now holds the 3Com Founders chair at the Laboratory for Computer Scie

commerce that stretched from China to Europe — was a highway for caravans of merchants laden with silk, gold, and glass, trading goods and sharing culture along the way. Like the Web, the Silk Road was not merely a single route, it had many different branches that connected different towns.

Tim Berners-Lee, the father of the Web, was the first to travel the hyperlinks of the Web. While working at CERN, the European Particle Physics Laboratory in Switzerland in the 1980s, Berners-Lee wrote a program called Enquire, which stored information using random associations and used hypertext to move around the Internet. In 1989, Berners-Lee proposed the World WideWeb, and online travel was underway.

Today, all you need is a modem, an Internet service provider, and a Web browser, and you are ready to explore this electronic Silk Road. Your Web browser is your golden tablet, providing passage between linked sites all over the world.

Browsing the World Wide Web is the Silk Road to learning essential Web site design. Looking at other's work, you quickly can recognize good and bad practices. The successful Web site must be innovative and effective to stand out. One way to achieve this effect is to use images and graphics in your Web page design. In good Web pages, images are not simply shown, they are integrated to furnish information, display pictures of goods and services, and permit navigation.

In this project, you will learn about the types of images used on the Web and master the graphics editing options necessary to include these images in your FrontPage web. FrontPage 2000 allows you to access the World Wide Web and select interesting and pertinent themes and backgrounds to add appeal to your pages. You will create a table with ease, and add graphics to which you assign hyperlinks to other pages in your web. Then, you can apply special formatting and effects to images using the Pictures toolbar. The Pictures toolbar contains buttons that perform actions such as rotating the image, adding text to an image, increasing or decreasing the brightness or contrast, or adding beveled edges. All of these elements ensure your success in developing a Web site that attracts and influences those browsing the Web and gets you noticed.

As travelers of the past learned of the treasures of the world on the Silk Road, you can experience the wealth of the Web as you gather the richness of ideas, insight, and design provided only by browsing the World Wide Web.

Calculate Purchase

Software

Click Here For More Help

Microsoft FrontPage 2000

Microsoft FrontPage 2000

Using Images, Hotspots, Bookmarks, and Excel to Create Web Pages

PROJECT 3

C A S E   P E R S P E C T I V E

The Bits 'n' Bytes computer club officers have reviewed the home page you created and would like to make some changes. Although they like the general approach, after seeing their paper design put on the screen, they want a design format more likely to capture someone's attention. They have asked you to come up with a scheme that is more colorful and attractive and is appropriate to apply to all of their Web pages. They suggest that perhaps a graphic background would be better and have supplied a graphic for possible use. Additionally, for the Discount page, they have supplied you with a Web page, exported from Excel, for calculating a purchase and would like you to incorporate it into their Web. Also for this page, they have provided a discounted price list from a local supplier who is willing to give club members a discount on purchases.

Introduction

Good Web pages do not merely display images, they integrate them and use them effectively. Images on Web pages are used to provide information, serve as decoration, display pictures of products or artistic works, and provide navigation.

Because images, graphics, and animation now are used so widely, it is important to take the time to learn about the types of images used on the Web and master the graphics editing options necessary to include these objects in your Web pages. You should know the characteristics, advantages, and disadvantages of each type of image file so that you can ascertain the best type of image to use for a particular situation.

Project 3 introduces you to using images and how to format them. You will create a transparent GIF image, an image map, and a bookmark. You also will see how easy it is in FrontPage to make significant changes to an entire Web site by applying a theme. You will create hotspots for an image map and link to an Excel worksheet to calculate totals.

The Web page you will develop in this project is the next page in the web for Bits 'n' Bytes computer club, the Discount page (Figure 3-1b). The Discount page consists of a long table of products. Clicking an image at the top of the Discount page immediately displays the corresponding section in the table below to which the image is linked. In Project 2, you created a hyperlink to this page from the (modified) Bits 'n' Bytes Home page (Figure 3-1a).

Then, using a worksheet exported from Excel (Figure 3-1c), you will include this page in your web that allows visitors to calculate their purchases from the Discount page. Before creating the Web page, you will modify the Bits 'n' Bytes Home page from the previous project to that shown in Figure 3-2 (on the next page). In addition, to help you in this process, some important concepts and definitions are presented.

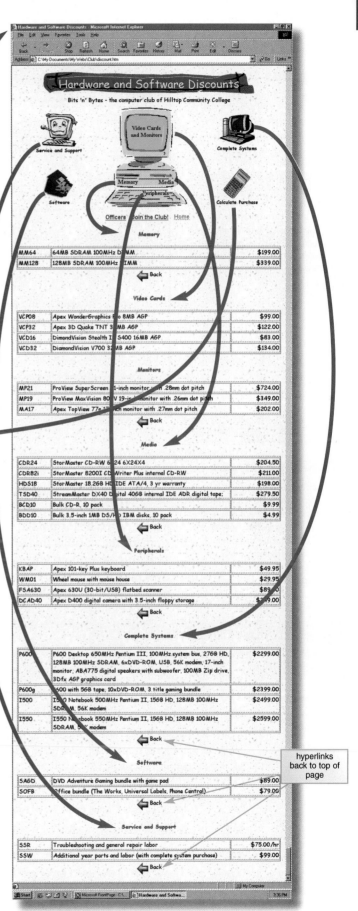

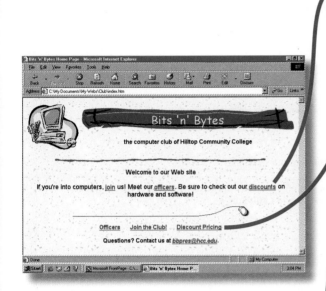

(a) Home Page

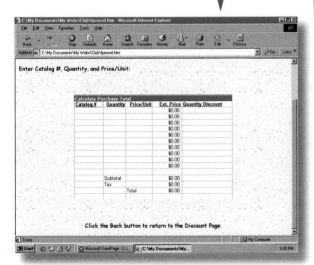

(c) Excel Worksheet

FIGURE 3-1

hyperlinks back to top of page

(b) Discount page with hyperlinks and bookmarks

Image File Formats

FrontPage will read BMP (Windows and OS/2), TIFF, TGA, RAS, EPS, PCX, PCD (Kodak Photo CD), and WMF formats. All of these must be converted when saved to GIF or JPEG, except PNG. Although FrontPage does support the PNG file format, many Web browsers cannot display PNG pictures without a special plug-in. In general, it is better to use only GIF or JPEG images on your Web pages.

Obtaining Images

You can browse the WWW and select any image to insert on your Web page. Be sure that you have permission to use the image before placing it on your FrontPage web as some images on the Web are copyrighted.

FIGURE 3-2

Image File Formats

Many different formats are used to represent images on computers. Table 3-1 shows some of the various image file formats. Numerous graphics editors and tools are available that allow you to create and edit images. For example, you can create your own custom buttons, bullets, dividers, and background images. FrontPage supports two types of image file formats: GIF and JPEG.

Table 3-1   Image File Formats

IMAGE FILE TYPE	DESCRIPTION
BMP	Windows bitmap file format – device-independent format, introduced with Windows 3.0 and increasingly supported by Windows applications.
EPS	Encapsulated postscript file format – an extension of the Postscript file graphics format developed by Adobe systems.
GIF	Graphic Interchange Format file format – a popular graphics exchange format used by the CompuServe Information Service and other online graphics sources. GIF is a licensed product for developers of commercial, for-profit software; however, for the nonprofit personal home page, a license agreement is not required.
JPEG	Joint Photographic Expert Group file format – used for true color 24-bit photographic images scanned or digitized from films.
PCX	Paintbrush file format – used in Windows Paintbrush and other paint programs and supported by many desktop publishing and graphics programs.
PNG	Portable Network Graphics file format – a file format for the lossless, portable, well-compressed storage of raster images.
RAS	Sun Raster file format – the raster image file format developed by Sun Microsystems, Inc.
TGA	Targa file format – a photo-realistic image format designed for systems with a Truevision display adapter.
TIF	Tagged Image File format – supported by many desktop publishing programs.
WMF	Windows Metafile format – a vector graphics format used mostly for word processing clip art.

Regardless of the file type, an image is displayed on a computer screen using small points of color called pixels. A **pixel**, or **picture element**, is the smallest addressable point on the screen. An image is formed on the screen by displaying pixels of different color. The combined group of different-colored pixels makes up the image. The **image file** contains the information needed to determine the color for each pixel used to display the image.

The **bit resolution** of an image refers to the number of bits of stored information per pixel. With an **8-bit image**, eight bits of information are stored for each pixel. Using the binary numbering system, you can represent up to 256 numbers using 8 bits. Thus, an 8-bit image can have a maximum of 256 colors, with each number representing a different color.

A **24-bit image** can have up to 16.7 million colors. These types of images have near-photographic quality. Each pixel, however, consumes three times as much storage as a pixel in an 8-bit image, which results in a larger file size for an image with the same number of pixels.

GIF Image Files

GIF stands for **Graphic Interchange Format**. GIF files use 8-bit resolution and support up to 256 colors. GIF files support indexed color image types, line art, and grayscale images.

Special types of GIF files, called **animated GIFs**, contain a series of images that are displayed in rapid succession, giving the appearance of movement. Special animated GIF editors are available to combine the series of images and set the display timing.

The GIF89a format contains a **transparency index**. This allows you to specify a transparent color, which causes the background of the Web page to display through the color that has been set as transparent. If you are using line art, icons, or images such as company logos, make sure they are in the GIF89a format. You then will be able to take advantage of the transparency features.

JPEG Image Files

JPEG stands for **Joint Photographic Expert Group**. The advantage to using JPEG files is the high-color resolution. JPEG supports 24-bit resolution, providing up to 16.7 million possible colors. If you are including photographic images in your Web page, they must use JPEG format because of the support for full color.

When you insert an image that is not in GIF or JPEG format, FrontPage automatically converts it to the GIF format if the image has eight or fewer bits of color. The image is converted automatically to JPEG format if the image has more than eight bits of color.

With FrontPage, you can import image files into the current FrontPage web, insert images in Web pages, align images with text, and create and edit image maps. The editing commands in FrontPage, such as crop, rotate, and resize, allow you to change the appearance of the image. In addition, you can change its brightness and contrast, make it black and white, or give the image beveled edges.

FrontPage can work with graphics editing programs such as the **Clip Art Gallery**, which is a tool for previewing and managing clip art, pictures, sounds, video clips, and animation. The Clip Art Gallery contains a collection of clip art and pictures you can insert into your Web pages. You used the Clip Art Gallery to create the Bits 'n' Bytes Home page in Project 2.

More About

GIF Files and Transparency

GIF images that are animated will not allow you to select a transparent color. An animated GIF image consists of several images that are displayed in rapid succession.

More About

Photographic Images

Be careful when using photographic images with 24-bit color. Not everyone on the WWW has a monitor and display adapter that supports 24-bit color. Try changing your Windows color setting to a lower bit resolution and displaying the Web page to see how the images look.

Modifying an Existing Web Page

Because the club officers did not want to keep their original design once they saw it on the computer, you want them to see some alternatives before the rest of the pages are developed. You decide on two approaches: applying a background graphic to the current design as suggested, and re-designing the look of the Home page by using a theme. Because applying these changes is an easy task in FrontPage, you decide to show both approaches and let the officers decide which they prefer.

To modify your initial Web page, you need to start FrontPage 2000 and then open the original FrontPage web. Start FrontPage 2000 using the steps summarized below.

TO START FRONTPAGE 2000

① Click the Start button on the taskbar. Point to Programs on the Start menu.

② Click Microsoft FrontPage on the Programs submenu.

The FrontPage window opens and an empty page displays.

Opening an Existing FrontPage Web

Perform the following steps to open the Bits 'n' Bytes FrontPage web created in Project 2. If you did not complete Project 2, see your instructor for a copy.

 To Open an Existing FrontPage Web

① **Click the Open button arrow on the Standard toolbar. Point to Open Web on the Open button menu.**

The Open button menu displays with the Open Web command selected (Figure 3-3).

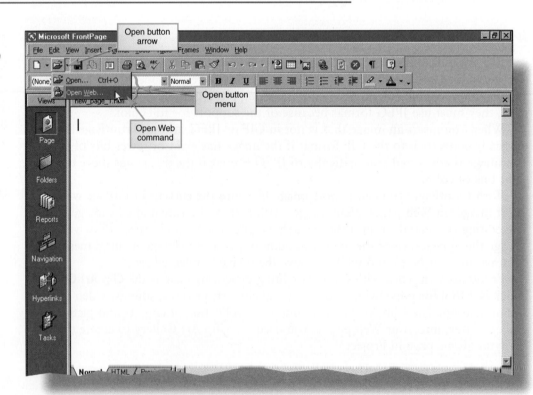

FIGURE 3-3

2 Click Open Web. When the Open Web dialog box displays, if necessary, click the Look in box arrow and select the folder location where you stored the web for project 2 (e.g., C:\My Documents\ My Webs\Club). Point to the Open button.

The Open Web dialog box displays with the Web folder selected (Figure 3-4). The new location displays in the text box. Use the drive and location that is appropriate for your environment.

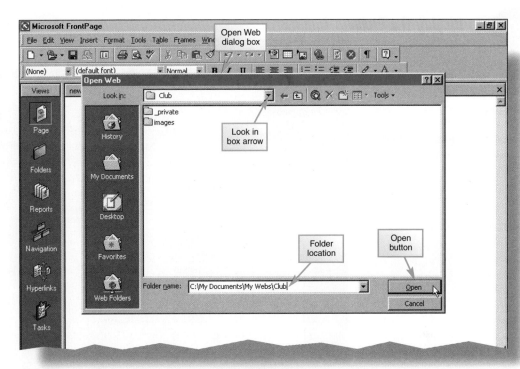

FIGURE 3-4

3 Click the Open button. Double-click the file index.htm in the Folder List.

The previous web is loaded and the file index.htm displays in Page view (Figure 3-5).

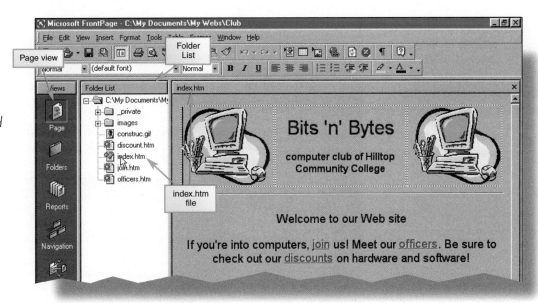

FIGURE 3-5

Other **Ways**

1. On File menu, click Open
2. Press ALT+F, O

The Pictures Toolbar

FrontPage has features for manipulating images within a Web page. The **Pictures toolbar** contains a set of buttons that perform actions such as rotating the image and changing the brightness and contrast. The buttons on the Pictures toolbar may be active or inactive, depending on the type of image and its context.

The Pictures toolbar can be hidden or displayed, depending on the setting on the View menu. Display the Pictures toolbar by following the steps on the next page.

Steps **To Display the Pictures Toolbar**

1 **Click View on the menu bar. Point to Toolbars.**

The View menu displays with the Toolbars command selected and the Toolbars submenu displaying (Figure 3-6). Visible toolbars are indicated with a check mark.

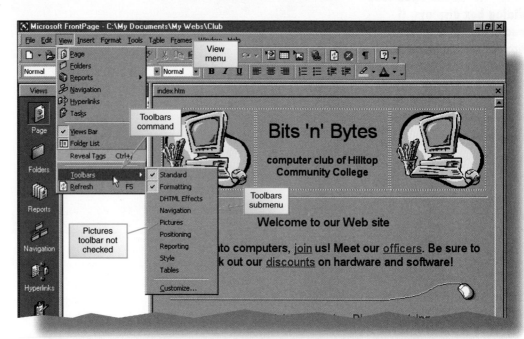

FIGURE 3-6

2 **If Pictures is not checked, click Pictures. If necessary, drag the Pictures toolbar to the position shown in Figure 3-7.**

The Pictures toolbar displays in the FrontPage window.

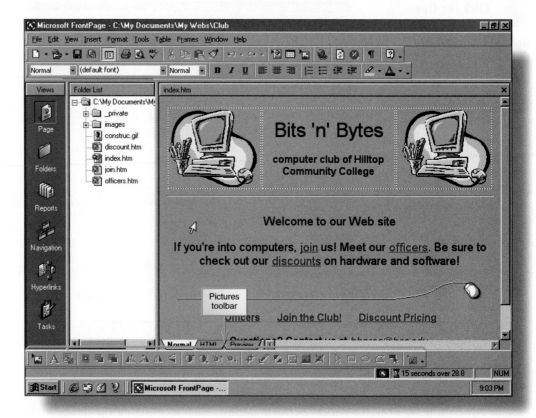

FIGURE 3-7

 Ways

1. Press ALT+V, T, select toolbar name, press ENTER

Even if the Pictures toolbar is not selected to be visible, it displays automatically whenever you select an image. Table 3-2 shows the buttons on the Pictures toolbar and a brief explanation of their purpose. Each button used in the project is discussed in more detail as it is encountered.

Table 3-2   Pictures Toolbar Buttons

BUTTON	BUTTON NAME	PURPOSE	BUTTON	BUTTON NAME	PURPOSE
	Insert Picture from File	Inserts a picture from a file		Crop	Crops an image
	Text	Adds text to an image		Set Transparent Color	Makes a color transparent
	Auto Thumbnail	Creates a thumbnail image of the selected picture		Black and White	Converts an image to black and white
	Position Absolutely	Assigns an absolute position to the selected element		Wash Out	Washes out an image
	Bring Forward	Moves the selected object up one level in the order of objects layered on the page		Bevel	Adds a bevel effect to an image's edges
	Send Backward	Moves the selected object down one level in the order of objects layered on the page		Resample	Resamples an image (changes the file size)
	Rotate Left	Rotates an image to the left		Select	Selects a hotspot on an image map
	Rotate Right	Rotates an image to the right		Rectangle	Draws a rectangular hotspot
	Flip Horizontal	Flips an image horizontally		Circle	Draws a circular hotspot
	Flip Vertical	Flips an image vertically		Polygon	Draws a polygonal hotspot
	More Contrast	Increases the contrast of an image		Highlight Hotspots	Highlights hotspots
	Less Contrast	Decreases the contrast of an image		Restore	Restores an image from a disk file
	More Brightness	Increases the brightness of an image		More Buttons	Adds or removes buttons from toolbar
	Less Brightness	Decreases the brightness of an image			

FrontPage does not allow you to edit an image directly. You need a separate image editor program to perform that activity. You can, however, specify that an image editor program starts automatically when you double-click an image. The **Options command** on the Tools menu includes a **Configure Editors sheet** on which you can identify an image editor program.

Background Images

Not all images make good tiled backgrounds because of their sizes and shapes. The edge of an image must flow smoothly from one copy to another in order to present a seamless background.

Applying a Background Image to a Web Page

The **background** of a Web page refers to the color or texture behind every object on the Web page. The default background is white. In Project 1, the background was specified as part of the theme that you applied to the web using the Themes view. In Project 2, you selected a color from a palette of available colors to use as the background.

FrontPage also allows you to specify a URL that points to an image file that is tiled, or repeated, across and down, to create the background of the Web page. This effect is similar to the wallpaper on your Windows desktop. You can specify an image file name within the current FrontPage web or the URL of any image file on the World Wide Web.

In keeping with your first approach to redesigning the club Home page, you will use the image provided by the club officers as a background to the current Web page. The following steps demonstrate how to use an image as a tiled background for a Web page.

 ## To Apply a Background Image to a Web Page

1 Click Format on the menu bar and then point to Background (Figure 3-8).

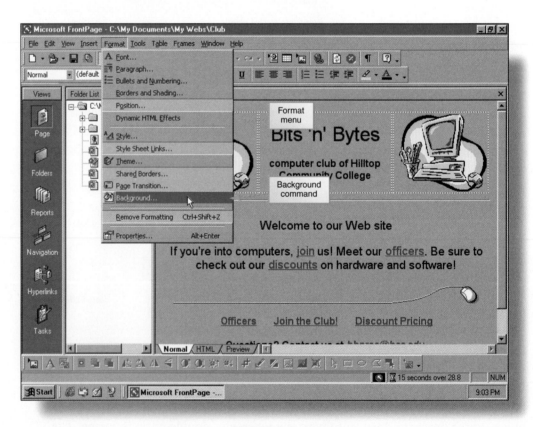

FIGURE 3-8

2 Click Background. When the Page Properties dialog box displays, if necessary, click the Background tab.

The Page Properties dialog box displays (Figure 3-9). The current background color displays in the Background tab sheet.

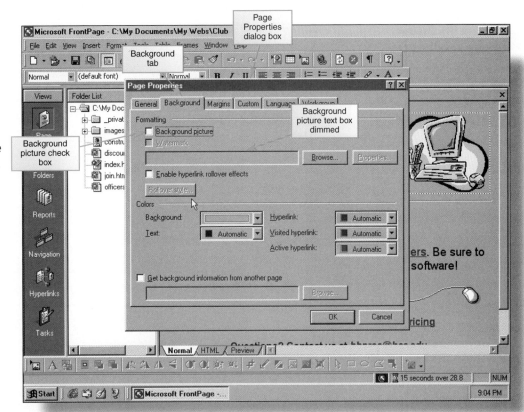

FIGURE 3-9

3 Click Background picture in the Formatting area to select it and then point to the Browse button.

The Background picture text box no longer is dimmed (Figure 3-10). You can click the text box to type a file name or URL, or click the Browse button to search for the file name or URL.

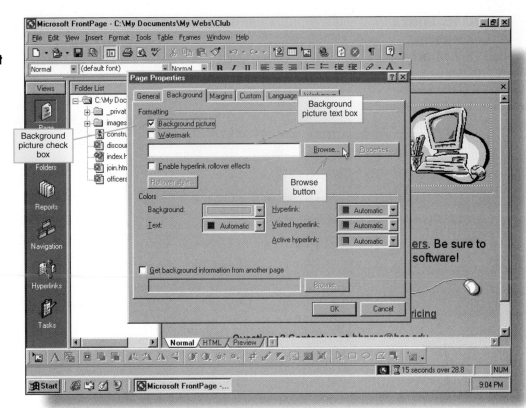

FIGURE 3-10

4 **Click the Browse button. When the Select Background Picture dialog box displays, point to the Select a file on your computer button.**

The Select Background Picture dialog box displays (Figure 3-11). You can select images stored on your computer or from the World Wide Web.

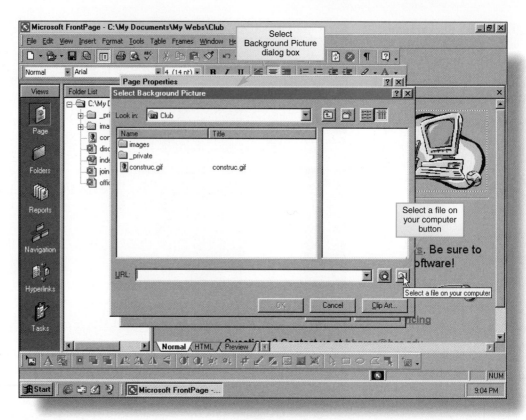

FIGURE 3-11

5 **Click the Select a file on your computer button. When the Select File dialog box displays, select the file binaryBack.jpg from the Project3 folder on the Data Disk. Point to the OK button.**

The image file is selected (Figure 3-12).

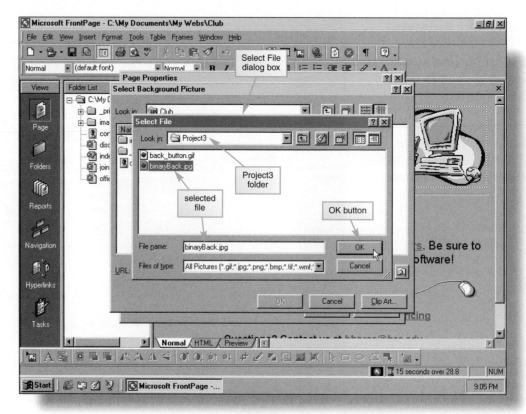

FIGURE 3-12

6 Click the OK button. When the Page Properties dialog box is again visible, point to the OK button.

The path to the image displays in the Background picture text box on the Page Properties dialog box (Figure 3-13).

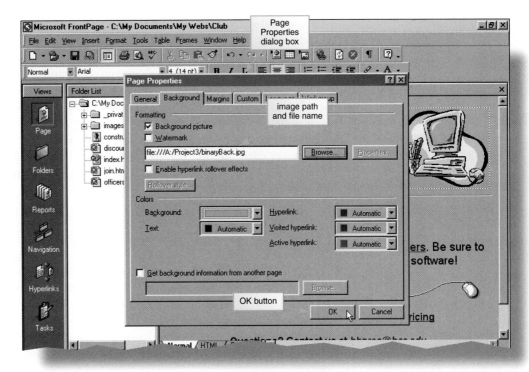

FIGURE 3-13

7 Click the OK button.

The FrontPage window displays with the image tiled across and down the page (Figure 3-14).

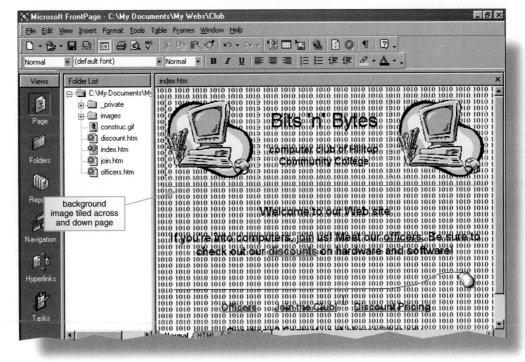

FIGURE 3-14

The binary number image has been tiled, or repeated, across and down the Web page. Not all images lend themselves to tiling. Trial and error is the best way to determine whether or not an image would make a good background.

Other Ways

1. Right-click Web page, click Page Properties on shortcut menu, click Background tab

2. Press ALT+O, K, I, B

You should consider carefully whether to download or simply point to images on the World Wide Web. Each choice poses problems. You must obtain permission before using an image or graphic that belongs to someone else. If you use a URL that points to an image on another Web server computer on the World Wide Web, someone could remove or rename the image file, or the Web server could be taken out of service. If this happens, your Web page background no longer will be available. Thus, it is best to save the image on your computer.

The current color scheme of the tiled binary number background is too bright and interferes with the text on the Web page. Using the Wash Out button on the Pictures toolbar will soften the colors of an image. The next section illustrates how to achieve this effect.

Washing Out an Image

Softening the color of the binary number background increases the ease with which the text can be read by users accessing the Web page. The **Wash Out button** creates a low-contrast, see-through version of an image with a washed out appearance.

Applying the wash out effect to an image permanently alters its look once you save your changes. If you need to keep a version that is not washed out, you must make a copy of the original image file or save this modified image to another location.

To apply the wash out effect to an image on the current page, select the image by clicking it and then click the Wash Out button. To apply the wash out effect to the background image on the current page, click the Wash Out button when no images are selected. Perform the following steps to apply the wash out effect to the binary number background.

More About

Washing Out Images

Many images, even washed out, are not effective as a background. If you wash out an image and decide that it still is not appropriate, then you can undo the effect as long as you have not saved your changes. If you do decide to wash out an image, be careful before permanently changing an image used on the Web. Many Web sites share image files to conserve disk space. If you change an image file and then publish it on the Web, other Web pages that use the same image could be affected.

Steps **To Wash Out an Image**

---

1 Point to the Wash Out button on the Pictures toolbar (Figure 3-15).

FIGURE 3-15

2 Click the Wash Out button. Point to the Save button on the Standard toolbar.

The binary number background image is washed out (Figure 3-16).

3 Click the Save button. When the Save Embedded Files dialog box displays, if necessary, select the images folder to save the background image. Click the OK button.

The modified binary number background image is saved in a new location, preserving the original on the floppy disk.

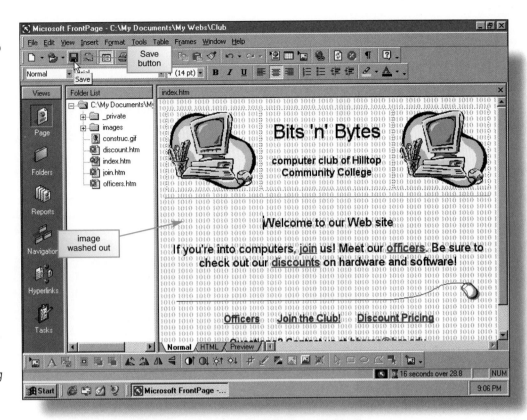

FIGURE 3-16

Applying the wash out effect to the background eliminates the problem of bright colors or contrasts interfering with the text on the Web page. It does not, however, mean that a given image can be made to work satisfactorily as a Web page background, especially for a page with text.

After meeting with club officers, they agree with you that this background may be more interesting than a plain color, but the theme which you suggest, named Loose Gestures, would be better yet. They also like your suggestion of using a banner on the pages and eliminating one of the two identical computer graphics on the Home page.

Applying a Theme to an Existing Web

Applying a theme to an existing web is essentially the same procedure used to apply a theme to a new web. When modifying a page that already contains certain graphic elements, such as a background color or image, be aware that applying a theme will permanently alter such existing properties. In fact, once a theme has been applied, you cannot access the background properties to apply an image or a color — they are under the control of the theme. You would need to remove or modify the theme to make such changes. Another thing to keep in mind when applying a theme is that once it is applied, you cannot undo the theme. You can effectively remove the theme by applying a theme selection of No Theme to the Web. This will set your Web pages to a white background with no background image. If you are not certain that you will want to use a theme, you might want to make a backup copy of your FrontPage web by saving it in an alternate location before applying the theme.

To apply a theme to an existing Web, perform the steps on the next page.

More *About*

Themes

Try to use an appropriate metaphor or theme on your Web pages. In addition to the themes provided in FrontPage, there often are themes available for free on the WWW. If none of these meet your needs, you can modify any theme in FrontPage to create your own new theme. Click the Modify button in the Themes dialog box and you can modify colors, graphics, and text in the theme.

TO APPLY A NEW THEME TO A FRONTPAGE WEB

1 Click Format on the menu bar and then click Theme.

2 Verify that the All Pages option button is selected.

3 Scroll to and then click the theme, Loose Gestures.

4 Click Vivid Colors. Verify that Active Graphics and Background picture are checked.

5 Click the OK button.

6 If a dialog box displays asking you to verify applying the theme, click Yes.

The theme Loose Gestures is applied to the FrontPage web (Figure 3-17).

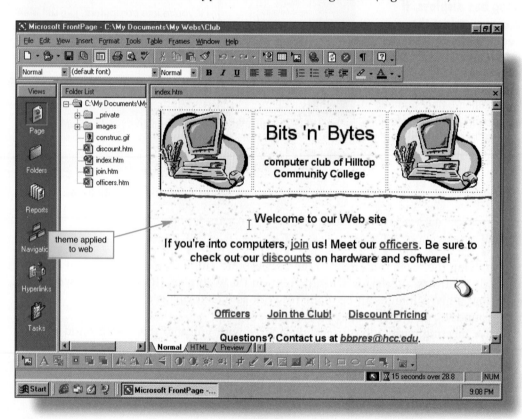

FIGURE 3-17

Inserting a Page Banner

In addition to applying a theme, you proposed changing the header of the Web page by adding a banner and by deleting one of the two computer images on either side of the club name. Currently, the header of the Web page is comprised of a table of three columns, with the leftmost and rightmost cells containing the computer graphic. Use the following steps to modify the header and insert a page banner.

Steps **To Insert a Page Banner**

1 **Position the mouse pointer above the rightmost cell of the table used as the header of the Web page and click to select the table column.**

The mouse pointer changes to a down arrow and the rightmost column (one cell) is selected (Figure 3-18). This action is needed to select the table cell and not just the image.

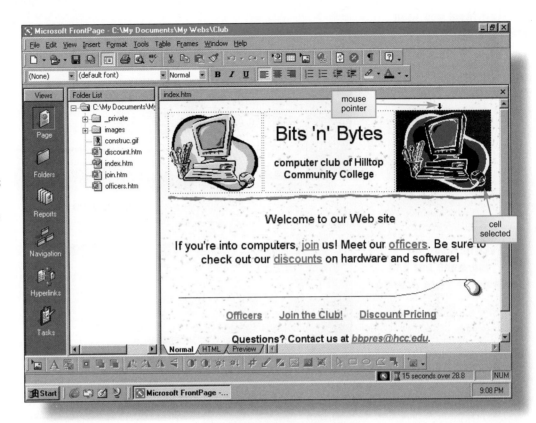

FIGURE 3-18

2 **Right-click the selected cell and then click Delete Cells on the shortcut menu.**

The rightmost cell and the image in it are deleted, reducing the table to two columns (Figure 3-19).

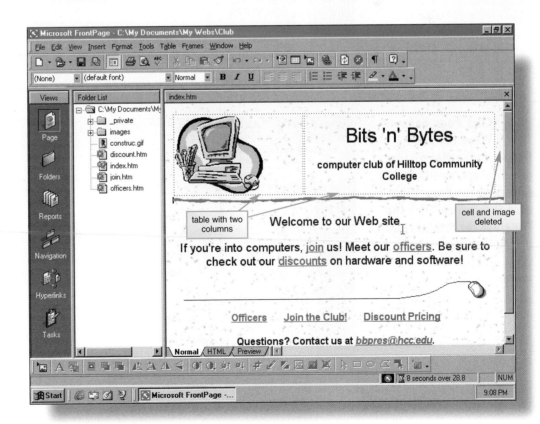

FIGURE 3-19

3 Drag through the words Bits 'n' Bytes to select them and then press the DELETE key.

The phrase is deleted (Figure 3-20).

FIGURE 3-20

4 Click Insert on the menu bar and then point to Page Banner.

The Insert menu displays (Figure 3-21).

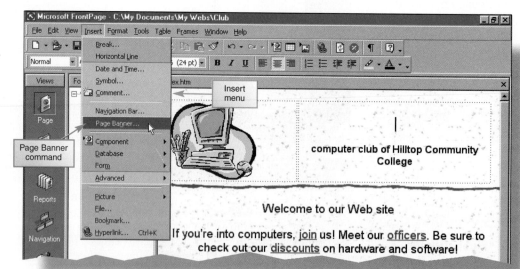

FIGURE 3-21

5 Click Page Banner. When the Page Banner Properties dialog dox displays, certify that Picture in the Properties area is selected. Click the Page Banner text box and delete the words Home Page. Point to the OK button.

The Page Banner Properties dialog box displays with the changes specified (Figure 3-22).

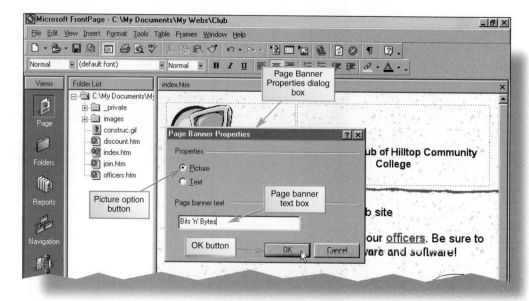

FIGURE 3-22

6 Click the OK button.

The Page Banner Properties dialog box closes and the new banner displays on the Web page (Figure 3-23).

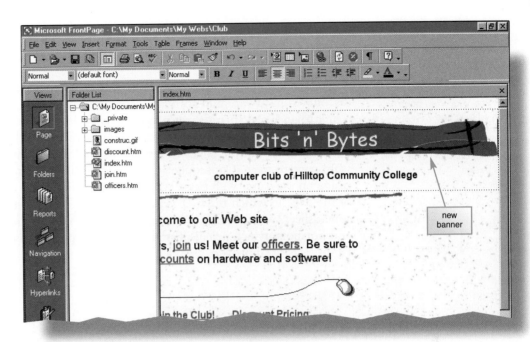

FIGURE 3-23

7 Type the at the beginning of the phrase that begins with computer club. Click the Save button on the Standard toolbar to save your changes.

The completed changes to the Web page are shown in Figure 3-24.

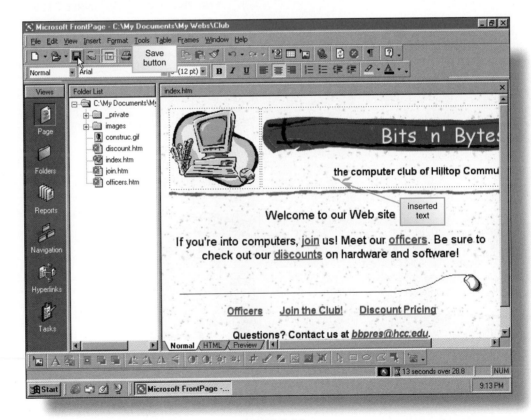

FIGURE 3-24

Other Ways

1. Press ALT+I, N

After showing these changes to the club officers, they agree that this is the best design yet and authorize you to continue work on the next page in the web, the Discount page.

Web Page Design

For more ideas to help in designing your Web page, visit the FrontPage 2000 More About Web page (www.scsite.com/fp2000/more.htm) and then click Web Page Design.

Designing the Web Page

For the Discount page, the club wants to have graphics as hyperlinks to each of the discounted hardware and software categories available from their supplier, as well as a link to an Excel spreadsheet page where a possible purchase can be totaled. Because discount prices are likely to change over time, club officers are concerned about having multiple pages to modify, as well as the time required in navigating from page to page. Consequently, they would like all discount pricing information to reside on the same Web page, with the hyperlinks displaying the appropriate section of the page in which the user is interested. The exception is the page with the Excel spreadsheet, which can be on a separate page. You discuss the use of an image map and hotspots, which are discussed later in this project, and the design shown in Figure 3-25 is approved.

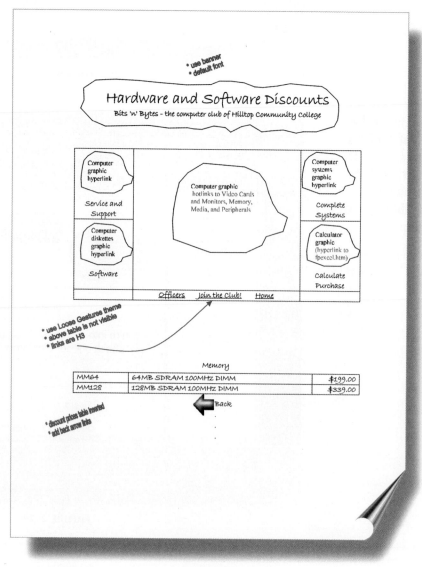

FIGURE 3-25

Adding a New Web Page to an Existing FrontPage Web

In the preceding project, you imported existing Web pages into your web. These pages indicated to the user that they were still under construction. This avoided having the user get an error from trying to access missing pages. To complete development of one of these pages, you could open the existing page and delete all items on the page, or simply delete the old one and create a new one.

More About

Deleting Pages

Deleting files locally does not remove them from the Web server. When you have deleted or moved files or folders in the web on your development computer, the next time you publish, FrontPage will prompt you about the corresponding files on the Web server.

Deleting an Existing Page from a Web

FrontPage's Folder List provides a simple way to manage files in a web using an interface much like that of the Windows Explorer. Files can be deleted or renamed in the same manner as with Explorer. Use care when deleting a file from your web, as this action permanently removes the file and cannot be undone. Perform the following steps to delete the file, discount.htm, from the web.

To Delete a File from a Web

1 **Right-click the file name, discount.htm, in the Folder List pane. Point to the Delete command on the shortcut menu.**

The file name is selected and the shortcut menu displays (Figure 3-26).

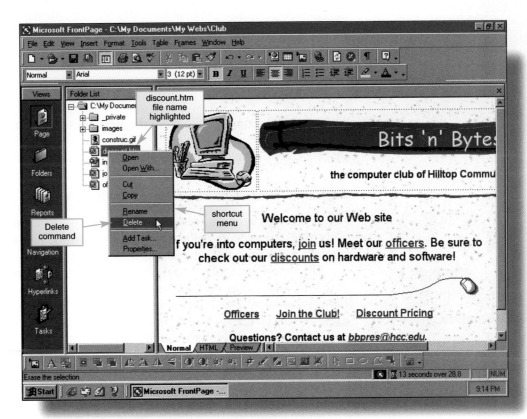

FIGURE 3-26

Click Delete. Click the Yes button in the Confirm Delete dialog box.

The file name discount.htm is deleted which removes it from the Folder List pane and from the web (Figure 3-27).

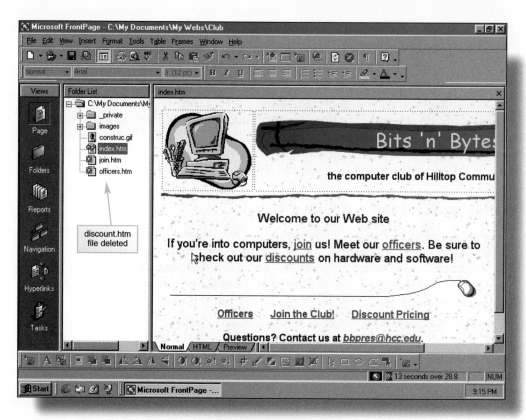

FIGURE 3-27

Other Ways

1. Click file name, press DELETE

Navigation View

You can move the page icons in Navigation view by dragging them to a new location. This allows you to reorganize the graphical tree diagram.

Because deleting the file from the web physically removes the file from your system, if you want to keep the file, but simply remove it from the current web, make a copy of the file in a location other than the current web folder.

Adding a New Web Page to a FrontPage Web

In previous projects, you used templates consisting of one or more pre-existing Web pages, or imported existing Web pages into your web. As you develop customized webs, you will want to add new Web pages to the web when the need arises.

The FrontPage toolbar contains the **New Page button** that you can use to add a new Web page to the current web. A new page can be added in Page, Folders, or Navigation view. If you are using navigation bars or banners in your web, as was done in Project 1, then you should add new pages after changing to Navigation view and then indicating the location of the new page by selecting a page icon in the Navigation pane. The new page icon will be inserted as a child below the selected page icon. This allows the navigation bars to be correctly updated by FrontPage and preserves the visual relationship in the graphical tree diagram in the Navigation pane.

When a new page is added in Page view, FrontPage displays the new page just as it does when an existing web first is opened. Such a new page does not show in the Folder List pane until it has been saved. Adding a new page in Navigation view, however, causes that page to be saved and added to the Folder List as soon as the view is refreshed.

Because you are going to use a banner on this page, you should add the page in Navigation view. Perform the following steps to insert a new page in Navigation view in the current FrontPage web.

Steps ## To Add a New Web Page to a FrontPage Web

1 **Click the Navigation button on the Views bar. If necessary, click the Bits 'n' Bytes Home page icon to select it. Point to the New Page button on the Standard toolbar.**

FrontPage displays in Navigation view (Figure 3-28).

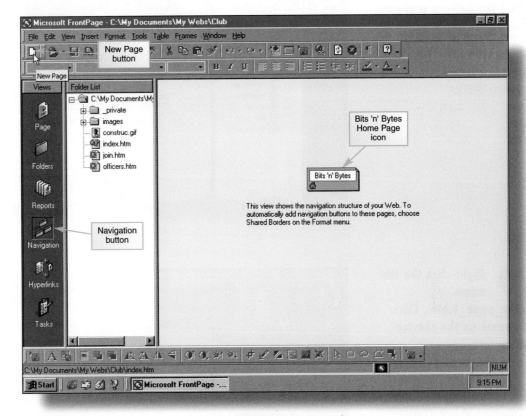

FIGURE 3-28

2 **Click the New Page button.**

A new page icon displays in the Navigation pane with a title of New Page 1 (Figure 3-29).

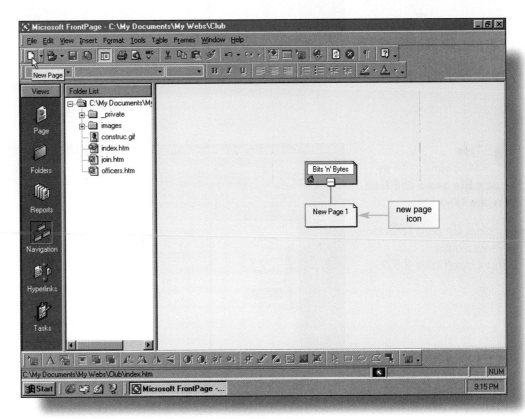

FIGURE 3-29

3 Click View on the menu bar and then click the Refresh command.

The new page displays in the Folder List pane as new_page_1.htm (Figure 3-30).

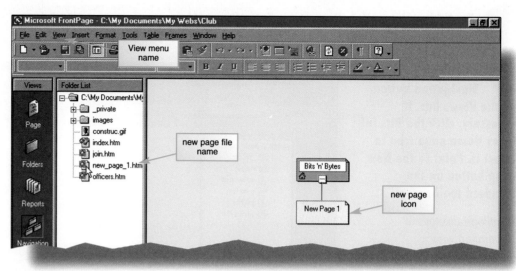

FIGURE 3-30

4 Right-click the file name new_page_1.htm. Click Rename on the shortcut menu.

The new_page_1.htm file name is highlighted and an edit text box displays around the file name (Figure 3-31).

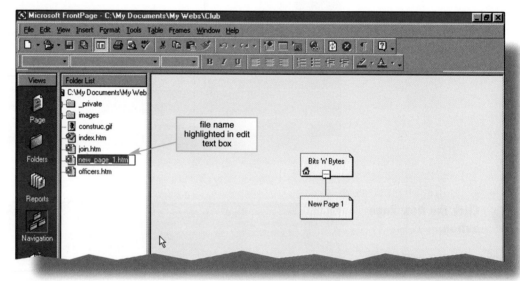

FIGURE 3-31

5 Type discount.htm as the new file name and then press the ENTER key.

The Folder List pane reflects the renamed file, discount.htm (Figure 3-32).

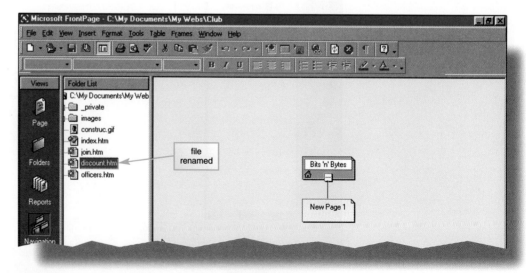

FIGURE 3-32

6 **Right-click the New Page 1 page icon. Click Rename on the shortcut menu and then type** Hardware and Software Discounts **in the edit text box. Press the ENTER key.**

The new title of the Web page displays in the page icon (Figure 3-33).

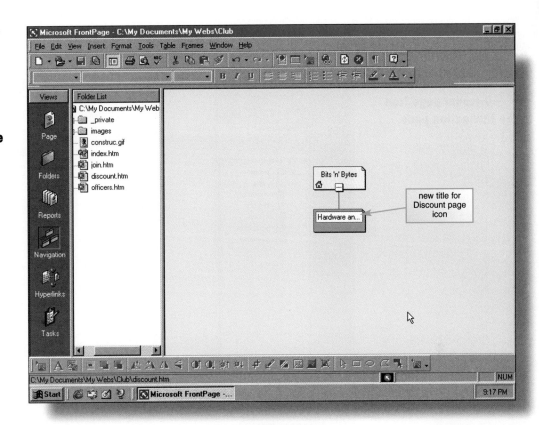

new title for Discount page icon

FIGURE 3-33

To control the location of the new Web page in the graphical tree diagram, you selected a Web page icon before clicking the New Page button. Because you clicked the top-level page, the New Page 1 page was added just below it, as shown in Figure 3-29 on page FP 3.25. If you were to insert another page with the Bits 'n' Bytes Home page selected, a New Page 2 would be added on the same level as the Discount page. If you were to click the Discount page and then click New Page, the New Page 2 would be added below the Discount page, creating a three-level graphical tree diagram.

Editing a New Web Page

The tasks to create the Discount page are in large part similar to steps you followed in creating the Bits 'n' Bytes Home page. You will use tables to align text and graphics, insert graphics from the Clip Art Gallery, and create hyperlinks on the page to other pages. New tasks will be creating hyperlinks to other locations on the Discount page itself, associating hyperlinks with images or sections of images, and incorporating the contents of another HTML file as part of the page. The HTML file is to be inserted into the current Web page below two tables which will hold other graphics and text. Perform the steps on the next page to edit the Discount page in Page view and add the required banner and tables.

Other Ways

1. On File menu click New, click Page
2. Press ALT+F, N, P
3. Press CTRL+N
4. Click New Page button arrow, click Page
5. Right-click Folder List pane, click New Page

More About

Importing Images

You can import an image simply by dragging the image from another Windows application to the Navigation or Folders view. You also may copy a file in Windows Explorer and paste it into the Folder List or the Contents pane while in Folders view.

To Edit a New Web Page

1 **Double-click the Discount page icon in the Navigation pane.**

FrontPage displays the Discount page in Page view (Figure 3-34).

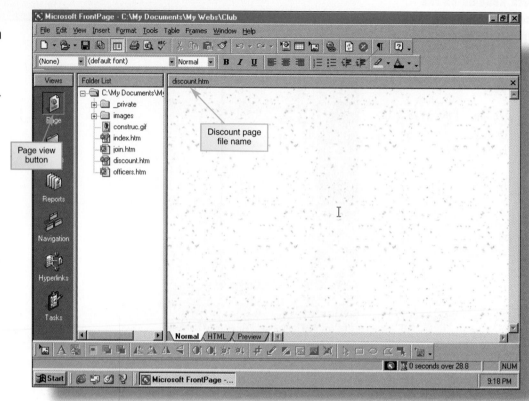

FIGURE 3-34

2 **Click the Insert Table button on the Standard toolbar and then insert a table with one row and one column. Right-click the single cell and select Cell Properties on the shortcut menu. In the Layout area, click the Horizontal alignment box arrow and then click Center. Point to the OK button.**

The Cell Properties dialog box displays (Figure 3-35).

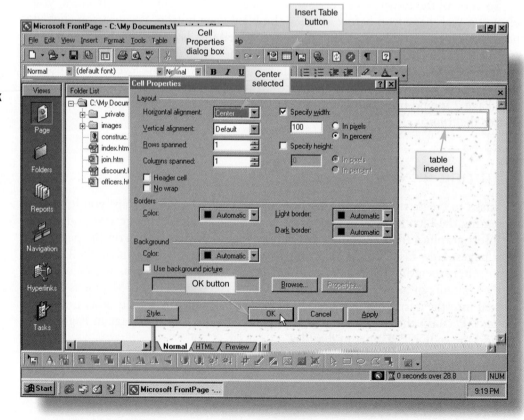

FIGURE 3-35

3 **Click the OK button. Click Insert on the menu bar. Point to Page Banner.**

The Insert menu displays (Figure 3-36).

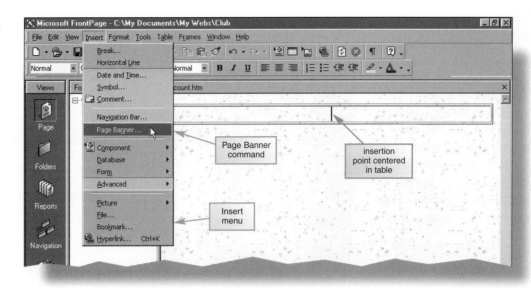

FIGURE 3-36

4 **Click Page Banner. When the Page Banner Properties dialog box displays, verify that Picture is selected in the Properties area. If necessary, type** Hardware and Software Discounts **in the Page banner text box. Point to the OK button.**

The Page Banner Properties dialog box displays (Figure 3-37).

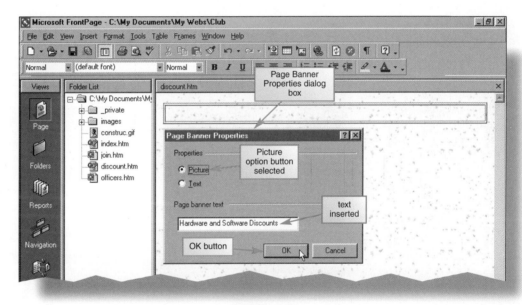

FIGURE 3-37

5 **Click the OK button. Hold down the SHIFT key and press the ENTER key. Type** Bits 'n' Bytes - the computer club of Hilltop Community College **as the text.**

The text displays below the page banner (Figure 3-38).

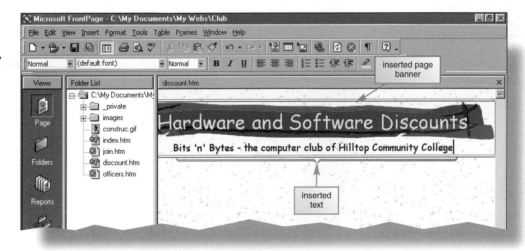

FIGURE 3-38

6 **Position the insertion point** below the table containing the banner. Click the Insert Table button on the Standard toolbar and then insert a table with three rows and three columns. Click the top center cell. Hold down the SHIFT key and click the middle center cell.

A 3x3 table is created with the selected cells highlighted (Figure 3-39).

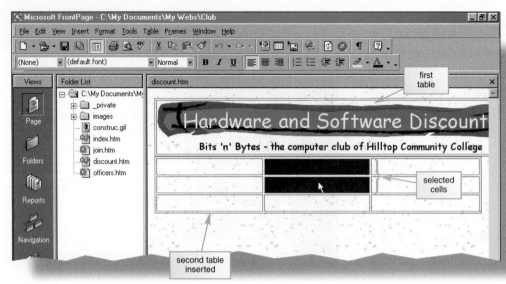

FIGURE 3-39

7 **Right-click one of the selected cells.** Point to Merge Cells on the shortcut menu.

The shortcut menu displays (Figure 3-40).

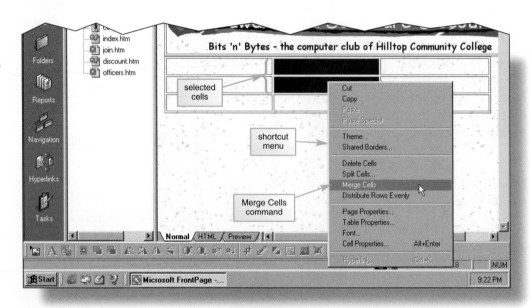

FIGURE 3-40

8 **Click Merge Cells.**

The selected cells are merged into a single cell (Figure 3-41).

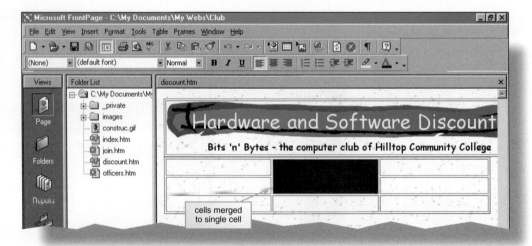

FIGURE 3-41

9 Right-click anywhere in the first table and point to Table Properties on the shortcut menu.

The shortcut menu displays (Figure 3-42).

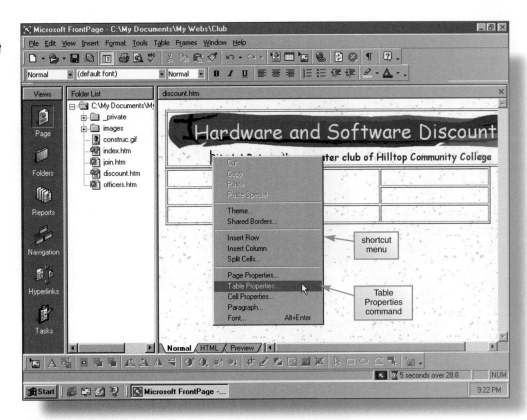

FIGURE 3-42

10 Click Table Properties. When the Table Properties dialog box displays, change the value in the Size box in the Borders area to zero (0). Point to the OK button.

Zero (0) displays in the Size box indicating that no visible border will display around the table cells (Figure 3-43).

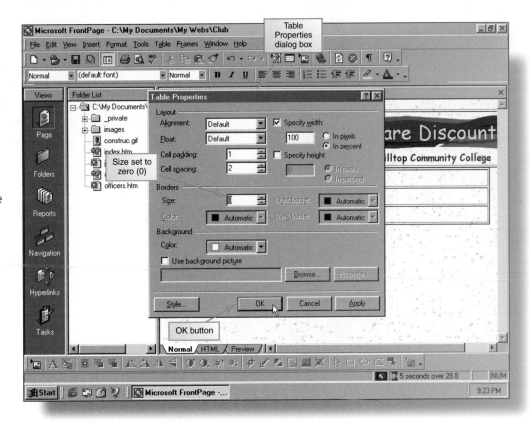

FIGURE 3-43

11 **Click the OK button.**

The table border is replaced with dashed lines (Figure 3-44).

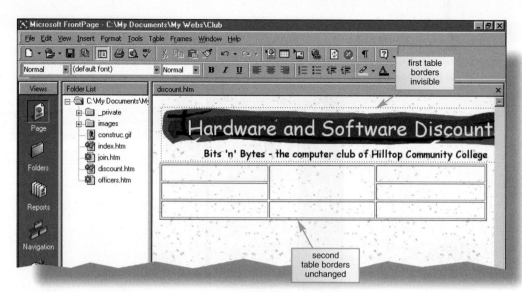

FIGURE 3-44

12 **Repeat Steps 9 through 11 for the second table.**

The table border for the second table is replaced with dashed lines (Figure 3-45).

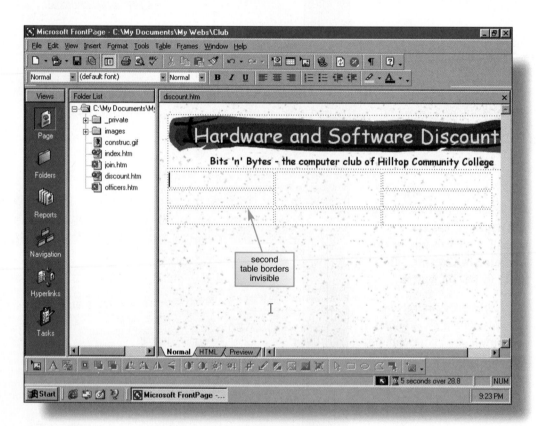

FIGURE 3-45

Inserting an HTML File into a Web Page

An HTML file containing the table of pricing information, table.htm, is provided on the Data Disk. It contains a series of tables with visible borders nested into cells of a table with invisible borders. The entire file is to be inserted into the current Web page below the two tables just added. To insert the HTML file, perform the following steps.

To Insert a File into a Web Page

1 **Position the insertion point at the bottom of the current page, below the last table added. Click Insert on the menu bar and then point to File.**

The insertion point is positioned where the contents of the inserted file will be added (Figure 3-46).

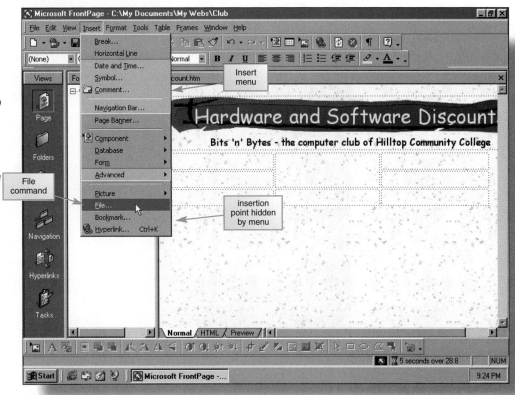

FIGURE 3-46

2 **Click File. When the Select File dialog box displays, select the file, table.htm, from the Project3 folder on the Data Disk. Point to the Open button.**

The Select File dialog box displays (Figure 3-47).

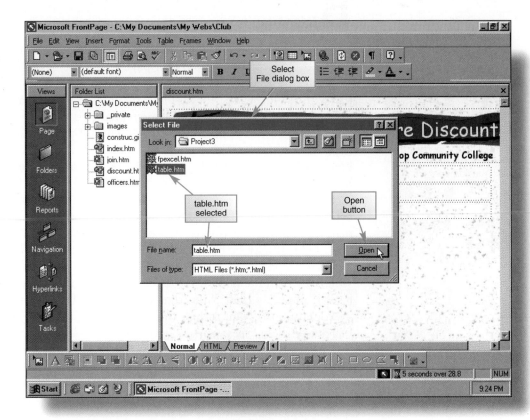

FIGURE 3-47

Click the Open button.

The contents of the file, table.htm, are inserted into the current Web page (Figure 3-48).

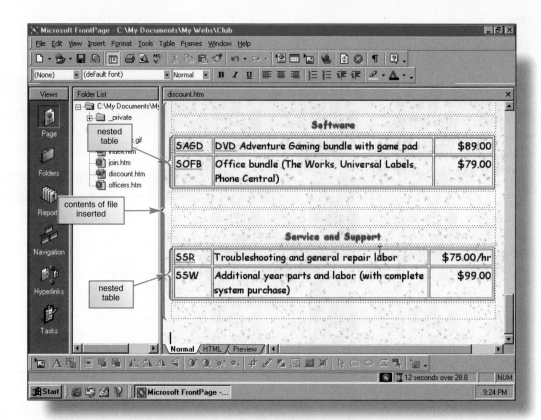

FIGURE 3-48

Other Ways

1. Press ALT+I, F

More About

Hyperlinks to Bookmarks

Hyperlinks to bookmarks do not have to be located on the same Web page as the bookmark. You can establish a hyperlink to a bookmark on another Web page first by selecting the page name in the Create Hyperlink dialog box and then selecting the desired bookmark on that page.

Bookmarks

When you create a Web page, it is natural to assume that you may have to create one or more hyperlinks from that page to another page. The ability to link from one Web page to other pages of interest is one of the most basic and powerful features of the World Wide Web. Not all links are created for the same purpose or in the same manner, however. In Project 1, you created two types of links. One type provided an e-mail link, so users could e-mail the owner of the page. Another type provided a hyperlink from one Web page to another. You also can create a hyperlink that has a bookmark as its destination. A **bookmark** is a location, or selected text, that you have marked on a page.

When designing a Web page, it is good to keep in mind how the user will interact with that page. If there are a number of links to relatively short pieces of information, and the user is likely to go back and forth from one page to another visiting these links, it may be better to place all of the information on a single Web page. This avoids having to reload each page as it is visited, which increases the perceived speed at which the pages can be reached. This approach must be balanced against having an overly large Web page, particularly if the user will not care to visit most of it. You also may want to link the user to a place in the Web page other than the top. In both of these cases, using a bookmark can help accomplish the task.

In FrontPage, if you have text that is bookmarked, the text is displayed with a dashed underline. If a location is bookmarked, the presence of a bookmark is indicated by a graphic flag icon . Perform the following steps to add a bookmarked location to the current Web page.

To Bookmark a Location in a Web Page

1 **Position the insertion point at the left of the banner at the top of the page. Click Insert on the menu bar and then point to Bookmark.**

The insertion point is positioned where the bookmark for this location is to be added (Figure 3-49).

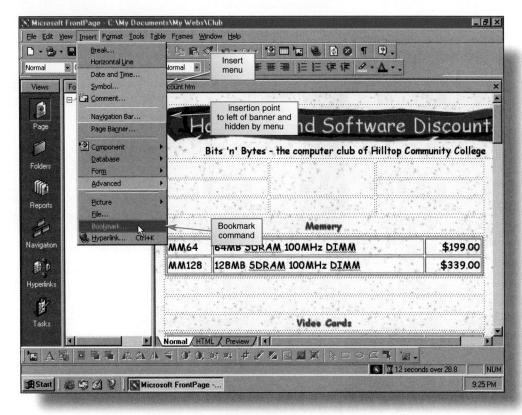

FIGURE 3-49

2 **Click Bookmark. When the Bookmark dialog box displays, type** Discount banner **in the Bookmark name text box. Point to the OK button.**

The Bookmark dialog box displays (Figure 3-50). The name of this bookmark is entered in the Bookmark name text box.

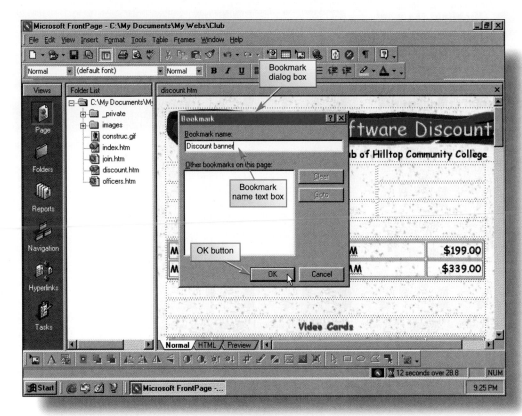

FIGURE 3-50

3 Click the OK button.

The Discount page displays with the bookmark flag icon, indicating the banner is a bookmarked location (Figure 3-51).

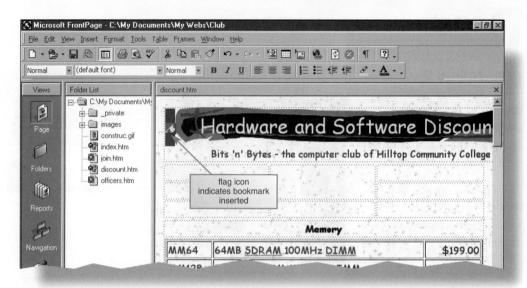

FIGURE 3-51

As previously discussed, text also can be bookmarked; once bookmarked, it displays with a dashed underline. Perform the following steps to add bookmarked text to the current Web page.

To Bookmark Text in a Web Page

1 Highlight the word, Memory, in the first row of the price list table previously inserted. Click Insert on the menu bar and then point to Bookmark.

The highlighted word, Memory, is the location for the bookmark that will be added (Figure 3-52).

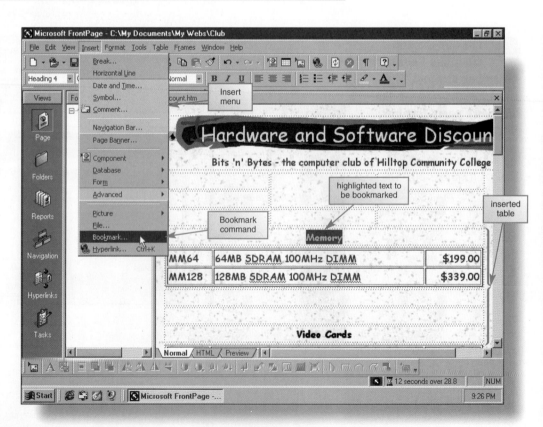

FIGURE 3-52

2 **Click Bookmark. When the Bookmark dialog box displays, point to the OK button.**

The Bookmark dialog box displays (Figure 3-53). The highlighted text is inserted automatically as the default name for this bookmark in the Bookmark name text box.

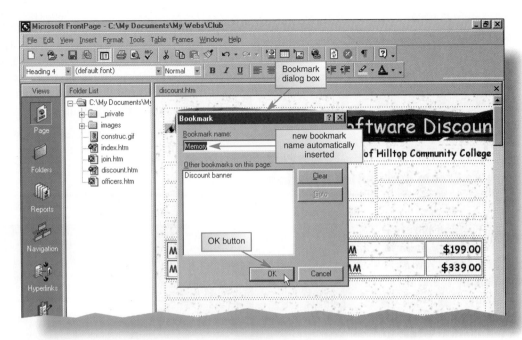

FIGURE 3-53

3 **Click the OK button.**

The Discount page displays, and the text, Memory, has a dashed underline, indicating that it is bookmarked (Figure 3-54).

4 **Repeat Steps 1 through 3 to bookmark each of the remaining text items listed in Table 3-3. Use the default name as the bookmark name in each case. Do not bookmark the word Monitors.**

FIGURE 3-54

Once users have followed a hyperlink to a bookmark on the same Web page, they could simply scroll back to return to the previous location. If the page is very long or if the original hyperlink was not at the top of the page, however, it may be tedious, at best, for the users to find their way back. It is common to provide a "Back button" link to take the user back to the location that linked to the bookmark. Although using the Back button in the Web browser could achieve the same visible effect, there is a subtle difference. Using the browser's Back button to return removes the current page from the browser's list of recently visited links. By using a Back button link, the list of links the user has followed recently is preserved, even though a different page is not really loaded.

Table 3-3 Bookmarked Text
Memory
Video Cards
Media
Peripherals
Complete Systems
Software
Service and Support

Use of a Back button link will work if only one hyperlink targets a given bookmark. If multiple hyperlinks target the same bookmark, there is no way to determine the source of the hyperlink to which the user should be returned. Because all of the links that target your text bookmarks will come from graphics near the top of the Web page, they may all target the same location for their Back button hyperlinks, the banner at the top of the page. Use the following steps to create a Back button link for each of the text bookmarks.

To Create Back Button Hyperlinks

1 **Position the insertion point in the first empty row after the Memory table. If necessary, right-click the cell. Select Cell Properties on the shortcut menu. In the Layout area, click the Horizontal alignment box arrow and then click Center. Click the OK button. Click Insert on the menu bar and then point to Picture. When the Picture submenu displays, point to From File.**

The Insert menu with the Picture submenu displays (Figure 3-55).

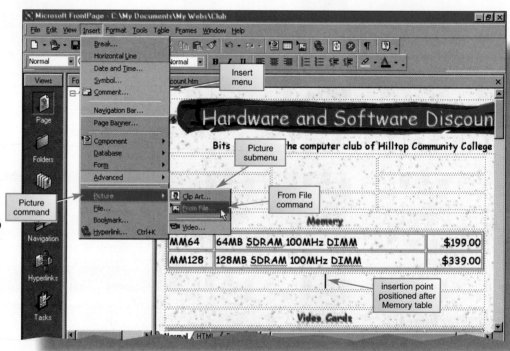

FIGURE 3-55

2 **Click From File. When the Picture dialog box displays, click the Select a file on your computer button. Select the file back_button.gif from the Project3 folder on the Data Disk. Click the OK button.**

The image of a left-pointing arrow contained in the back_button.gif file, is inserted (Figure 3-56).

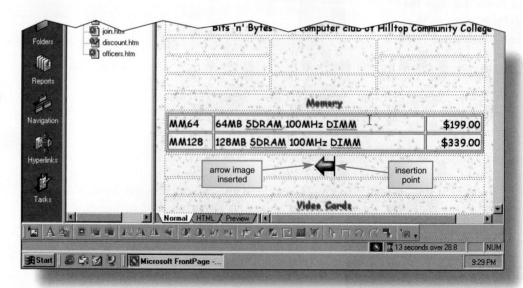

FIGURE 3-56

3 To the right of the arrow image, press the SPACEBAR once and type Back as the text. Right-click the arrow image. Point to Picture Properties on the shortcut menu.

The shortcut menu displays (Figure 3-57).

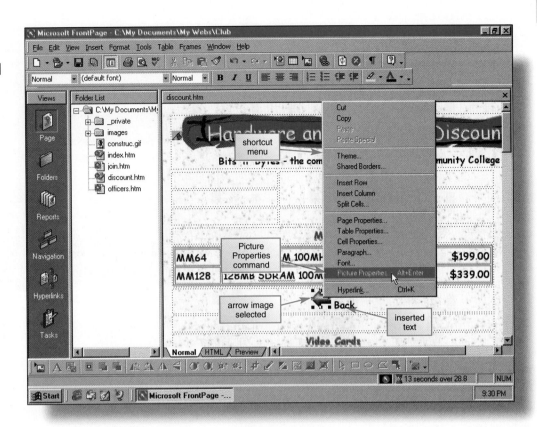

FIGURE 3-57

4 Click Picture Properties. If necessary, when the Picture Properties dialog box displays, click the Appearance tab. In the Layout area, click the Alignment button arrow and then click Middle in the Alignment box. Point to the OK button.

The Appearance sheet in the Picture Properties dialog box displays (Figure 3-58).

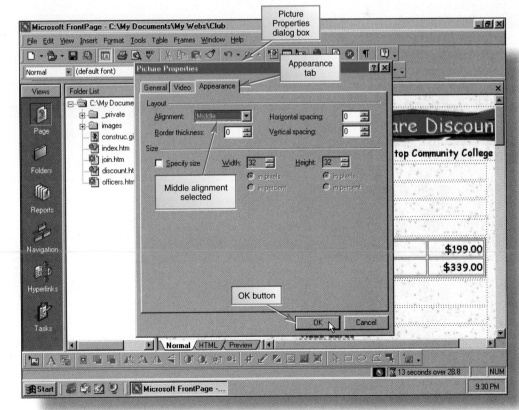

FIGURE 3-58

5 Click the OK button. Right-click the arrow image. Point to Hyperlink on the shortcut menu.

The shortcut menu displays (Figure 3-59).

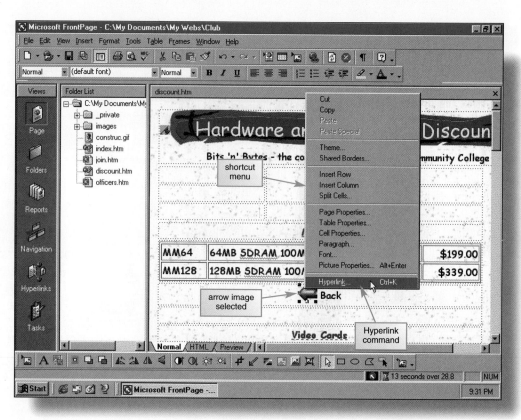

FIGURE 3-59

6 Click Hyperlink. When the Create Hyperlink dialog box displays, click the Bookmark box arrow in the Optional area and then click Discount banner in the Bookmark list. Point to the OK button.

The Create Hyperlink dialog box displays with Discount banner in the Bookmark box in the Optional area (Figure 3-60). The URL changes after the bookmark is selected.

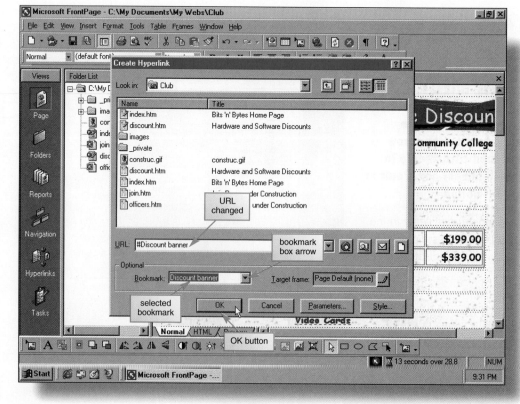

FIGURE 3-60

7 Click the OK button. Select the arrow image and the text, **Back**. Press CTRL+C to copy both the arrow image and the text.

The arrow and text are selected and copied (Figure 3-61).

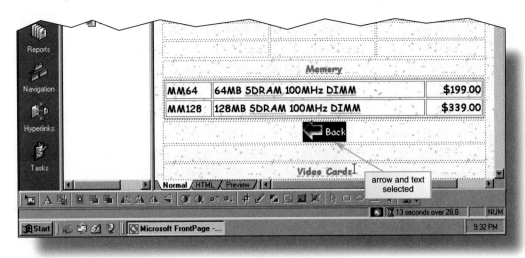

FIGURE 3-61

8 Position the insertion point in the first empty row after the Monitors table. If necessary, right-click the cell and select Cell Properties. In the Layout area, click the Horizontal alignment box arrow and then click Center. Click the OK button. Press CTRL+V to paste both the arrow image and the text.

The arrow image and text are pasted (Figure 3-62).

9 Repeat Step 8 for each of the remaining visible tables listed in Table 3-4. Save the Web page and any embedded files.

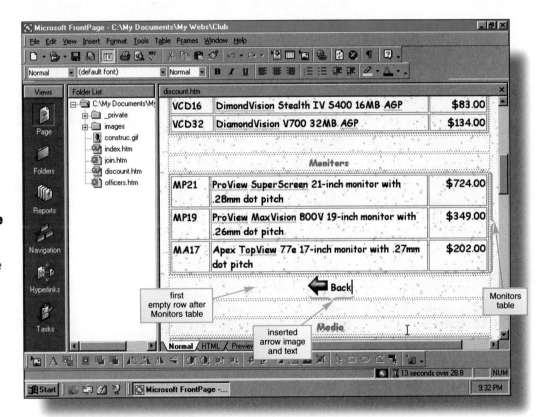

FIGURE 3-62

Table 3-4 Nested Tables
Memory
Monitors
Media
Peripherals
Complete Systems
Software
Service and Support

Using Images with Hyperlinks

In previous projects, you used images to enhance your pages artistically. They may have communicated an idea and as such were useful, but they had no direct function on the pages. For your hyperlinks, you used text. In this project, several images will be used as hyperlinks to other locations.

More *About*

Resampling an Image

Because resampling stores a new copy of the image in the image file, you may want to make a backup copy of the original image file, in case you save an unwanted change accidentally. You can retrieve a fresh copy from the backup and continue with your development.

Resizing and Resampling an Image

Sometimes an image you want to use is too small or too large to fit within the space you have set aside for it in your Web page design. You can resize an image, shrinking or stretching it, by selecting the image and dragging its handles until it becomes the desired size. This was done in Project 2 with the computer image on the Bits 'n' Bytes Home page. You also may specify the width and height of the image directly.

Resizing an image does not automatically change the size of the image file. It changes only the HTML tags for the image, so the browser actually does the shrinking or stretching when the image is displayed. This is an advantage for small images that you have stretched to a larger size. The small image file takes less time to load than if the file contained the image at its larger size.

Conversely, for images you have made smaller, the file still contains the image at its original size, and it still must be loaded even though the browser displays a smaller version of the image. To take advantage of the download performance brought about by a smaller image, you must resample the image. **Resampling** an image stores the image in the file at its new size.

Once an image has been resampled as a smaller size it may appear better at the smaller size than before it was resampled. Once the resampled file is saved, trying to stretch it back to its original size will result typically in a poorer quality image. In both cases, this is due to the amount of information needed in the file to display the image at the given size. In the first case, too much information was provided for a smaller image. In the second, information was lost in the resampling that is needed for the larger displayed image. If you are going to resample an image but may need the larger version later, then make a backup copy.

Images in this project can be resized and resampled as needed. The new images will be saved in the images folder of the project when the project is saved. The original images will remain in the Clip Art Gallery. Perform the following steps to insert, resize, and resample the five remaining images for this project.

 To Insert, Resize, and Resample an Image

1 Position the insertion point in the top leftmost cell of the second table on the page. If necessary, click the Center button on the Formatting toolbar.

The Discount page displays with the insertion point in the top leftmost cell of the second table (Figure 3-63).

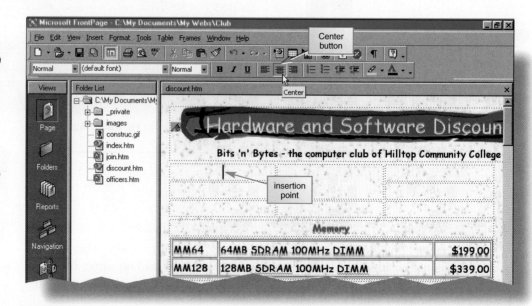

FIGURE 3-63

2 Click Insert on the menu bar. Point to Picture. Click Clip Art. Search for an appropriate computer image to indicate service needed, or another image of your choice. Click the image and point to the Insert clip button on the Pop-up menu.

The Clip Art Gallery window opens (Figure 3-64). Your preview of pictures may be different.

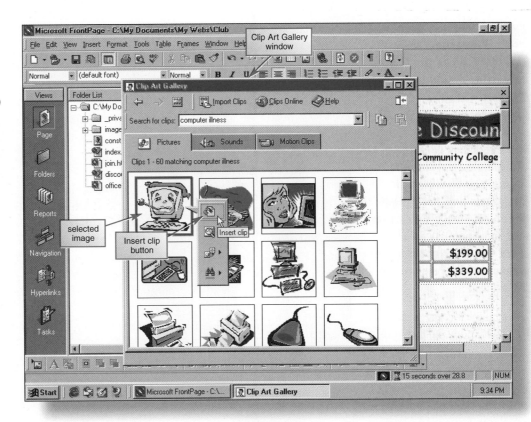

FIGURE 3-64

3 Click the Insert clip button. If necessary, resize the image using the sizing handles. Right-click the image and point to Picture Properties on the shortcut menu.

The image is inserted. The shortcut menu displays (Figure 3-65).

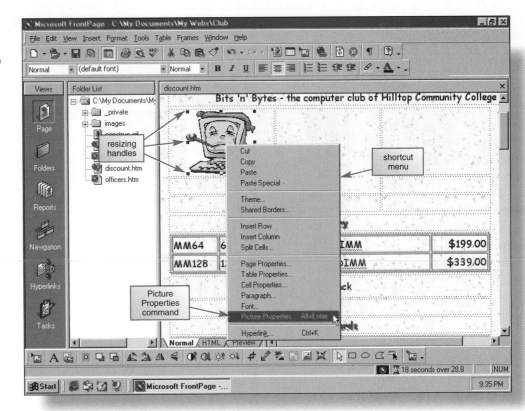

FIGURE 3-65

Microsoft **FrontPage 2000**

Click Picture Properties. If necessary, when the Picture Properties dialog box displays, click the Appearance tab. In the Size area, verify that the Specify size check box contains a check mark. If necessary, change the Width box to 104 pixels and the Height box to 93 pixels. Be certain that the Keep aspect ratio check box does not contain a check mark. Point to the OK button.

The Appearance sheet of the Picture Properties dialog box displays (Figure 3-66).

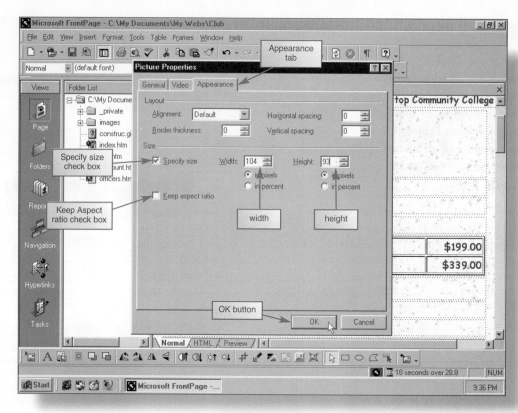

FIGURE 3-66

Click the OK button. With the image still selected, click the Resample button on the Pictures toolbar. Position the insertion point to the right of the image. Hold down the SHIFT key and press the ENTER key. Select a font size of 2 (10 pt). Click the Bold button on the Formatting toolbar. Type Service and Support **to enter the text.**

The resized and resampled image displays with its text (Figure 3-67).

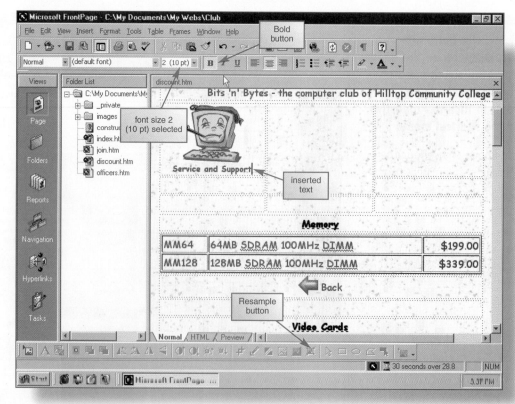

FIGURE 3-67

Repeat Steps 1 through 5 to insert, resize, and resample the remaining images. Use the height and width values and the text listed in Table 3-5 for the remaining images.

The completed pictures are shown in Figure 3-68. Your images may be different.

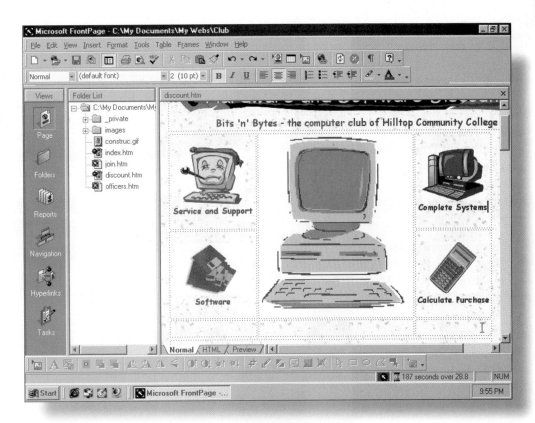

FIGURE 3-68

Creating a Transparent Image

A **transparent image** sometimes is referred to as a **floating image** because it appears to float on the Web page. To make an image transparent, you select one of the colors in the image to be the **transparent color**. The transparent color is replaced by the background color or image of the page.

An image can have only one transparent color. If you select another transparent color, the first transparent color reverts to its original color. Use the **Set Transparent Color button** on the Pictures toolbar to make a selected color transparent. When you click the Set Transparent Color button, the mouse pointer changes to the **Set Transparent Color pointer**. You then click a color on the image to make it transparent.

To make an image transparent, it must be in the GIF file format. FrontPage will ask you if you want to convert a JPEG image to GIF format if you try to make a JPEG image transparent. Because GIF supports a maximum of only 256 colors, you may lose some image quality by converting from JPEG to GIF.

The procedure for making a transparent image is to select the image and then choose the transparent color using the Set Transparent Color pointer. To set the color white around the sides of each of the five images as the transparent color so that the background shows through, perform the steps on the next page.

Table 3-5 Text and Sizes for Images		
TEXT	*WIDTH*	*HEIGHT*
Service and Support	104	93
Software	126	84
[no text]	254	292
Complete Systems	102	84
Calculate Purchase	77	83

To Create a Transparent Image

1 **Click the computer image in the top leftmost cell of the second table on the page to select it. Click the Set Transparent Color button on the Pictures toolbar. Position the mouse pointer over the image.**

Sizing handles display around the image to indicate that it is selected (Figure 3-69). The mouse pointer changes to the Set Transparent Color pointer when it is moved over the image. You may get a message indicating the file will be converted to GIF format. If so, click the OK button.

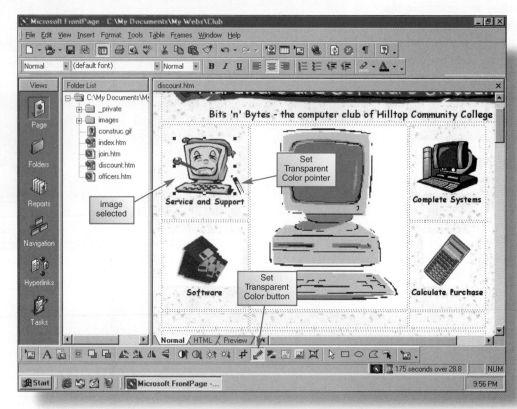

FIGURE 3-69

2 **Click the color white surrounding the image.**

The color white becomes transparent and is replaced by the background (Figure 3-70). The mouse pointer is restored to the normal block arrow pointer and the Set Transparent Color button no longer is selected.

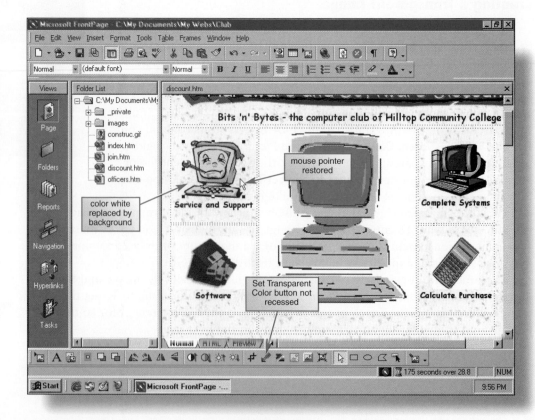

FIGURE 3-70

(3) **Repeat Steps 1 and 2 for each of the other four remaining images in the table.**

The table displays with all image background colors set to transparent (Figure 3-71).

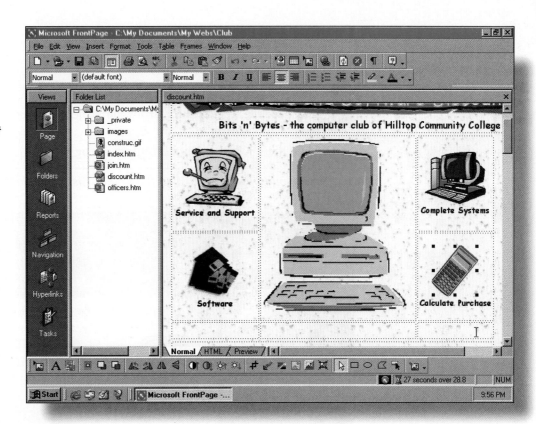

FIGURE 3-71

You must take care when selecting a color to be transparent. If the color appears in other sections of the image, it will become transparent in the other sections as well, and this might have an unexpected or undesirable effect. If you look closely at some of the images in this table, you may see the background showing where you would not expect it.

In many cases, it is not significant because you have to look very carefully to see it. You could run into problems if, for example, you have a purple background and an image containing a face. If you make white the transparent color, it could result in a face with purple eyes and purple teeth.

Assigning a Hyperlink to an Image

As was noted earlier, previous projects used text as hyperlinks. This project also will use images as hyperlinks. Now that the five images have the desired appearance, it is time to make them function as hyperlinks. Three of the images will link to other locations on this same Web page; that is, to a bookmark. One of the images will need to link to a page containing an Excel spreadsheet. That page should be imported into the web before establishing the hyperlink. Later in the project, you will make some modifications to that page. For now, it simply will be imported into the current web. To import the existing Web page, perform the steps on the next page.

Displaying Images

Current computers allow you to specify the number of bits of color your computer will display. If the number is smaller than the bit resolution of an image, the image will not display properly. Right-click the desktop to see the current setting for your computer monitor.

TO IMPORT A WEB PAGE

1 Click file on the menu bar and then click Import.

2 Click the Add File button in the Import dialog box.

3 Select the file, fpexcel.htm, from the Project3 folder on the Data Disk. Click the Open button.

4 Click the OK button in the Import dialog box.

The file, fpexcel.htm, is added to the Folder List pane (Figure 3-72).

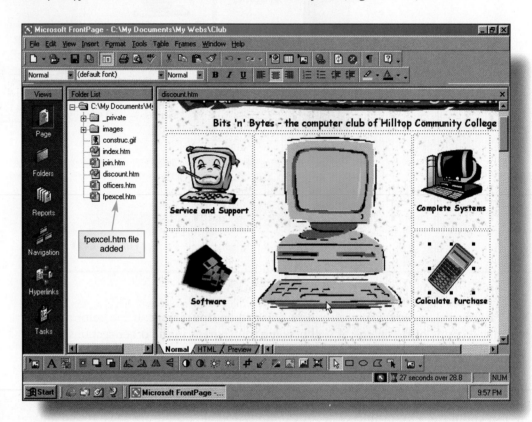

FIGURE 3-72

As noted earlier, three of the images will link to bookmarks on this same Web page. One will link to the Excel page just imported. To set up the images with hyperlinks, perform the following steps.

Steps **To Assign a Hyperlink to an Image**

1 **Right-click the Calculate Purchase image. Point to Hyperlink on the shortcut menu.**

Sizing handles display around the image to indicate that it is selected (Figure 3-73). The shortcut menu displays.

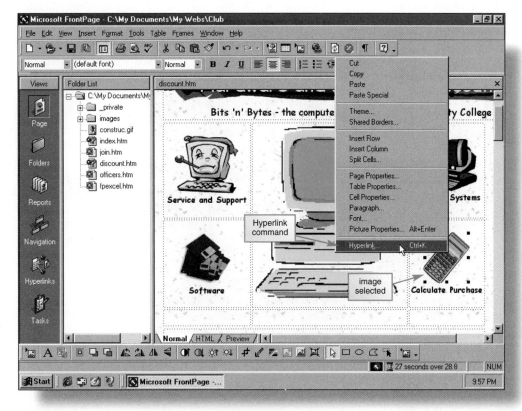

FIGURE 3-73

2 **Click Hyperlink. If necessary, when the Create Hyperlink dialog box displays, click the Look in box arrow and select the Web folder location. Select the file, fpexcel.htm. Point to the OK button.**

The URL in the Create Hyperlink dialog box changes to fpexcel.htm after the file is selected (Figure 3-74).

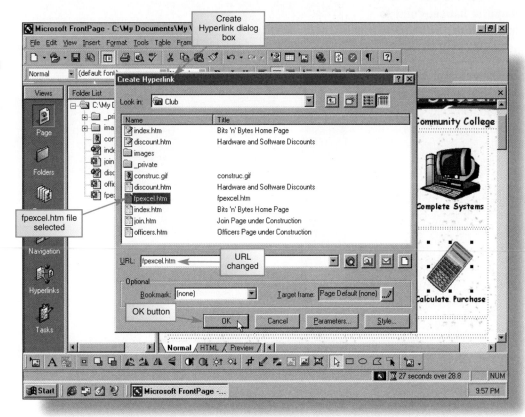

FIGURE 3-74

3 **Click the OK button. Position the mouse pointer over the image.**

The new URL for the image hyperlink displays on the status bar (Figure 3-75).

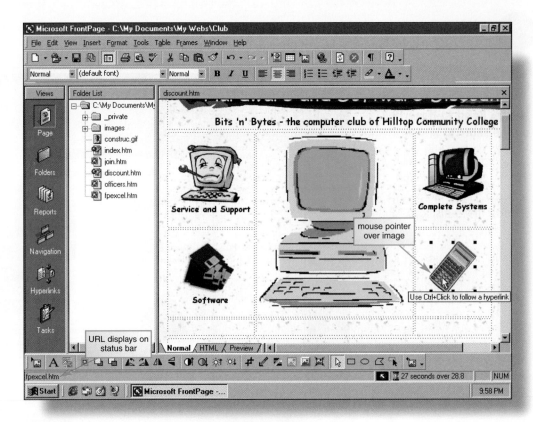

FIGURE 3-75

4 **Right-click the Service and Support computer image. Point to Hyperlink on the shortcut menu.**

Sizing handles display around the image to indicate that it is selected (Figure 3-76). The shortcut menu displays.

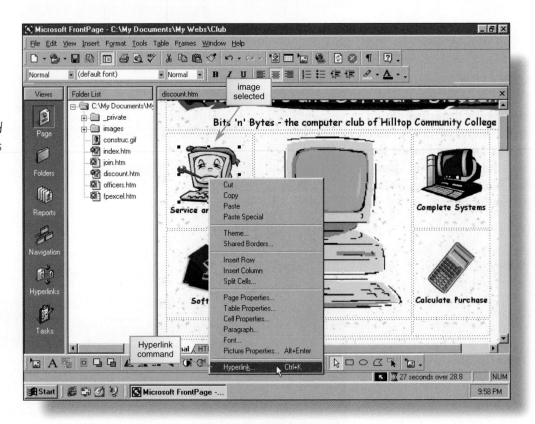

FIGURE 3-76

5 Click Hyperlink. When the Create Hyperlink dialog box displays, click the Bookmark box arrow in the Optional area and then click Service and Support in the Bookmark list. Point to the OK button.

The URL in the Create Hyperlink dialog box changes after the bookmark is selected (Figure 3-77).

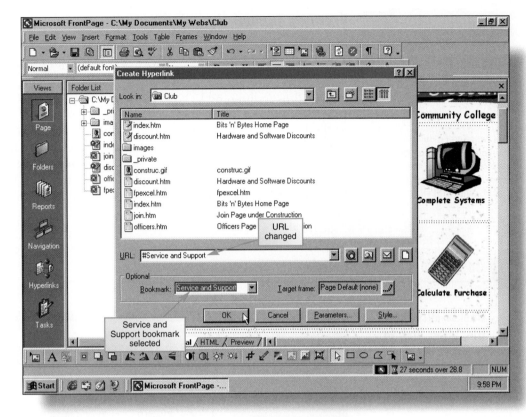

FIGURE 3-77

6 Click the OK button. Position the mouse pointer over the image.

The new URL for the image hyperlink displays on the status bar (Figure 3-78).

7 Repeat Steps 4 through 6 for the remaining two image hyperlinks for Software and Complete Systems. The center image will be addressed later.

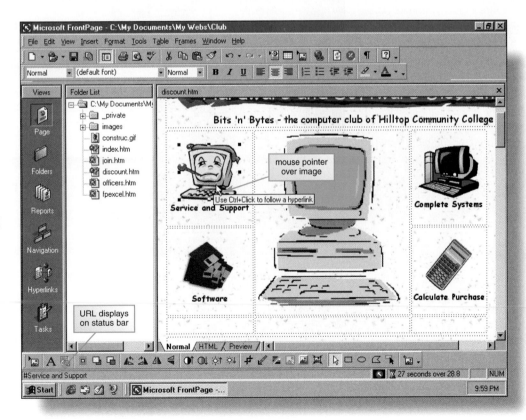

FIGURE 3-78

More About

Copying and Pasting

You can copy images into a Web page by dragging the image from another Windows application to FrontPage. You also can use the Copy and Paste commands on the Edit menu, or use the shortcut keys, CTRL+C and CTRL+V.

Creating Textual Hyperlinks

Even though this project is using graphics for hyperlinks, it also will use some textual hyperlinks. In the same way that links on the Home page are provided to link to the Officers, Join, and Discount pages, the Discount page also should have links to the Officers, Join, and Home pages. This way users can navigate to the same pages from the Discount page as they could from the Home page. Obviously, a link to the Discount page is not necessary, and so it is replaced by a link to the Home page. It is a good idea to keep the same order for these links as they have on the Home page, because users will expect to see them in the same relative positions. The links on the Home page can be copied and pasted onto the Discount page; only the last link needs to be changed. Follow the steps below to create text hyperlinks to the other pages in this web.

Steps To Create a Text Hyperlink

1 **Double-click the file, index.htm, to open the page. Highlight the three text links and press CTRL+C to copy them. Point to the Close button for the page.**

The three text hyperlinks are highlighted (Figure 3-79).

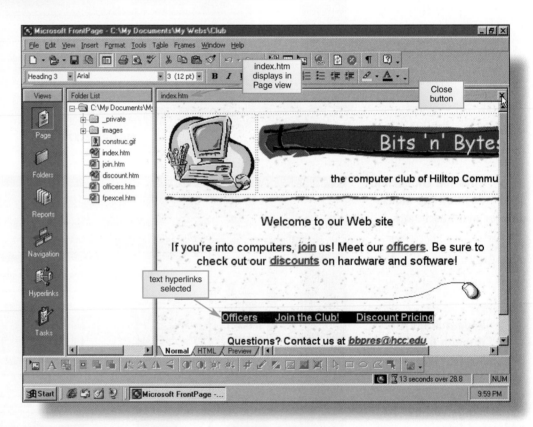

FIGURE 3-79

2 Click the Close button. Position the insertion point in the center cell of the last row of the second table. If necessary, click the Center button on the Formatting toolbar. Press CTRL+V to paste the copied hyperlinks.

Three text hyperlinks are pasted on the Discount page (Figure 3-80).

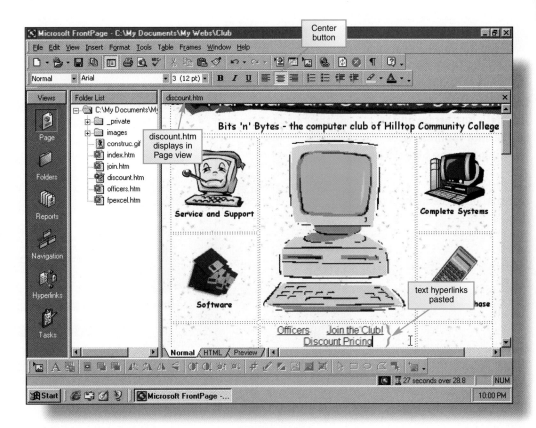

FIGURE 3-80

3 Highlight the text Discount Pricing and type Home as the text. Right-click the text, Home. Click Hyperlink Properties on the shortcut menu and in the Edit Hyperlink dialog box, select the file, index.htm. Point to the OK button.

The URL in the Edit Hyperlink dialog box changes to index.htm (Figure 3-81).

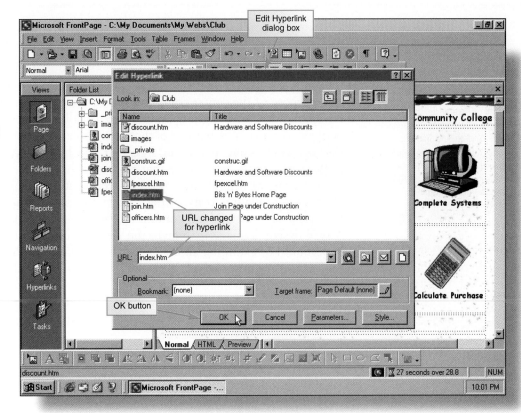

FIGURE 3-81

4 Click the OK button. Delete three spaces between each of the hyperlinks. Highlight all three hyperlinks and click the Style box arrow on the Formatting toolbar. Click Heading 3 in the Style list.

The text hyperlinks on the Discount page are completed (Figure 3-82).

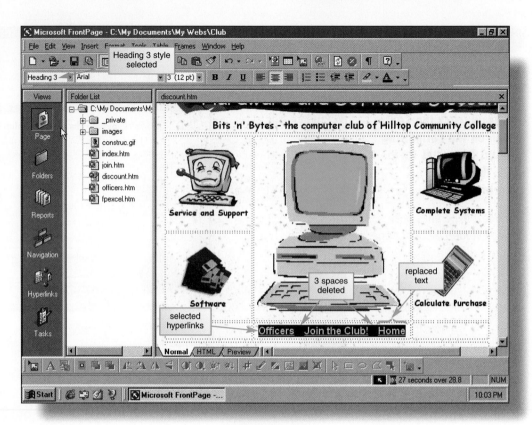

FIGURE 3-82

Image Maps

The purpose of the center computer image is to serve as an image map. **Image maps** are special graphic images containing areas called hotspots. A **hotspot** is a specially designated portion of the image that is set up as a hyperlink. Clicking one of the hotspots is the same as clicking a regular text hyperlink. The hotspot lets you jump to the URL that is defined for that region of the image.

Image maps provide new ways to create interactive Web pages. They provide an alternative to plain text hyperlinks. They also allow you to economize on images, because a single image can contain multiple hotspots and, thus, multiple hyperlinks. A well-designed image map gives the viewer clues about the destination of each hyperlink. For example, an art gallery might have an image containing a diagram of the various rooms in which different types of art are exhibited. Clicking a room displays another Web page containing images of related works of art. A college or university could have an image containing a map of the campus with hotspots defined for each building. Clicking a building would display another Web page describing the building.

When creating an image map, you want to use a motif, or metaphor, for your images. For example, a campus map of different buildings might be used for obtaining navigation assistance. A bookshelf with books listing different topics might be used in a help desk application.

Defining Hotspots

To create an image map, you first decide on an image to use and then you define hotspots on the image. Finally, you assign URLs to each hotspot.

Hotspots can be circles, rectangles, or irregularly shaped areas called polygons. You designate hotspots using the hotspot buttons on the Pictures toolbar. For example, when you click the Rectangle button, the mouse pointer changes to a pencil pointer. To draw a rectangular hotspot, click and hold one corner of the desired rectangle, drag to the opposite corner, and then release the mouse button. The Create Hyperlink dialog box automatically opens so that you can enter the target URL that will be assigned to the hotspot. You also can add text to an image and then create hyperlinks for the text making it, in effect, a labeled rectangular hotspot. When adding hotspots other than as text, the Create Hyperlink dialog box automatically is invoked. This is not done for text, because text may be added to an image without making it a hotspot.

The computer image has several hotspots. A large area on the screen of the computer, two rectangular areas on the computer body, and an irregular shape surrounding the keyboard. Each of these also will have text descriptions to direct the user. Perform the following steps to add text and hotspots to the image, making it an image map.

 Steps ## To Create an Image Map by Adding Hotspots to an Image

1 **If necessary, click the center computer image to select it and then click the Text button on the Pictures toolbar.**

A resizable text box displays in the computer image (Figure 3-83).

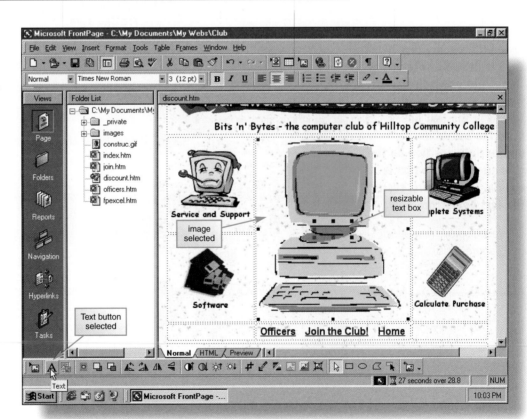

FIGURE 3-83

2 Type Memory **in the text box. Drag the text box to an appropriate position on the graphic where the text is visible. If necessary, resize the text box accordingly.**

The text displays in the text box (Figure 3-84).

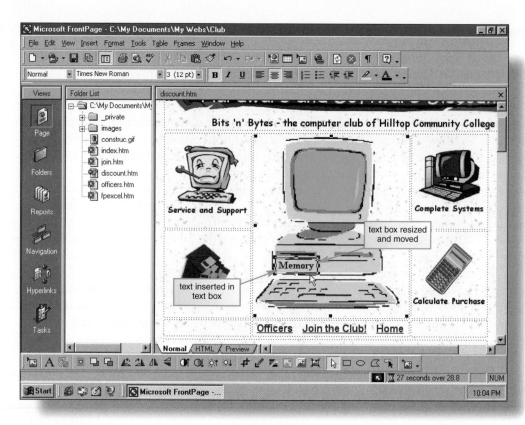

FIGURE 3-84

3 **Click the Text button on the Pictures toolbar. Type** Media **in the text box. Drag the box to an appropriate position on the graphic where the text is visible. If necessary, resize the text box accordingly.**

The text displays in the text box (Figure 3-85).

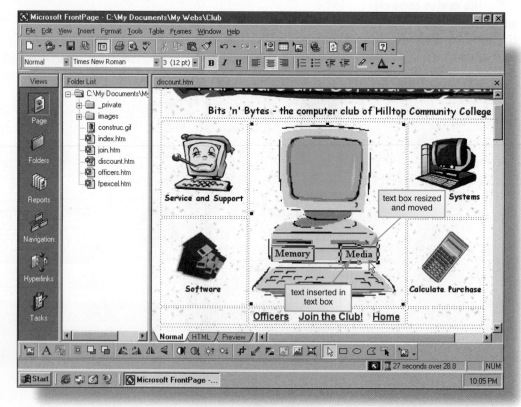

FIGURE 3-85

4 Click the Text button on the Pictures toolbar. Type `Peripherals` in the text box. Drag the text box to an appropriate position on the graphic where the text is visible.

The text displays in the text box (Figure 3-86). If the text is longer than the text box, a warning may sound, but the text box will expand automatically to fit the text entered.

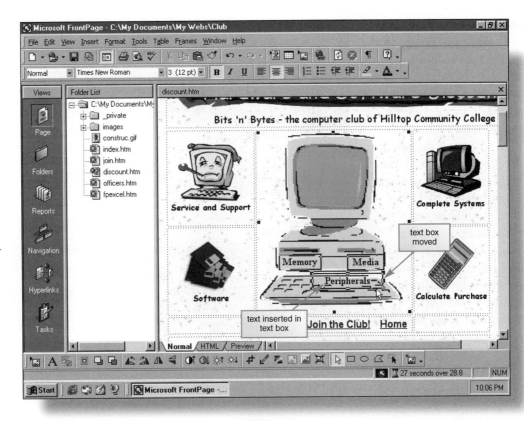

FIGURE 3-86

5 Click the Text button on the Pictures toolbar. Type `Video Cards` and then press the ENTER key. Type `and Monitors` in the box. Drag the text box to an appropriate position on the graphic where the text is visible. If necessary, resize the text box accordingly.

The text displays in the text box (Figure 3-87).

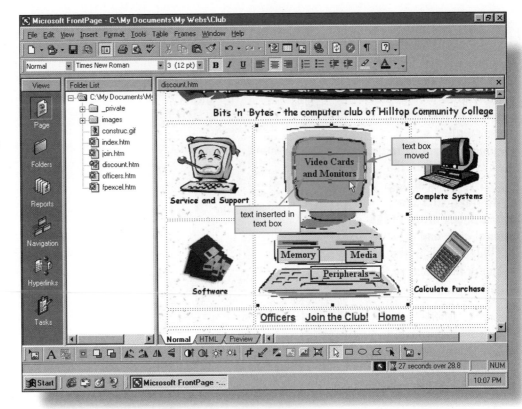

FIGURE 3-87

6 Click the Polygonal Hotspot button on the Pictures toolbar. Carefully draw around the perimeter of the image keyboard, using a single click to create a new edit point with each change of direction. When you have completed tracing around the perimeter, click the starting point to complete the hotspot. When the Create Hyperlink dialog box displays, click the Bookmark box arrow in the Optional area and then click Peripherals in the Bookmark list. Point to the OK button.

The Create Hyperlink dialog box displays (Figure 3-88). The URL in the Create Hyperlink dialog box changes after the bookmark is selected.

FIGURE 3-88

7 Click the OK button. Click the Polygonal Hotspot button on the Pictures toolbar. Carefully draw around the perimeter of the image screen, creating a polygonal hotspot as in the previous step. When the Create Hyperlink dialog box displays, click the Bookmark box arrow in the Optional area and then click Video Cards in the Bookmark list. Point to the OK button.

The Create Hyperlink dialog box displays (Figure 3-89). The URL in the Create Hyperlink dialog box changes after the bookmark is selected.

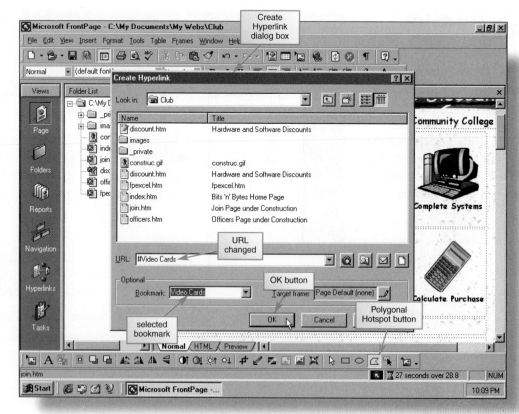

8 Click the OK button.

FIGURE 3-89

You successfully have created hotspots on an image map. When creating hotspots using the circle, rectangle, or polygon buttons on the Pictures toolbar, the Create Hyperlink dialog box automatically displays as soon as you release the mouse button after drawing the hotspot using the pencil pointer. This did not happen when you inserted the text in the previous steps because you could add text to an image without making the text a hotspot. You must add the target URLs to text hotspots manually.

Adding Image Map Targets

Once the text hotspots are defined, assigning the target URLs is the same as setting up a regular hyperlink. Perform the following steps to assign target URLs to the text hotspots in the computer image map.

 To Specify the Target of an Image Map Hotspot

Double-click the Memory text hotspot. When the Create Hyperlink dialog box displays, click the Bookmark box arrow in the Optional area and then click Memory in the Bookmark list. Point to the OK button.

The URL in the Create Hyperlink dialog box changes after the bookmark is selected (Figure 3-90).

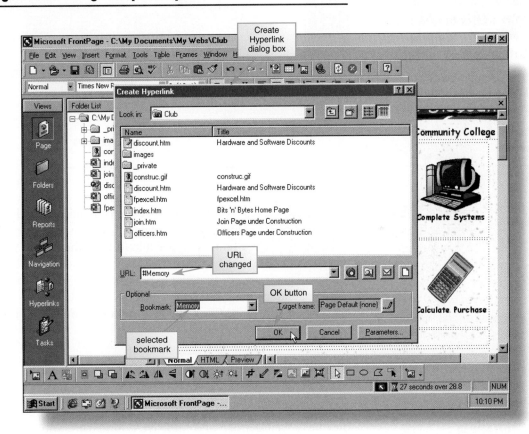

FIGURE 3-90

② Click the OK button and then double-click the Media text hotspot. Click the Bookmark box arrow in the Optional area and then click Media in the Bookmark list. Point to the OK button.

The Create Hyperlink dialog box displays (Figure 3-91). The URL in the Create Hyperlink dialog box changes after the bookmark is selected.

③ Click the OK button. Click the Save button on the Standard toolbar to save the changes. Save embedded files in the Images folder.

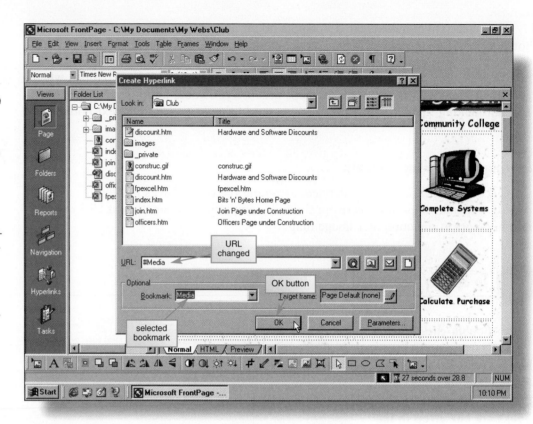

FIGURE 3-91

The two text boxes, Video Cards and Monitors, and Peripherals, do not need to have hyperlinks associated with them, as they are positioned entirely over polygonal hotspots that already have hyperlinks. When the mouse pointer is positioned over one of these two text boxes, the URL of the underlying hotspot displays on the status bar. This indicates that the hyperlink of the underlying hotspot will be followed.

Image maps are an excellent way to present links visually in an intuitive and user-friendly fashion. Creating your own image maps is not hard to do, but requires some careful preparation.

Image Map Hotspots

You can set a default hyperlink for any area on the image map that does not have a hotspot defined. Click the General tab in the Picture Properties dialog box.

Highlighting Image Map Hotspots

The hotspots on the computer image map are easy to see because you added text descriptions to the image map and, in the case of the computer screen and keyboard, they have well-defined and intuitive boundaries. Some image maps will not have any text or image features associated with hotspots. Locating the hotspot outlines can be difficult in these instances.

The Pictures toolbar includes the **Highlight Hotspots button** that toggles between displaying hotspots only and displaying the image and the hotspot. Perform the following steps to highlight the hotspots on the computer image map.

Steps: To Highlight Hotspots in an Image Map

1 **If necessary, click the computer image used as an image map. Click the Highlight Hotspots button on the Pictures toolbar.**

The image becomes white, and the hotspots are revealed with black outlines (Figure 3-92). In this view, you easily can see the hotspots.

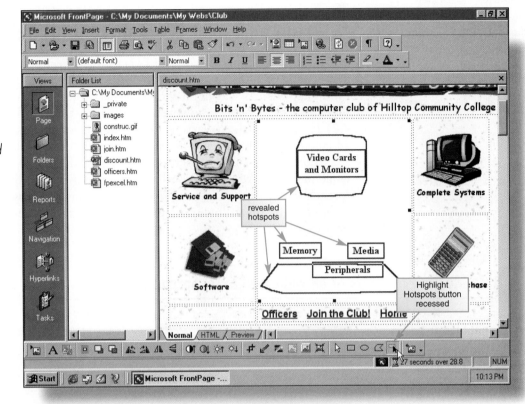

FIGURE 3-92

2 **Click the Highlight Hotspots button.**

The computer image redisplays (Figure 3-93).

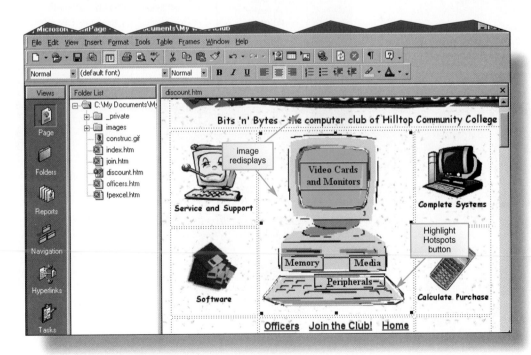

FIGURE 3-93

Saving Images

Be sure to remove from the
images folder any unused
image files you imported or
downloaded from the Web.
Image files take up disk space
on the development computer
as well as the Web server.

The Highlight Hotspots button is useful when image features make it difficult to
see the hotspot outlines that are superimposed on the image.

Using an Excel Worksheet in a Web

It is possible to embed a working Excel spreadsheet in a Web page. It is a simple
matter to save an Excel file as an HTML file. That file then can be imported into a
FrontPage web, as was done earlier in this project. To interactively use the spreadsheet page in a browser, however, the user must have Microsoft Internet Explorer
4.01 or later and the Microsoft Office Web Components. If the page is opened with
an incompatible browser, a message to this effect is displayed.

Additionally, some properties of an embedded Excel spreadsheet can be modified
while in FrontPage. With FrontPage, you can directly edit and set properties for the
spreadsheet in Page view, even if you do not have Microsoft Excel installed on your
computer. Use the following steps to modify some properties for the Excel page
imported earlier.

Steps To Modify Properties of an Embedded Excel Spreadsheet

1 **Double-click the
file fpexcel.htm in
the Folder List pane.**

*The page fpexcel.htm
displays in Page mode
(Figure 3-94).*

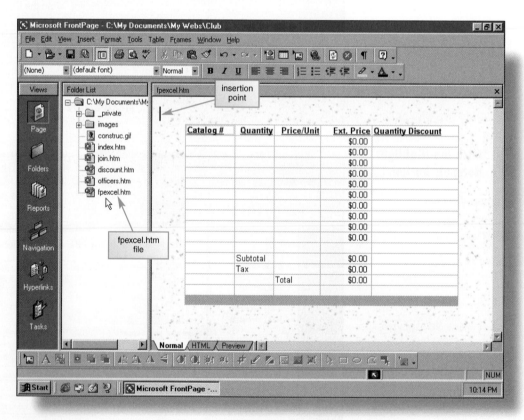

FIGURE 3-94

2 Position the insertion point at the top of the page, above the spreadsheet. Type Enter Catalog #, Quantity, and Price/Unit: **and then press the ENTER key.**

The spreadsheet is moved down, below the entered text (Figure 3-95).

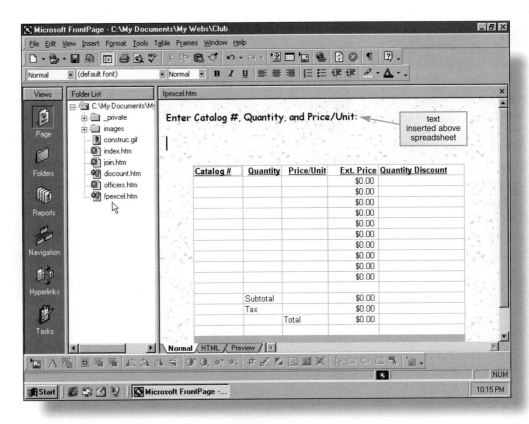

FIGURE 3-95

3 Position the insertion point below the spreadsheet. Press the ENTER key. If necessary, click the Center button on the Formatting toolbar. Type Click the Back button to return to the Discount Page. **to enter the text.**

The text is entered below the spreadsheet (Figure 3-96).

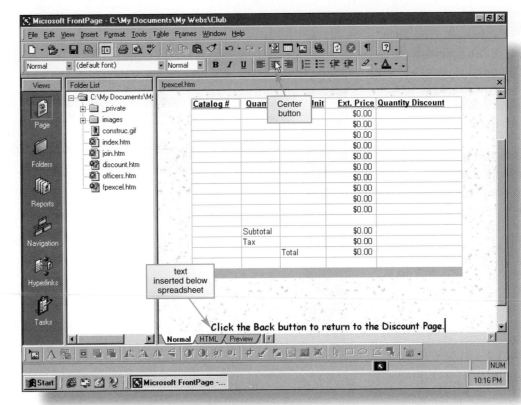

FIGURE 3-96

4 Click the spreadsheet to select it. Right-click the spreadsheet and click Property Toolbox on the shortcut menu. When the Spreadsheet Property Toolbox displays, click Show/Hide in the Spreadsheet Property Toolbox to display the Show/Hide menu and then point to the Title bar button.

The Spreadsheet Property Toolbox with the Show/Hide menu displays (Figure 3-97).

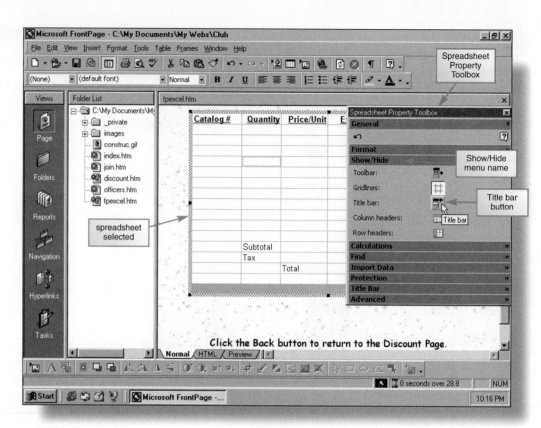

FIGURE 3-97

5 Click the Title bar button. Click Title bar in the Spreadsheet Property Toolbox to display the Title Bar menu and then click in the Title text box. Type Calculate Purchase Total in the Title text box and then press the ENTER key. Point to the Close button on the Spreadsheet Property Toolbox.

The Title bar button in the Spreadsheet Property Toolbox is selected, a title bar displays on the spreadsheet, and the text entered in the Title bar text box displays on the spreadsheet title bar (Figure 3-98).

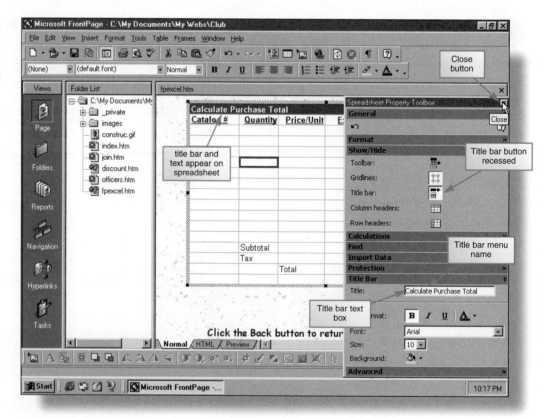

FIGURE 3-98

6 **Click the Close button on the Spreadsheet Property Toolbox. Click the Save button on the Standard toolbar to save your work.**

The completed spreadsheet page displays in Page mode (Figure 3-99).

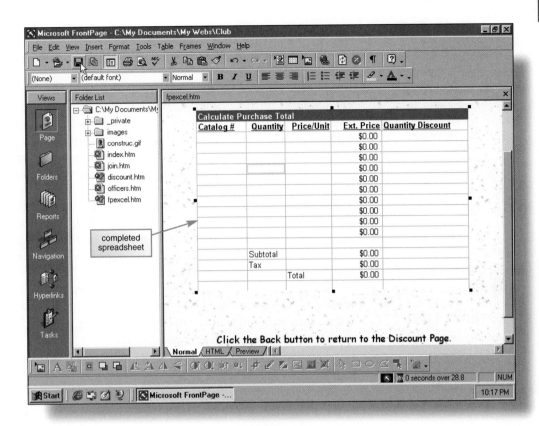

completed spreadsheet

FIGURE 3-99

As you can see, many properties of an Excel spreadsheet can be modified in FrontPage, even if you do not have Excel installed on your machine. You even may insert an Excel spreadsheet component and build the spreadsheet from scratch, or you may import one already created, as was done here.

Hyperlink Status

Be aware that if you choose to check the status of all the hyperlinks in the current web, it could take a significant length of time. FrontPage not only will look in the current web, but also will look on the World Wide Web following hyperlinks to make sure the targets exist.

Hyperlinks View

If Hyperlinks view reveals a misspelled hyperlink, you can load the page in FrontPage by double-clicking the page icon in Hyperlinks view and then quickly correcting the hyperlink.

Displaying the Hyperlinks in a FrontPage Web

Recall in Project 2 during the construction of the Bits 'n' Bytes Home page, you created links to three other Web pages with file names of discount.htm, join.htm, and officers.htm. You will have completed the discount.htm file by completing the activities in this project. The other two hyperlinks point to the remaining temporary "under construction" pages which you imported in Project 2. These files were imported so that the corresponding hyperlinks would not point to nonexistent files. Hyperlinks that point to nonexistent files are referred to as **broken hyperlinks**.

Several reasons exist for encountering broken hyperlinks. The file that is the target of the hyperlink could have been deleted, renamed, moved to another folder, or moved to another Web server. The Web server on which the file resides could have its Internet address changed, could be out of service for some period of time, or could be permanently out of service.

Keeping track of broken hyperlinks in a small web like the Bits 'n' Bytes web is simple, because it contains only a few hyperlinks. When developing very large webs, with many files and hyperlinks, however, it would be very difficult to try to remember which hyperlinks are broken.

The **Hyperlinks view** in FrontPage alleviates this problem. It displays in a graphical format the Web pages and their hyperlinks and indicates which hyperlinks are broken. Perform the following step to display the Hyperlinks view and determine whether the Bits 'n' Bytes web has any broken hyperlinks.

Steps To Display the Hyperlinks in a FrontPage Web

1 **Make sure that you have saved all changes. Double-click the file index.htm in the Folder List pane. Click the Hyperlinks button on the Views bar. If necessary, click the plus sign on the discount.htm icon to display its links.**

FrontPage displays the web in Hyperlinks view (Figure 3-100). The plus sign on the discount.htm icon turns to a minus sign.

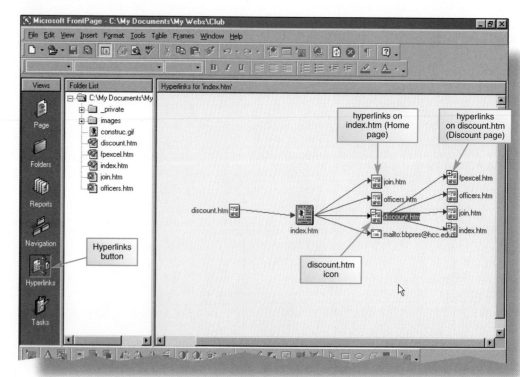

FIGURE 3-100

The Hyperlinks view displays a graphical diagram of the hyperlinks in the current FrontPage web starting with the top-level page. In this web it is the Bits 'n' Bytes Home page, index.htm, which displays the hyperlinks shown in Figure 3-100. Hyperlinks exist from the Home page to the Join page, the Officers page, and the Discount page, as well as a mailto: link. The Discount page contains one hyperlink to the page containing the Excel spreadsheet. None of the hyperlinks is broken. A broken hyperlink displays like any other hyperlink, except that it shows as a broken line. You can select another page in the web to view its hyperlinks by double-clicking the page icon in the graphical diagram.

You can use the Hyperlinks view to verify quickly which links, if any, are broken in the current FrontPage web.

Testing Pages by Previewing in a Browser

When you have completed your Web page, you should test the results to see how they will appear in an actual Web browser. Although FrontPage has a Preview tab, it still is better to make a final test in an actual browser. In fact, it is preferable to test your pages in all browsers that you have available, in addition to any you believe that your users may have available. For the most part, testing with Microsoft Internet Explorer and Netscape Navigator covers the majority of users.

To test your Web pages in a browser installed on your machine, you could save your latest changes, perhaps exit FrontPage, and then manually start your browser and load the web you are testing. FrontPage makes it easy to test with a browser without ever exiting FrontPage, however. To test your Web pages in your browser, perform the steps on the next page.

To Preview Web Pages in a Browser

 1 **Click Preview in Browser on the File menu.**

The Preview in Browser dialog box displays and lists browsers installed on your machine (Figure 3-101). Your list of browsers may be different.

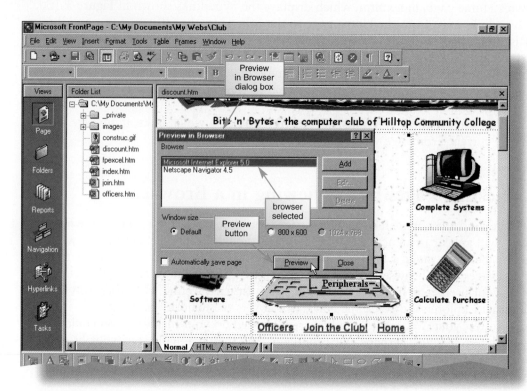

FIGURE 3-101

2 **Select the browser you want to use, if more than one is available. Click the Preview button.**

The selected browser is started and loads the current Web page (Figure 3-102). If you have not saved your latest changes to disk, FrontPage will prompt you to save your changes before loading the browser.

FIGURE 3-102

Publishing Changes to a FrontPage Web

In Project 2, the Bits 'n' Bytes web was published on the World Wide Web. You since have added two Web pages and the accompanying image files to the FrontPage web. For these new Web pages to be available on the World Wide Web, you must publish the Bits 'n' Bytes web again.

When you publish a FrontPage web that has been published before, FrontPage will install only those parts of the web that are new or that have changed since the last time the web was published. This reduces the amount of data transfer that takes place, which is good for webs with many folders, Web pages, and files.

The following steps summarize how to publish changes to a FrontPage web. Be sure to substitute your own URL or an error will occur. If you do not know what URL to use, ask your instructor.

TO PUBLISH CHANGES TO A FRONTPAGE WEB

1 Click the Publish Web button on the Standard toolbar.

2 Type `ftp://www.hcc.edu/computer/club` in the Specify the location to publish your web to text box. If your Web server has the Microsoft FrontPage Server Extensions installed on it, you can publish using HTTP (HyperText Transfer Protocol). Otherwise, you must publish your web using FTP (File Transfer Protocol).

3 Click the Publish button.

4 Type your FTP user name and password. Click the OK button.

5 Click the Done button.

You now can view the Discount page by entering http://www.hcc.edu/computer/club/discount.htm in any browser and pressing the ENTER key. Be sure to test the hyperlink to the Home page and from the Home page to the Discount page.

More About

Microsoft Certification

The Microsoft Office User Specialist (MOUS) Certification program provides an opportunity for you to obtain a valuable industry credential — proof that you have the FrontPage 2000 skills required by employers. For more information, visit the Shelly Cashman Series MOUS Web page at www.scsite.com/off2000/cert.htm.

Quitting FrontPage

When you have published the Bits 'n' Bytes web, you can quit Microsoft Front-Page. Perform the following step to quit FrontPage.

TO QUIT FRONTPAGE

1 Click the Close button on the FrontPage title bar.

The FrontPage window closes and the Windows desktop displays.

CASE PERSPECTIVE SUMMARY

The officers of the Bits 'n' Bytes computer club are pleased with the resulting design of their Web pages. Although they were concerned about requesting such wholesale changes, they are impressed that you could incorporate the changes so quickly. They believe that you clearly have met their goal to make the club pages more colorful and attractive. They are very satisfied with the way in which you included the Excel spreadsheet page and the discount price list. They also found your choice of graphics for the hyperlinks and image map to be most appropriate.

Project Summary

In this project, you learned how to insert a new Web page into a FrontPage web. You learned about image file formats. You created a tiled background from an image file. You inserted bookmarks in a Web page. You created transparent images and resampled images to change their file size. You created an image map and assigned target URLs to the hotspots. After inserting a Web page with an Excel spreadsheet, you modified its properties. You learned how to display the status of the hyperlinks used in the Web pages of the current FrontPage web. Finally, you previewed your web in a browser.

More About

Quick Reference

For a table that lists how to complete the tasks covered in this book, visit the Office 2000 Web page (www.scsite.com/off2000qr.htm) and then click Microsoft FrontPage 2000.

What You Should Know

Having completed this project, you now should be able to perform the following tasks:

▶ Add a New Web Page to a FrontPage Web *(FP 3.25)*
▶ Apply a Background Image to a Web Page *(FP 3.12)*
▶ Apply a New Theme to a FrontPage Web *(FP 3.18)*
▶ Assign a Hyperlink to an Image *(FP 3.49)*
▶ Bookmark a Location in a Web page *(FP 3.25)*
▶ Bookmark Text in a Web Page *(FP 3.36)*
▶ Create a Text Hyperlink *(FP 3.52)*
▶ Create a Transparent Image *(FP 3.46)*
▶ Create an Image Map by Adding Hotspots to an Image *(FP 3.55)*
▶ Create Back Button Hyperlinks *(FP 3.38)*
▶ Delete a File from a Web *(FP 3.23)*
▶ Display the Hyperlinks in a FrontPage Web *(FP 3.66)*
▶ Display the Pictures Toolbar *(FP 3.10)*
▶ Edit a New Web Page *(FP 3.28)*
▶ Highlight Hotspots in an Image Map *(FP 3.61)*
▶ Import a Web Page *(FP 3.48)*
▶ Insert a File into a Web Page *(FP 3.33)*
▶ Insert a Page Banner *(FP 3.19)*
▶ Insert, Resize, and Resample an Image *(FP 3.42)*
▶ Modify Properties of an Embedded Excel Spreadsheet *(FP 3.62)*
▶ Open an Existing FrontPage Web *(FP 3.8)*
▶ Preview Web Pages in a Browser *(FP 3.68)*
▶ Publish Changes to a FrontPage Web *(FP 3.69)*
▶ Quit FrontPage *(FP 3.69)*
▶ Specify the Target of an Image Map Hotspot *(FP 3.59)*
▶ Start FrontPage 2000 *(FP 3.8)*
▶ Wash Out an Image *(FP 3.16)*

Apply Your Knowledge

⊕ Project Reinforcement at www.scsite.com/off2000/reinforce.htm

1 Adding and Modifying a Spreadsheet

Instructions: Start FrontPage 2000 and perform the following steps with a computer.

1. Open the one-page web, RegSales, that you modified in Project 2. If you did not complete that assignment, see your instructor for a copy. Edit the Home page (index.htm).

2. In the first bulleted line, after Unit Sales, type and Commissions as the text.

3. Position the insertion point below the table you previously entered. Click Insert on the menu bar and then point to Component. Click Office Spreadsheet.

4. Highlight and copy the data in the table, including row and column titles. Paste the data into the spreadsheet.

5. Click the table. Click Table on the menu bar. Point to Select. Click Table on the submenu. Click Edit on the menu bar. Click Delete.

6. Use the Spreadsheet Property Toolbox to make the following modifications: change the font size to 10 for all of the pasted row and column titles; change the number format to currency and right-align all numeric data.

7. Copy the column headings from cells B1 through D1 to cells G1 through I1. Copy the row headings from cells A2 through A6 to cells F2 through F6. Right-adjust all column headings.

8. In cell A1, type Unit Sales with a font size of ten (10). In cell F1, type Commissions with a font size of ten (10).

9. In cell G2 of the spreadsheet, type =B2*.01 as the formula. Copy this formula and paste it into all cells to the right and below G2 through row I and column 6.

10. Adjust the table and cell borders by dragging.

11. Use the Spreadsheet Property Toolbox to hide the spreadsheet toolbar, gridlines, title bar, column headers, and row headers.

12. The completed project is shown in Figure 3-103. Save the Web page. Print the Web page, write your name on it, and hand it in to your instructor.

Apply Your Knowledge

⊕ **Project Reinforcement at www.scsite.com/off2000/reinforce.htm**

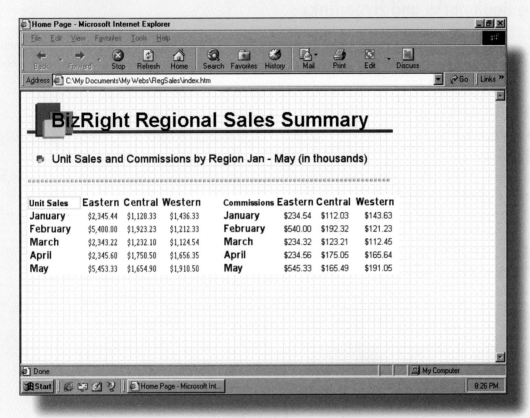

FIGURE 3-103

In the Lab

1 **Using Bookmarks and Hyperlinks**

Problem: You like the Web page created in the previous project for your automobile parts mail-order business, but want to enhance it by adding a parts list page. Initially, you want to set up a table with the categories of parts grouped together, and a list of categories at the top of the page linking to each group.

Instructions: Perform the following activities to create the Parts 'n' Parcel Parts page.

1. Start FrontPage and open the Parts 'n' Parcel web. If you did not complete that assignment, see your instructor for a copy.
2. Create a new page. Save it as parts.htm. Copy and paste the top table with its graphics and the horizontal line from the Home page to the Parts page. Place a bookmark, Parts Top, in the table's left cell.
3. Below the table, type Select Parts by Category: and then click the Center button on the Formatting toolbar. Below this, insert a two row, five column table.
4. Enter the text listed in Table 3-6 into the cells of the table as shown in Figure 3-104. Use the table background color as shown. Insert a second horizontal line graphic.

Table 3-6	Text and Sizes for Images	
Accessories	Cooling System	Filters
Auto Body	Engine	Tires & Wheels
Batteries	Electrical	Tune-up
Brakes	Exhaust	Tools

5. Center both horizontal graphics.
6. Below the second horizontal line graphic, insert a table with 24 rows and a single column. Beginning with the first row, insert in every other row a text item from Table 3-6. Mark each of the text items with bookmarks. In each of the other rows, type Return to Top as the text. Right-adjust the text and make it a hyperlink to the Page Top bookmark.
7. Use the Table Properties to set the alignment of both tables to Center and set their widths to match that of the horizontal line graphic.
8. Make each of the text items entered in Step 4 a hyperlink to its corresponding bookmark.
9. Save the Web page. Print the Web page, write your name on it, and hand it in to your instructor.

In the Lab

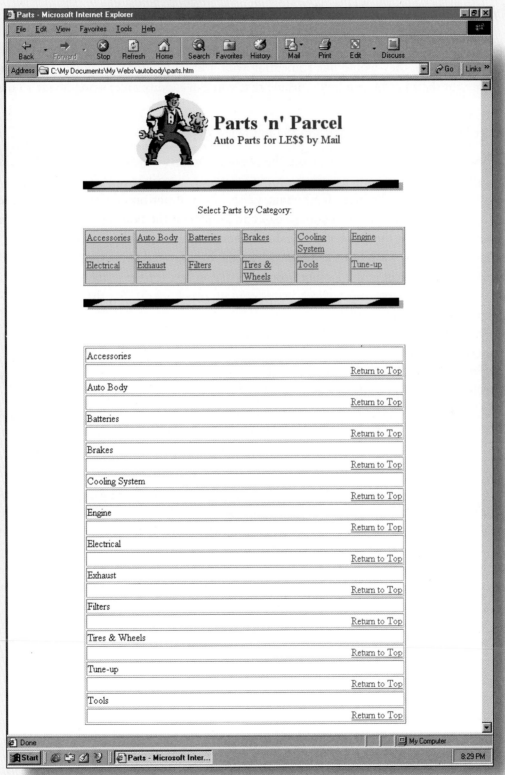

FIGURE 3-104

In the Lab

2 Modifying Images in a Web Page

Problem: The Westchester Little League team for whom you made a Web page would like a background other than plain white. Predictably, they would like something with a baseball motif. Although you have no images that are appropriate for their background, you decide that you can modify an existing image to meet their requirements.

Instructions: Start FrontPage 2000 and perform the following steps using a computer.

1. Open the Westchester Little League web from the previous project. If you do not have that assignment, see your instructor for a copy.
2. Highlight the phrase, … for the love of the game. Click the Bold button on the Formatting toolbar.
3. From the Clip Art Gallery, insert a new, small baseball graphic at the bottom of the page. Although it can be the same image used for the baseball links, do not simply copy a graphic from the page.
4. Using the Pictures toolbar, wash out the image. Make the background color transparent.
5. Display the Appearance sheet in the Picture Properties dialog box for the graphic. Make certain that the Specify size and the Keep aspect ratio check boxes contain check marks. Set the width to 15 pixels. Click the OK button. Resample the graphic.
6. Click the Save button. Be sure to save the new embedded image in the Images folder with a unique name. Delete the image from the page.
7. In the Page Properties dialog box, set the Background picture to the unique file name you used in Step 6 above for saving the new embedded image.
8. Set the background color transparent for images that need it. Your page should resemble Figure 3-105.
9. Save the Web page. Print the Web page, write your name on it, and hand it in to your instructor.

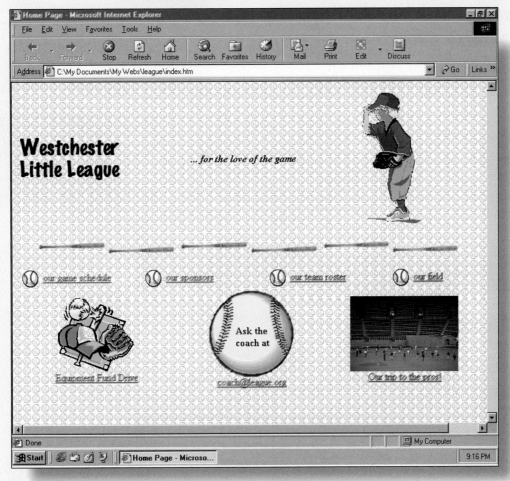

FIGURE 3-105

In the Lab

3 Image Maps and Graphic Hyperlinks

Problem: WorldWide Travel wants some additions to the Web page you created in Project 2. They want some image maps on the Home page and would like you to start a Travel Packages page.

Instructions: Start FrontPage 2000 and perform the following steps using a computer.

1. Open the WorldWide Travel web from Project 2. If you did not complete that assignment, see your instructor for a copy.
2. Add a new Web page. Type `Travel Packages` at the top of the page. Below, on three separate lines, type `Cruises`, `Vacations`, and `International Trips`. Make these bookmarks. Between each of these, place a list of your favorite places that would correspond to these headings. See Table 3-7 for some suggestions. Put a link to the Home page at the end. Save the page as travelPkgs.htm.

Table 3-7 Sample Travel Packages	
TRAVEL PACKAGES	*CRUISES (BOOKMARK)*
Grand Canyon	Bahaman Breeze
Southern Charm (Atlanta area)	Alaskan Breeze
Whitewater Rafting	Hawaiian Pineapple
Canadian Mounted (horseback riding)	U.S. Virgin Islands
Politico (Washington, D.C.)	Riverboat (Mississippi River)
VACATIONS (BOOKMARK)	*INTERNATIONAL TRIPS (BOOKMARK)*
Florida - Disney World	Paris and surrounding area
Florida - Space Adventure	Southern France
Colo. Springs & Rocky Mt Natl Pk	Spain
Hawaii	Ireland
Southern California Surfin'	Switzerland
New York City	Brazil
Las Vegas	Madagascar

3. Open the Home page, index.htm. Below the links under Plan Your Own, insert a small graphic from the Clip Art Gallery representing a hotel room and link to the same page as the Reserve a Room link. Also insert a graphic representing a car rental and link to the same page as the Rent a Car link. Resize and resample graphics as necessary. See Figure 3-106 for an example.
4. Use the Polygon Hotspot button to draw a hotspot around each of the two airplane images at the top of the page. Link one to the same link as the Book a Flight link and the other to the Find Flight Info link.
5. Use the Rectangular Hotspot button to draw a hotspot around the beach graphic at the center of the page. Link it to SunnyPlaces.htm.
6. Use the Circular Hotspot button to draw a hotspot around the shopping graphic under Travel Packages. Link it to travelPkgs.htm, which was created in Step 2.

In the Lab

7. Change each of the three links Shop for Cruises, Shop for Vacations, and Shop for International Trips, by editing the hyperlink and selecting travelPkgs.htm. After selecting travelPkgs.htm and before clicking the OK button, also select the appropriate bookmark for each hyperlink, as created in Step 2, using either Cruises, Vacations, or International Trips. This links a hyperlink on one page to a bookmark on another page.

8. Save the Web page. Print the Web page, write your name on it, and hand it in to your instructor.

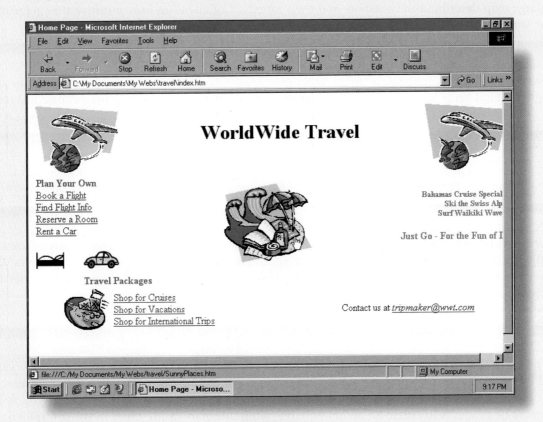

FIGURE 3-106

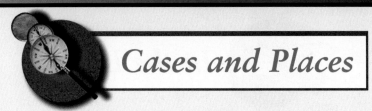

Cases and Places

The difficulty of these case studies varies:
◗ are the least difficult; ◗◗ are more difficult; and ◗◗◗ are the most difficult.

1 ◗ You can learn about the use of image maps by studying how other Web developers use them. Find and print three Web pages, each containing an image map. Write a report that includes a diagram for each image map describing the hotspots and their targets. Comment on how intuitive the image map was, or was not, for the user.

2 ◗ Not all the clip art, buttons, dividers, and other images you find on the Web are free. Some of it is copyrighted. Find three Web sites with free images. Locate their policies on the use of their images and report your findings.

3 ◗◗ In addition to images, you also can include sound and movies on your Web pages. Search the Internet for libraries of sounds and movies. Create a Web page containing links to some of these resources.

4 ◗◗ Graphics editors, such as Windows Paint, allow you to create and edit images. Many editors are available for download on the Internet. Find out about two different free or shareware graphics editors and two different commercial graphics editors. Discuss which one of each type you would prefer and why, in terms of their features. Include information such as the types of supported image file formats and special effects.

5 ◗◗◗ The GIF89a format supports special images called animated GIFs. These animated images support limited movement. Search the Internet to learn how to create an animated GIF. From your research, answer the following questions: What types of animated GIF editors are available? Would you need any other items or products to create an animated GIF? What alternatives are there to using GIF89a?

6 ◗◗◗ Use the Internet to find the current formal specification for HTML. Also determine if formal specifications exist for the JPEG and GIF file formats. Write a report that briefly describes the contents of GIF and JPEG files. Are any new techniques or features being considered for inclusion in the next set of specifications?

7 ◗◗◗ Image maps can be created using one of several different styles. These styles include client-side, server-side, NCSA, CERN, and Netscape. Research the different image map styles and write a report describing each format and when you might use each one.

Microsoft **FrontPage 2000**

Microsoft FrontPage 2000

P R O J E C T

Creating and Using Interactive Forms on the Web

You will have mastered the material in this project when you can:

O B J E C T I V E S

- Describe forms and the types of form fields
- Describe available form handlers
- Describe the methods and format used to send form data
- Add a new Web page in Page view
- Manage files in Folders view
- Insert a form in a Web page
- Insert a form in a table
- Insert a table in a form
- Insert a text box in a form
- Modify the properties of a text box
- Insert a drop-down menu in a form
- Modify the properties of a drop-down menu
- Create a nested table
- Insert a radio button in a form
- Assign text as a label for a radio button
- Modify the properties of a radio button
- Insert a check box in a form
- Assign text as a label for a check box
- Modify the properties of a check box
- Adjust form button properties
- Choose a form handler
- Modify HTML code directly in FrontPage
- Print a Web page in FrontPage

Online Connection

Rediscover Old Friends and Former Classmates

W hen your class reunion approaches or you happen to come across an old yearbook, do you ever wonder what happened to your high school class president, the cheerleading captain, your best friend in homeroom, or a childhood sweetheart? It would be fun to know.

Now, you may be able to find a friend or former classmate with the help of ClassMates™, a unique service on the Internet. The site is the brainchild of Randy Conrads, who devised the concept while perusing the list of America Online and Prodigy subscribers in search of former class-mates. He found the name of a friend he had not seen in many years, and the two subse-quently met. Then, in Conrads's words, he became "the first spammer" in 1995 by

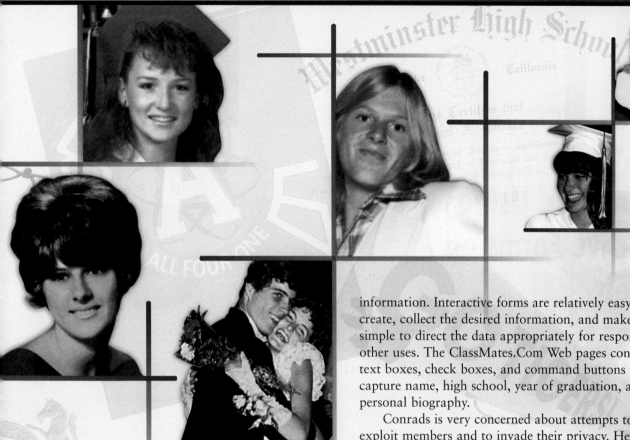

contacting every AOL and Prodigy subscriber and asking for participants in his alumni matching project.

The response was overwhelming, and Conrads found himself trying to manage the thousands of people expressing an interest. As a nonprogrammer setting up a computer business on a UNIX server, his early efforts in database design and report generation soon became inadequate and outdated. Conrads's son convinced him to buy an IBM-compatible computer and use FrontPage to design the effective ClassMates.Com site.

Today, more than 3.1 million alumni are registered with ClassMates.Com, and nearly 10,000 people join each day. Registration is free and allows members a way to contact registrants and a way for registrants to scan the database to search for familiar names from a specific high school in a particular graduating class. Membership for a small fee is required to participate in activities, such as contacting high school friends, acquiring reunion information, and other member services.

When registering, users enter data in interactive forms similarly to the membership form you will create in Project 4 for the Bits 'n' Bytes computer club. The form contains controls that provide a means for interested visitors to supply contact and academic

information. Interactive forms are relatively easy to create, collect the desired information, and make it simple to direct the data appropriately for response or other uses. The ClassMates.Com Web pages consist of text boxes, check boxes, and command buttons that capture name, high school, year of graduation, and personal biography.

Conrads is very concerned about attempts to exploit members and to invade their privacy. He does not allow advertisers to sell products to members, nor does he allow the members to distribute the data for any commercial purpose, except for planning a class reunion.

While a traditional class reunion involves face-to-face contact, ClassMates.Com schedules online virtual class reunions for alumni scattered throughout the world. For example, one such reunion for a Miami high school included participants dialing in from a New Jersey hotel, a military base in Australia, and Singapore.

The site includes message boards that allow former schoolmates to reminisce about high school experiences, friends, teachers, and hangouts and view photos and celebrity yearbooks. These features are popular for graduates who have moved to different parts of the country or world.

Conrads calls business on the Web, "a tremendous opportunity field," even for computer users with little Web page authoring experience. He adds, "FrontPage allows people like me to put a site together."

Each day he receives hundreds of letters and e-mail messages from members delighted with the service. Several classmates have reunited and then married, and Conrads even attended one of these weddings. Judging from this positive response, increasingly more friends and classmates are making the online connection.

Microsoft FrontPage 2000

Creating and Using Interactive Forms on the Web

CASE PERSPECTIVE

The officers of the Bits 'n' Bytes computer club are pleased with your progress on the club Web pages. They are satisfied with the Discount Pricing page and order form. They particularly liked your changes to the theme for the site.

Now they would like a Web page developed that accepts membership requests. This page should allow visitors to the Bits 'n' Bytes site who are interested in joining the club to provide details that include contact information and academic status.

The officers want information on potential members to be separated from other e-mail such as requests or comments so they can respond quickly and appropriately to interested students. They also are considering collection of the contact data into a database. For this reason, they want some structure to the data collected, rather than simply providing a link to e-mail this information. Furthermore, with unstructured e-mail, a potential member might omit some requested information. With your FrontPage experience, you inform them that it is relatively easy to create the interactive form they want; thus allowing them to collect the desired information, eliminate irrelevant data, and then direct it appropriately.

Introduction

In previous projects, you created Web pages that go in one direction: from you to your reader. Most of the flow of information over the Web uses this technique. A Web server sends the majority of Web pages to your computer for viewing without any way for you to send information or data back to the Web server.

A method does exist, however, for providing feedback and interaction with Web pages. Special HTML objects, called forms, provide two-way communication between you and a Web server. Using forms, you can order products, do banking, engage in live conversations, leave comments or suggestions, and use Web search engines. Forms make a Web page **interactive**. Users can respond to a Web site by filling in forms and submitting them.

Project Four — Creating and Using an Interactive Form

In this project, you will learn how to use forms and form fields by creating the Bits 'n' Bytes Join page shown in Figure 4-1a. The Join page will be used to collect information from prospective club members. That information is sent by e-mail, as illustrated in Figure 4-1b, to an address of your choosing when the prospective member clicks the Send button on the form. You created hyperlinks to this page from the Bits 'n' Bytes Home page. Before you begin creating the Join page, you should familiarize yourself with some important concepts and definitions about forms.

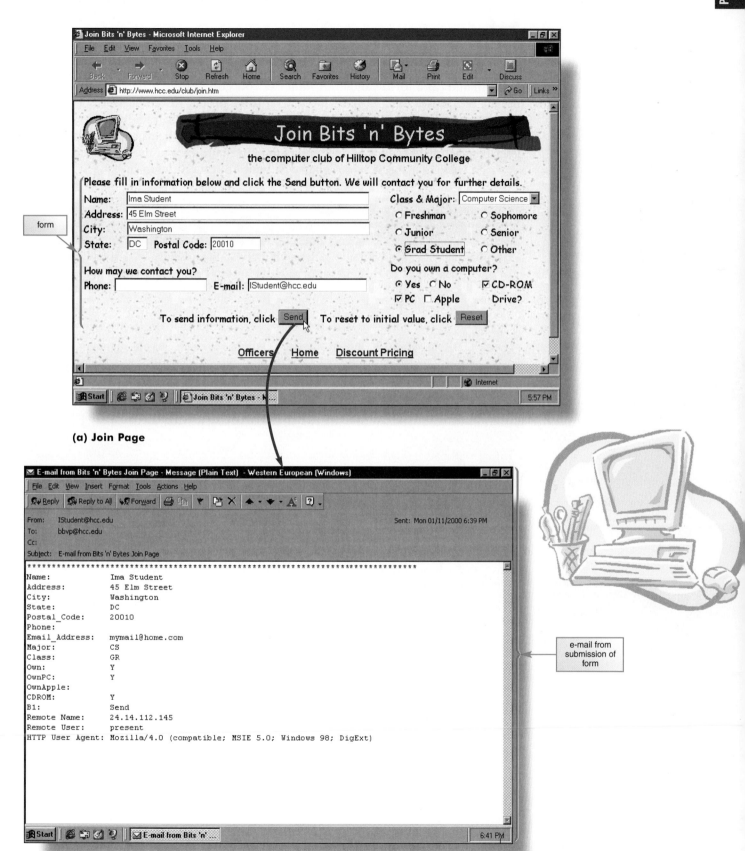

(a) Join Page

(b) E-mail from Join Page

FIGURE 4-1

HTML Forms

Two components are required to send data using forms: (1) a Web page containing the form and (2) a form handler. A **form** is a collection of input fields on a Web page that enables a user to enter data and send it to be processed on the Web server by a form handler. The **form fields** can be text boxes, check boxes, radio buttons, drop-down menus, or buttons. Table 4-1 lists the available form fields and briefly describes each field type. The user enters data in the form and sends it to the Web server by clicking a specially-designated Submit button on the form.

Table 4-1 FrontPage Form Fields	
FORM FIELD	**DESCRIPTION**
Radio button	A form field that presents you with a selection you can choose by clicking an option button. Radio buttons are used to present a set of one or more mutually exclusive options, one of which typically is set by default. Selecting a new radio button on the form deselects the currently selected radio button.
Check box	A form field you can select by clicking a box. In check boxes, you can choose none, one, or more of a set of options.
One-line text box	A form field that allows you to enter alphanumeric text. You can type a maximum of 500 characters. If you type nothing in the text box, the text box name is returned without any data.
Drop-down menu	A form field that presents a list of selections in a drop-down list box style. You can use it to present a wide variety of choices — more than radio buttons can handle effectively. You can configure a drop-down menu to allow single or multiple selections.
Scrolling text box	A form field in which users can type multiple lines of free-form text. You can set the properties of the scrolling text box to have 999 columns and 999 rows.
Button	Each form has two default buttons: Submit, which sends a form to the Web server and Reset, which sets each form field back to its original default contents.

A typical form is composed of one or more form fields, along with a Submit button and a Reset button. The **Submit button** sends the completed form to the Web server for processing. The **Reset button** clears the fields and sets them back to their original default condition. The user simply fills in the form and then clicks the Submit button to send the data to be processed.

Because you can have more than one form on a Web page, you could have more than one Submit button on a Web page. You must use caution when using multiple forms on a Web page. When you click the Submit button for one of the forms, only those form fields in that form are sent to the Web server. Form fields that are not part of that form are ignored. You would have to click every Submit button in every form to send all the form fields on the Web page. With every Submit button you click, a separate collection of data is sent back to the Web server. Each collection of data contains only the data that was entered in the fields for one of the forms on the Web page.

Some applications might require several forms on a Web page. This allows you to have the same Web page return one of several potential sets of data and process the data differently depending on which Submit button the user clicks. Whenever a user clicks the Submit button, the server processes the data on the form using a form handler program.

Microsoft Certification

The Microsoft Office User Specialist (MOUS) Certification program provides an opportunity for you to obtain a valuable industry credential — proof that you have the FrontPage 2000 skills required by employers. For more information, visit the Shelly Cashman Series MOUS Web page at www.scsite.com/off2000/cert.htm.

Form Handlers

A form handler provides a means for collecting information entered on a form. A **form handler** is a program that resides on the server and is executed when a user submits a form using the Submit button that is part of each form. The form handler normally is not visible to a user.

Form handler programs are highly dependent on the computer operating system and Web server software. Because of this, writing form handler programs can be a complex process and requires advanced programming skills.

You can use one of several available techniques when deciding how to handle the form data. Several standard techniques are available on the Web. In addition, FrontPage has several form handlers included in the FrontPage extensions that can be installed on the Web server computer. Table 4-2 describes the standard Web techniques as well as the extensions available with FrontPage. The most popular way of handling forms is to use the **Common Gateway Interface**, or **CGI**. In addition to the standard techniques, you can have the data e-mailed to an e-mail address.

Table 4-2 Standard and FrontPage Form Handlers	
FORM HANDLER	**DESCRIPTION**
CGI	Common Gateway Interface - A standard method of extending Web server functionality by executing programs or scripts on a Web server in response to Web browser requests.
ISAPI	Internet Server Application Program Interface - A Web server application development interface developed by Process Software and Microsoft Corporation that can be used in place of CGI.
NSAPI	Netscape Server Application Program Interface - A Web server application development interface developed by Netscape Communications Corporation.
ASP	Active Server Page - A method for creating programs that execute on a Web server, first available on the Microsoft Internet Information Server 3.0.
Discussion Form Handler	A FrontPage form handler that allows users to participate in an online discussion. The Discussion Form Handler collects information from a form, formats it into an HTML page, and adds the page to a table of contents and text index.
Registration Form Handler	A FrontPage form handler that allows users to register themselves automatically for access to a service implemented as a World Wide Web site. The Registration Form Handler adds the user to the service's authentication database, then gathers optional information from the form and stores it in one of many supported formats.
Save Results Form Handler	A FrontPage form handler that gathers information from a form and stores it in one of a selection of formats or sends the information to an e-mail address.

CGI Scripts

CGI is a universal way to execute programs on the Web. CGI programs can be written in one of several available programming languages such as Perl, Java, or Visual Basic. These programs frequently are called **CGI scripts**.

CGI scripts begin executing after the user supplies data by filling in the form fields and then clicking the Submit button. The browser sends the data fields from the form to the Web server. The name of the CGI script is stored in the form. The CGI script processes the data and sends back a confirmation Web page.

More About

CGI Scripts

A form is not required to use a CGI script. You can use a hyperlink that points to a CGI script to generate dynamic Web pages based on real-time data.

The CGI script can perform many different functions with the data, including retrieving or updating data from a database, storing data in a series of data files, or executing other programs. When finished, the CGI script usually returns information to the browser in the form of a new HTML document indicating the status of the form processing.

You can choose a form handler that will append the data to a data file, send the data to an e-mail address, or immediately process the data with a user-supplied CGI program. If you use the FrontPage handlers rather than a custom form handler, such as a CGI script or sending the data directly to an e-mail address, a server that has the FrontPage Server Extensions installed is required. Regardless of the technique you choose to process the data, two basic formats, or methods, are used to send data to be processed: Get and Post.

Get and Post Methods

When the viewer fills in the form fields and then clicks the Submit button, the data is sent in plain ASCII text in a **name=value** format, with the name of the field first, followed by an equal sign, and then followed by the data the user entered in the field. Values that have embedded spaces have those spaces replaced with '+' signs, to indicate that this text is concatenated together to form a single value. Names cannot have spaces in them, so when assigning a name to a field, uppercase and lowercase letters, along with underscores, are used to make the names more readable. Figure 4-2 shows the format of the collection of name=value pairs from a sample form. Each name=value pair is separated by an ampersand (&). The creator of the Web page assigns names to the form fields.

```
Full_Name=Ima+Student&Address=45+Elm+Street&City=Washington&State=DC&P
ostal_Code=20010&Phone=&Email_Address=IStudent@hcc.edu&Major=CS&Class=
GS&Own=Yes&OwnPC=Y&OwnApple=&CDROM=Y
```

FIGURE 4-2

The way in which the form handler reads the information depends on which one of the two methods is used to send the form. The **Get method** stores the name=value pairs in an environment variable called QUERY_STRING. The form handler program must contain instructions to access the QUERY_STRING environment variable in order to read the name=value pairs.

The **Post method** reads the name=value pairs as input directly to the form handler from a standard input stream. A **stream** is similar to a data file. Most programs have a standard input and a standard output stream automatically defined when they are compiled.

Post is the preferred method, as most programs can be written to read from the standard input stream with little effort and remain portable across different computer platforms. Reading environment variables can require sets of instructions that are unique to each computer platform, requiring more programming effort to migrate the programs from one computer system to another.

Regardless of the method you choose to handle the form, the steps to use the form remain the same: you fill in the form by typing data in the text boxes, clicking radio buttons and check boxes, and selecting items from menus. You then send the data on the form by clicking the Submit button. A default Web page normally is sent confirming the reception of the data by the form handler. You can supply a customized Web page containing the confirmation information.

CGI Script Languages

On UNIX systems, most CGI scripts are written in C or Perl. On Windows systems, most CGI scripts are written in Visual Basic or Visual C.

Get and Post

Other related information about forms data, such as the length of the data string and the Internet address of the computer sending the data, are available in environment variables.

Designing a Form

The Bits 'n' Bytes computer club will use the form on the Web page to obtain useful information from potential members, such as their name and address, their academic status with the school, and some basic information about computer ownership. The forms data will be handled using an electronic mail account. Figure 4-3 illustrates the design for the Join Web page.

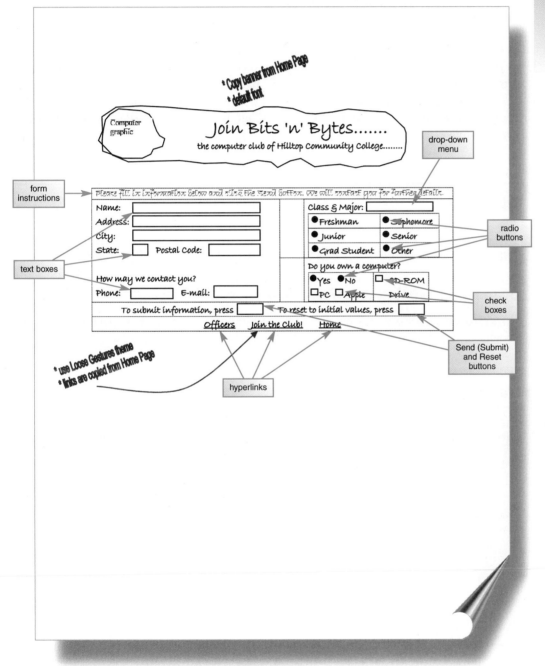

FIGURE 4-3

The form shown in Figure 4-3 on the previous page consists of four logical sections. The purpose of each section is to obtain a certain type of information. The number and purpose of the sections in your form design will depend on the types of information you are requesting and any design concerns and issues for the Web page.

When designing a form for a Web page, lay out the input fields in the order you would read a book – from left to right and top to bottom. You can use tables to organize and control the spacing of the form fields on the Web page.

Adding and Deleting Web Pages

Before beginning any work on a form, you first must add a new page to the Bits 'n' Bytes FrontPage web. Because an under-construction Join page previously was added to this FrontPage web, this Join page either should be modified, as was done for the previous project, or deleted and a new Join page created.

To delete an existing Web page and add a new Web page, you need to start FrontPage and then open the original FrontPage web. Start FrontPage using the following steps .

TO START FRONTPAGE

1 Click the Start button on the taskbar. Point to Programs on the Start menu.

2 Click Microsoft FrontPage on the Programs submenu.

The FrontPage window opens and an empty page displays (see Figure 4-4).

Opening an Existing FrontPage Web

Perform the following steps to open the Bits 'n' Bytes FrontPage web created in Project 3. If you did not complete Project 3, see your instructor for a copy.

 Steps **To Open an Existing FrontPage Web**

1 **Click the Open button arrow on the Standard toolbar. Point to Open Web on the Open Web button menu.**

The Open Web button menu displays with the Open Web command highlighted (Figure 4-4).

FIGURE 4-4

2 Click Open Web. When the Open Web dialog box displays, if necessary, click the Look in box arrow and select the folder location where you stored the web for Project 3 (e.g., C:\My Documents\ My Webs\Club). Point to the Open button.

The Open Web dialog box displays with the web folder selected (Figure 4-5). The new location displays in the text box. Use the drive and location that is appropriate for your environment.

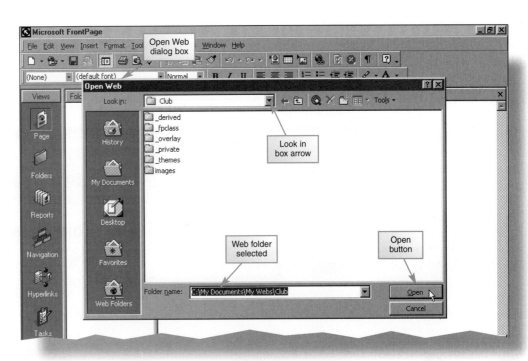

FIGURE 4-5

3 Click the Open button. Double-click the file join.htm in the Folder List.

The previous web is loaded and the file join.htm displays in Page view (Figure 4-6).

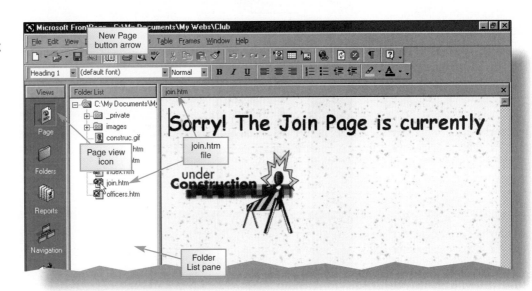

FIGURE 4-6

Other Ways

1. On File menu click Open
2. Press ALT+F, O
3. Press CTRL+O

Adding a New Page in Page View

FrontPage makes it very easy to add new pages to your FrontPage web. You may have noticed that a new page is displayed automatically when an existing FrontPage web is opened. It is likely that you would not want to add an additional page to your web every time you open it in FrontPage. Consequently, if you do not make any modifications to this displayed page before changing pages, views, or quitting FrontPage, it is not saved. If you open an existing page and then close it, the new page may no longer display. If, at such a time, you want to create another new page, doing so only requires that you click a single button. This is the same procedure that you used in Project 3 to add a new page when in Navigation view.

Use the following steps to add a new page to an existing web in Page view.

 To Add a New Page in Page View

1 **Click the New Page button arrow on the Standard toolbar. Point to Page on the New Page button menu.**

The New Page button menu displays with the Page command highlighted (Figure 4-7).

FIGURE 4-7

2 **Click Page.**

A new page displays in Page view (Figure 4-8). The new page name is not listed in the Folder List pane.

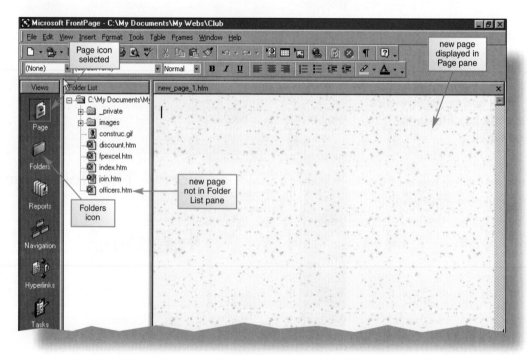

FIGURE 4-8

 Other Ways

1. On File menu point to New, click Page on New submenu
2. Press ALT+F, N, P
3. Press CTRL+N
4. Right-click Folders List pane, click New Page on shortcut menu

Managing Files in Folders View

FrontPage has several ways by which you can manage the files in your FrontPage web. The Folder List panel displays the files included in the current web. Operations on these files, such as renaming or deleting files, can be done in the Folder List, as we have already seen. There is also another view, **Folders view**, which not only allows for similar file management, but also displays additional information about files in the current web, such as file size, title, when the file was last modified, and who last modified it.

Display the FrontPage web in Folders view by following these steps.

To Display Files in Folders View

 Point to the Folders icon on the Views bar.

The page currently displays in Page view (Figure 4-9).

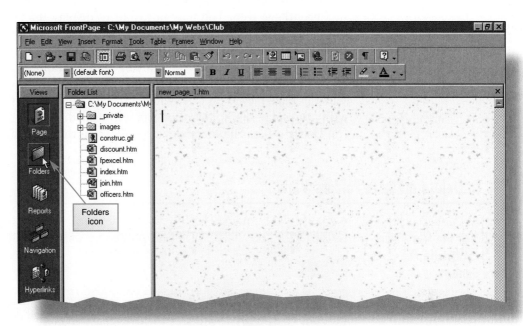

FIGURE 4-9

 Click the Folders icon.

The pages in the FrontPage web display in Folders view (Figure 4-10).

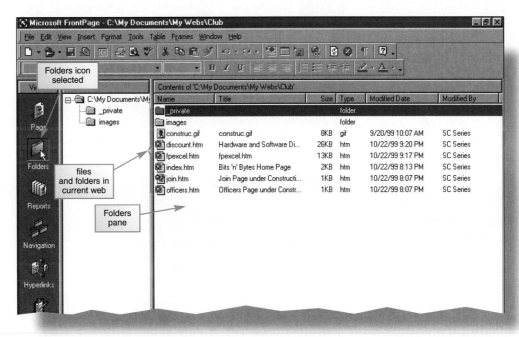

FIGURE 4-10

1. On View menu click Folders
2. Press ALT+V, F

The new page just created does not display in Folders view in Figure 4-10. This is because it was not saved. For a new page created in another view to display in Folders view, it must be saved before switching to Folders view. Notice that the individual files in the web display in detail in the Folders pane, and therefore, the Folder List pane does not show the individual files; only folders. The Folder List pane is a subset of the more expanded Folders view.

Deleting Files in Folders View

Folders view provides an alternative to using the Folder List pane to manage files in a FrontPage web. You may not want to display the Folders List pane in Page view, particularly if you are using a monitor with a display size less than 17 inches. By not using the Folders List pane, you can enlarge the area of your screen available for editing in Page view. Both Folders view and the Folders List pane allow for deleting, adding, and renaming files in much the same way. If you hide the Folders List pane when in Page view, you can switch either to Folders view to manage files, or you can easily redisplay the Folders List pane, if needed.

Delete a file in Folders view by following these steps.

 To Delete a File in Folders View

1 **Click the file name join.htm in the Folders pane.**

The file is highlighted in the Folders pane (Figure 4-11).

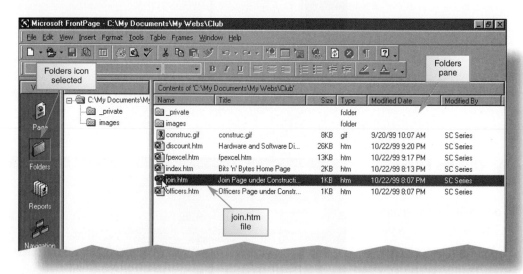

FIGURE 4-11

2 **Press the DELETE key. When the Confirm Delete dialog box displays, point to the Yes button.**

The Confirm Delete dialog box displays, indicating the file to be deleted (Figure 4-12).

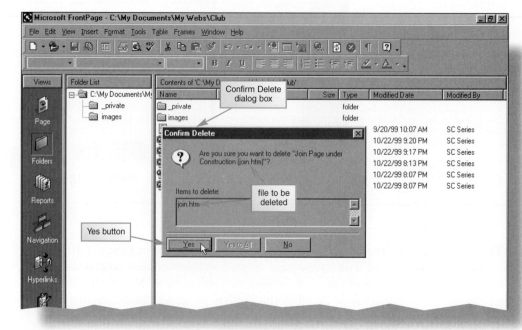

FIGURE 4-12

3 Click the Yes button.

The Confirm Delete dialog box closes and the selected file is deleted (Figure 4-13).

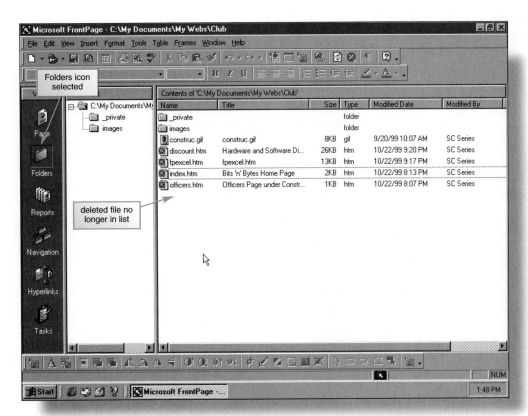

FIGURE 4-13

Other Ways

1. On Edit menu click Delete
2. Press ALT+E, D

If you delete a file that is referenced by a hyperlink on a different page, that hyperlink is broken, and will display as such when the page with the broken hyperlink displays in Navigation view. Adding a new file with the same name as the deleted file will cause the broken hyperlink to be repaired. It then will reference an existing file.

Adding and Renaming Files in Folders View

While viewing the web in Folders view, you may add a new page to a FrontPage web. Adding a page in this view causes the page to be saved and added to the list of files in the web as soon as you rename the new page or change views. When you add a new page in Folders view, FrontPage supplies a default name for the page and the page title and allows you to change the name of the new page immediately. You may also change the name later. The New Page button is accessible in all views allowing you to add a new page at anytime. Adding a new page in any view other than Navigation or Folders view automatically changes the view to Page view.

Add a new file in Folders view by following the steps on the next page.

Steps **To Add and Rename a File in Folders View**

 Click the New Page button while in Folders view.

A new file is added to the file list in the Folders pane. The name of the new file is highlighted (Figure 4-14).

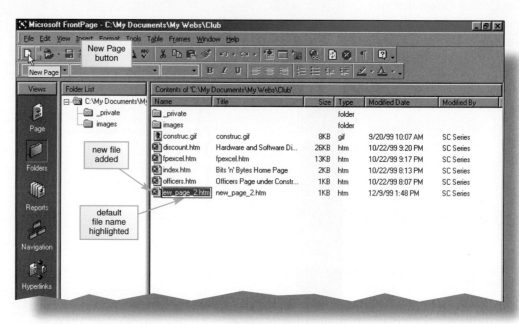

FIGURE 4-14

 **Type** join.htm **as the new file name and then press the ENTER key.**

The file name and the title both change to join.htm (Figure 4-15).

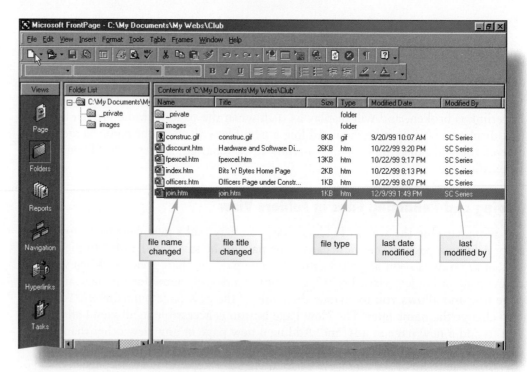

FIGURE 4-15

1. On File menu point to New, click Page on New submenu
2. Press ALT+F, N, P
3. Right-click Folders pane, click New Page on shortcut menu

Adding a new page in this manner causes FrontPage to use the supplied file name as the default title for the new Web page. You likely will want to change the title, as the title displays in the title bar of the Web browser when the page is viewed.

To modify the title of a Web page in Folders view, use the following steps.

Steps | **To Modify a Page Title in Folders View**

1 **Click the title of the page to be modified.**

The page title of join.htm is highlighted and an edit text box appears around the page title (Figure 4-16).

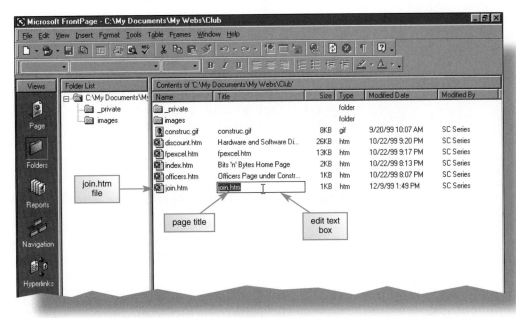

FIGURE 4-16

2 **Type** Join Bits 'n' Bytes **as the new page title. Press the ENTER key.**

The Folders pane reflects the new title for the page (Figure 4-17).

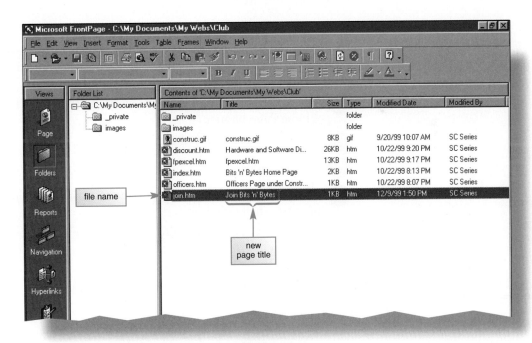

FIGURE 4-17

Other Ways

1. On File menu click Properties, click General tab

If you did not rename the file when it was created, you may change the name of the file in the same manner as you changed the title. After selecting the line containing the file you want to change, simply click the name to select it and then type a new name. When renaming a file, FrontPage determines if other pages reference the current file name and, if so, will prompt for permission to update any such links accordingly.

More *About* 2000

Format Painter

To copy character or paragraph formatting without copying the selected text, you can use the Format Painter. Select the text that has the format you want to copy, click the Format Painter button on the Standard toolbar, and then select the text where you want to apply the selected formatting.

Editing a New Web Page

When creating a new Web page, you likely will want some similarity between the new page and existing pages in the FrontPage web. Applying a theme allows certain aspects, such as the color scheme, to be carried over to new pages. You also may want to have similar page banners and hyperlinks on each page. FrontPage provides Navigation bars that automatically provide continuity in hyperlinks, as was done in Project 1. Even without using Navigation bars, you can copy elements, such as hyperlinks and page banners, from one Web page to another. To maintain continuity among pages, you can copy the page banner from the Bits 'n' Bytes Home page using Windows copy and paste facilities.

Copying and Pasting Objects from Another Web Page

In FrontPage, the procedure to copy objects consists of opening the target Web page, opening the source Web page, selecting the objects to be copied, placing them on the Clipboard, and then pasting them into the target Web page. The target Web page, the Join page, already is open. To complete the procedure, you now must open the source Web page, copy the selected object, and then paste the contents of the Clipboard into the target Web page. The following steps summarize how to copy the two-cell table containing the Bits 'n' Bytes Home page banner and graphic and paste it into the Join Web page.

TO COPY AND PASTE OBJECTS FROM ANOTHER WEB PAGE

1. Click the Page icon on the Views bar. In the Folder List pane, double-click the file index.htm to open it.

2. Select the two-cell table row containing the clip art image and the Bits 'n' Bytes Home Page banner.

3. Press CTRL+C to copy the selected objects.

4. In the Folder List pane, double-click the file join.htm to open it.

5. If necessary, click in the Page pane to position the insertion point. Press CTRL+V to paste the copied objects.

6. Position the insertion point at the beginning of the text, the computer club. Press the BACKSPACE key. Hold down the SHIFT key and then press the ENTER key.

7. Click the Navigation icon on the Views bar. Drag the file join.htm from the Folder List pane to the Navigation pane. Position it under the Home page icon.

8. Click the Page icon on the Views bar. Resize the graphic to just fit within the table. Drag the column border left as needed.

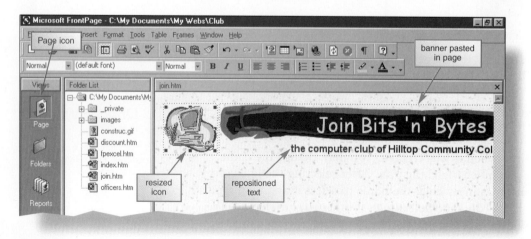

FIGURE 4-18

Figure 4-18 shows the FrontPage window after the copy and paste operation is completed. The Copy and Paste commands save time and work as you develop Web pages.

As in previous projects, this project uses tables to control spacing of objects on the Web page. In this case, one table contains the form and the hyperlinks to other pages, while additional tables are used within the form to position form fields and text. Although no name is associated with a given table in FrontPage, it can be helpful for discussion to reference them by the order in which they were created. The banner and graphic pasted earlier are in a table. The next table to add is the second table for this page, or table-T2. The following steps summarize how to add a table, table-T2, to the Join page.

TO ADD A TABLE TO A WEB PAGE

1 Position the insertion point below the first table containing the page banner. Click the Insert Table button on the Standard toolbar and then drag through two rows and one column (a 2 x 1 table).

2 Click the mouse button.

3 Right-click the table and then click Table Properties on the shortcut menu. When the Table Properties dialog box displays, type 0 in the Size text box in the Borders area, and then click the OK button.

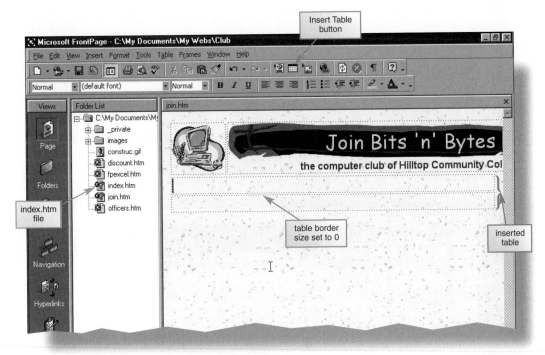

FIGURE 4-19

Figure 4-19 shows the FrontPage window after the insert table operation is completed.

The table just inserted, table-T2, will contain the interactive form in the top row and hyperlinks to other pages in this web in the bottom row. Copying and pasting the hyperlinks from the Home page to the Join page is done in the same manner as the table containing the page banner, table-T1.

Use the steps on the next page to copy and paste the hyperlinks from the Home page to the Join page.

To Copy and Paste Hyperlinks from Another Web Page

1 Double-click the file index.htm in the Folder List pane. Select the entire line containing the hyperlinks to other pages in the web.

The Home page index.htm is opened and the line containing the hyperlinks is highlighted (Figure 4-20).

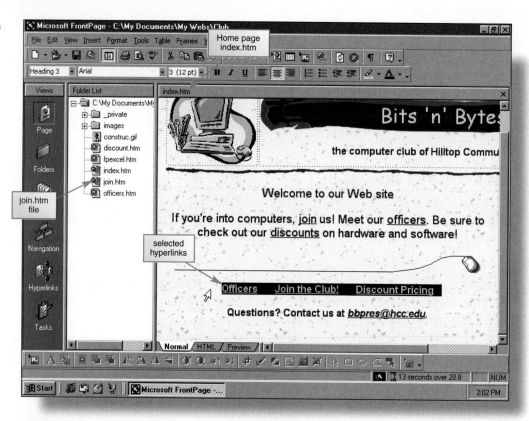

FIGURE 4-20

2 Press CTRL+C to copy the selected line. In the Folder List pane, double-click the file join.htm to open it.

The hyperlinks are copied and the Join page join.htm is opened (Figure 4-21).

FIGURE 4-21

3 **Click in the last row of table-T2 to position the insertion point. Press CTRL+V to paste the copied line.**

If you copied and pasted the entire line properly, the links will display centered and in the same font as on the Home page. The insertion point will be on a line following the links (Figure 4-22).

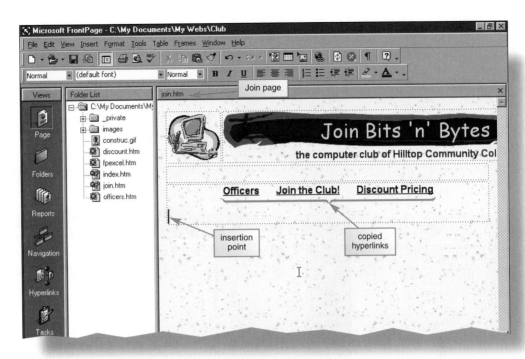

FIGURE 4-22

4 **Press the BACKSPACE key to remove the extra line.**

The Join page displays with the hyperlinks properly positioned (Figure 4-23).

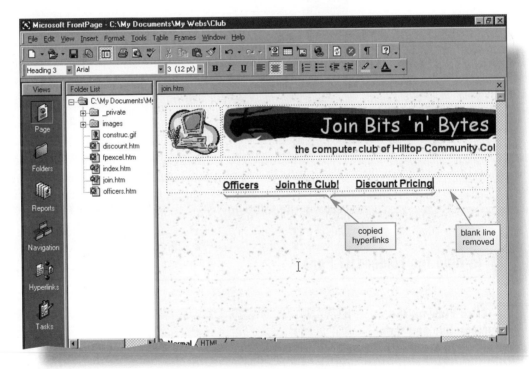

FIGURE 4-23

Other Ways

1. On Edit menu click Copy; on Edit menu click Paste
2. Press ALT+E, C; press ALT+E, P

Copies of the hyperlinks from the Home page have been pasted into the Join page. The hyperlink to the Join page must be changed, however, because a page has no need to link to itself. Rather, it must be replaced with a link back to the Home page, with the text modified to reflect this change. The steps on the next page change the text and the URL of a hyperlink.

TO MODIFY THE TEXT AND URL OF A HYPERLINK

1 Select the entire text of the Join the Club! hyperlink. Type Home as the new name.

2 Right-click the hyperlink. Click Hyperlink Properties on the shortcut menu.

3 In the Edit Hyperlink dialog box, select the file index.htm as the new URL. Click the OK button. Point to the Home hyperlink.

The URL of the modified link on the Join Page displays in the status bar (Figure 4-24).

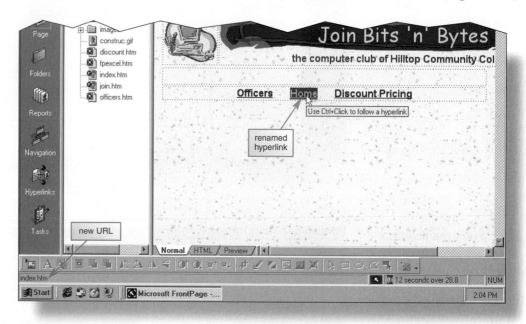

FIGURE 4-24

As was indicated earlier, the Folders List pane can be hidden to provide additional space for editing the page. When the form fields and text are added later, having a larger area for editing the page will make positioning such elements easier. Perform the following steps to hide the Folder List pane.

To Hide the Folder List Pane

1 **Click View on the menu bar and then point to Folder List.**

The View menu displays with the Folder List icon recessed, indicating that the Folder List pane currently is displayed (Figure 4-25).

FIGURE 4-25

Click Folder List.

FrontPage displays the current page in Page view with the Folder List pane hidden (Figure 4-26). This command is a **toggle**, *so repeating the same steps will redisplay the Folder List pane.*

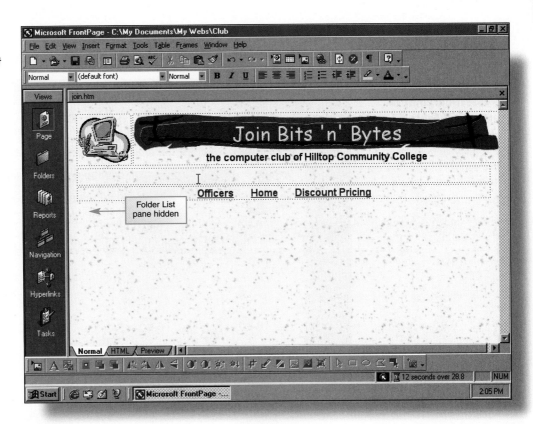

FIGURE 4-26

Other Ways

1. Click Folder List button on Standard toolbar
2. Press ALT+V, E

With table-T1 containing the page banner and graphic and table-T2 containing the hyperlinks to other pages in the web, this page now is ready to have the form and form fields added to it, which will provide the mechanism for feedback from the user.

Inserting a Form in a Web Page

Recall that a form typically consists of one or more form fields along with Submit and Reset buttons. FrontPage automatically creates the Submit and Reset buttons when you insert the form in the Web page. You also can insert a form by inserting any of the form fields outside of an existing form. Within a given form on a Web page, you may have many form fields, but you will have only one Submit button and only one Reset button.

Inserting a Form in a Table

Although FrontPage automatically creates the form when you insert the first form field on the Web page, you also can insert a form before inserting any form fields. In both cases, FrontPage inserts on the Web page a form HTML tag, along with the HTML tags describing the form field you inserted, if any. Additional form fields subsequently can be added to the existing form. A form can be added to a Web page without using a table. Just as a table was used to control positioning of text in previous projects, however, the same technique is useful for a page with a form, whether the text is external to the form or within the form. Perform the steps on the next page to insert a form in table-T2 on the Join page.

To Insert a Form in a Table

1 Position the insertion point in the first row of table-T2 on the form.

The insertion point displays in the first row of the second table on the Join page (Figure 4-27).

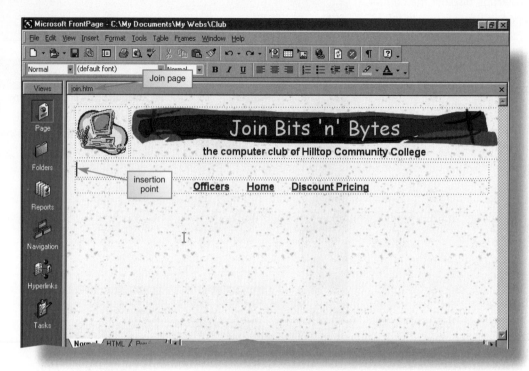

FIGURE 4-27

2 Click Insert on the menu bar and then point to Form. When the Form submenu displays, point to Form.

The Form submenu displays showing the form fields that can be added to a page (Figure 4-28).

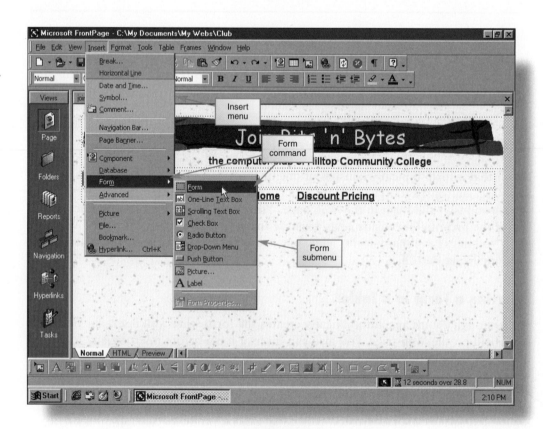

FIGURE 4-28

3 Click Form on the Form submenu.

A form is inserted in the first row of table-T2 (Figure 4-29). FrontPage adds the Submit and Reset buttons automatically.

FIGURE 4-29

Inserting a Table in a Form

The use of a table to contain the form allows better positioning of the form with respect to text outside the form. Within the form, a table also is useful to position text and form fields. A **table** allows a physical grouping of related fields and text, although it does not affect the function of the form in the collection of data. In each cell of this third table, table-T3, you will place several form fields and in some cases, an additional table. To ensure that table-T3 is part of the form, you must insert the form on the Web page before inserting the table.

If you insert the table first, followed by the form, the form location is inside one of the table cells, as was done with table-T2. Inserting form fields in another table cell (table-T2) would insert another form, complete with its own Submit and Reset buttons. On this form, you want the viewer to be able to send all the information he or she enters by clicking only one Submit button. Remember that each Submit button controls only those fields within the same form. The following steps summarize how to insert a table, table-T3, in the form just created.

TO INSERT A TABLE IN A FORM

1 If necessary, position the insertion point before the Submit button in the form.

2 Click the Insert Table button on the Standard toolbar and then drag through four rows and three columns. Click the mouse button.

3 Right-click the table and then click Table Properties on the shortcut menu. When the Table Properties dialog box displays, type 0 in the Size text box in the Borders area and then click the OK button.

4 Merge the columns of the top row into a single column. Merge the columns of the bottom row into a single column. Merge row 2 and row 3 of column 1 into a single row.

5 Highlight the Submit and Reset buttons. Cut and paste them into the last row of the table.

6 To allow for better positioning of text and form fields, delete the extra lines, if any, at the bottom of the form and at the bottom of the table and narrow the width of the center column. Adjust the width of the table created in step 2 to a little less than that of the form so that it is easier to distinguish between the two.

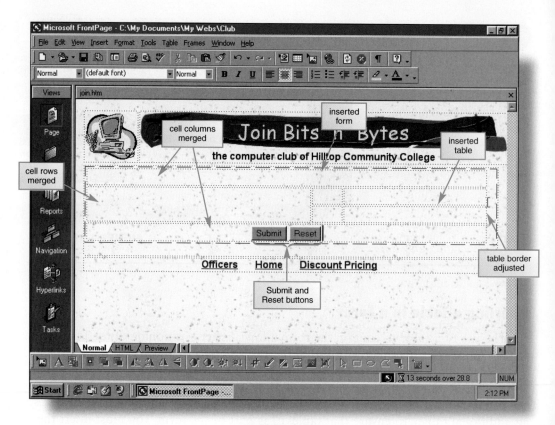

FIGURE 4-30

Figure 4-30 shows the form with the table, table-T3, added and with the indicated adjustments made.

Inserting Text in a Form

Some text in a form is often needed for descriptive reasons, to give instructions to the user as to the actions they should take. Adding text is as simple as positioning the insertion point and typing. Using tables, as in this project, is helpful for controlling the position of the text. The following steps summarize how to insert descriptive text in the form just created.

TO INSERT TEXT IN A FORM

1. Position the insertion point in row 1 of table-T3. Type Please fill in information below and click the Send button. We will contact you for further details.

2. Position the insertion point in row 4 of table-T3, before the Submit button. Type To send information, click. Make certain to include a space between the last word and the button.

3. Position the insertion point between the Submit button and the Reset button. Insert 4 spaces.

4. Type To reset to initial values, click before the Reset button. Make certain to include a space between the last word and the button.

5. If necessary, click the Center button on the Standard toolbar to center the line.

Figure 4-31 shows the form with the added text and with the last line centered.

More About

Spell Checking Text

You can check the spelling of text you insert in the Web page by clicking the Check Spelling button on the Standard toolbar.

More About

Formatting Lists

As another type of formatting, you can insert multi-level bulleted or numbered lists in your text. On the Format menu, click Bullets and Numbering. Click the Numbers tab to add a numbered list or the Picture Bullets tab to use pictures for the bullets. If your page does not have a theme applied, a tab for Plain Bullets may be selected. Use the Decrease Indent and Increase Indent buttons on the Formatting toolbar to move selected list items up or down a level.

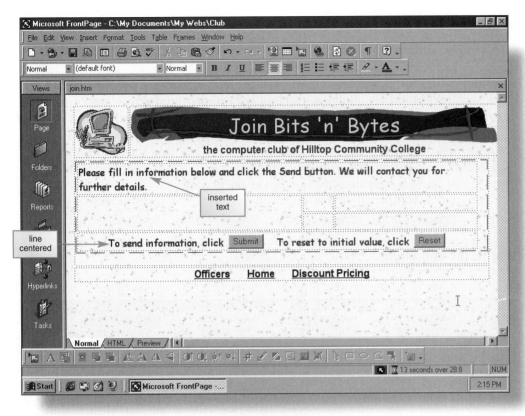

FIGURE 4-31

Adding Data Collection to a Form

Although a form is created with Submit and Reset buttons, they are of little value until the form is given the capability of collecting data from the user. This is done by means of form fields. **Form fields** allow the user to enter text, initiate actions by clicking buttons, and make choices by means of drop-down lists (menus), option (radio) buttons, and check boxes.

The two steps to inserting a form field on a Web page are (1) add the form field and any accompanying descriptive text and (2) adjust the properties of the form field. Place subsequent form fields for the same form within the dashed lines that indicate the boundaries of the form. Recall that you insert new objects at the location of the insertion point. Inserting an object at any other location causes the insertion of a new form with its own Submit and Reset buttons. Although you can create a Web page with several forms on it, this might not be what you want. You will notice that as you insert form fields, they contain no text label. Inserting a form field inserts only the form field object, such as a radio button or text box. You are responsible for providing the specific labels for the form fields you insert. As you do, you can associate the text as the label for a particular field, so when the user clicks the label text, the form field is selected. This makes it easier for users to select small items such as radio buttons and check boxes.

Because form fields of the same type have the same set of properties, when multiple instances are needed, it is often easier to create one instance, set the property values, copy the form field, and then paste the needed copies. This is particularly true when a number of the properties need to be modified from their default values. Although some properties, such as the field name, still may need to be changed for each instance, the number of individual changes you need to make for each copy may be decreased.

Positioning Form Fields

As you insert form fields in a form, it is best to preview the page in a browser to determine form field positioning. This is especially true for wide text fields that cannot be wrapped. They may display on a different line when editing, yet display on the same line in the browser.

Inserting Text Box Form Fields in a Form

Remember that Table 4-1 on page FP 4.6 indicates two types of text boxes are available in FrontPage for use on a form: a scrolling text box and a one-line text box. A **scrolling text box** is used when multiple lines of text are to be entered by the user. Such text boxes are shown with vertical and horizontal scroll bars. A **one-line text box** is used when only a single line of text is to be entered. Although it does not have a scroll bar, a one-line text box may accommodate entered text that is longer than the box displays on the form. The width of the box and the length of text it will accept are independent property values that can be set for each one-line text box. In this project, only one-line text boxes are needed.

Perform the following steps to insert one-line text box form fields in a form.

 Steps

To Insert Text Box Form Fields in a Form

1 **Position the insertion point in the second row and first column of table-T3, the table in the form. Type** Name: **followed by five spaces.**

The inserted text displays in the second row and first column of the table in the form on the Join page (Figure 4-32).

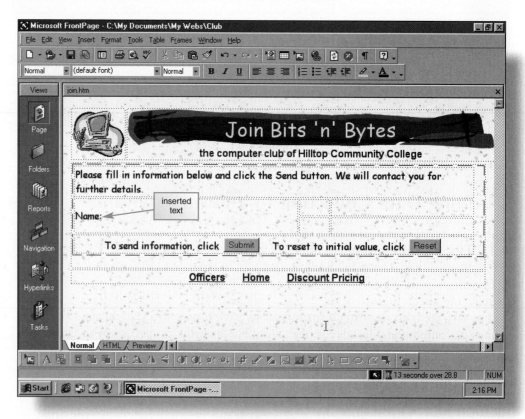

FIGURE 4-32

2 Click Insert on the menu bar and then point to Form. When the Form submenu displays, point to One-Line Text Box.

The Form submenu displays (Figure 4-33).

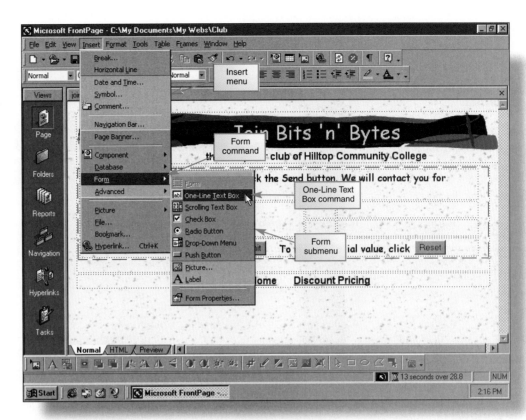

FIGURE 4-33

3 Click One-Line Text Box.

A one-line text box is inserted on the form with a default length (Figure 4-34).

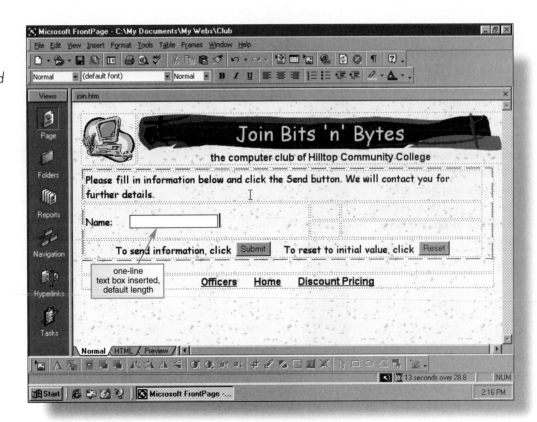

FIGURE 4-34

4 Right-click the text box. When the shortcut menu displays, point to Form Field Properties.

The text box form field is selected and a shortcut menu displays (Figure 4-35).

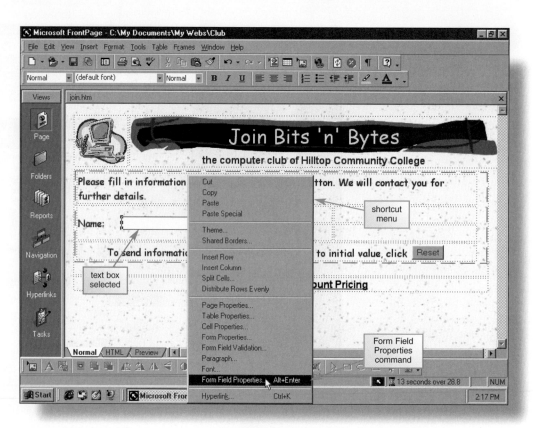

FIGURE 4-35

5 Click Form Field Properties. When the Text Box Properties dialog box displays, type Full, an underscore (_), and Name in the Name text box (the Name property cannot have spaces), type 55 in the Width in characters text box, and type 1 in the Tab order text box. Point to the Validate button.

The Text Box Properties dialog box displays with the changes indicated (Figure 4-36).

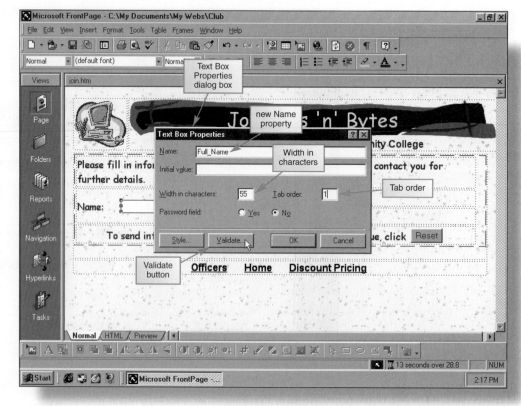

FIGURE 4-36

6 Click the Validate button. When the Text Box Validation dialog box displays, click Required in the Data length area and type Name in the Display name text box. Point to the OK button.

The Text Box Validation dialog box displays with the changes indicated (Figure 4-37).

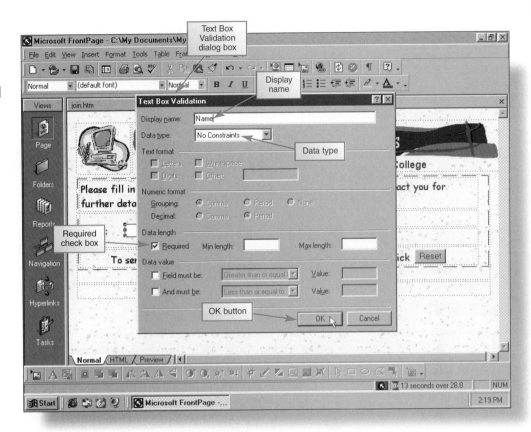

FIGURE 4-37

7 Click the OK button in the Text Box Validation dialog box. Click the OK button in the Text Properties dialog box. If necessary, click the text box to select it. Press CTRL+C to copy the text box and its properties and validations.

The entered text and the text box display in the form (Figure 4-38).

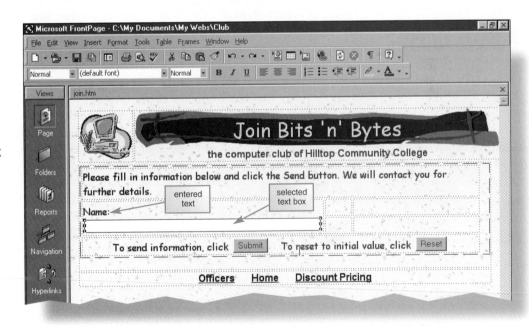

FIGURE 4-38

Other Ways

1. Press ALT+I, M, T

You have inserted a text box field on a form successfully. The form requires several other text box fields for all the information that the club needs about potential members. The steps on the next page describe how to insert the remaining text box fields on the Join Web page.

Microsoft **FrontPage 2000**

TO ENTER THE REMAINING TEXT BOX FIELDS

1 Position the insertion point after the Name text box. Hold down the SHIFT key and then press the ENTER key. Type Address: followed by a space. Press CTRL+V to insert the copied text box. Right-click the Address text box. Click Form Field Properties on the shortcut menu. When the Text Box Properties dialog box displays, type Address in the Name text box. Verify that 55 is the value in the Width in characters text box. Press the TAB key three times and then type 2 in the Tab order text box. Click the Validate button. When the Text Box Validation dialog box displays, verify that the Required check box in the Data length area is checked. Type Address in the Display name text box. Click the OK button in each dialog box.

2 Position the insertion point after the Address text box. Hold down the SHIFT key and then press the ENTER key. Type City: followed by seven spaces. Press CTRL+V to insert the copied text box. Right-click the text box. Click Form Field Properties on the shortcut menu. When the Text Box Properties dialog box displays, type City in the Name text box. Press the TAB key and then type Washington in the Initial value text box. Verify that 55 is the value in the Width in characters text box. Press the TAB key twice then type 3 in the Tab order text box. Click the Validate button. When the Text Box Validation dialog box displays, verify that the Required check box in the Data length area is selected. Type City in the Display name text box. Click the OK button in each dialog box.

3 Position the insertion point after the City text box. Hold down the SHIFT key and then press the ENTER key. Type State: followed by five spaces. Press CTRL+V to insert the copied text box. Right-click the text box. Click Form Field Properties on the shortcut menu. When the Text Box Properties dialog box displays, type State in the Name text box. Press the TAB key and then type DC in the Initial value text box. Press the TAB key and then type 3 in the Width in characters text box. Press the TAB key then type 4 in the Tab order text box. Click the Validate button. When the Text Box Validation dialog box displays, verify that the Required check box in the Data length area is selected. Type State in the Display name text box. Select Text in the Data type list. Check Letters in the Text format area. In the Data length area, type 2 in the Min length text box and type 2 in the Max length text box. In the Data value area, click Field must be, select Greater than or equal to in the list, and type AA in the Value text box. On the next line, click And must be, select Less than or equal to in the list, and type ZZ in the Value text box. Click the OK button in each dialog box.

4 Position the insertion point after the State text box. Press the SPACEBAR two times. Type Postal Code: followed by one space. Press CTRL+V to insert the copied text box. Right-click the text box. Click Form Field Properties on the shortcut menu. When the Text Box Properties dialog box displays, type Postal, underscore (_), and Code in the Name text box. Press the TAB key and then type 20010 in the Initial value text box. Press the TAB key and then type 10 in the Width in characters text box. Press the TAB key then type 5 in the Tab order text box. Click the Validate button. When the Text Box Validation dialog box displays, verify that the Required check box in the Data length area is selected. Type Postal Code in the Display name text box. Select Text in the Data type list. Click Letters, Digits, and Other in the Text format area, and type a hyphen (-) in the Other text box. In the Data length area, type 5 in the Min length text box and type 10 in the Max length text box. Click the OK button in each dialog box.

More About

Text Boxes

A text box can be configured as a password field. When a user enters data in the field, the field will display a series of asterisks rather than the text actually entered as data.

5 Position the insertion point after the Postal Code text box. Press the ENTER key. Type How may we contact you? and then hold down the SHIFT key and press the ENTER key. Type Phone: followed by one space. Press CTRL+V to insert the copied text box. Right-click the text box. Click Form Field Properties on the shortcut menu. When the Text Box Properties dialog box displays, type Phone in the Name text box. Press the TAB key twice and then type 20 in the Width in characters text box. Press the TAB key then type 6 in the Tab order text box. Click the Validate button. When the Text Box Validation dialog box displays, select Text in the Data type list. Click Digits and Other in the Text format area, and type ( ) (with no spaces) in the Other text box. Type Phone in the Display name text box. Click Required in the Data length area to deselect the check box. Click the OK button in each dialog box.

6 Position the insertion point after the Phone text box. Press the SPACEBAR two times. Type E-mail: followed by one space. Click Insert on the menu bar and then point to Form. When the Form submenu displays, click One-Line Text Box. Right-click the text box. Click Form Field Properties on the shortcut menu. When the Text Box Properties dialog box displays, type E-mail, underscore (_), and Address in the Name text box. Press the TAB key twice and then type 27 in the Width in characters text box. Press the TAB key then type 7 in the Tab order text box. Click the OK button.

7 Click the Save button on the Standard toolbar to save your changes.

The Web page displays as shown in Figure 4-39. The labels, properties, and validations for the form fields are listed in Table 4-3 on the next page.

More About

Hidden Form Fields

To include information in a form that you do not want users to see, you can add hidden form fields. For example, if you use the same custom form handler for several different forms, you could use a hidden field to identify each form.

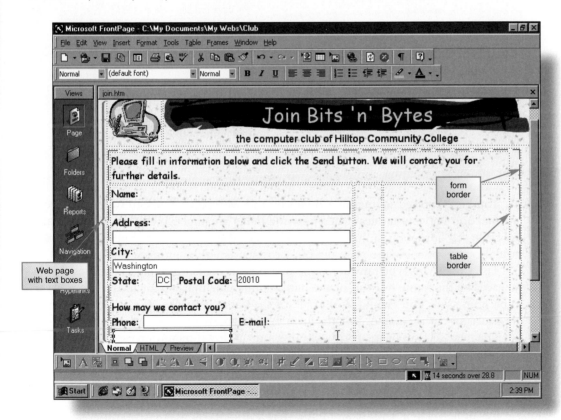

FIGURE 4-39

Table 4-3   Labels, Properties, and Validations for Text Box Form Fields

LABEL	PROPERTY VALUES TO SET	VALIDATIONS TO SET
Name:	Name = Full_Name Width = 55 Tab order = 1	Display name = Name In Data length area, click Required
Address:	Name = Address Width = 55 Tab order = 2	Display name = Address In Data length area, click Required
City:	Name = City Initial Value = Washington Width = 55 Tab order = 3	Display name = City In Data length area, click Required
State:	Name = State Initial Value = DC Width = 3 Tab order = 4	Display name = State Data type = Text In Text format area, click Letters In Data length area, click Required, Min length = 2, Max length = 2 In Data value area, check Field must be, select Greater than or equal to, set Value to AA; check And must be, select Less than or equal to, set Value to ZZ
Postal Code:	Name = Postal_Code Initial Value = 20010 Width = 10 Tab order = 5	Display name = Postal Code Data type = Text In Text format area, click Digits, click Letters, click Other, in Other text box, type hyphen (-) In Data length area, click Required, Min length = 5, Max length = 10
Phone:	Name = Phone Width = 20 Tab order = 6	Display name = Phone Data type = Text In Text format area, click Digits, click Other, in Other text box, type ( ), and - characters
E-mail:	Name = Email_Address Width = 26 Tab order = 7	Display name = E-mail

More About

Form Fields

Inserting a field outside a form causes a new form to be created by default with its own Submit and Reset buttons, with the new field inserted inside the form. You can disable this feature, however, if you want to use fields with scripts rather than inside forms. Click Page Options on the Tools menu, and then on the General sheet, click Automatically enclose form fields within a form to deselect the check box.

More About

Drop-Down Menus

Drop-down menus allow you to present a large number of choices in a small space. The choices do not display unless the user clicks the menu box arrow. When a choice is selected, the list of choices is hidden once again.

You have entered several text boxes on the Web page. You can toggle between Normal and Preview modes to see how the fields are aligned. Use the SPACEBAR and the table cell borders to adjust the text boxes to display as desired on the Web page. You also may preview the page in your browser as you align page elements.

The values you typed in the Name text box in the Form Field Properties dialog box will be the name portion of the name=value pair that is sent to the Web server to be processed. You should keep track of the names you use, so you do not duplicate any of the names in later form field properties.

The next section of the form contains a drop-down menu, or list box, that will indicate the major of potential club members.

Inserting a Drop-Down Menu in a Form

Recall in Table 4-1 on page FP 4.6 that a **drop-down menu** is useful when you have a variety of choices, particularly when more are available than can be handled using radio buttons. Use radio buttons when you have a small number of items.

With drop-down menus, you give each item a name and then assign a list of menu choices to the menu. You can order the menu choices by most-frequently occurring to least-frequently occurring, alphabetically, or in another sequence.

When the viewer makes a selection and clicks the Submit button, the menu name and the value associated with the selected menu choice are sent. You can select a default menu item that will be returned automatically if the viewer makes no selection. You also can make a menu item that cannot be selected by the user but is descriptive only, forcing him or her to make a selection. The following steps show how to insert a drop-down menu in the form.

More About 2000

Drop-Down Menus

To allow the selection of more than one choice, you can alter the properties of a menu. This is an alternative method to using a group of check boxes.

 Steps **To Insert a Drop-Down Menu Form Field in a Form**

---

1 **Position the insertion point in the second row and third column of table-T3, the table in the form. Type** Class & Major: **followed by a space.**

The inserted text displays in the second row and third column of the table in the form on the Join page (Figure 4-40).

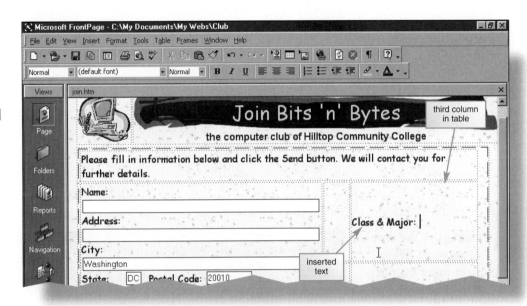

FIGURE 4-40

---

2 **Click Insert on the menu bar and then point to Form. When the Form submenu displays, point to Drop-Down Menu.**

The Form submenu displays (Figure 4-41).

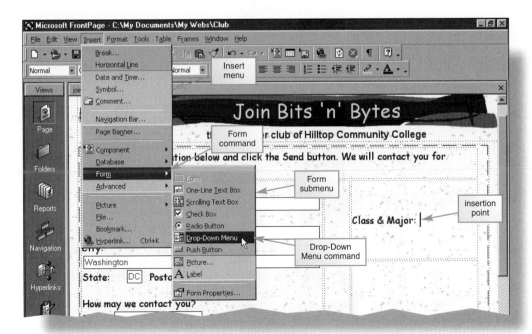

FIGURE 4-41

Click Drop-Down Menu.

A drop-down menu is inserted on the form with a default size (Figure 4-42).

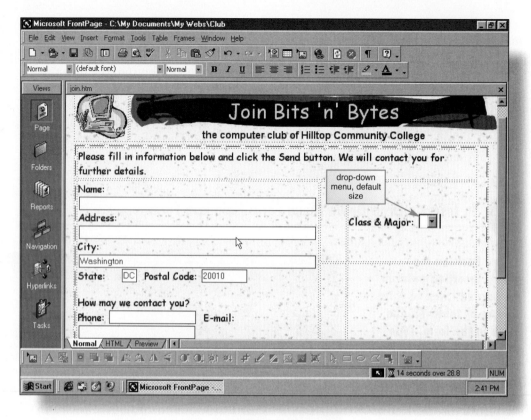

FIGURE 4-42

Right-click the drop-down menu. When the shortcut menu displays, point to Form Field Properties.

The drop-down menu form field is selected and a shortcut menu displays (Figure 4-43).

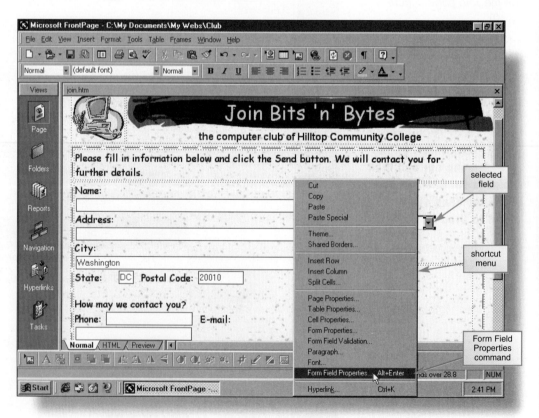

FIGURE 4-43

⑤ **Click Form Field Properties. When the Drop-Down Menu Properties dialog box displays, type** Major **in the Name text box. Point to the Add button.**

The Drop-Down Menu Properties dialog box displays (Figure 4-44).

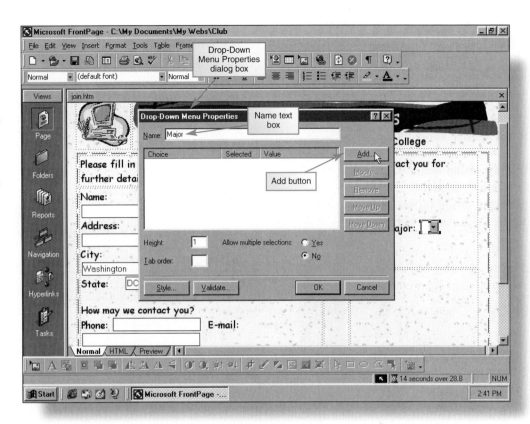

FIGURE 4-44

⑥ **Click the Add button. When the Add Choice dialog box displays, type** Select a Major **in the Choice text box. If necessary, click Not Selected in the Initial state area. Point to the OK button in the Add Choice dialog box.**

The Add Choice dialog box displays with the changes indicated (Figure 4-45).

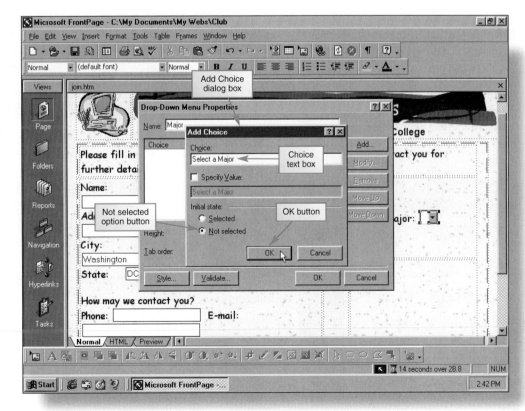

FIGURE 4-45

7 Click the OK button. Click the Add button. When the Add Choice dialog box displays, type Computer Info Sys in the Choice text box. Click Specify Value and then type CIS in the Specify Value text box. If necessary, click Not Selected in the Initial state area. Click the OK button.

The Drop-Down Menu Properties dialog box displays with the two choices added (Figure 4-46).

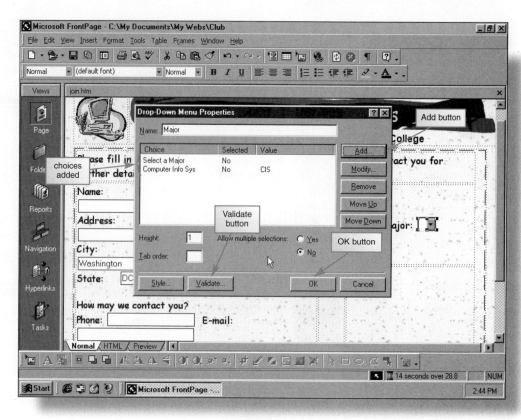

FIGURE 4-46

8 Repeat Step 7 for the remaining choices listed in Table 4-4 on page FP 4.40. Click the OK button in the Add Choice dialog box. Type 8 in the Tab order text box. Point to the Validate button.

The Drop-Down Menu Properties dialog box displays with all of the choices added (Figure 4-47).

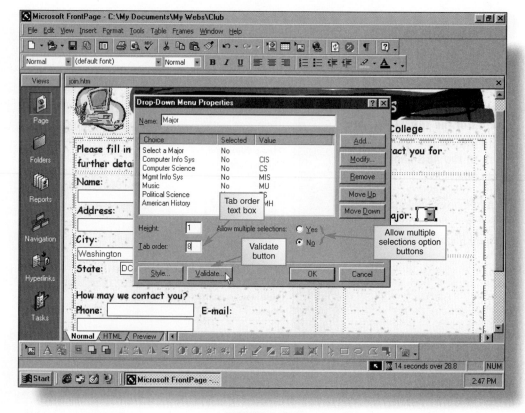

FIGURE 4-47

9 **Click the Validate button. When the Drop-Down Menu Validation dialog box displays, click Data required. Click Disallow first choice. Type** Select Major **in the Display name text box. Point to the OK button in the Drop-Down Menu Validation dialog box.**

The Drop-Down Menu Validation dialog box displays with the changes indicated (Figure 4-48).

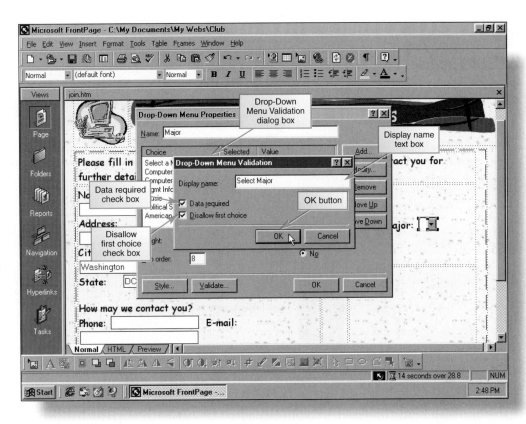

FIGURE 4-48

10 **Click the OK button. Verify that the Allow multiple selections No option button is selected. Point to the OK button in the Drop-Down Menu Properties dialog box.**

The Drop-Down Menu Validation dialog box closes, and the values entered are visible in a text box in the Drop-Down Menu Properties dialog box (Figure 4-49).

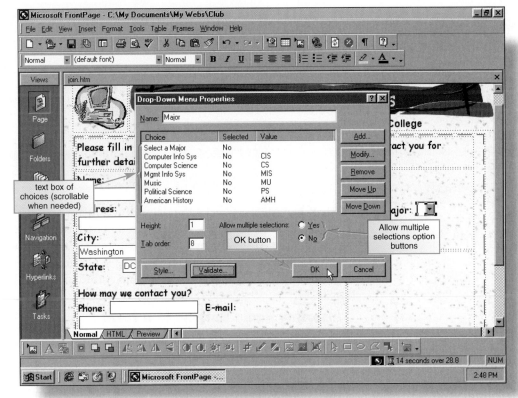

FIGURE 4-49

11 **Click the OK button. Click the Save button to save your changes.**

The first value entered is visible in the drop-down menu in the form (Figure 4-50). You should periodically save changes as you proceed through the project.

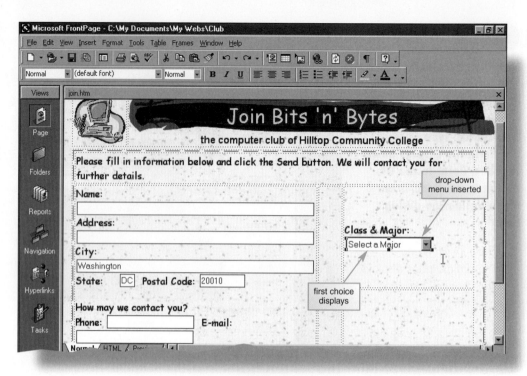

FIGURE 4-50

Other Ways

1. Press ALT+I, M, D

Table 4-4	Choices for Major Drop-Down Menu Form Field	
CHOICE TEXT BOX	**SPECIFY VALUE**	**INITIAL STATE**
Select a Major	not checked	Selected
Computer Info Sys	checked, value=CIS	Not selected
Computer Science	checked, value=CS	Not selected
Mgmt Info Sys	checked, value=MIS	Not selected
Music	checked, value=MU	Not selected
Political Science	checked, value=PS	Not selected
American History	checked, value=AMH	Not selected

When the user clicks the drop-down menu arrow, the choices just entered will display in the order they were entered. The Drop-Down Menu Properties dialog box includes the Move Up or Move Down button that allows you to move a given choice higher or lower in the list, or to delete it altogether. You also may modify a choice previously entered to change its name, value, or initial state.

Inserting Radio Buttons in a Form

Recall in Table 4-1 on page FP 4.6 that a **radio button** is useful when you must choose from among a small set of mutually exclusive options. Each radio button in a form consists of the radio button and an accompanying label. As indicated earlier, entered text can be associated as the label for a form field so that clicking the text is like clicking the form field for the user. The radio button and its label take up space on the Web page, so radio buttons are not a good choice if you have a large number of items from which to select. In such cases, a drop-down menu is the better choice.

As has been done with text, another table, table-T4, will be created to help control positioning of the radio buttons on the form. The radio buttons later will be inserted into the cells of this table. The table itself will be inserted within the cell of an already existing table, thus providing a **nested table**. You saw an example of a nested table in Project 3, where the table was imported into the project. In this case, you will create the nested table. The following steps summarize creating a nested table.

TO CREATE A NESTED TABLE

1. Right-click the table cell containing the drop-down menu. Click Cell Properties on the shortcut menu. When the Cell Properties dialog box displays, select Top in the Vertical alignment list in the Layout area. Click the OK button.

2. If necessary, position the insertion point just after the drop-down menu in table-T3. Click the Insert Table button on the Standard toolbar and then drag through three rows and two columns. Click the mouse button.

3. Right-click the table and then click Table Properties on the shortcut menu. When the Table Properties dialog box displays, type 0 in the Size text box in the Borders area. Click the OK button.

Figure 4-51 shows the FrontPage window after the nested table is inserted.

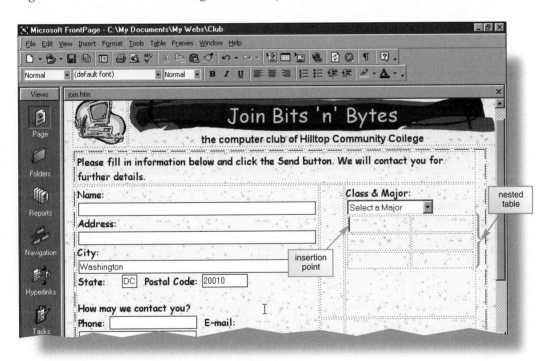

FIGURE 4-51

Related radio buttons are defined in a group. The group of buttons is given a name. The associated value assigned to the group name depends on which radio button the viewer selects.

The process of inserting radio buttons begins with the insertion and labeling of the first radio button. The label should indicate accurately which of the mutually exclusive options that radio button represents. You then adjust the properties of the radio button, assigning it to a group and identifying the value that will be sent to the Web server when a viewer clicks the Submit button.

Perform the steps on the next page to insert a radio button in a form.

Steps **To Insert a Radio Button Form Field in a Form**

1 If necessary, position the insertion point in the first row and first column of table-T4, the nested table just created. Click Insert on the menu bar and then point to Form. When the Form submenu displays, point to Radio Button.

The Form submenu displays (Figure 4-52).

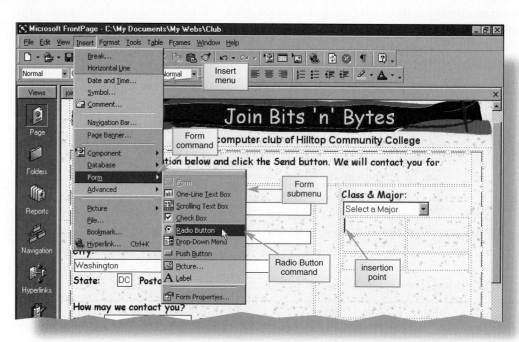

FIGURE 4-52

2 Click Radio Button.

The inserted radio button displays on the form (Figure 4-53).

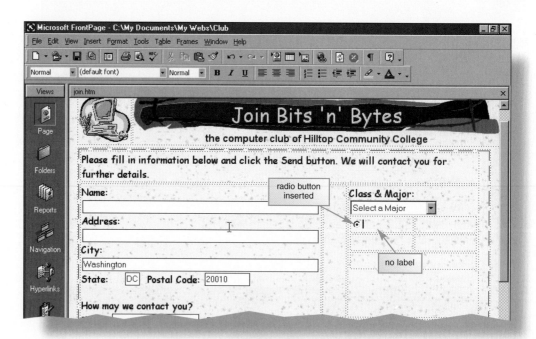

FIGURE 4-53

1. Press ALT+I, M, R

    Recall that inserting a form field inserts only the form field object, as with this radio button. You must provide a label for each form field you insert. Furthermore, just typing text next to the form field does not associate the text as a label for the field. You explicitly have to assign the text entered as the label for the field. Perform the following steps to attach a label to the radio button.

To Assign a Label to a Radio Button Form Field

1 **Type** Freshman **to the right of the radio button. Drag through both the radio button and the text to select them together. Click Insert on the menu bar and then point to Form. When the Form submenu displays, point to Label.**

The Form submenu displays (Figure 4-54).

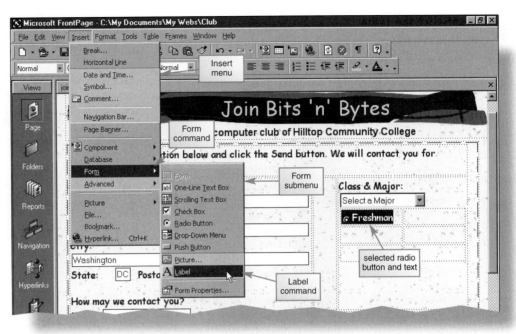

FIGURE 4-54

2 **Click Label.**

The selected text displays with a box around it, indicating that it is a label for the corresponding radio button form field (Figure 4-55).

FIGURE 4-55

Other Ways

1. Press ALT+I, M, L

Finally, you need to set some properties for the radio button, such as the value that will be returned when the radio button is selected, whether the radio button is selected by default (initial state), and the group with which the radio button will be associated. Remember that radio buttons are **mutually exclusive**; that is, selecting any radio button in a given group will deselect all of the others in that same group. Perform the steps on the next page to modify the properties of a radio button.

To Modify the Properties of a Radio Button Form Field

1 **Right-click the radio button. When the shortcut menu displays, point to Form Field Validation.**

The radio button form field is selected and a shortcut menu displays (Figure 4-56).

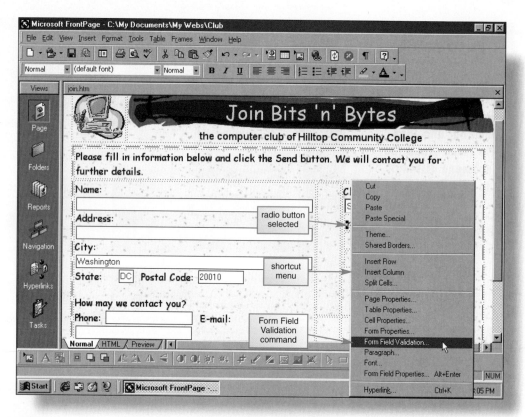

FIGURE 4-56

2 **Click Form Field Validation. When the Radio Button Validation dialog box displays, click Data required and then type** Class Rank **in the Display name text box. Point to the OK button.**

The Radio Button Validation dialog box displays with the indicated changes (Figure 4-57).

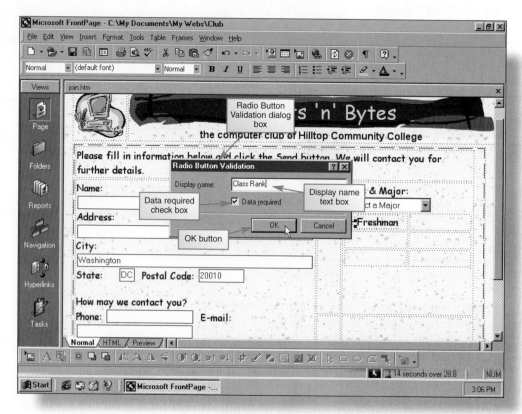

FIGURE 4-57

3 Click the OK button. Right-click the radio button. When the shortcut menu displays, point to Form Field Properties.

The radio button form field is selected and a shortcut menu displays (Figure 4-58).

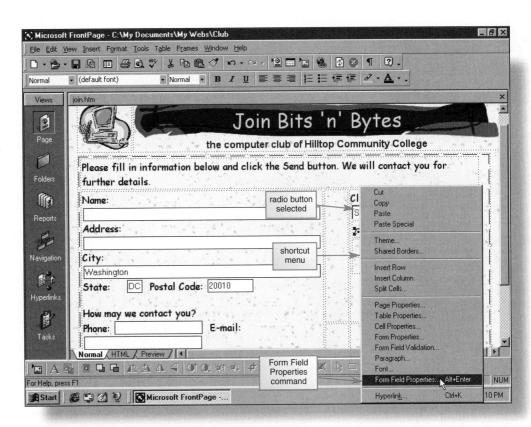

FIGURE 4-58

4 Click Form Field Properties. When the Radio Button Properties dialog box displays, type `Class` in the Group name text box, and then type `FR` in the Value text box. Verify that the Initial state Selected option button is selected. Type `9` in the Tab order text box. Point to the OK button.

The Radio Button Properties dialog box displays (Figure 4-59).

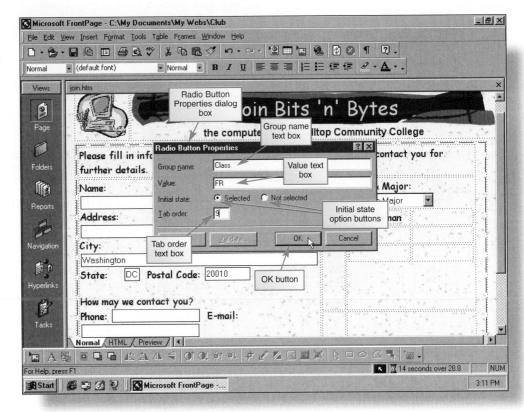

FIGURE 4-59

5 Click the OK button. For each of the radio button fields listed in Table 4-5, add the button, its label, and modify its properties accordingly. Note that the Group name for these radio buttons is determined automatically from the last value entered. Because they all belong to the same group, the validation values are already set.

The dialog boxes close and all of the Class group radio buttons and their labels display on the form (Figure 4-60).

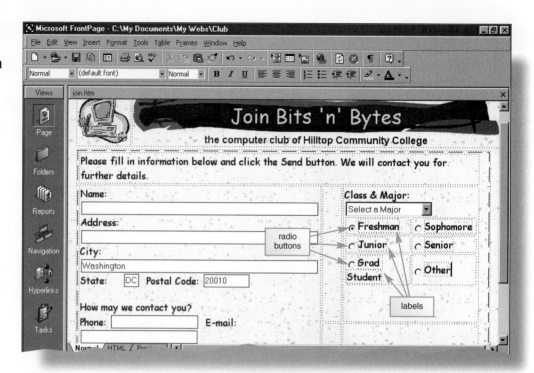

FIGURE 4-60

Other Ways

1. On Format menu click Properties
2. Press ALT+O, I
3. Press ALT+ENTER

Table 4-5	Radio Button Fields for Class Group		
LABEL	**VALUE**	**INITIAL STATE**	**TAB ORDER**
Freshman	FR	Selected	9
Sophomore	SO	Not selected	10
Junior	JR	Not selected	11
Senior	SR	Not selected	12
Grad Student	GS	Not selected	13
Other	OT	Not selected	14

You have inserted radio buttons successfully in a form on a Web page. The data you supplied in the Value text box will be sent to the form handler when the Submit button is clicked. In this form, the values of the buttons happen to be two character codes to represent the class of students. The same values as the labels of the buttons could have been used (with the elimination of any space characters), but this would increase the amount of data sent back to the form handler for processing.

Because the text for each of the radio buttons was associated as a label, rather than having to click the radio button directly, the user can click the text and the radio button will be selected. This makes selection a little easier for those users who may be mouse-challenged.

Because these radio buttons all have the same group name, in this case, Class, only one radio button can be selected, and only one value will be sent when a viewer clicks the Submit button. For example, if a viewer clicks Senior, the name=value pair is Class=SR, because Class is the name of the group of radio buttons, and the value associated with the Class radio button is the text, SR.

In Figure 4-59 on page FP 4.45, notice the two options in the Initial state area of the Radio Button Properties dialog box. The Initial state option indicates whether this radio button is active automatically when the viewer first displays the Web page. **Selected** means the radio button is displayed initially on the form as active. **Not selected** means the radio button is displayed initially on the form as inactive.

You should decide which radio button is chosen most frequently, and then set its initial state to Selected. This saves the viewer some time when filling out the form, as the radio button most frequently chosen already is active; allowing the viewer to move on to the other fields.

FrontPage allows you to create other groups of radio buttons by assigning different group names representing other data values that can be sent. Be sure to keep the groups of radio buttons together, slightly separating each group. You do not want to confuse the viewer with an unorganized collection of unrelated radio buttons.

Another group of radio buttons is to be added to the form. For help in aligning text, another nested table is needed first. To add the last table, table-T5, to the form, perform the following steps.

TO ENTER THE REMAINING TABLE FOR THE FORM

1 Position the insertion point in column 3, row 3 of table-T3. Type Do you own a computer?

2 Click the Insert Table button on the Standard toolbar and then drag through two columns and one row. Click the mouse button.

3 Right-click the table and then click Table Properties on the shortcut menu. When the Table Properties dialog box displays, type 0 in the Size text box in the Borders area. Click the OK button.

Figure 4-61 shows the FrontPage window after the insert table operation is completed. The table just inserted, table-T5, will contain the last two radio buttons and the check boxes for the form.

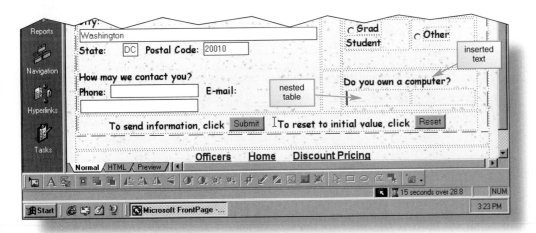

FIGURE 4-61

Now the last group of radio buttons can be added to the form. The first radio button added for this group will show a group name matching that of the last radio button inserted. After the group name is updated, any subsequent radio buttons added to the form will belong to this new group, unless the group name is modified again. It is important to make certain that this new group of radio buttons has a unique group name, different from the first group. Otherwise, all of the radio

More About

Radio Buttons

You should always indicate one radio button in a group as the default; that is, being initially selected, even though FrontPage does not force you to do so. Because radio buttons in a group are mutually exclusive, pre-selecting one button reduces confusion for your users and may reduce their data entry time.

buttons, regardless of where they are placed in the form, would all belong to the same group. In addition, when the user selects a choice in a given group, that action deselects all other radio buttons in the same group.

TO ENTER THE REMAINING RADIO BUTTONS

1 If necessary, position the insertion point in column 1 of table-T5. Click Insert on the menu bar and then point to Form. When the Form submenu displays, click Radio Button.

2 Type Yes as the label for the radio button followed by two spaces. Drag through both the radio button and the label text to select them together. Do not select the trailing spaces. Click Insert on the menu bar and then point to Form. When the Form submenu displays, click Label.

3 Right-click the radio button and then click Form Field Properties on the shortcut menu. When the Radio Button Properties dialog box displays, type Own in the group name text box and type Y in the Value text box. Verify that the Initial state Selected option button is selected. Type 15 in the Tab order text box and then click the OK button.

4 Position the insertion point after the label and trailing spaces. Click Insert on the menu bar and then point to Form. When the Form submenu displays, click Radio Button.

5 Type No as the label for the radio button. Hold down the SHIFT key and then press the ENTER key. Drag through both the radio button and the label text to select them together. Click Insert on the menu bar and then point to Form. When the Form submenu displays, click Label.

6 Right-click the radio button and then click Form Field Properties on the shortcut menu. When the Radio Button Properties dialog box displays, verify that Own is the group name. Type N in the Value text box. Verify that the Initial state Not selected option button is selected. Type 16 in the Tab order text box. Click the Validate button. When the Radio Button Validation dialog box displays, click Data required and then type Ownership in the Display name text box. Click the OK button in each dialog box.

The Web page displays with the remaining radio buttons as shown in Figure 4-62.

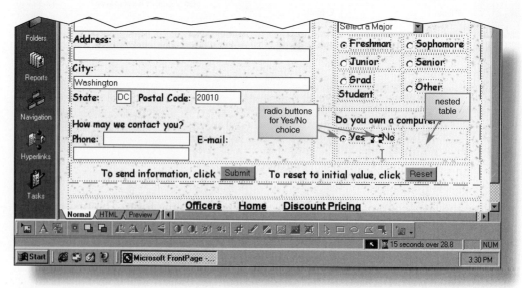

FIGURE 4-62

Inserting Check Boxes in a Form

Recall in Table 4-1 on page FP 4.6 that you use a **check box** to choose zero, one, or more choices from a set of options. The viewer can select more than one check box. Unlike radio buttons, check boxes are not mutually exclusive; that is, selecting one check box does not deselect another check box. Each check box that is selected has its name=value pair returned. If a box is not checked, nothing will be returned for that check box. This is unlike text boxes, which will return the name label even though nothing was typed in the text box. Perform the following steps to insert a check box in the form.

More About

Check Boxes

You can assign a group of related check boxes the same name and then differentiate them by their values. This way of naming them causes them to function similarly to radio buttons.

 Steps ## To Insert a Check Box Form Field in a Form

1 If necessary, position the insertion point under the Yes radio button of table-T5. Click Insert on the menu bar and then point to Form. When the Form submenu displays, point to Check Box.

The Form submenu displays (Figure 4-63).

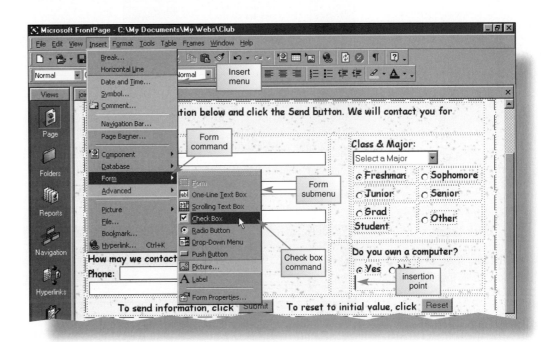

FIGURE 4-63

2 Click Check Box. Type PC as the label for the check box followed by two spaces.

The inserted check box and its label text display on the form (Figure 4-64).

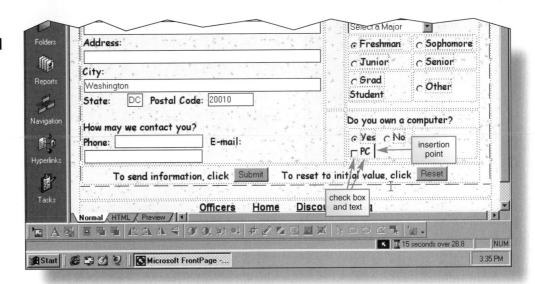

FIGURE 4-64

Drag through both the check box and the label text to select them together. Click Insert on the menu bar and then point to Form. When the Form submenu displays, point to Label.

The Form submenu displays (Figure 4-65).

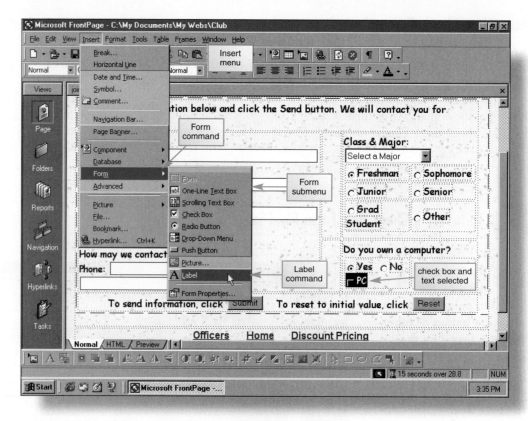

FIGURE 4-65

 Click Label.

The selected text now has a box around it, indicating that it is a label for the corresponding check box form field (Figure 4-66).

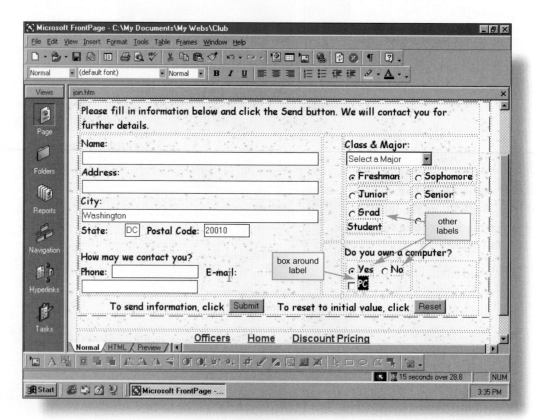

FIGURE 4-66

5 Right-click the check box and then point to Form Field Properties on the shortcut menu.

The check box form field is selected and a shortcut menu displays (Figure 4-67).

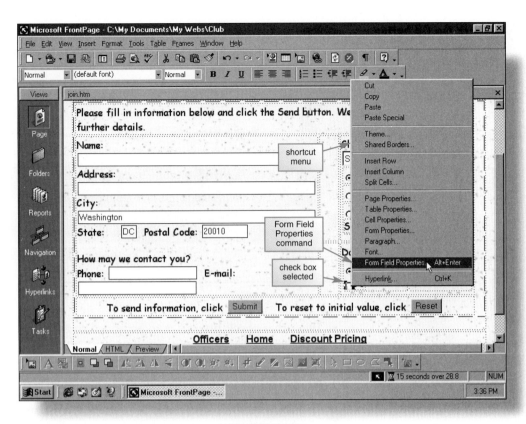

FIGURE 4-67

6 Click Form Field Properties. When the Check Box Properties dialog box displays, type OwnPC in the Name text box and type Y in the Value text box. Verify that the Initial state Checked option button is selected. Type 17 in the Tab order text box. Point to the OK button.

The Check Box Properties dialog box displays with the indicated changes (Figure 4-68).

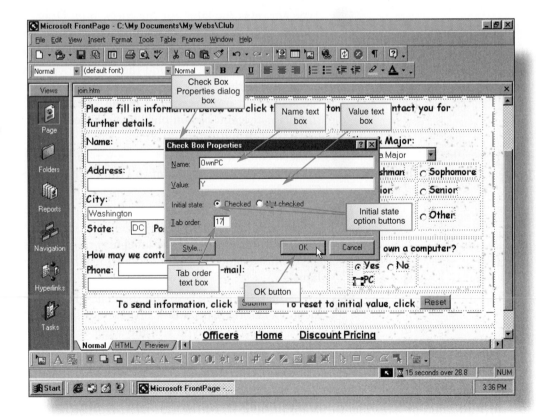

FIGURE 4-68

Microsoft FrontPage 2000

7 **Click the OK button.**

The dialog boxes close and the check box and its label appear on the form (Figure 4-69).

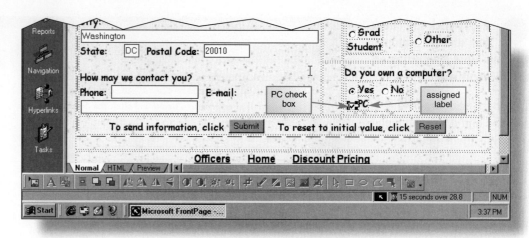

FIGURE 4-69

Other Ways

1. Press ALT+I, M, C

Two other check boxes are to be added to the form. The following steps add the remaining check boxes.

TO ENTER THE REMAINING CHECK BOXES

1 Position the insertion point after the PC label and the trailing spaces. Click Insert on the menu bar and then point to Form. When the Form submenu displays, click Check Box.

2 Type Apple as the label for the check box. Drag through both the check box and the label text to select them together. Click Insert on the menu bar and then point to Form. When the Form submenu displays, click Label.

3 Right-click the check box and then click Form Field Properties on the shortcut menu. When the Check Box Properties dialog box displays, type OwnApple in the Name text box and type Y in the Value text box. Verify that the Initial state Not checked option button is selected. Type 18 in the Tab order text box. Click the OK button.

4 Click in column 2 of table-T5 to position the insertion point. Click Insert on the menu bar and then point to Form. When the Form submenu displays, click Check Box.

5 Type CD-ROM, hold the SHIFT key and then press the ENTER key, insert four spaces and then type Drive? as the label for the check box. Drag through both the check box and all of the label text to select them together. Click Insert on the menu bar and then point to Form. When the Form submenu displays, click Label.

6 Right-click the check box and then click Form Field Properties on the shortcut menu. When the Check Box Properties dialog box displays, type CD-ROM in the Name text box and type Y in the Value text box. Verify that the) Initial state Checked option button is selected. Type 19 in the Tab order text box. Click the OK button.

7 Drag table borders and columns to adjust the form the way you want it to display on the Web page.

The Web page displays with the remaining check boxes and tables resized as shown in Figure 4-70.

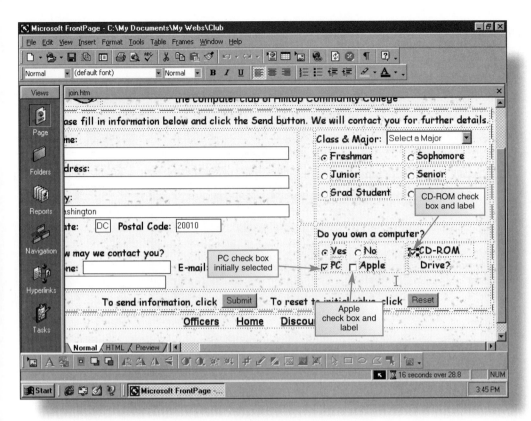

FIGURE 4-70

You have inserted check boxes in a form successfully. Notice the Check Box Properties dialog box shown in Figure 4-68 on page FP 4.51 contains no Validate button. Check boxes only can be checked or unchecked, and obviously cannot be required, so nothing needs validation.

The form is almost complete. The last two steps are to adjust the properties of the Submit and Reset buttons as needed, and to adjust the properties of the form itself.

Adjusting Form Button Properties

Two buttons usually display on every form. The buttons are Submit and Reset. The purpose of the **Submit button** is to indicate that the data entered on the form should be sent back to the Web server. Recall that the data will be in the form of name=value pairs separated by ampersands (&).

The purpose of the **Reset button** is to clear any data typed in text boxes, clear any check boxes, and change any radio buttons and menu items back to the default choices. This allows an individual to clear the form and start over.

In addition, you can add other buttons to the form and assign actions to be performed by clicking the button. The **Push Button command** on the Forms submenu allows you to add other buttons to the form. The default label for a new button is Button.

You can adjust the properties of the form buttons, such as the data value they will return, or the text label that will display in the button. In some cases, the default labels will be sufficient and no changes will be needed. Perform the steps on the next page to alter form button properties and change the text labels of the buttons.

More About

The Submit Button

Although most forms have a Submit button, you can create a form without any buttons. After filling in the data fields, the user simply presses the ENTER key to send the form data.

Steps: To Set Form Button Properties

1 **Right-click the Submit button and then click Form Field Properties on the shortcut menu.**

The Push Button Properties dialog box displays (Figure 4-71).

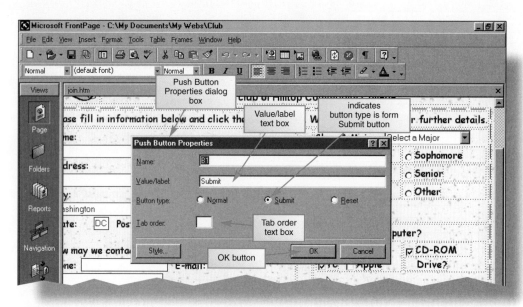

FIGURE 4-71

2 **Drag through the Value/label text box and then type Send in the text box. Type 20 in the Tab order text box. Point to the OK button.**

The old label text is replaced and the tab order is set to 20 (Figure 4-72).

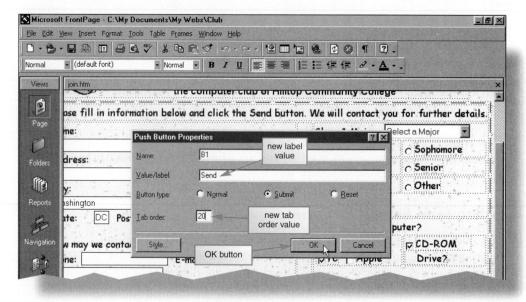

FIGURE 4-72

3 **Click the OK button.**

The new text label displays in the button (Figure 4-73).

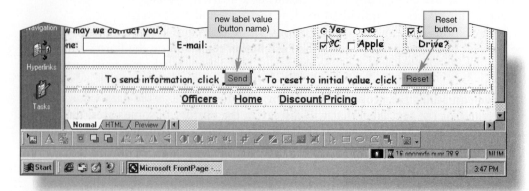

FIGURE 4-73

4 **Right-click the Reset button. Click Form Field Properties on the shortcut menu.**

The Push Button Properties dialog box displays (Figure 4-74).

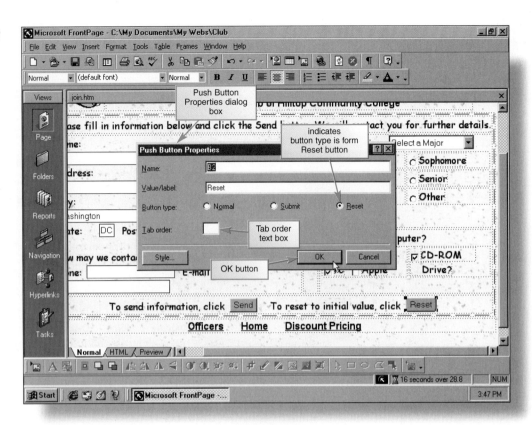

FIGURE 4-74

5 **Type 21 in the Tab order text box. Point to the OK button.**

The tab order is set to 21 (Figure 4-75).

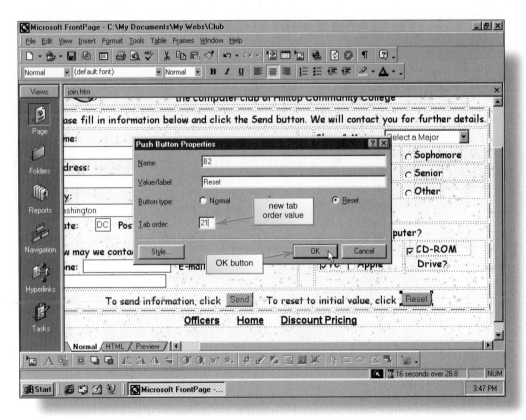

FIGURE 4-75

Click the OK button.

The completed form displays (Figure 4-76).

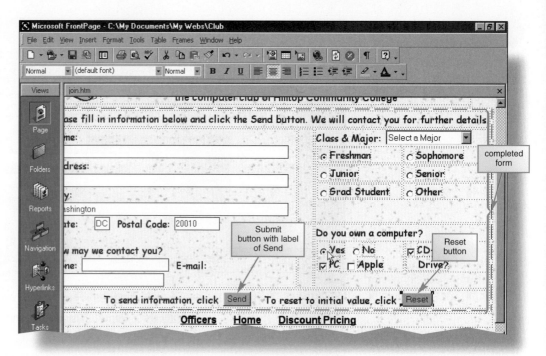

FIGURE 4-76

In the Push Button Properties dialog box shown in Figure 4-74 on the previous page, you can set a button type to be Normal, Submit, or Reset. You can use the **Normal type** to add other buttons to the form. You can assign a script to be run if a user clicks the Normal button. Be sure to give the button a name and label that correctly indicates its purpose.

When a user clicks the Submit button, it sends the form and initiates the form handler. When the form has been completely designed, you must decide how the form will be handled when a user clicks the Submit button.

Choosing the Form Handler for the Form

After a user fills out the form and clicks the Submit button, the form data is sent back to the Web server, where an appropriate form handler will be invoked to process the form data. Table 4-2 on page FP 4.7 lists the choices you have available when deciding what to do with the form data once it is sent.

Recall that the form data for the Join page is sent to an electronic mail account. You must provide the electronic mail address where the form data will be sent. The electronic mail address is contained in the form HTML tag in the Web page.

Setting the Form Properties and Form Handler

Most modern Web server software has the necessary capabilities of sending form data using electronic mail. FrontPage has additional features, or **extensions**, that provide several options to send form data. These include sending form data to a text file, to an electronic mail address, to a database, or to another form handler on the server, either a custom form handler or a specialized FrontPage form handler. FrontPage inserts special HTML codes in the form's Web page to implement the additional features. Perform the following steps to modify the form properties and choose a form handler.

To Set Form Properties

 **Right-click the form. Point to Form Properties on the shortcut menu.**

A shortcut menu displays (Figure 4-77). The *Form Properties command* allows you to change the form handler, as well as set other form properties.

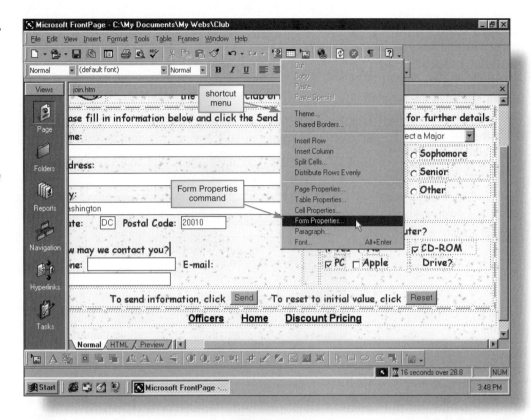

FIGURE 4-77

Click Form Properties.

The Form Properties dialog box displays (Figure 4-78). The *Form Properties dialog box* contains text boxes and option buttons that control what type of form handler you want to use with the form data.

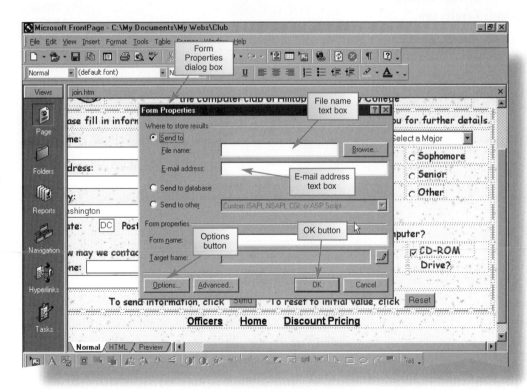

FIGURE 4-78

3 Drag through the text in the File name text box and then press the DELETE key. Click the E-mail address text box and then type your e-mail address in the text box. If you do not have an e-mail address, ask your instructor which e-mail address to use. Point to the Options button.

The Form Properties dialog box displays with the above changes (Figure 4-79).

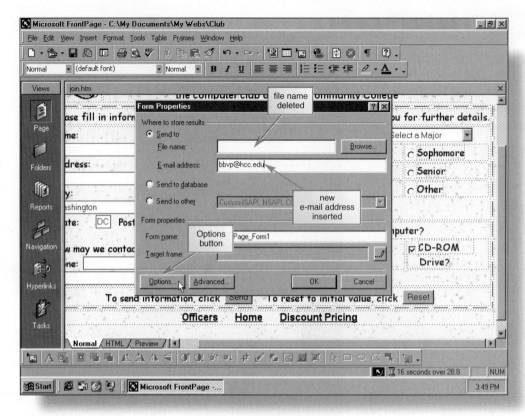

FIGURE 4-79

4 Click the Options button. Click the E-mail Results tab.

The Options for Saving Results of Form dialog box displays with the E-mail Results tab sheet shown (Figure 4-80).

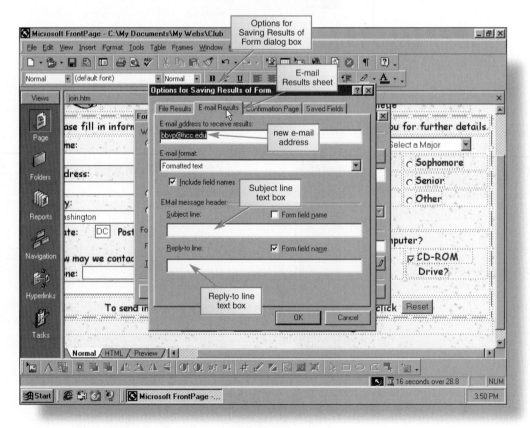

FIGURE 4-80

5 In the Subject line text box type E-mail from Bits 'n' Bytes Join Page. **The Form field name check box should not be checked. In the Reply-to line text box type** Email_Address **(use an underscore not a space; if you used a different name for the user e-mail address, enter that name instead.) The Form field name check box should be selected, as this text box contains the name of a form field. If you do not remember the name you used, you can locate them by clicking the Saved Fields tab. Point to the OK button.**

The E-mail Results tab sheet displays with the indicated changes (Figure 4-81).

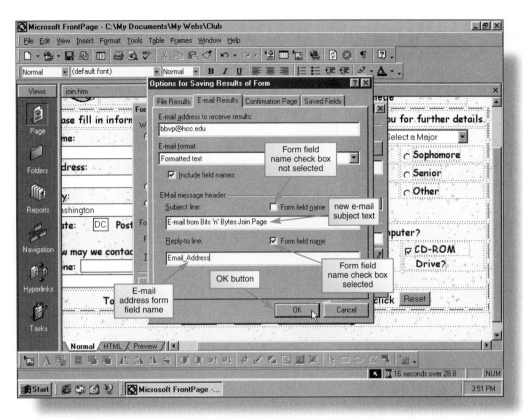

FIGURE 4-81

6 **Click the OK button in the Options for Saving Results of Form dialog box. Click the OK button in the Form Properties dialog box. When the Microsoft FrontPage dialog box displays, point to the No button.**

A Microsoft FrontPage dialog box displays indicating the server extensions have not been installed (Figure 4-82). It asks you whether you want to remove the e-mail address you just entered.

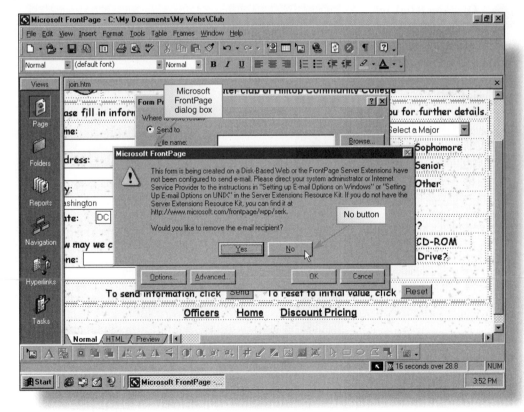

FIGURE 4-82

7 **Click the No button.**

The dialog boxes close and FrontPage displays the current page in Page view (Figure 4-83).

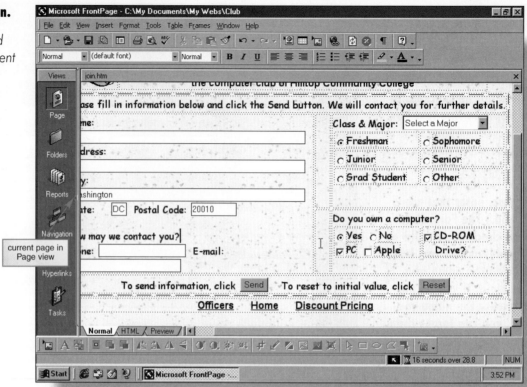

FIGURE 4-83

8 **Click the HTML tab at the bottom of the FrontPage window. If necessary, scroll toward the top of the Web page until the form HTML tag displays.**

The HTML source for the Join Web page displays (Figure 4-84). The form HTML tag displays with WEBBOT-SELF in the action tag.

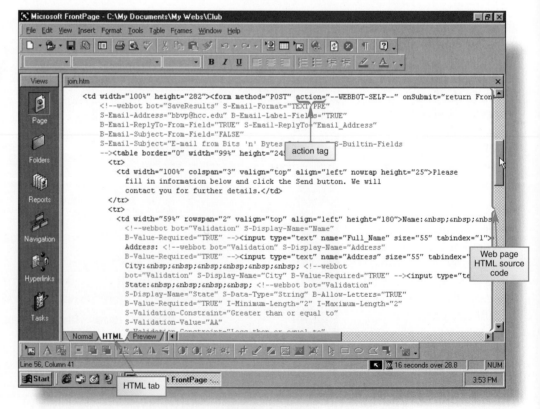

FIGURE 4-84

The Options for Saving Results of Form dialog box shown in Figure 4-80 on page FP 4.58 contains several tabbed sheets. The **Confirmation Page sheet** provides options for customizing both a confirmation page returned to the user after he or she submits the form and a failure page if an error occurs. Both are optional, as default pages are provided. The **Saved Fields sheet** allows you to choose which form fields actually are saved, as well as additional information, such as the date and time the form was submitted, the browser type, remote computer name, and user name.

You can see in the action HTML tag the reference to WEBBOT-SELF. This is the reference to the FrontPage extensions. The green HTML tags just below are the information that would be used by the FrontPage extensions to send the form data to an e-mail address. FrontPage assumes you will be using its extensions and inserts HTML tags in the Web page to take advantage of them.

Modifying HTML Code Directly

The FrontPage extensions must be installed on the Web server computer before they can be used. You might be working with a Web server, however, that does not have the Microsoft FrontPage extensions installed. This means you cannot take advantage of the special features that FrontPage has for handling forms data.

Modifying HTML Code on the HTML Sheet

Fortunately, sending form data using electronic mail is possible without the FrontPage extensions. You can change the HTML to use the basic e-mail facilities for forms and not rely on the FrontPage extensions being installed on the Web server. You will, however, have to edit the HTML directly, removing the references to the extensions that FrontPage inserts in your Web page when choosing electronic mail as the forms handler, and inserting the HTML tag for electronic mail. If you do not remove the special HTML code, the Web server software will not know what to do with your form data, and your form data will not be mailed correctly. FrontPage allows you to modify HTML code directly by using the HTML tab in the FrontPage window. Perform the steps on the next page to modify the form HTML directly in order to remove the FrontPage e-mail extension references and insert the electronic mail-HTML tag.

More About 2000

HTML Code

For resources to help you understand HTML in your Web pages better, visit the FrontPage 2000 More About Web page (www.scsite.com/fp2000/more.htm) and click HTML.

To Modify HTML Code

1 In the form tag, point to the data portion of the action= tag, beginning, "--WEBBOT.

The mouse pointer is positioned at the beginning of the text that will be replaced (Figure 4-85).

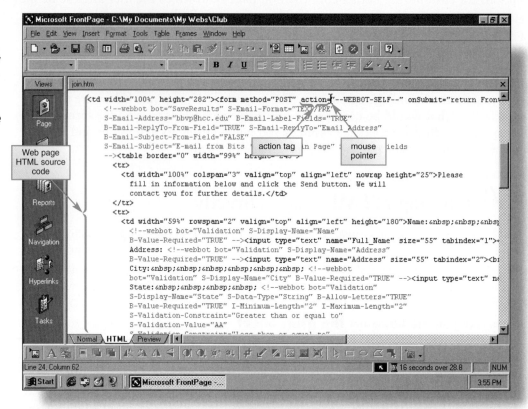

FIGURE 4-85

2 Drag through the text up to the > character just before the <table> tag.

The selected text is highlighted (Figure 4-86). The > character just before the <table> tag is the ending character of the <form> tag. Do not select it.

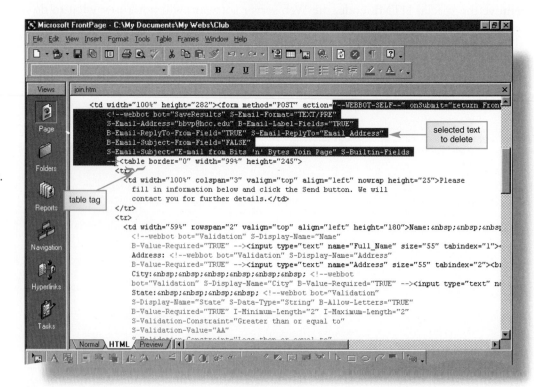

FIGURE 4-86

3 **Press the DELETE key.**

The selected text is deleted from the Web page (Figure 4-87).

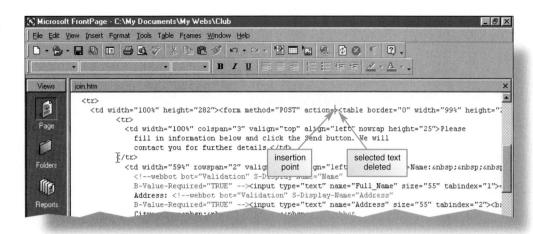

FIGURE 4-87

4 **Type** "mailto:bbvp @hcc.edu" **on the HTML Web page. Be sure to substitute your own e-mail address where you see bbvp@hcc.edu, and include the quotation marks. If you do not know which e-mail address to use, ask your instructor.**

The e-mail address displays in the action= tag (Figure 4-88). The table tag should display just after the e-mail address you typed. Be sure you have left no extra spaces, or have not removed too many characters, or your form will have errors.

5 **Click the Normal tab to display the Web page in Normal view.**

The HTML view closes and the Web page displays in Normal view.

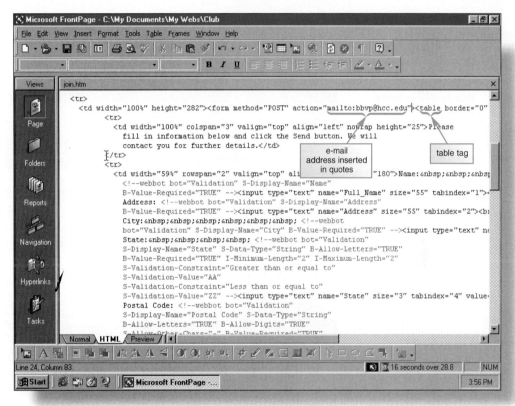

FIGURE 4-88

You have modified the form on the Join Web page to use e-mail as the form handler. Notice in the Form Properties dialog box, shown in Figure 4-78 on page FP 4.57, that you can select Send to other to use CGI scripts, or one of the other available form handling protocols. When a custom script is chosen as the form handler, the Options button allows you to specify the CGI script to be run when a user clicks the Submit button.

Saving the Web Page

When the editing of the Web page is complete, you should save it on disk. The step below saves the Web page.

TO SAVE THE WEB PAGE

 ① Click the Save button on the Standard toolbar.

The Web page is saved in the club folder on drive C (or the drive where you originally opened this web).

Other Ways

1. On File menu click Save
2. Press ALT+F, S
3. Press CTRL+S

Printing the Web Page

After saving the Web page on disk, you can print it. Perform the following steps to print the Join page.

Steps To Print the Web Page

① **Ready the printer. Click File on the menu bar and then point to Print.**

The File menu displays with the Print command highlighted (Figure 4-89).

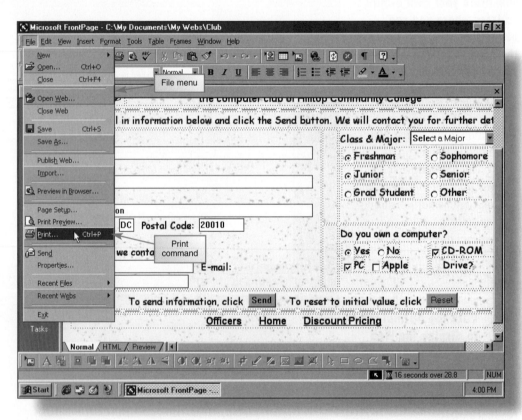

FIGURE 4-89

2 **Click Print. Point to the OK button.**

The Print dialog box displays (Figure 4-90).

3 **Click the OK button.**

When the printer stops, retrieve the printout.

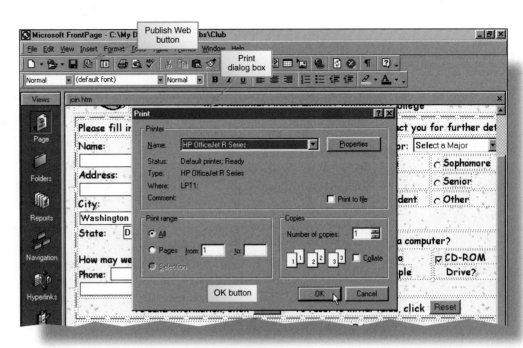

FIGURE 4-90

Publishing Changes to a FrontPage Web

In Project 3, changes to the Bits 'n' Bytes Web page were published on the World Wide Web. Because you have made additional changes to the FrontPage web, you must publish the Bits 'n' Bytes web again.

When you publish a FrontPage web that has been published before, FrontPage will install only those parts of the web that are new or have changed since the last time the web was published. This reduces the amount of data transfer that takes place, which is good for webs with many folders, Web pages, and files.

The following steps publish changes to a FrontPage web. Be sure to substitute your own URL or an error will occur. If you do not know what URL to use, ask your instructor.

TO PUBLISH CHANGES TO A FRONTPAGE WEB

1 Click the Publish Web button on the Standard toolbar.

2 When the Publish Web dialog box displays, type `ftp://www.hcc.edu/computer/club` in the Specify the location to publish your web to text box. If your Web server has the Microsoft FrontPage Server Extensions installed, you can publish using HTTP (hypertext transfer protocol). Otherwise, you must publish the web using FTP (file transfer protocol).

3 Click the Publish button.

4 Type your FTP user name and password. Click the OK button.

5 Click the Done button.

You now can view the Join page by entering http://www.hcc.edu/computer/club/join.htm in any browser and then pressing the ENTER key. Be sure to test the hyperlink to the Home page and from the Home page to the Join page.

More About

Publishing Changes

When making changes to a FrontPage web, if the changes are made directly to the Web site by opening the web on the server in FrontPage, you do not have to perform the publishing step. Only a copy of the web remains on the server, however, without a local copy for backup.

More About

Quick Reference

For a table that lists how to complete the tasks covered in this book, visit the Office 2000 Web page (www.scsite.com/off2000qr.htm) and then click Microsoft FrontPage 2000.

QUITTING FRONTPAGE When you have published the Bits 'n' Bytes web, you can quit Microsoft FrontPage. Perform the following step to quit FrontPage.

TO QUIT FRONTPAGE

 Click the Close button on the FrontPage title bar.

The FrontPage window closes and the Windows desktop displays.

CASE PERSPECTIVE SUMMARY

The officers of the Bits 'n' Bytes computer club are impressed with the different options available for collecting and saving data from potential members. While they are using only e-mail to handle form data now, they are intrigued by some of the database options available using the FrontPage extensions. They continue to be very satisfied with the progress of their Web site and look forward to development of the next page for the site.

Project Summary

Having completed Project 4, you now are ready to create interactive forms and use them to obtain information from the viewers of your Web pages. In this project, you learned about forms and form handlers. The project presented different types of form handlers. You learned about the Get and Post methods of sending form data. The format in which form data is sent was described. You learned how to create nested tables to help position form elements. You learned how to insert radio buttons, text boxes, drop-down menus, and check boxes in a form. You learned how to adjust the properties of the different types of form fields. Finally, you learned how to adjust the properties of the form and specify the form handler to be used to process the data from the form.

What You Should Know

Having completed this project, you now should be able to perform the following tasks:

- Add a New Page in Page View *(FP 4.12)*
- Add a Table to a Web Page *(FP 4.19)*
- Add and Rename a File in Folders View *(FP 4.16)*
- Assign a Label to a Radio Button Form Field *(FP 4.43)*
- Copy and Paste Hyperlinks from Another Web Page *(FP 4.20)*
- Copy and Paste Objects from Another Web Page *(FP 4.18)*
- Create a Nested Table *(FP 4.41)*
- Delete a File in Folders View *(FP 4.14)*
- Display Files in Folders View *(FP 4.13)*
- Enter the Remaining Check Boxes *(FP 4.52)*
- Enter the Remaining Radio Buttons *(FP 4.48)*
- Enter the Remaining Table for the Form *(FP 4.47)*
- Enter the Remaining Text Box Fields *(FP 4.32)*
- Hide the Folder List Pane *(FP 4.22)*
- Insert a Check Box Form Field in a Form *(FP 4.49)*
- Insert a Drop-Down Menu Form Field in a Form *(FP 4.35)*
- Insert a Form in a Table *(FP 4.24)*
- Insert a Radio Button Form Field in a Form *(FP 4.42)*
- Insert a Table in a Form *(FP 4.25)*
- Insert Text Box Form Fields in a Form *(FP 4.28)*
- Insert Text in a Form *(FP 4.26)*
- Modify a Page Title in Folders View *(FP 4.17)*
- Modify HTML Code *(FP 4.62)*
- Modify the Properties of a Radio Button Form Field *(FP 4.44)*
- Modify the Text and URL of a Hyperlink *(FP 4.22)*
- Open an Existing FrontPage Web *(FP 4.10)*
- Print the Web Page *(FP 4.64)*
- Publish Changes to a FrontPage Web *(FP 4.65)*
- Quit FrontPage *(FP 4.66)*
- Save the Web Page *(FP 4.64)*
- Set Form Button Properties *(FP 4.54)*
- Set Form Properties *(FP 4.57)*
- Start FrontPage *(FP 4.10)*

Apply Your Knowledge

1 Adding Security to a Web Page

Note: This assignment requires access to a server with FrontPage extensions installed.

Instructions: Start FrontPage 2000 and perform the following steps with a computer.

1. Open the one-page web RegSales that you modified in Project 3. If you did not complete that assignment, see your instructor for a copy.
2. Publish the local web to a server with FrontPage extensions installed. Close the local web.
3. Open the web on the server where you just published it. It must be opened on the server, not locally, or the security tools will not be available.
4. Click Tools on the menu bar, point to Security, and then click Permissions on the Security submenu.
5. In the Permissions – FP2000/RegSales dialog box, click Unique permissions for this web. Click the Apply button. The permissions are updated on the server.
6. Click the User tab. Click Only registered users have Browse access. Click the Add button.
7. In the Add Users dialog box, type Sales01 in the Name text box. Type topgun in the Password text box and also in the Confirm password text box. Note that for increased security, asterisks appear in place of the letters as you type in a password. If you are using a Windows NT Server running IIS (Internet Information Services), you cannot add users; you must select existing users from a list provided by domain or group from the server. Additionally, your webs must be hosted on an NTFS partition, not a FAT partition. See FrontPage Help for further details.
8. In the Allow users to area, click Browse this web as the appropriate level of access for this user. Click the OK button.
9. The added user name and his or her access rights display in the Permissions dialog box. Click the OK button. The changes are updated to the server.
10. Test your page by opening your browser and pointing it to the web you just published. You should be asked to supply a user name and password before you can browse this web.
11. The project is shown in Figure 4-91 on the next page with the Permissions – FP2000/RegSales dialog box displayed. Save the Web page. Print the Web page, write your name on it, and hand it in to your instructor.

(continued)

Apply Your Knowledge

➕ Project Reinforcement at www.scsite.com/off2000/reinforce.htm

Adding Security to a Web Page *(continued)*

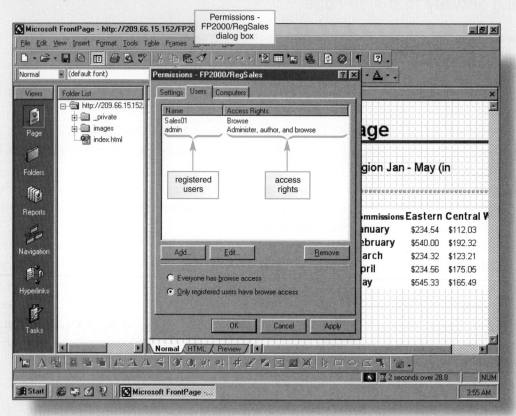

FIGURE 4-91

In the Lab

1 Using Form Fields to Collect Data

Problem: Your Parts Web page created earlier for your automobile parts mail-order business, is working out quite well, but you need to be able to collect delivery information from customers. Fortunately, your Home page already has a link to a Delivery page. Now you just need to develop it. Note: to fully implement this assignment, you need access to a Web server with FrontPage extensions.

Instructions: Perform the following activities to create the Parts 'n' Parcel Delivery page.

1. Start FrontPage and open the Parts 'n' Parcel web from Project 3. If you did not complete that assignment, see your instructor for a copy.

In the Lab

2. Create a new page. Save it as delivery.htm. Copy and paste the top table with its graphics and the horizontal line from the Home page to the Delivery page.
3. Below the table, insert a form. In the form, insert fields for Name, Address, City, State, and Postal Code. Insert two groups of radio buttons, one for delivery options (U.S. Mail, UPS, FedEx, etc.) and another for major credit card options, such as MasterCard, Visa, Discover, etc. Insert two text fields (double entry to avoid mistakes) for the user to enter a credit card number. These fields should be password-protected. Use tables as necessary to align items. Enter appropriate labels for fields.
4. Enter a check box field to allow the user to select insurance for the delivery and indicate the insurance rate (e.g., $3 per each $100 or fraction thereof ordered).
5. Insert a scrolling text box for entry of the order. Indicate that the user should enter part numbers and brief descriptions for items ordered.
6. Type Place Order as the label for the Submit button. Type Clear Form as the label for the Reset button.
7. Set the form handler to add the data sent to a text file.
8. Make appropriate text captions and labels for fields. Your page should resemble the one shown in Figure 4-92.
9. Save and publish the Web page. Print the Web page, write your name on it, and hand it in to your instructor.

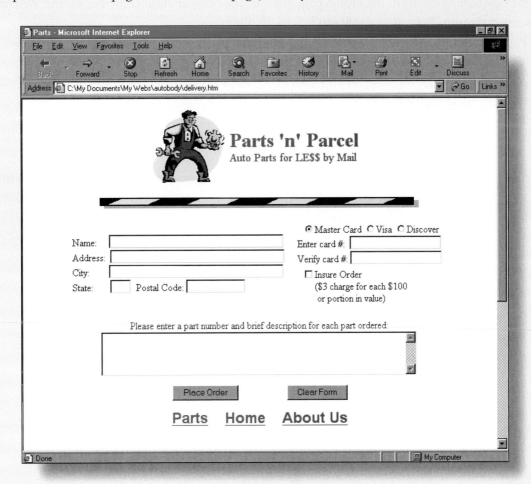

FIGURE 4-92

In the Lab

2 Adding a Discussion Forum to a Web

Problem: Rather than repeatedly answer e-mails containing the same questions, the coach of the Westchester Little League team would like a discussion forum added to the League Web site. He also would like the link on its Home page changed from an e-mail link to a hyperlink to the Welcome page of the discussion forum.

Instructions: Start FrontPage 2000 and perform the following steps using a computer.

1. Open the Westchester Little League web from Project 3. If you do not have that assignment, see your instructor for a copy.
2. Click File on the menu bar and then point to New. Click Web on the New submenu. When the New dialog box displays, double-click the Discussion Web Wizard icon. Click Add to current web and then click the OK button.
3. Follow the instructions in the Discussion Web Wizard, selecting the defaults. For the descriptive title, type Ask The Coach! Select Subject, Comments for the fields for the Submission form. Allow anyone to post articles and order them from oldest to newest. Do not make the Table of Contents page the Home page. Select Subject, Size, Date, and Score for the Search Form. Select Dual interface for the Frames Options.
4. Copy the baseball image from the Home page (or use one of your choice) for use on the Welcome page of the discussion forum. Place it in a table to help with alignment.
5. In the Page Properties dialog box, set the background color for each of the pages in the discussion forum to an appropriate color. This may be seen as the team color, matching a color from the inserted baseball image. Be sure to change the color of all pages in the discussion forum, including the version on the No Frames tab of the Discussion page.
6. Edit the Home page, removing the e-mail link and text. Modify the text in the baseball image to reflect the title of the discussion forum. Make the entire image a hyperlink to the Welcome page of the discussion forum.
7. Click the Save button on the Standard toolbar. Be sure to save new embedded images, if any, in the images folder with unique names. Your discussion Welcome page and modified Home page should resemble those in Figure 4-93a and Figure 4-93b.
8. Publish the Web pages. Print the new Web pages and the modified Home page, write your name on them, and hand in your work to your instructor.

In the Lab

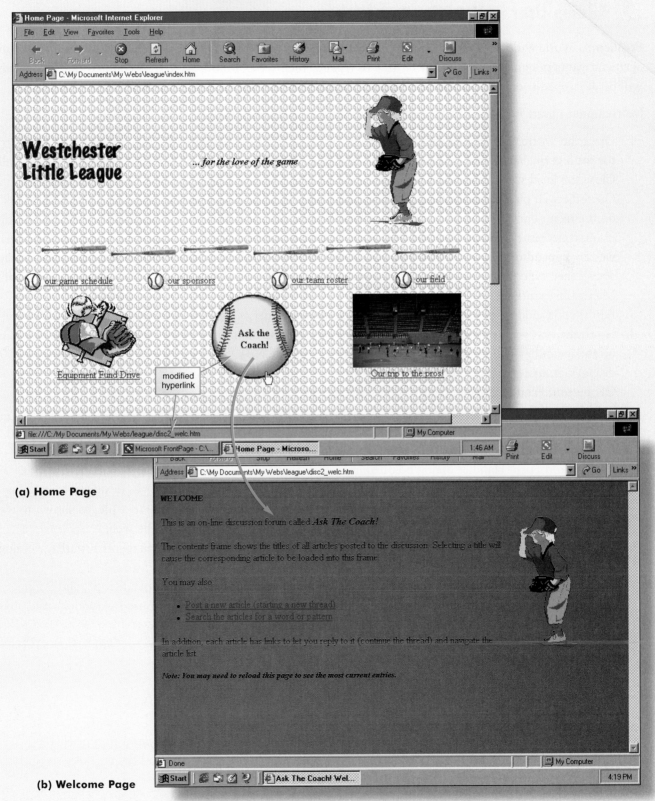

(a) Home Page

(b) Welcome Page

FIGURE 4-93

In the Lab

3 Adding User Registration to a Web

Problem: WorldWide Travel wants to encourage additional business for its Web site. As an incentive, the management wants potential customers to be able to register themselves for access to a discounted fares page, which will be developed soon. This assignment requires access to a Web server with FrontPage extensions.

Instructions: Start FrontPage 2000 and perform the following steps using a computer.

1. Open the WorldWide Travel web from Project 3. If you did not complete that assignment, see your instructor for a copy. Verify that you have published the local web to a server with FrontPage extensions installed. Close the local web.

2. Open the web on the server where you just published it. It must be opened on the server, not locally. Click File on the menu bar and then point to New. Click Web on the New submenu. When the New dialog box displays, if necessary, double-click the One Page Web icon. Specify a location under the location of the current web by appending the new web name (e.g., if the location of your current web is http://www.myserver.com/Travel then type http://www.myserver.com/Travel/Discounts as the new location). A second copy of Microsoft FrontPage will open.

3. Edit the file index.htm to reflect a discount page that is under construction. Save and then close this web.

4. Go to the first web, opened in step 2. This web now will be the root web for the Discounts web. Click File on the menu bar and then point to New. Click Page on the New submenu. When the New dialog box displays, if necessary click the General tab, double-click the User Registration icon and then click the OK button. FrontPage will create a Registration Page with a user registration form and assign to it the registration form handler.

5. Right-click the form and then click Form Properties on the shortcut menu. Note that Send to other and Registration Form Handler already are selected. Click the Options button. When the Options for Registration Form Handler dialog box displays, click the Registration tab. In the Web name text box, type Discounts which is the name of the subweb previously created. Click the File Results tab and note the location of the saved results in the File name text box and the format of the text file, as shown in the File format list. By default, the text file will be located in the _private folder of the web.

6. Click the OK button in each of the dialog boxes. Click the OK button in the Microsoft FrontPage dialog box.

7. Customize the form by adding fields such as Full Name, Address, City, State, Postal Code, and Phone. Modify other text as appropriate and delete unwanted text on the page. Customize instructions and change field labels as needed. Save the form as register.htm.

8. Modify the form Page Properties and type You can automatically register yourself for savings! for the title.

9. Open the Home page, index.htm. In the empty table cell above the e-mail link, Type Register for Discounts! Highlight and make this a hyperlink to register.htm. See Figures 4-94a and 4-94b for an example of the modified Home page and Registration page.

10. Save all Web pages. Because the pages were modified on the server, you do not need to republish the Web. Print the Home page and Registration page, write your name on them, and hand them in to your instructor.

In the Lab

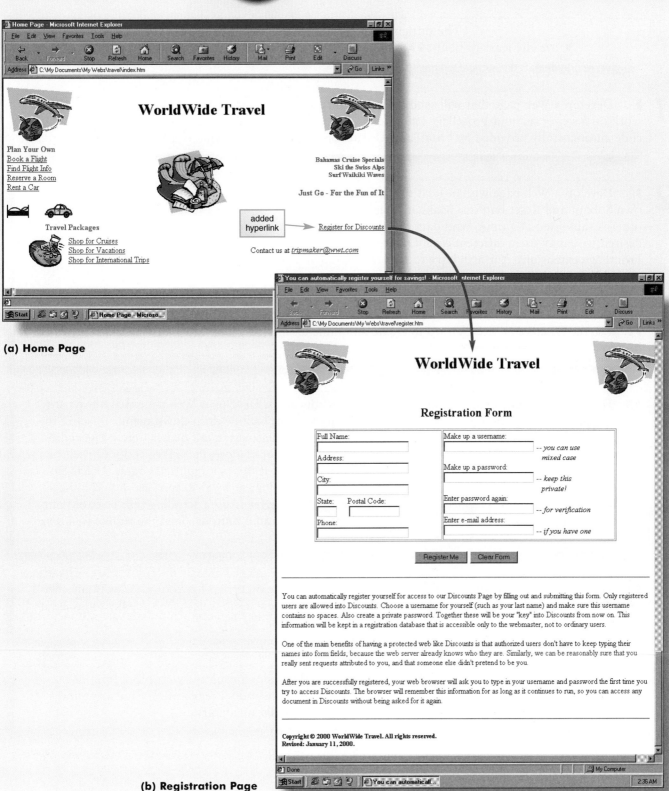

(a) Home Page

(b) Registration Page

FIGURE 4-94

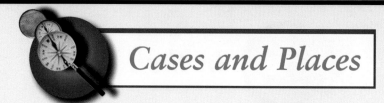

Cases and Places

The difficulty of these case studies varies:
▶ are the least difficult; ▶▶ are more difficult; and ▶▶▶ are the most difficult.

1 ▶ Develop a Web page that will send data from a form to an e-mail address of your choice. It should work on a server without FrontPage extensions. You will have to remove the e-mail extensions HTML code automatically provided by FrontPage. Use at least three different types of form fields in the form.

2 ▶ Develop a Web page with at least two different forms on the same page. Each form will have its own Submit and Reset buttons. Make it visually clear that the forms are exclusive - only one or the other is submitted at a time. Send data from either form to an e-mail address of your choice. If so desired, you may use a different e-mail address for each form. It should work on a server without FrontPage extensions. You will have to remove the e-mail extensions HTML code automatically provided by FrontPage.

3 ▶▶ Use the Discussion Web Wizard to create an online discussion group for your class. Let entries be browsed or posted by anyone.

4 ▶▶ Feedback from class participants is important to educators. Develop a Web page that allows students to provide evaluations for courses in a university system. Include drop-down menus to select the department, the course number, section, and the term (e.g., fall semester, fall quarter, etc.). Use radio buttons in groups to allow choices for class rank (Freshman, Sophomore, etc.), the school of their major, the gender of the student, their expected grade, and to indicate if this is a required course. Use radio buttons to select responses to the set of questions as shown in Figure 4-95. Responses should indicate Strongly Agree, Agree, Undecided, Disagree, and Strongly Disagree. Add a scrolling text box for comments. Use appropriate captions. Assign labels to appropriate radio buttons. Send the results to a text file.

5 ▶▶▶ Use the Discussion Web Wizard to create an online discussion group for your class as in number 3 above, but now limit participation to registered users. Add a few users to test the site. Try to access it without a valid user name and/or password.

6 ▶▶▶ Use the Discussion Web Wizard to create an online discussion group for your class, limiting participation to registered users as in number 5 above. This time, add a registration page using the Registration template to allow users to add themselves to the discussion group.

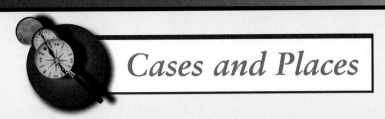

Cases and Places

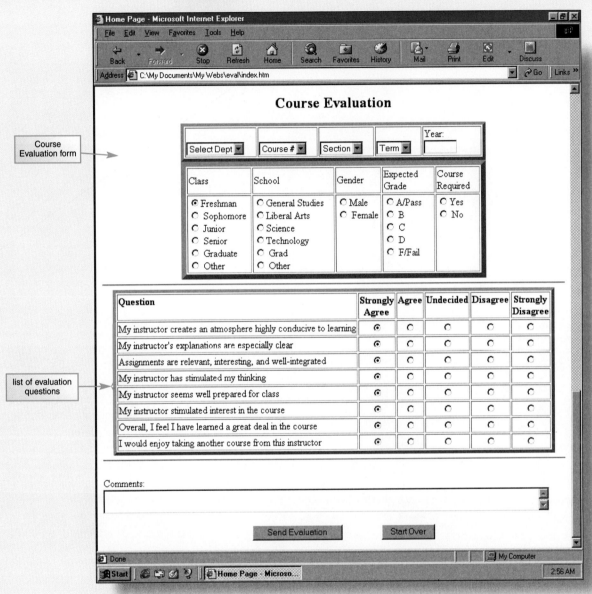

Course
Evaluation form

list of evaluation
questions

FIGURE 4-95

Microsoft FrontPage 2000

PROJECT

5

Using Frames in Web Pages

You will have mastered the material in this project when you can:

- Describe frames Web pages and explain how they work
- Import files into an existing FrontPage web
- Use a frames template
- Save a frames Web page
- Use an existing Web page as the initial page in a frame
- Adjust the size of a frame
- Create an initial Web page for a frame
- Use tables in a frame to position elements
- Modify properties of a frame
- Modify properties of a frames page
- Create hyperlinks to pages in a frame
- Display the No Frames view
- Add a bevel effect to an image
- Open the target of a link in a different frame
- Use a Word document as a URL
- Create a thumbnail image from a larger image
- Use Find and Replace across a Web site
- Use reporting features of FrontPage
- Verify hyperlinks in a web

Web Page Design Flexibility

FrontPage Leads the Way

O n his first day as New Media Architect, Eric Horr was given the assignment by his manager at Ericsson, Inc. to help more than one thousand employees share information in the company and with the rest of the world as soon as possible. For Eric it was not a problem; he would use his FrontPage web development skills.

Working at Ericsson's Research Triangle Park (RTP) facility in North Carolina, Horr was recruited specifically to enhance the company's intranet, consisting of more than 4,000 pages of jumbled information the day he arrived. The task was monumental, but Horr was prepared.

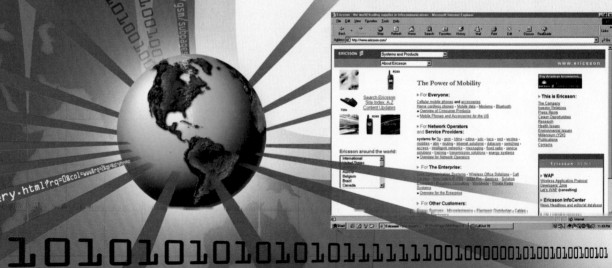

ERICSSON

Submit Search

Swedish-based Ericsson is a world-leading supplier of telecommunications and data communications equipment, offering advanced communications solutions for mobile and fixed networks, as well as consumer products. Ericsson has more than 100,000 employees, representation in 140 countries, and the world's largest customer base in the telecommunications field. Ericsson connects nearly 40 percent of the world's mobile callers.

Its largest single market is the United States, where demand for its mobile telephones and cellular systems has driven the company's profits skyward. European countries account for 50 percent of the company's net sales.

Horr worked with the information systems group, who had developed this initial intranet, to devise a solution. First, he analyzed the situation. The RTP site supports Ericsson's worldwide workforce in various business units, including research and development, quality assurance, sales, marketing, and human resources. Employees use Microsoft Office applications and access the intranet to collaborate on projects, obtain benefits information, manage deadlines, project sales, and develop marketing strategies.

The problem was that the intranet lacked organization and had limited capabilities. Employees could not perform a global search and replace or a global spell check, so verifying information or correcting data, such as an employee's new telephone number, had to be done manually, page by page. Navigational links were difficult to verify and individual pages were unstructured.

Horr believed that FrontPage was the obvious software to resolve these difficulties because he was familiar with the program and the employees were familiar with Microsoft Office applications. He developed a two-step process to complete the task. First, he created a new FrontPage web, and second, he moved the root directory for the existing site into FrontPage.

In creating the intranet, he decided to bypass FrontPage's default themes, which you learned about in Project 1. Instead, in four hours, he created the initial custom theme using unique backgrounds, graphics, and templates that reflect Ericsson's image and mission.

The new intranet consists of 2,000 pages, which is less than one-half the number of pages on the original intranet. Part of this reduction occurred because employees used FrontPage to sort files and eliminate duplicate pages. It contains tables and frames resembling those you will create in Project 5.

Horr delegated the task of posting information to each RTP business unit. Training was minimal if the Web administrators already were familiar with Microsoft Office applications. These employees claim they now can create Web content up to 50 percent more quickly using FrontPage instead of the former system.

Thus far, you have learned to use templates, add graphics, and design forms. Now, with your knowledge of creating frames in this project, you will enhance your skills and develop spectacular Web sites quickly and efficiently.

Microsoft FrontPage 2000

Using Frames in Web Pages

P R O J E C T

5

CASE PERSPECTIVE

The work you have done on the Web site for the Bits 'n' Bytes computer club is almost complete. One additional page for the initial web is needed, the club Officers page. For this page, the officers want to include some informal pictures and information about themselves, as well as a link to the Draft Charter, which describes their official roles. The charter is in draft form, and the officers want members to be able to view it, print it, and save it. The Charter then can be edited for use in future meetings. Consequently, they have provided the draft as a Word document, not in HTML. You have been given a number of graphic files, with most of them already incorporated on individual pages for each officer. The exceptions are some vacation photos taken by the Treasurer. He wants these photos included on his personal page, but was concerned about their size. For that reason, you decide to provide a thumbnail of the pictures, which will allow a user to link to the original picture if desired. Likewise, you decide to use frames for ease of navigation between pages, avoiding necessary reloading of large graphics.

Introduction

You have created Web pages consisting of single pages with links to other single pages. While this is fairly simple, it allows your users to view only one page at a time. The reason is that normal Web pages display in the entire browser window. Each new Web page replaces the previous Web page in the browser. Using frames gives you the ability to divide the browser window into multiple regions, or panes. A **frame** is an independent region within a browser window that can act independently of other regions in the window. Frames originally were created by Netscape as an HTML extension and now are a part of the HTML specification. Each frame can be given an individual URL, so it can load information independent of the other frames on the page; can be given a name, allowing it to be targeted by other URLs, and; can resize dynamically if the user changes the window's size, or can have its sizing disabled, ensuring a constant frame size.

Frames provide greater flexibility in Web page design. With frames, you can display several Web pages in the same browser window with each Web page displaying in its own frame. Also, if your pages share many of the same links, it may involve a lot of duplication to create and maintain these links when they are in normal pages. With frames, you can use a page in one frame to control what displays within another frame. Thus, you could put the common links in one frame where they would always be displayed, and display the target Web pages in another frame, where each new target page displayed would replace the previous one. A typical example of a frames application might be displaying a table of contents consisting of hyperlinks in one frame and displaying the corresponding Web pages in another. You can place products for sale in one frame and display the accompanying descriptions and details in another. You can place vocabulary words in one frame and display their definitions in another.

Elements the user always should see, such as copyright notices and title graphics, can be placed in a static frame by using frames. As the user navigates the site, the static frame's contents remain fixed, even though adjoining frames redraw. Placing frames side by side also would allow queries to be posed and answered on the same page, with one frame holding the query form and another presenting the results.

Frames are defined in HTML with the FRAMESET and FRAME tags. Although browsers that are compliant with the current HTML specification now handle frames, you may get requests from browsers that do not support them or possibly from users that prefer a nonframes version. Many sites that use frames may have an alternative scheme of pages for such nonframe requests.

Project Five — Creating and Using Frames

Creating and coordinating frames is a more complex process than creating regular, nonframe Web pages. Not only must you create the frames Web page, but you also must have an initial, default Web page for each frame in the browser window. In addition, all the Web pages that can be displayed in the various frames must exist. Normally, hyperlinks for these pages are located in one or more of the frames.

To facilitate this process, Microsoft FrontPage includes several ready-to-use frame templates, each of which contains a variety of frames of various sizes. Recall from Project 1 that a **template** is one or more Web pages that have been organized and formatted with a basic framework of content on which new Web pages can be built. You can select from one of the templates and customize it to suit your needs and even save the customized version as a new template. In addition, you can resize the existing frames in the template, and you can add new frames using the mouse and/or special key combinations.

In this project, you will learn how to use frames by creating the club Officers pages shown in Figures 5-1a through 5-1d on the next two pages. The Officers pages introduce the three officers of the club to the public. The pages use frames to display personal information as well as selected pictures of each officer. You created hyperlinks to the main Officers page from the Bits 'n' Bytes Home page. Before you begin modifying the Officers page, however, you should familiarize yourself with some important concepts and definitions about frames.

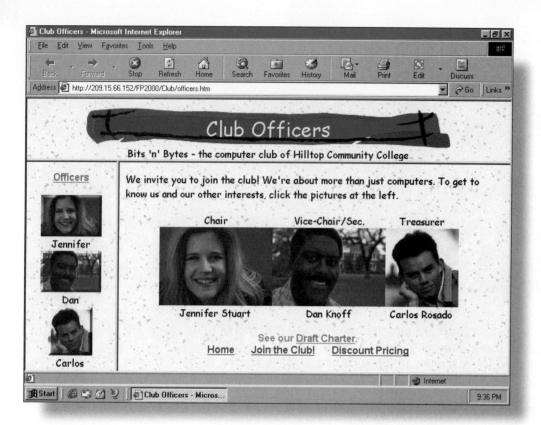

(a) Frames Web Page

(b) Chair Personal Information Web Page

FIGURE 5-1

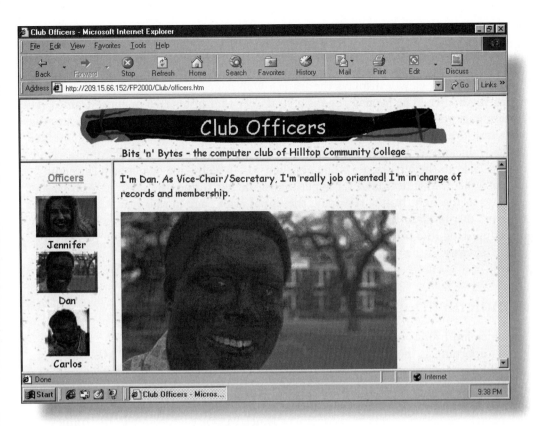

(c) Vice-Chair Personal Information Web Page

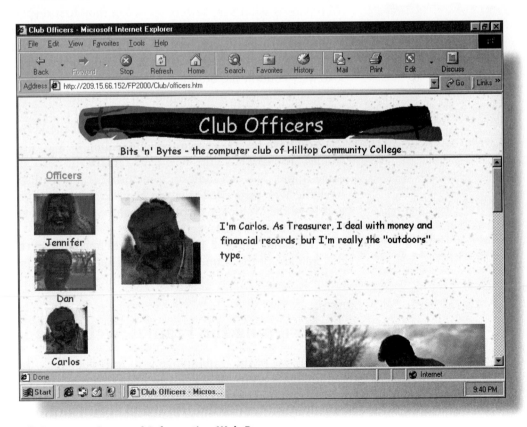

(d) Treasurer Personal Information Web Page

FIGURE 5-1 (continued)

Using Frames Pages

To use frames, a viewer displays the frames Web page by clicking a hyperlink or supplying a URL. The **frames page** is a container that holds two or more frames. The frames page itself has no visible content. It simply specifies which other pages to display and how to display them. An initial Web page displays in each frame contained in the frames page. For example, in a two-frame Web page, a table of contents page may display in the left frame, while another initial Web page displays in the right frame. When the viewer clicks a hyperlink in the left frame, the selected Web page displays in the right frame, replacing the initial Web page in that frame. The table of contents displayed in the left frame remains the same. The viewer can select another hyperlink from the table of contents and the corresponding Web page replaces the page currently in the right frame.

Implementing Frames

Implementing frames requires the coordination of several Web pages. The first, and most important, is the frames page. The frames page contains the HTML tags describing the number, sizes, and orientation of the frames that will display in the browser window. It also contains the URLs of the initial Web pages that will display in each frame. Normally, it has no other HTML content.

Next, one complete HTML document is needed for each frame in the frames page. This HTML document will serve as the **initial Web page** for that frame. This Web page is what the viewers see when they first display the frames page.

Finally, you need the **target Web pages** that could be displayed in a frame. Hyperlinks to these Web pages could display somewhere within one of the initial Web pages. These hyperlinks not only contain the URL of the target Web page, but also may contain the destination frame, referred to as a **target frame**, as one of its tags. This allows you to designate which frame to use to display the Web page. Also, a default frame target may be specified for all links within a particular frame by a special **base target** tag in the header section of the HTML document.

You have several choices when deciding how to display Web pages when using frames. You can have the Web page replace the currently displayed Web page in the same frame. You can indicate some other frame to display the Web page. You can have the Web page use the entire browser window. You can open another window and have the Web page display in the new browser window, keeping the original window's contents intact.

You can create the initial Web pages and the target Web pages before or during the creation of the frames Web page. The frames template has buttons that allow you to select a preexisting page or create a new page.

Designing the Frames Web Page

The purpose of the frames page is to introduce the officers of the Bits 'n' Bytes computer club. This frames page will include three frames, one with hyperlinks to Web pages containing personal information about each officer. This page is named the Officers page. Figure 5-2(a) and 5-2(b) illustrate the design.

More About

Web Page Design

For more ideas to help in designing your Web page visit the FrontPage 2000 More About Web page (www.scsite.com/fp2000/more.htm) and click Web Page Design.

More About

Designing Frames Pages

Although most modern browsers support frames, some users either may not have the latest browser version, or may not like to use frames. To appeal to the broadest market, you may want to offer an alternative set of pages for your site that does not use frames. By doing so, users can choose the format they want to employ for viewing your site.

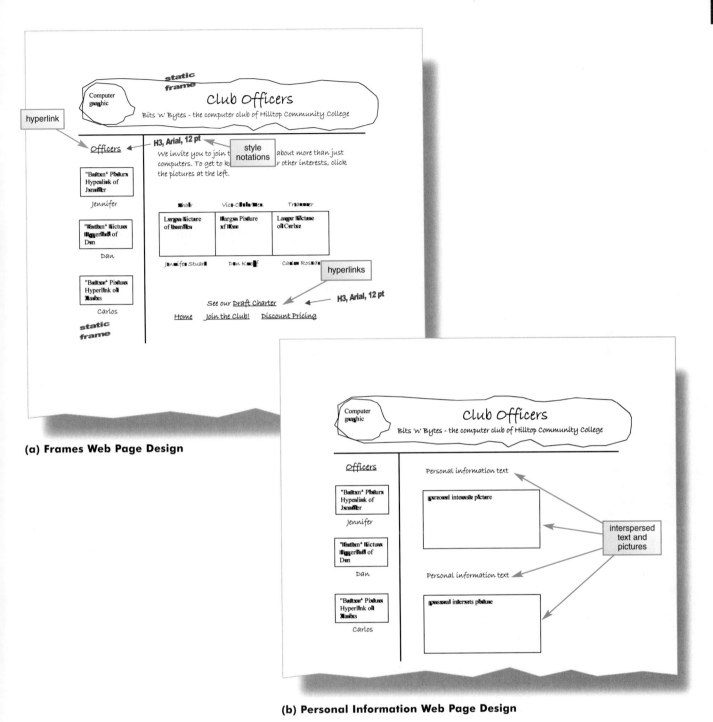

(a) Frames Web Page Design

(b) Personal Information Web Page Design

FIGURE 5-2

The frames Web page design shown in Figure 5-2(a) illustrates three frames. The top frame contains a simple heading similar to the one used with other pages in the Bits 'n' Bytes web. The contents of this frame will remain the same while the frames page is displayed.

The left frame contains a list of images that are hyperlinks to the personal information Web pages of the officers. The contents of this frame will remain the same while the frames page is displayed. At the top of the frame is a hyperlink to the Officers page. This hyperlink will redisplay the Officers page with its initial Web pages in the frames.

The right frame initially will contain a small graphic image of each officer, their respective names, and the title of each office. Similarly to previous pages developed for this web, links exist to the Home page, the Join page, and the Discounts page. Finally, a hyperlink is provided to a draft charter for the club. The target of this hyperlink is not an HTML document, but a Word document, which will be opened by the browser. The contents of this frame will change depending on which hyperlink a viewer clicks in the left frame.

The personal information Web page design in Figure 5-2(b) on the previous page, illustrates the general design used for the personal information Web page for each officer. The web consists of three personal information Web pages, one for each officer. All together, seven Web pages will be required to implement this design: the frames page, the three initial Web pages, and the three personal information Web pages. With the design of the page completed, you now can implement the design using Microsoft FrontPage.

Importing Files into an Existing Web

The development of a Web page using frames involves a great amount of effort. The content of each frame is a complete Web page. If you are the only person doing the development work, you are solely responsible for all the initial Web pages, as well as any Web pages for which you have hyperlinks in your frames Web page.

The Officers Web page in this project requires seven Web pages to implement frames. In order for you to complete the project within a reasonable amount of time, four of the seven Web pages are available on the Data Disk. To obtain a copy of the Data Disk, follow the instructions on the inside back cover of this book.

You will create the frames Web page and two initial Web pages that are part of the frames Web page. The four other Web pages are supplied on the Data Disk for this textbook. Image files used by these pages and by the pages you will create also are contained on the Data Disk. You will import these files to complete the Officers Web page. Later, you will make some modifications to one of the personal information Web pages.

Perform the following steps to start FrontPage and then open the Bits 'n' Bytes FrontPage web from Project 4. If you did not complete Project 4, see your instructor for a copy.

TO START FRONTPAGE AND OPEN AN EXISTING WEB

1 Click the Start button on the taskbar. Point to Programs on the Start menu.

2 Click Microsoft FrontPage on the Programs submenu.

3 Click the Open button arrow on the Standard toolbar. Click Open Web on the Open Web button menu.

4 When the Open Web dialog box displays, if necessary, click the Look in box arrow and select the folder location where you stored the web for Project 4 (e.g., C:\My Documents\My Webs\Club).

5 Click the Open button. If necessary, click the Folder List button on the Standard toolbar to display the Folder List pane.

The Bits 'n' Bytes web is loaded and a new blank page displays in Page view (Figure 5-3).

M *re* **About** *2000*

Frames Compatibility

If the commands for inserting or using frames appear dimmed on menus, or the Frames Pages tab does not appear in the New dialog box, check for browser compatibility. On the Tools menu, click Page Options, and then click the Compatibility tab. To enable frames and frames pages, click the Frames check box to select it. Verify also that you have not selected a target browser that does not support frames. Frames are automatically disabled by default when you target your web for compatibility with Microsoft Web TV in the Browsers text box.

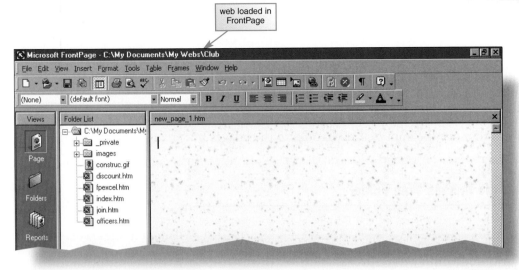

FIGURE 5-3

As you can see in the Folders List pane, a file named officers.htm already exists. This is the Under Construction page imported in Project 2. This file will be replaced with the frames page created in this project. Once replaced, the Under Construction graphic file, constru.gif, also shown in the Folders List pane, no longer will be needed.

Before you begin developing the Officers Web page, you should include the Web pages and their accompanying image files from the Data Disk into the current FrontPage web. You cannot simply copy the files to the web, as FrontPage will not recognize and include the pages automatically. You will use the Import command as you did in Project 2 and Project 3 to import new, already existing Web pages and other Web resource files into an existing web.

The following steps import the required files into the Bits 'n' Bytes web.

TO IMPORT FILES INTO AN EXISTING FRONTPAGE WEB

1 Insert the Data Disk in drive A. Click File on the menu bar and then click Import.

2 Click the Add File button in the Import dialog box.

3 Select all of the files from the Project5 folder on the Data Disk. Click the Open button.

4 Click the OK button in the Import dialog box.

The files are added to the Folder List pane (Figure 5-4).

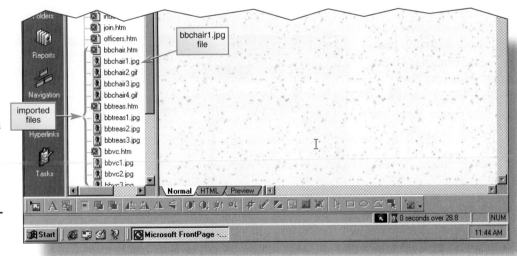

FIGURE 5-4

1. Press ALT+F, M

Figure 5-4 on the previous page shows the Folder List pane after the import operation is completed. Not only were Web pages imported, but also images used by those pages, along with a Word document to be used later in this project. They were all imported into the same directory as the Web pages. While not absolutely necessary, it is useful to organize image files in the same folder. Perform the following steps to move the imported image files to the images folder.

Steps To Move Image Files to the Images Web Folder

1 Click the Folders icon on the Views bar. When the page displays in Folders view, hold down the CTRL key and click each of the imported graphic files to select them. If necessary, scroll down to select additional files.

The page displays in Folders view and the imported image files are highlighted (Figure 5-5).

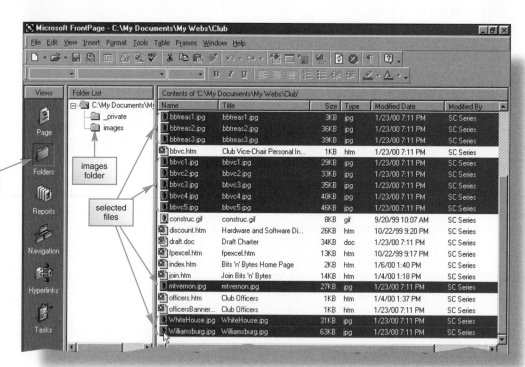

FIGURE 5-5

2 Drag and drop the selected files in the Folders pane into the images folder. Click the Page icon on the Views bar to return to Page view.

The imported image files are moved to the images folder and references to each are updated automatically (Figure 5-6).

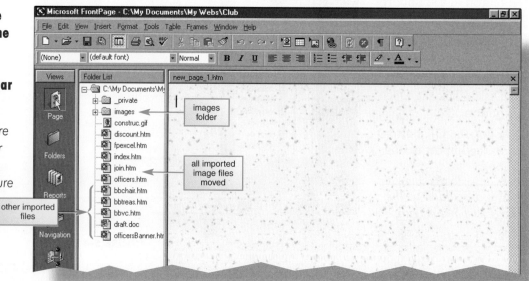

FIGURE 5-6

While it may be advantageous to keep all image files together, it is most important that references to these images within Web pages be correct. If you move or rename files outside of FrontPage, references to these files within Web pages, such as hyperlinks or references to graphic images, may become broken. Moving or renaming files within FrontPage assures that such references will be maintained, as FrontPage modifies references to the files automatically.

Using Frames Templates

FrontPage comes with ten frames templates. The templates vary in the number, orientation, and size of the contained frames. The **frames templates** provide layouts such as a simple table of contents, a small header at the top, a small footer at the bottom, and a window split into any number of horizontal or vertical frames.

Creating a Frames Page Using a Frames Template

You should choose a template that best satisfies your design requirements. You then can alter the size and number of frames within the template until you have the exact size and number of frames you need.

When using a frames template, FrontPage opens a new document and places the template within the new document. When you save this document, you will replace the officers.htm Web page you added earlier as an "under construction" page. Perform the following steps to create a frames page using a frames template.

Moving Files

If you have only a few files to move to another folder in your web, you can drag and drop files in the Folder List pane just as you did in Folders View. However, using this method is limited to only one file at a time.

Page Transition

FrontPage provides other ways besides frames to give a new look to your Web pages. Click Page Transition on the Format menu to create a special effect that is displayed when a site visitor enters or leaves a page.

 To Create a Frames Page Using a Frames Template

1 **Click File on the menu bar and then point to New. Point to Page on the New submenu.**

The New submenu displays with the Page command highlighted (Figure 5-7).

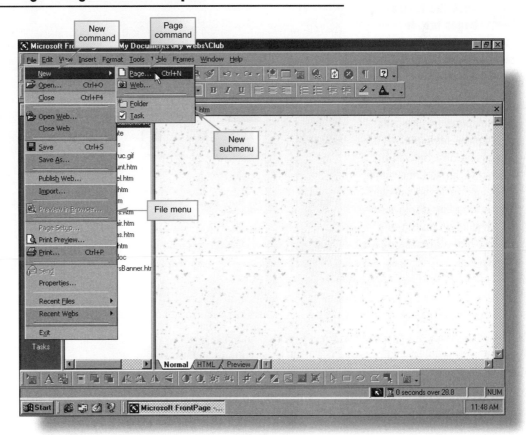

FIGURE 5-7

2 Click Page. When the New dialog box displays, point to the Frames Pages tab.

The New dialog box displays (Figure 5-8).

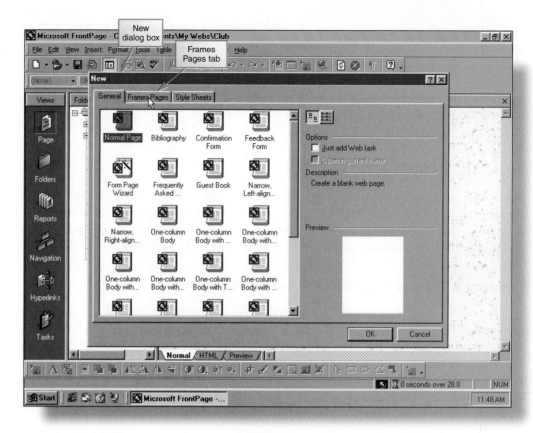

FIGURE 5-8

3 Click the Frames Pages tab. If necessary, click the Banner and Contents icon. Point to the OK button.

The Frames Pages tabbed sheet displays (Figure 5-9). Each frames template appears as an icon with a descriptive name underneath. A description of the selected frames template displays in the Description area and a preview of the frames page is displayed.

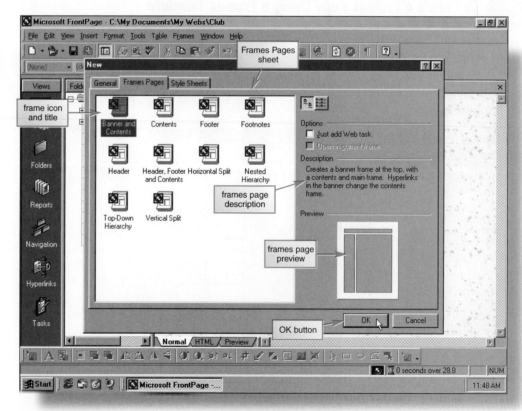

FIGURE 5-9

Click the OK button.

*A new frames page displays
with three frames: a banner
frame, a contents frame, and
a main frame (Figure 5-10).*

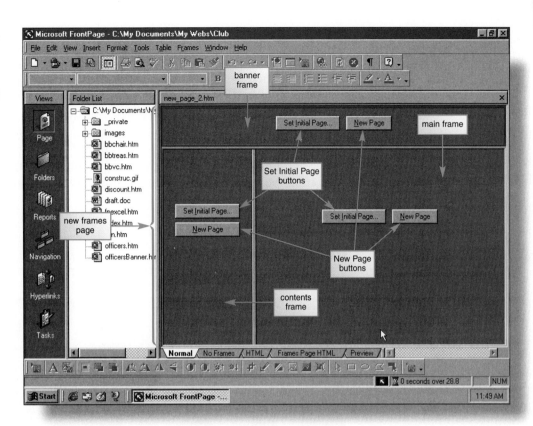

FIGURE 5-10

Figure 5-10 shows the added frames page. Note that each frame has two
buttons. The **Set Initial Page button** allows you to select a preexisting Web page as the
initial Web page for that frame. The page can be from the current FrontPage web,
another Web page on the Web server where the frames page will be published, or
any page on the World Wide Web.

The **New Page button** allows you to create a new Web page, right in the frame, to
display as the initial Web page for that frame.

Recall that each frame contains an entire Web page. Notice the blue highlighted
border surrounding the top frame shown in Figure 5-10. The **blue highlighted border**
indicates the current active frame. Activities such as special formatting, inserting
objects, and saving will be performed on the Web page in the active frame. You can
change the active frame simply by clicking the desired frame. The highlighted border
will surround the frame you clicked.

Two additional tabs display at the bottom of the window in Figure 5-10. The **No
Frames** tab displays the Web page that the user will see if the browser does not support frames. The No Frames tab will be discussed later in the project.

The **Frames Page HTML tab** displays the HTML source code for the frames Web
page. The **HTML tab** displays the HTML source code for the Web page in the current
active frame.

Saving the Frames Web Page

You now are ready to create the initial Web pages that will display in each
frame. Before you begin, however, you should save the frames Web page.

FrontPage keeps track of whether or not you saved a file. If you create the initial Web pages and then try to save them, you will be prompted twice – once for the initial Web page and once for the frames page. This happens every time you try to save, until you finally do save the frames page. Saving the frames page first prevents the second prompt from appearing, saving you time and possibly preventing confusion over which page is being saved.

Before you can save the frames Web page, you must select it to make it the active page. You can select the frames page to be the current active page by clicking any of the frames borders. The blue highlighted border will surround the entire window, indicating the frames page is the current active page. Perform the following steps to save the frames Web page.

 To Save the Frames Web Page

1 **Click the border between any of the frames to select the frames Web page as the current active page. Point to the Save button on the Standard toolbar.**

The highlighted border surrounds the frames page in the Web page (Figure 5-11).

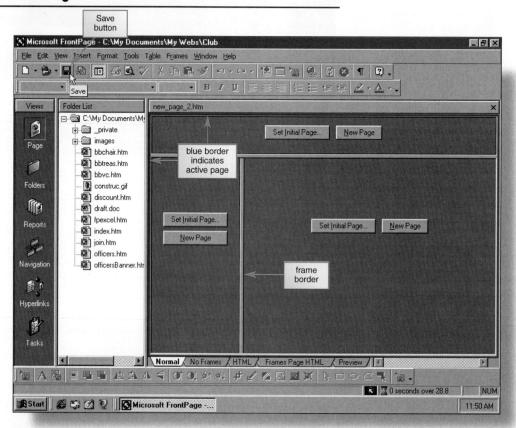

FIGURE 5-11

2 **Click the Save button on the Standard toolbar.**

The Save As dialog box displays with a default name for the new frames page (Figure 5-12). A graphic map indicates the frames page as the frame to be saved.

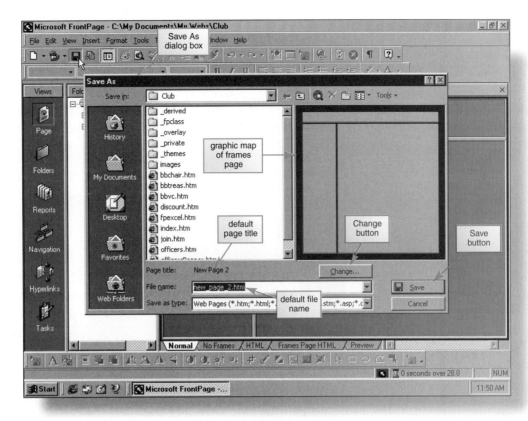

FIGURE 5-12

3 **If necessary, scroll down the file list until the officers.htm file displays. Click the officers.htm file. Click the Change button. When the Set Page Title dialog box displays, type** Club Officers **in the Page title text box and then point to the OK button.**

The Set Page Title dialog box displays with Club Officers typed in the Page title text box (Figure 5-13).

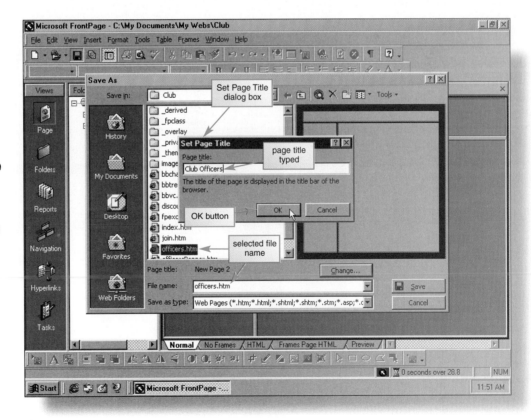

FIGURE 5-13

4 **Click the OK button.**

The Set Page Title dialog box closes and the Page title in the Save As dialog box is set to Club Officers (Figure 5-14).

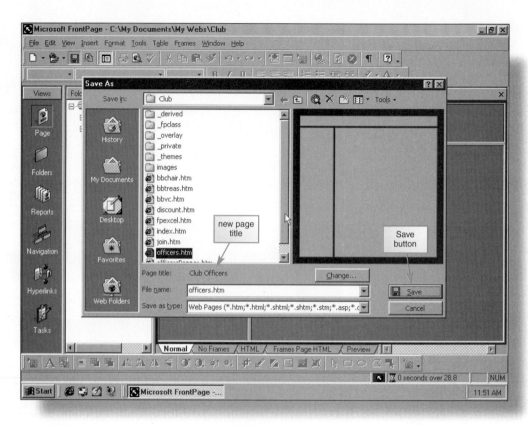

FIGURE 5-14

5 **Click the Save button in the Save As dialog box. When the Microsoft FrontPage dialog box displays, point to the Yes button.**

A Microsoft FrontPage dialog box displays asking if you want to replace the officers.htm file (Figure 5-15).

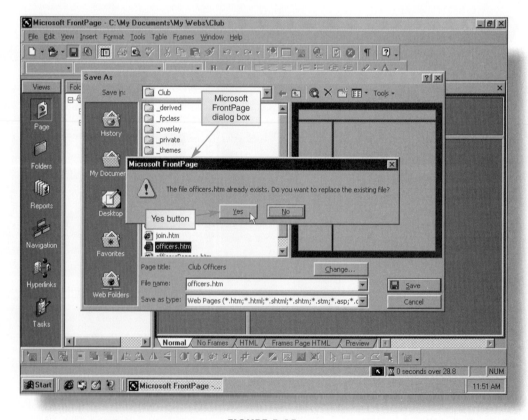

FIGURE 5-15

6 **Click the Yes button.**

The frames Web page is saved using the file name officers.htm (Figure 5-16).

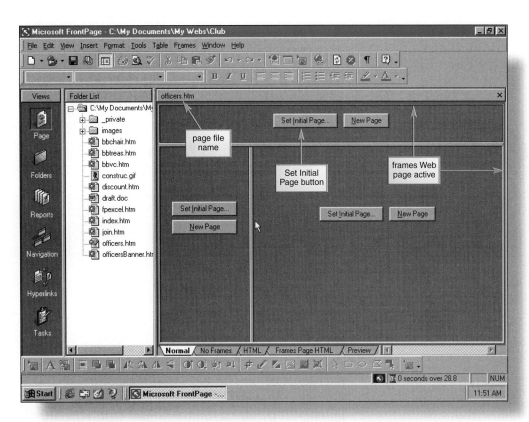

FIGURE 5-16

Other Ways

1. On File menu click Save
2. Press ALT+F, S
3. Press CTRL+S

With the frames page saved, you will not be prompted to save it every time you save one of the other Web pages you will develop in this project. The next step is to set the initial Web page for the banner frame.

Creating an Initial Web Page for a Frame

You can make a Web page with frames in one of several ways. The frames template gives you a choice of selecting an already existing Web page, or creating a new Web page, to use as the initial Web page for a frame.

You can create the frames page and then create the initial Web page for each frame within the frames page. This is the process you will use to create the initial main and contents Web pages.

You also can create each individual Web page before working on the frames page. Then you simply can use the Set Initial Page button in the frames template to provide the URL to the Web page to be used as the initial Web page for the frame. This is the method that you will use to implement the banner frame, which will contain a static heading for the frames page. **Static** means it never changes.

Using an Existing Web Page as the Initial Page in a Frame

This technique provides flexibility in the design process. You can assign responsibility for different Web pages to different individuals or work groups. The pages can be developed simultaneously, reducing the time it takes to implement complex frames pages.

When all initial Web pages and all target Web pages already exist, creating the frames Web page is a short, simple process. Simply select a template, arrange the frame borders if necessary, identify the initial Web pages, and then save and test the frames page. Perform the following steps to use an existing Web page as the initial Web page in a frame.

 ## To Use an Existing Web Page as the Initial Page in a Frame

1 **Click the Set Initial Page button in the top frame.**

The Create Hyperlink dialog box displays (Figure 5-17). The top frame becomes the current active frame.

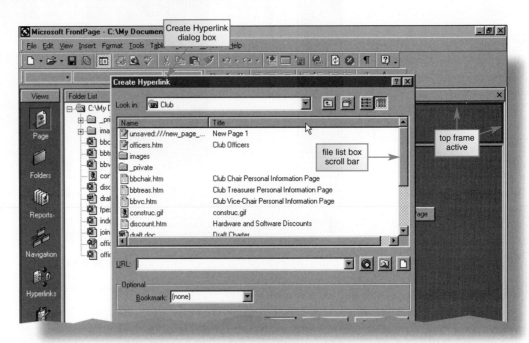

FIGURE 5-17

2 **If necessary, scroll down the file list until the file officersBanner.htm, which was imported earlier, displays. Click the file officersBanner.htm. Point to the OK button.**

The officersBanner.htm file name displays in the URL text box (Figure 5-18).

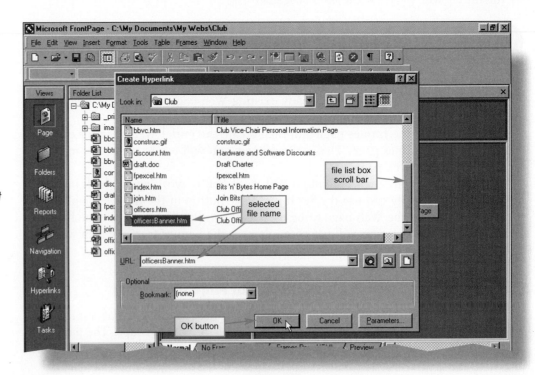

FIGURE 5-18

3 Click the OK button.

The officersBanner.htm file displays in the top frame of the frames page (Figure 5-19). The banner graphic will not display until the page has been added to the Navigation view.

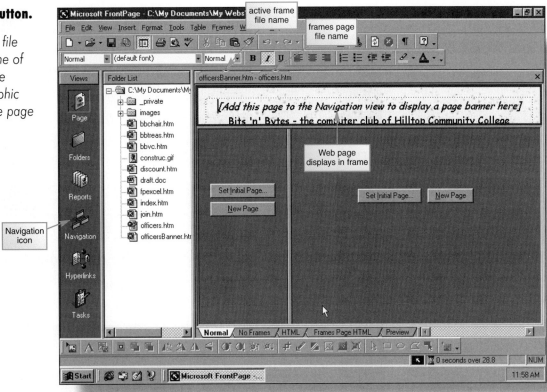

FIGURE 5-19

4 Click the Navigation icon on the Views bar. Point to the officersBanner.htm file in the Folders List pane.

The current web displays in navigation view (Figure 5-20).

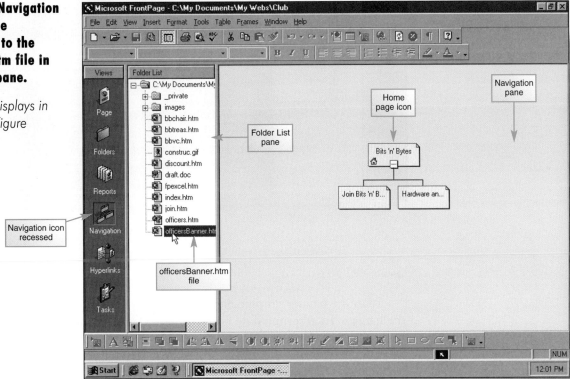

FIGURE 5-20

5 Drag and drop the officersBanner.htm file from the Folders List pane into the Navigation pane under the Bits 'n' Bytes Home page icon.

An icon for the officersBanner.htm file displays in the Navigation pane (Figure 5-21).

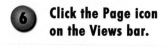

Page icon

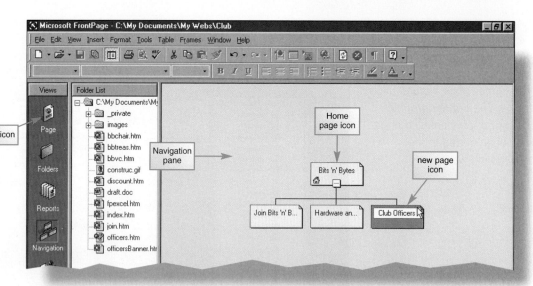

FIGURE 5-21

6 Click the Page icon on the Views bar.

The frames page displays in Page view. The officersBanner.htm file displays with a banner graphic in the top frame of the frames page (Figure 5-22).

Page icon recessed

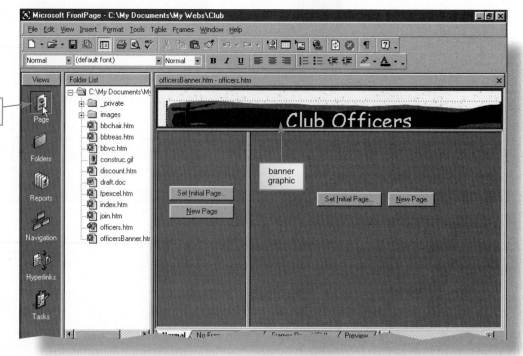

FIGURE 5-22

With the banner graphic now displaying, you cannot see the text that is under the banner. To accommodate both the banner and the text, the frame size of the top frame must be adjusted.

Adjusting the Size of a Frame

You can adjust the size of a frame by dragging the frame border to the desired location. In this instance, you can increase the size of the top frame so the text will display with the banner graphic and without the need for a scroll bar. Perform the following steps to adjust the size of a frame.

Steps · To Adjust the Size of a Frame

1 Point to the horizontal frame border below the top frame.

The mouse pointer changes to a double-headed arrow, indicating that the border can be resized (Figure 5-23).

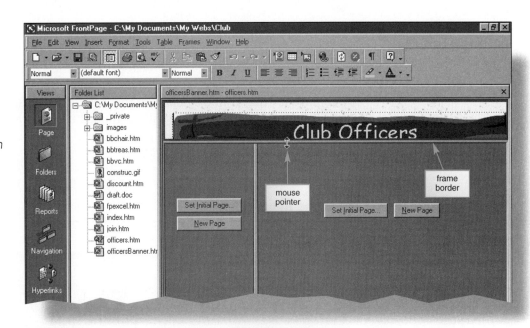

FIGURE 5-23

2 Drag the border down until the text in the top frame partially is visible.

The frame border is resized (Figure 5-24). You can deter-mine the required location when you preview your web in a browser.

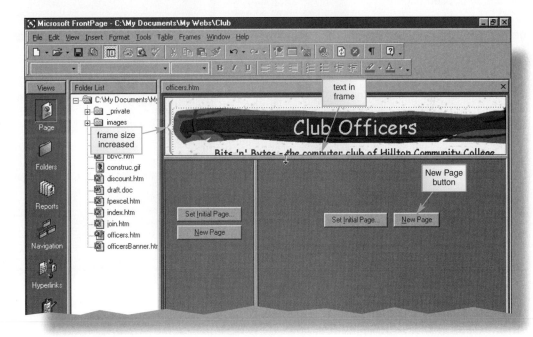

FIGURE 5-24

You can decrease the size of a frame in the same fashion – simply by dragging the frame border until the frame is the desired size.

It is not necessary to save this Web page because it already exists. You imported it to the frames folder in previous steps. The frames page has changed, however, and should be saved. Perform the step on the next page to save the changes to the frames page.

Other Ways

1. On Frames menu click Frame Properties, type new size values
2. Right-click frame, click Frame Properties on shortcut menu, type new size values
3. Press ALT+R, P, type new size values

TO SAVE CHANGES TO THE FRAMES PAGE

1 Click the Save button on the Standard toolbar.

Creating a New Page for an Initial Page in a Frame

The steps for creating a new Web page are the same as performed in previous projects. With a frames template, you can indicate that you want to create a new Web page for that frame by clicking the New Page button in the desired frame. All the objects and text you insert will be applied to that frame only. Perform the following step to create the initial Web page that will display in the main frame when the viewer first displays the frames page.

 To Create a New Page in the Main Frame

1 **Click the New Page button in the right, or main, frame.**

A new Web page displays in the main frame with the current theme applied (Figure 5-25). The right frame becomes the current active frame and the insertion point is located in this Web page.

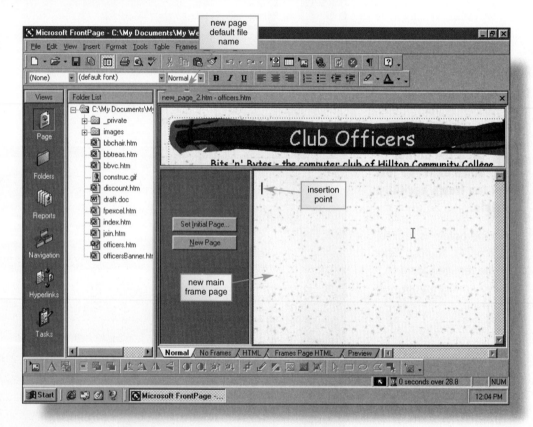

FIGURE 5-25

This Web page now can be modified just as you modified previous Web pages by inserting the required text, table and hyperlink to the draft charter document. Because the targets of the other hyperlinks have to be modified, they will be added later. Refer to the design illustrated in Figure 5-2(a) on page FP 5.9 for the contents of this frame. Perform the following steps to insert text and a table in the initial Web page for the main frame.

TO INSERT TEXT AND A TABLE IN THE MAIN FRAME INITIAL PAGE

1 If necessary, click the Web page in the main frame to position the insertion point. Using the default font, type `We invite you to join the club! We're about more than just computers. To get to know us and our other interests, click the pictures at the left.`

2 Press the RIGHT ARROW key to position the insertion point on the next line. Click the Insert Table button on the Standard toolbar and then insert a 3 by 3 table.

3 If necessary, click the cell in the first row of the first column of the table. Hold down the SHIFT key and then click the cell in the third row of the third column to select all cells.

4 Right-click the table and then click Cell Properties on the shortcut menu.

5 When the Cell Properties dialog box displays, click the Horizontal alignment box arrow in the Layout area and then click Center. If necessary, click Specify width to deselect the check box. Click the OK button.

6 Click the cell in the first row of the first column. Type `Chair`. Press the RIGHT ARROW key to position the insertion point in the next cell. Type `Vice-Chair/Sec.` and then press the RIGHT ARROW key. Type `Treasurer`. Click the cell in the third row and first column. Type `Jennifer Stuart` and then press the RIGHT ARROW key. Type `Dan Knoff` and then press the RIGHT ARROW key. Type `Carlos Rosado` in the third column.

7 Position the insertion point below the table. Click the Center button on the Formatting toolbar. Click the Style box arrow and then click Heading 3 in the Style list. Click the Font box arrow and then click Arial or a font of your choice. Click the Font Size box arrow and then click 3 (12 pt). Type `See our Draft Charter`. Press the END key to position the insertion point at the end of the line. Hold down the SHIFT key and then press the ENTER key.

8 Type `Home` and then press the SPACEBAR seven times. Type `Join the Club!` and then press the SPACEBAR seven times. Type `Discount Pricing` as the final entry for that line.

The main page displays in the frames page with the added table and text (Figure 5-26).

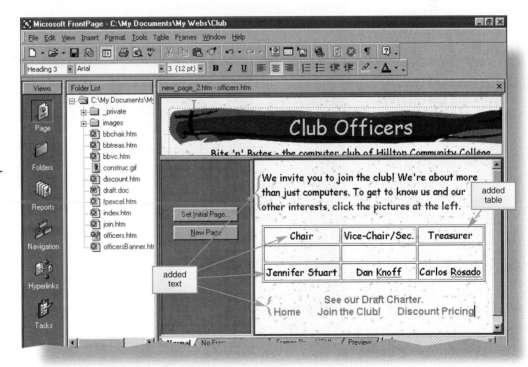

FIGURE 5-26

The table is almost complete. According to the design, small pictures of each of the officers need to be inserted into the center row of cells. Perform the following steps to insert pictures of each officer using the images files imported earlier.

 To Insert Pictures from a File into a Table

1 Click the cell in the second row and first column to position the insertion point. Point to the Insert Picture From File button on the Pictures toolbar.

The insertion point is positioned in the table (Figure 5-27).

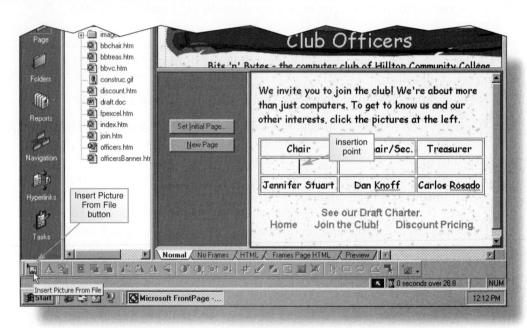

FIGURE 5-27

2 Click the Insert Picture From File button. When the Picture dialog box displays, if necessary, scroll down the file list until the bbchair1.jpg file displays. Click bbchair1.jpg and then point to the OK button.

The Picture dialog box displays with the bbchair1.jpg file selected (Figure 5-28). A preview of the picture displays.

FIGURE 5-28

3 **Click the OK button.**

The selected image displays in the table cell (Figure 5-29).

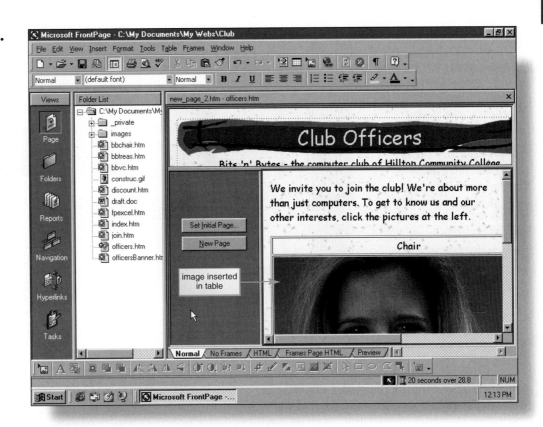

FIGURE 5-29

4 **Click the image to select it. Drag the sizing handles to resize the image to approximate the size shown in Figure 5-30. Click the Resample button on the Pictures toolbar to resample the resized image.**

The resized image displays in the table cell (Figure 5-30). Recall that resizing an image does not alter the image itself, only the HTML code; however, resampling an image results in a modified image file.

FIGURE 5-30

5 **Repeat Steps 1 through 4 to insert the remaining two pictures in their respective table cells. Use the bbvc1.jpg file for the cell in the second column and the bbtreas1.jpg file for the cell in the third column. Remember to resample each picture.**

The inserted images display in the table (Figure 5-31).

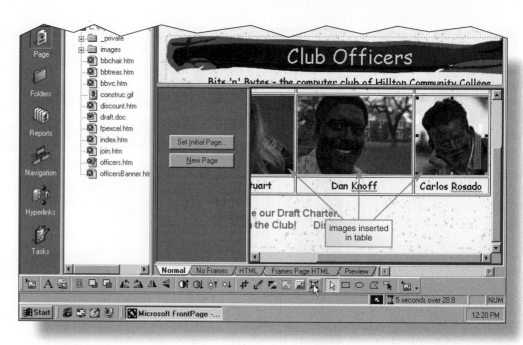

FIGURE 5-31

The last step to complete the table is to modify certain table properties. You are familiar with setting the table border size property to zero in order to make the table invisible. Some other properties need to be set, however, to center the table horizontally on the page and to allow the browser to resize the table to fit the contents in the table cells. Perform the following steps to modify the table properties.

Steps **To Modify Table Properties**

1 **Right-click the table and then point to Table Properties on the shortcut menu.**

The shortcut menu displays (Figure 5-32).

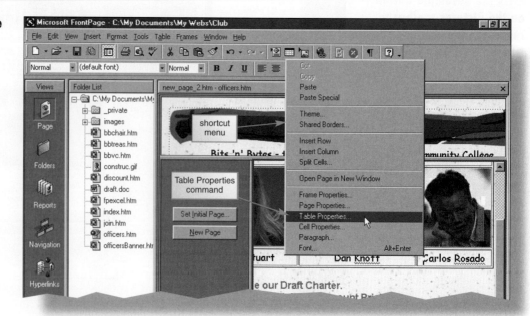

FIGURE 5-32

2 **Click Table Properties. When the Table Properties dialog box displays, click the Alignment box arrow in the Layout area and then click Center. Click Specify width to deselect the check box. Type 0 in the Cell padding text box and type 0 in the Cell spacing text box in the Layout area. Type 0 in the Size text box in the Borders area. Point to the OK button.**

The Table Properties dialog box displays with the changes (Figure 5-33).

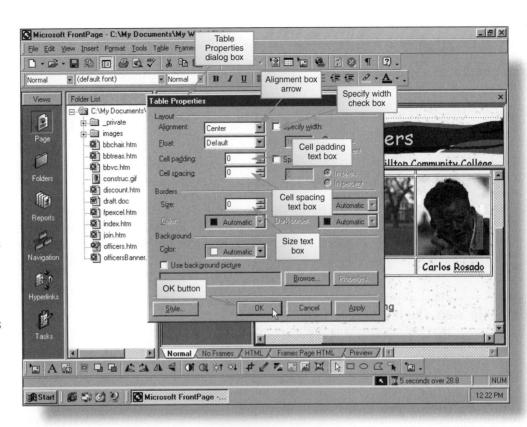

FIGURE 5-33

3 **Click the OK button.**

The completed table displays (Figure 5-34).

FIGURE 5-34

Other Ways

1. On Table menu point to Properties, click Table

2. Press ALT+A, R, T

Except for the hyperlinks to be added later, the main frame Web page is complete. Because the Web page was created rather than imported, you should save it before continuing. Make a habit of saving your work periodically. Although FrontPage will indicate if changes have not been saved when you quit, unsaved work can be lost due to outside factors, such as an unexpected loss of power. In addition to making a habit of periodically saving your work, another reason exists for saving the main frame Web page at this point. It will be used as a target for a hyperlink in the contents frame, and so needs to be saved with a given file name.

Saving the Initial Web Page

Recall that each frame displays an entire Web page. You developed the main frame Web page directly in the frame. You must save this Web page in the FrontPage web. By default, the Web page in the current active frame will be saved. Recall that the blue highlighted border indicates the current active frame.

 To Save the Initial Web Page

1 **Click the Save button on the Standard toolbar.**

The Save As dialog box displays (Figure 5-35). A graphic map of the current active frame is highlighted. This indicates which Web page will be saved. You want to use a file name that is representative of the function of this Web page in the frames page.

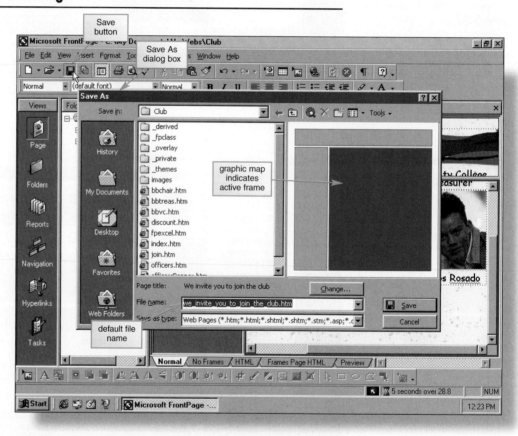

FIGURE 5-35

2 Type
officersMain.htm
**in the File name text box.
Point to the Change button.**

*The new file name displays in
the File name text box (Figure
5-36).*

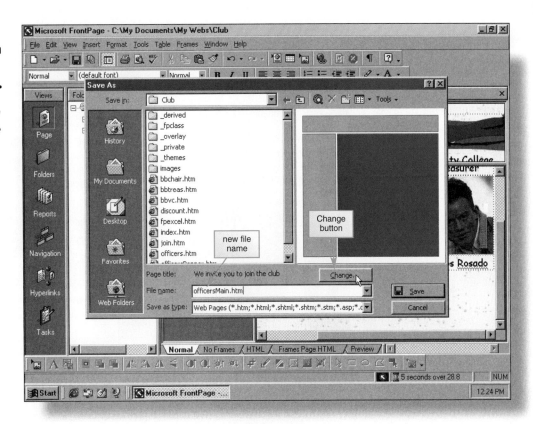

FIGURE 5-36

3 **Click the Change
button. When the
Set Page Title dialog box
displays, type** Officers
main page **in the Page
title text box and then
point to the OK button.**

*The new title displays in the
Page title text box (Figure
5-37).*

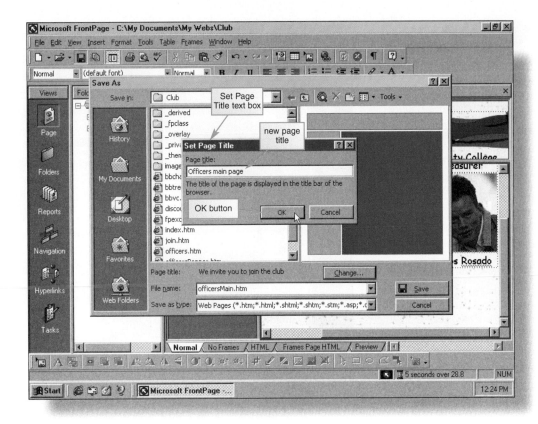

FIGURE 5-37

4 Click the OK button. Point to the Save button in the Save As dialog box.

The Page title in the Save As dialog box is set to Officers main page (Figure 5-38).

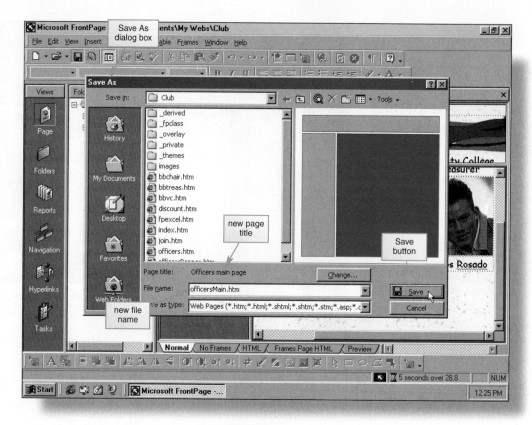

FIGURE 5-38

5 Click the Save button in the Save As dialog box.

The Save Embedded Files dialog box displays (Figure 5-39). The names of the three embedded picture files are highlighted. The bbchair1.jpg picture displays in the Picture preview.

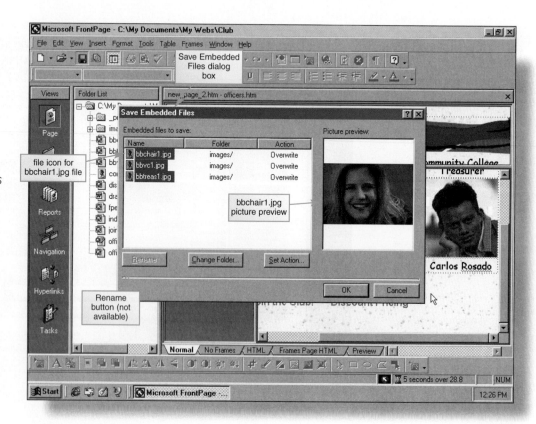

FIGURE 5-39

6 Click the icon to the left of the bbchair1.jpg file name. Point to the Rename button.

The file bbchair1.jpg is highlighted and the Rename button becomes available (Figure 5-40).

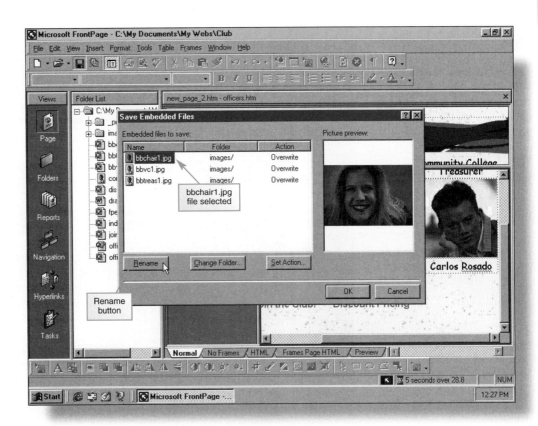

FIGURE 5-40

7 Click the Rename button. Type bbchair1Main.jpg as the new name. Click the icon to the left of the bbvc1.jpg file name. Point to the Rename button.

The file name is changed to bbchair1Main.jpg, the action changes from Overwrite to Save, and the file bbvc1.jpg is highlighted (Figure 5-41). The picture displays in the Picture preview.

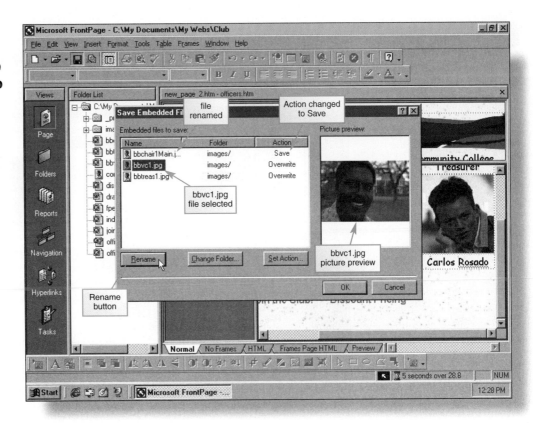

FIGURE 5-41

8 **Click the Rename button. Type** bbvc1Main.jpg **as the new name. Click the icon to the left of the bbtreas1.jpg file name. Point to the Rename button.**

The file name is changed to bbvc1Main.jpg, the action changes from Overwrite to Save, and the file bbtreas1.jpg is highlighted (Figure 5-42). The picture displays in the Picture preview area.

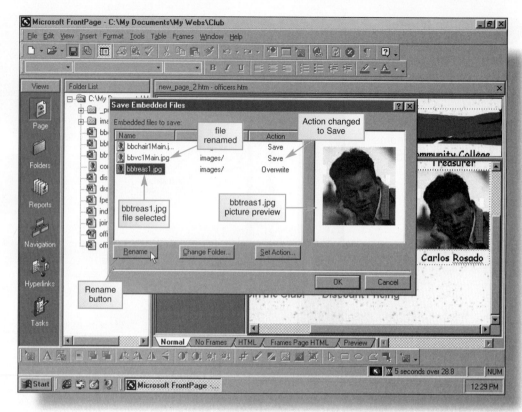

FIGURE 5-42

9 **Click the Rename button. Type** bbtreas1Main.jpg **and then press the ENTER key. Point to the OK button.**

The file name is changed to bbtreas1Main.jpg and the action changes from Overwrite to Save (Figure 5-43).

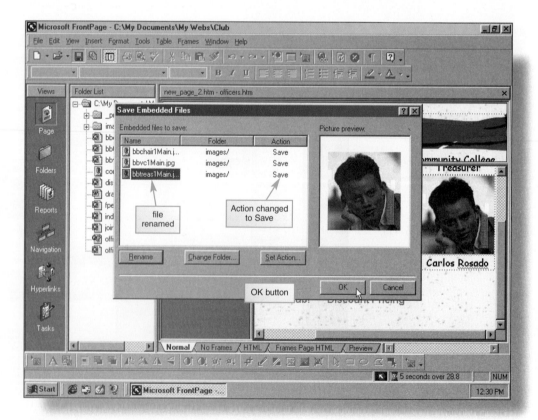

FIGURE 5-43

10 **Click the OK button.**

The embedded image files are saved and the completed Web page displays (Figure 5-44).

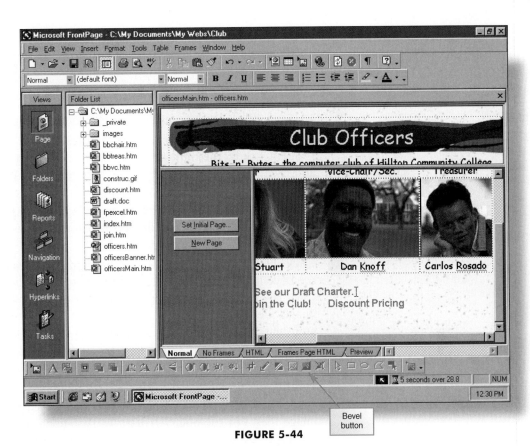

Bevel
button

FIGURE 5-44

You have created one of the initial Web pages for a frame, right within the frame itself. Creating the other initial Web pages is similar to the preceding steps. The next page is the table of contents Web page, which will be displayed as the initial Web page for the left frame. According to the design, this page will contain a text hyperlink and three images used as hyperlinks. The images are similar to the ones used in the main frame, but have beveled edges to give them the appearance of buttons. Perform the steps below to create the contents frame Web page and insert the text and images.

TO CREATE THE CONTENTS FRAME WEB PAGE

1 Click the New Page button in the left frame.

2 Click the Center button on the Formatting toolbar. Click the Style box arrow and then click Heading 3 in the Style list. Click the Font box arrow and then click Arial or a font of your choice. Click the Font Size box arrow and then click 3 (12 pt). Type Officers and then press the ENTER key.

3 Click the Insert Picture From File button on the Pictures toolbar. When the Picture dialog box displays, if necessary, scroll down the file list until the file bbchair1.jpg displays. Click bbchair1.jpg and then click the OK button.

4 Click the image to select it. Drag the sizing handles to resize the image. Click the Bevel button on the Pictures toolbar to add a bevel border to the image. Click the Resample button on the Pictures toolbar to resample the modified image. Click to the right of the image to deselect it. Hold down the SHIFT key and then press the ENTER key. Type Jennifer below the picture.

5 Hold down the SHIFT key and then press the ENTER key. Click the Insert Picture From File button. When the Picture dialog box displays, if necessary, scroll down the file list until the file bbvc1.jpg displays. Click bbvc1.jpg and then click the OK button.

6 Click the image to select it. Drag the sizing handles to resize the image. Click the Bevel button on the Pictures toolbar to add a bevel border to the image. Click the Resample button on the Pictures toolbar to resample the modified image. Click to the right of the image to deselect it. Hold down the SHIFT key and then press the ENTER key. Type Dan below the picture.

7 Hold down the SHIFT key and then press the ENTER key. Click the Insert Picture From File button. When the Picture dialog box displays, if necessary, scroll down the file list until the file bbtreas1.jpg displays. Click bbtreas1.jpg and then click the OK button.

8 Click the image to select it. Drag the sizing handles to resize the image. Click the Bevel button on the Pictures toolbar to add a bevel border to the image. Click the Resample button on the Pictures toolbar to resample the modified image. Click to the right of the image to deselect it. Hold down the SHIFT key and then press the ENTER key. Type Carlos below the picture.

9 Click the Save button on the Standard toolbar. When the Save As dialog box displays, type officersTOC.htm in the File name text box. Click the Save button.

10 When the Save Embedded Files dialog box displays, rename each of the three image files. For the bbchair1.jpg file, type bbchair1Btn.jpg. For the bbvc1.jpg file, type bbvc1Btn.jpg, and for the bbtreas1.jpg file, type bbtreas1Btn.jpg. Click the OK button.

The contents Web page is saved and displays with the inserted elements (Figure 5-45).

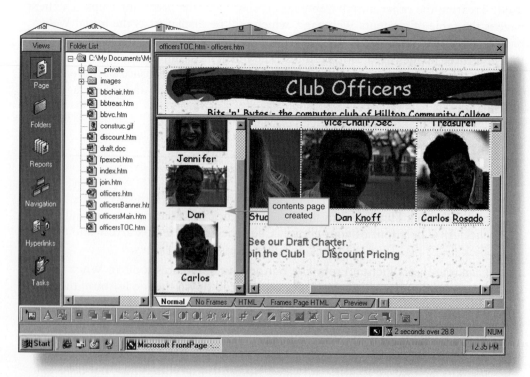

FIGURE 5-45

Modifying Properties of Frames and Frames Pages

Earlier, you adjusted the size of a frame by dragging its border. While this sets the initial size of the frame, other properties affect how that frame displays in the browser, including the size of the frame and how the user may view the frame contents.

Modifying the Properties of a Frame

The appearance of a frame within a frames page is affected by properties of the frame itself and properties of the frames page. Setting certain frame properties determines whether the frame has a fixed appearance or whether the user can manipulate the frame appearance when viewing it in a browser. Decisions about frame properties should be made carefully because they can affect the ability of the user to see all of the frame content.

Some decisions, such as whether the frame should display with scroll bars, are made on a frame-by-frame basis. This is because some frames will not need scroll bars while other frames, even in the same frames page, may need them. A frame can be set to always show scroll bars, never show scroll bars, or show them only if needed.

Other decisions, such as allowing the frame to be resized in a browser, are made for multiple frames together, even though the property value is set for an individual frame. For example, if one frame is set to be resizable and the frames around it are not resizable, then the setting for that one frame has no effect.

Perform the following steps to modify the properties of a frame.

 To Modify Frame Properties

1 **Right-click the contents frame. Point to Frame Properties on the shortcut menu.**

The shortcut menu displays (Figure 5-46).

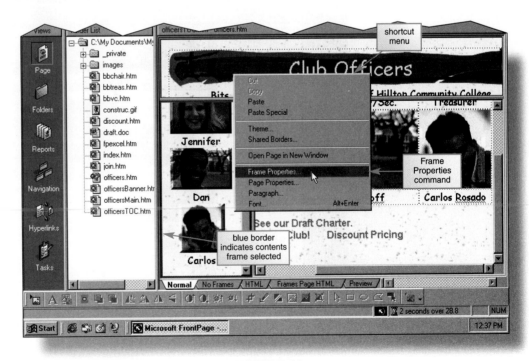

FIGURE 5-46

2 Click Frame Properties. When the Frame Properties dialog box displays, click the Show scrollbars box arrow in the Options area and then click Never. If necessary, click Resizable in Browser to select the check box. Point to the OK button.

The Frames Properties dialog box displays with the changes (Figure 5-47).

FIGURE 5-47

3 Click the OK button.

The contents frame displays without scroll bars (Figure 5-48).

FIGURE 5-48

Modifying the Properties of the Frames Page

Certain properties of the frames page itself also have an effect on frames appearance. The amount of padding displayed between frames is a property of the frames page, not the individual frames. Whether or not borders are shown between frames also is a frames page property. To modify the properties of the frames page, perform the following steps.

 To Modify Frames Page Properties

1 **Click the border between any of the frames to select the frames Web page as the current active page. Click File on the menu bar and then point to Properties.**

The highlighted border surrounds all the frames in the Web page (Figure 5-49).

FIGURE 5-49

2 **Click Properties.
When the Page
Properties dialog box
displays, point to the
Frames tab.**

*The Page Properties dialog
box displays (Figure 5-50).*

FIGURE 5-50

3 **Click the Frames
tab. If necessary,
type 1 in the Frame
Spacing text box. Point to
the OK button.**

*The Frames tabbed sheet dis-
plays (Figure 5-51).*

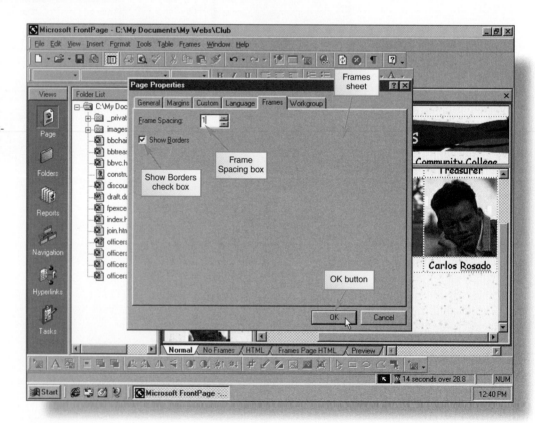

FIGURE 5-51

4 **Click the OK button.**

The modified frames page displays (Figure 5-52).

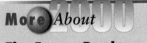

FIGURE 5-52

The contents frame Web page has been created and properties were set to affect how it is displayed. Currently, the frame contains no hyperlinks, however, to allow users to navigate to new pages. Before creating these hyperlinks, it is useful to have some background regarding the choices for a target frame for a hyperlink.

Setting Targets for Hyperlinks in Frames

Creating a hyperlink in a frame page is done just as with any other page. While hyperlinks in regular pages cause the current page to be replaced with a new page, hyperlinks in frames usually display pages in another frame, leaving the original page with the hyperlink unaffected. The hyperlinks in the contents Web page will cause other Web pages to display in the right, or main, frame. This is the typical case, which was established as the default by the template used to create the frames page.

Hyperlinks also can be modified to display pages in frames or windows other than the default target. You can display a Web page in the same frame as the Web page containing the hyperlink, in a different frame on the frames Web page, in the entire browser window thus replacing the frames page, or in a new browser window. The available choices for a target frame are predefined frame settings that are understood by all Web browsers that support frames. Table 5-1 on the next page shows the common settings.

More About

The Frame Borders

If you do not want the borders between frames to be visible when the frames page is displayed, click Properties on the File menu, and then click the Frames tab on the Page Properties dialog box. Click the Show Borders check box to uncheck it.

Table 5-1   Common Settings for Frame Targets

FRAME TARGET	DESCRIPTION
Page Default	Specifies that the page pointed to by the hyperlink should be displayed in the default target frame for the active page. This is the recommended method of specifying target frames for hyperlinks.
Same Frame	Sets the target frame of the hyperlink to the same frame that contains the hyperlink. Use this setting to override the page's default target frame.
Whole Page	Sets the target frame of the hyperlink to the entire Web browser window.
New Window	Specifies that a new Web browser window should be launched on the user's desktop, and the page that is the target of the hyperlink should be displayed in the new Web browser window.
Parent Frame	Specifies that the page pointed to by the hyperlink should be displayed in the frame that contains the current frameset tag. This is an advanced feature.

More About

Frames Template Description

The description for the selected frames template usually will indicate when hyperlinks in one frame affect the contents of another frame. Typically, the frame or frames to contain the hyperlinks as well as the target frame are all identified in the frames page description.

More About

Overriding a Base Target

A hyperlink in a frame can still target a location other than that identified in a base target tag. The HTML code for the individual hyperlink overrides the base target tag with a target value of its own. When editing properties of a hyperlink, FrontPage provides common target settings for the frame target, or you can supply a custom target.

Creating Hyperlinks to Pages in Frames

The purpose of the contents page is to present a list of hyperlinks to Web pages to the viewer. As noted earlier, these hyperlinks can link to Web pages in the same FrontPage web, to other Web pages on the same Web server, or to any Web page on the World Wide Web. For these hyperlinks, the target Web pages display in the right, or main, frame.

The frames template sets the main frame as the base target for hyperlinks in the contents frame. Figure 5-53 shows the HTML code in the header section of the contents frame. The **base target** tag sets the default target for hyperlinks in this frame Web page. Because of this tag, creating hyperlinks to pages that will display in the main frame is just like the steps for creating hyperlinks you have performed in previous projects. You do not have to indicate that the main frame should be the target because it has been set as the default. Perform the following steps to create the contents page hyperlinks and main page hyperlink to Web pages that display in the default frame.

```
<head>
<meta http-equiv="Content-Language" content="en-us">
<meta http-equiv="Content-Type" content="text/html; charset=windows-1252">
<meta name="GENERATOR" content="Microsoft FrontPage 4.0">
<meta name="ProgId" content="FrontPage.Editor.Document">
<title>Officers</title>
<base target="main">
<meta name="Microsoft Theme" content="loosegst 111, default">
</head>
```

FIGURE 5-53

Steps **To Create Hyperlinks Targeting the Default Frame**

1 Drag through the text Officers at the top of the contents frame. Right-click the highlighted text. Point to Hyperlink on the shortcut menu.

The text is highlighted and the shortcut menu displays (Figure 5-54).

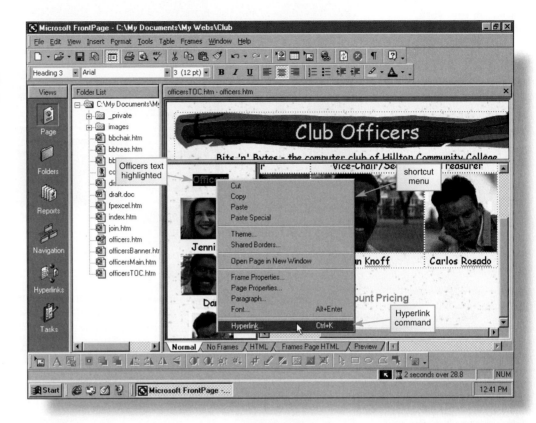

FIGURE 5-54

2 Click Hyperlink. When the Create Hyperlink dialog box displays, if necessary, scroll down the file list until the officersMain.htm file displays. Click the file officersMain.htm and then point to the OK button.

The Create Hyperlink dialog box displays and the file name officersMain.htm displays in the URL text box (Figure 5-55). This is the file name of the new Web page created earlier for the main frame. The Target frame text box indicates that the target frame for this hyperlink is the Page Default, which is the main page.

FIGURE 5-55

3 **Click the OK button. Position the mouse pointer on the word, Officers.**

The officersMain.htm URL displays on the status bar when the mouse pointer is positioned on the Officers hyperlink text (Figure 5-56).

FIGURE 5-56

4 **Right-click the top picture in the contents frame. Point to Hyperlink on the shortcut menu.**

The picture is selected and the shortcut menu displays (Figure 5-57).

FIGURE 5-57

5 Click Hyperlink. When the Create Hyperlink dialog box displays, if necessary, scroll down the file list until the file bbchair.htm displays. Click the file bbchair.htm and then point to the OK button.

The Create Hyperlink dialog box displays and the file name bbchair.htm displays in the URL text box (Figure 5-58). The Target frame text box indicates that the target frame for this hyperlink is the Page Default, which is the main page.

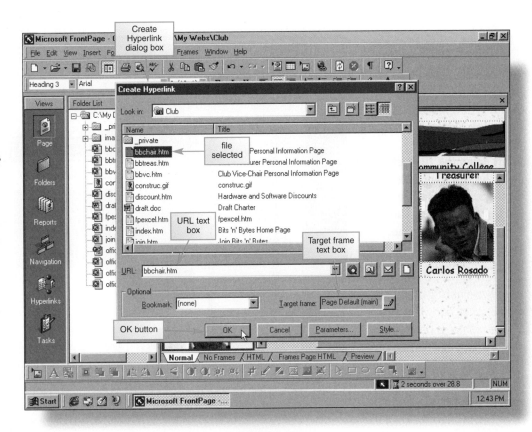

FIGURE 5-58

6 Click the OK button. Position the mouse pointer on the image.

The bbchair.htm URL displays on the status bar when the mouse pointer is positioned on the image hyperlink (Figure 5-59).

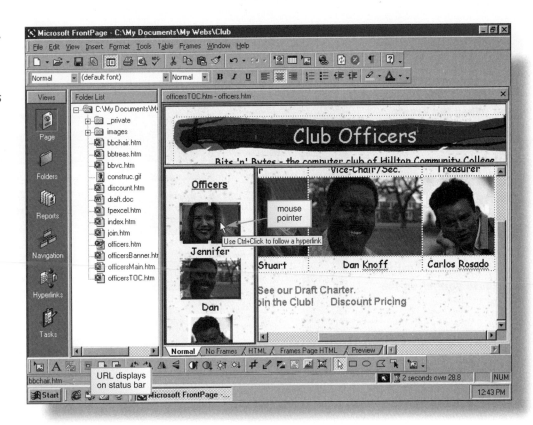

FIGURE 5-59

7 **Right-click the second picture in the contents frame. Click Hyperlink on the shortcut menu. When the Create Hyperlink dialog box displays, if necessary, scroll down the file list until the file bbvc.htm displays. Click the file bbvc.htm and then click the OK button. Position the mouse pointer on the image.**

The bbvc.htm URL displays on the status bar when the mouse pointer is positioned on the image hyperlink (Figure 5-60).

FIGURE 5-60

8 **Right-click the third picture in the contents frame. Click Hyperlink on the shortcut menu. When the Create Hyperlink dialog box displays, if necessary, scroll down the file list until the file bbtreas.htm displays. Click the file bbtreas.htm and then click the OK button. Click the Save button on the Standard toolbar. Position the mouse pointer on the image.**

The bbtreas.htm URL displays on the status bar when the mouse pointer is positioned on the image hyperlink (Figure 5-61). Changes to the page are saved.

FIGURE 5-61

9 Drag through the words Draft Charter in the main frame. Click the Hyperlink button on the Standard toolbar. When the Create Hyperlink dialog box displays, if necessary, scroll down the file list until the draft.doc file displays. Click draft.doc and then click the OK button. Position the mouse pointer on the text.

The draft.doc URL displays on the status bar when the mouse pointer is positioned on the text hyperlink (Figure 5-62).

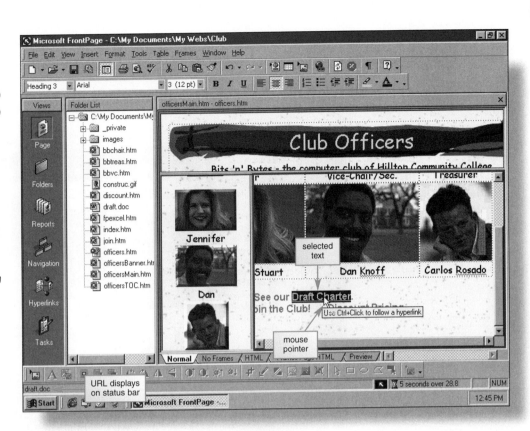

FIGURE 5-62

Other Ways

1. Select text or image, on Insert menu click Hyperlink
2. Select text or image, press ALT+I, H
3. Select text or image, press CTRL+K

The contents page now is complete. It contains a list of images that are hyperlinks to the personal information Web pages of the officers and text that is a hyperlink to the main Officers page.

The hyperlink created in the main page references an object that is not a Web page. When the user clicks this hyperlink, the browser will need to open a Word document. Depending on the browser used, you may need to have the appropriate helper application, in this case, Word, defined in the browser as the application to use to open the document. In other cases, the browser may be able to open the document directly.

The remaining hyperlinks in the main page now must be created. They will display Web pages in the entire browser window, replacing the frames page.

Creating a Hyperlink to a Whole Page

In addition to targeting pages for individual frames, a hyperlink in a frame can be used to display a Web page in an entire browser window instead of a frame. This is the purpose of the hyperlinks in the main frame for the Home, Join, and Discounts pages. Unlike the contents page, the initial main page does not have a base target tag. It still has a default target, however, itself. If these hyperlinks used the default target frame established by the template, then their target pages would display in the main frame only. This would give the Web pages a cascading effect that is not desired. To avoid displaying their target Web pages in the frame, these hyperlinks must indicate a target other than the default target frame.

Perform the following steps to create hyperlinks using the Whole Page setting.

 To Create a Hyperlink to a Whole Page

1 **Drag through the text Home below the table in the main frame. Right-click the highlighted text. Point to Hyperlink on the shortcut menu.**

The text is highlighted and the shortcut menu displays (Figure 5-63).

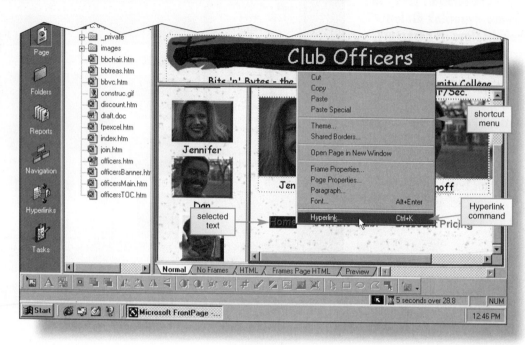

FIGURE 5-63

2 **Click Hyperlink. When the Create Hyperlink dialog box displays, if necessary, scroll down the file list until the index.htm file displays. Click index.htm and then point to the Change Target Frame button.**

The Create Hyperlink dialog box displays and the file name index.htm displays in the URL text box (Figure 5-64).

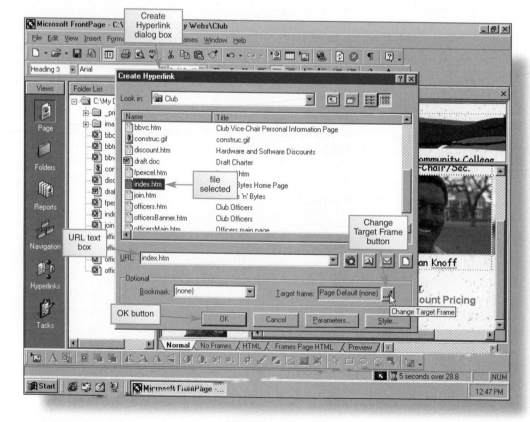

FIGURE 5-64

The Officers hyperlink now will redisplay the entire frames page when clicked. Alternatively, in this instance, the link could have been made to display only the initial main page, and then the target could have been left as the default.

All the initial Web pages have been created and applied to frames in the frames page. The frames Web page is almost complete. Next, you can provide special HTML code in the No Frames view, for viewers who are using browsers that do not support frames.

Displaying the No Frames View

Initially, only the Netscape 2.0 browser supported frames. Since then, support for frames has been added to the formal HTML specifications, and all modern browsers support them. It is possible, however, that some viewers still use older versions of browsers that do not support frames.

If you display a frames page in a browser that does not support frames, the results can be unpredictable. This problem is detected, and special HTML code is displayed instead.

The **No Frames HTML code** is contained inside the frames Web page and usually states that your browser does not support frames. It can be a complete, nonframes Web page and supply hyperlinks to other nonframes versions of the Web pages used in your frames page. You can customize the No Frames HTML code by displaying the No Frames view. Perform the following steps to display the No Frames view.

No Frames View

HTML code inserted into the No Frames View is displayed only for browsers that do not accommodate frames pages. Browsers that are frames compatible do not display this view. To allow your users to select whether to view frames, include a hyperlink on the frames page to a version of your page that does not use frames.

 To Display the No Frames View

1 Click the No Frames tab at the bottom of the FrontPage window.

The Web page displays in No Frames view (Figure 5-69).

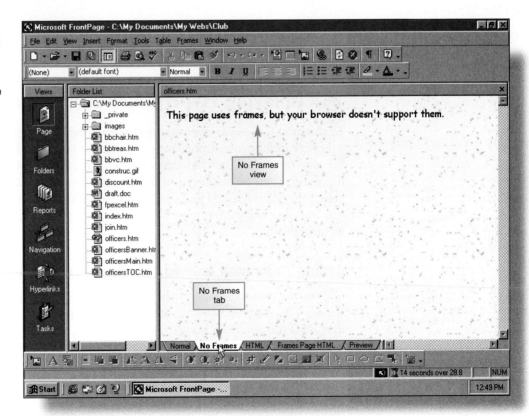

FIGURE 5-69

Click the Normal tab.

The frames Web page redisplays in Normal view (Figure 5-70).

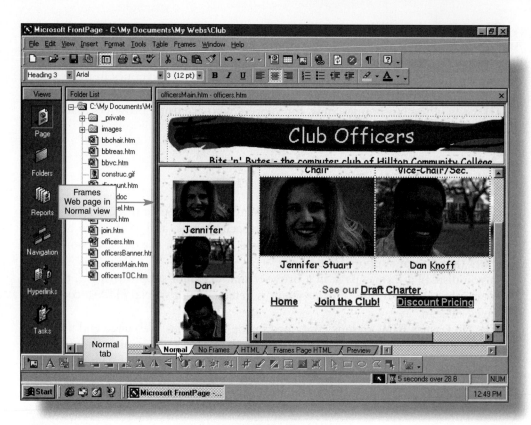

FIGURE 5-70

You can edit the No Frames HTML code as you would any other Web page. This feature is becoming less important as the use of the older browsers diminishes.

Displaying Hyperlinked Pages in a Frame

To this point, the only Web pages that have been displayed are those initial Web pages created for the frames page. The pages targeted by the hyperlinks created earlier were imported, but have not been edited or displayed. By clicking the hyperlinks, these pages can be displayed in their target frame and then edited as any other Web page. Alternatively, you can double-click the file name in the Folder List and then edit it as any other Web page. In this manner, however, the page does not display in its target frame.

Adding Thumbnail Images to a Web Page

For the personal page of the Bits 'n' Bytes club Treasurer, three images need to be added. These are vacation photos supplied in JPEG format. Recall from Project 3 that **JPEG** images often are used for photographic quality pictures. Because JPEG images can be quite large and can take a long time to load, especially if the Web page contains several images, thumbnail images often are made for larger JPEG images. For this reason, it was decided to add a thumbnail image to the Web page rather than the original image. A **thumbnail image** is a small image that is a hyperlink to a larger version of the same picture. Creating a thumbnail version of a JPEG image can speed up the time it takes to load a Web page.

When you create a thumbnail image, a small version of the image is created and stored in a file. The full-sized version of the image is replaced by the small version of the image on the Web page. The small version of the image then is set up as a hyperlink to the full-sized image. When you click the thumbnail image, the full-sized version of the file is loaded in your browser.

You use the **Auto Thumbnail button** on the Pictures toolbar to create a thumbnail image. FrontPage allows you to set options for creating thumbnail images. You can choose whether the image will be created with a border and, if so, you can set the border thickness. Also, you may indicate if the image will be created with a beveled edge, and you may set a default size for the image. Perform the following steps to create a thumbnail image for the vacation photos of the club Treasurer.

 To Add a Thumbnail Image to a Web Page

1 **Hold down the CTRL key and then click the image hyperlink of the Treasurer in the contents frame. If necessary, scroll down the main frame to the third table in the page.**

The personal information Web page for the club Treasurer displays in the right frame (Figure 5-71). In the third table, the text already is added, and the cells in the second row are empty.

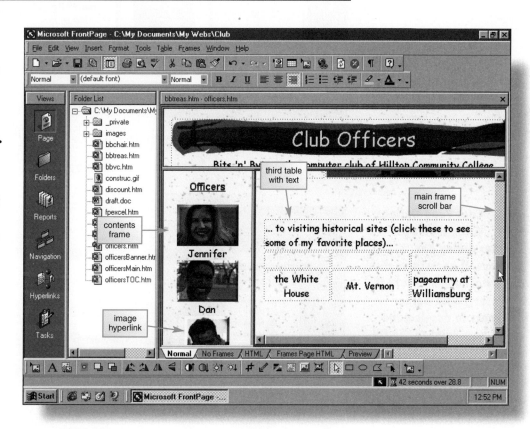

FIGURE 5-71

2 Click Tools on the menu bar. Point to Page Options.

The Tools menu displays (Figure 5-72).

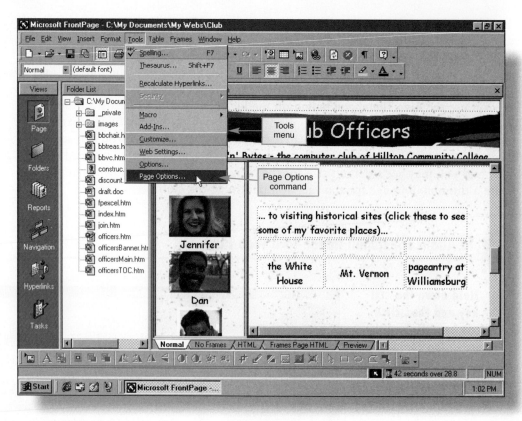

FIGURE 5-72

3 Click Page Options. When the Page Options dialog box displays, if necessary, click the AutoThumbnail tab. If necessary, click Border thickness to deselect the check box. Point to the OK button.

The AutoThumbnail sheet displays with the indicated changes (Figure 5-73).

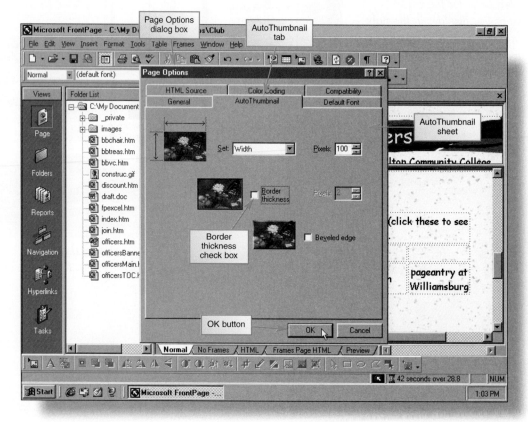

FIGURE 5-73

4 **Click the OK button. Click in column one and row two of the third table to position the insertion point. Point to the Insert Picture From File button on the Pictures toolbar.**

The insertion point displays in the table (Figure 5-74).

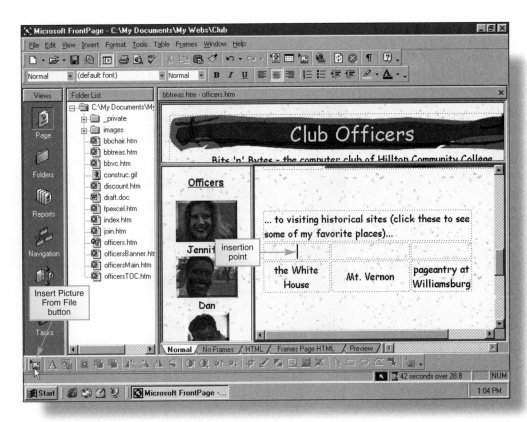

FIGURE 5-74

5 **Click the Insert Picture From File button. When the Picture dialog box displays, if necessary, scroll down the file list until the WhiteHouse.jpg file displays. Click WhiteHouse.jpg and then point to the OK button.**

The Picture dialog box displays with the file WhiteHouse.jpg selected (Figure 5-75). A preview of the image displays.

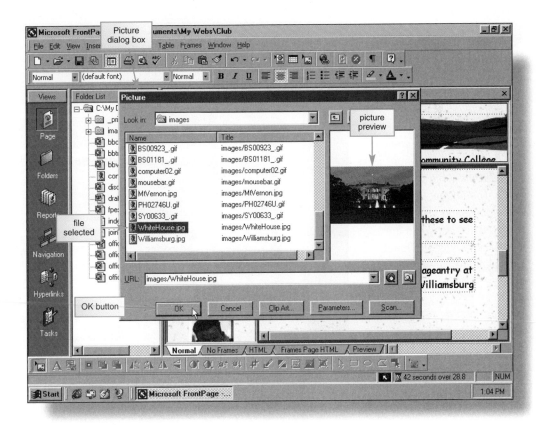

FIGURE 5-75

6 **Click the OK button. Click the image to select it. Point to the Auto Thumbnail button on the Pictures toolbar.**

The selected image displays in the table cell (Figure 5-76). Sizing handles indicate the picture is selected.

FIGURE 5-76

7 **Click the Auto Thumbnail button to make a thumbnail image of the larger image. Position the mouse pointer on the image.**

A thumbnail image is created and replaces the original image in the table (Figure 5-77). The images/ WhiteHouse.jpg URL displays on the status bar when the mouse pointer is positioned on the image hyperlink.

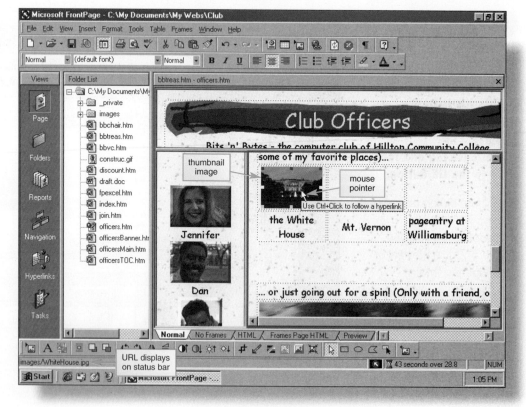

FIGURE 5-77

8 Repeat Steps 5 through 7 to insert the remaining two thumbnail pictures in their respective table cells. Use the file MtVernon.jpg for the cell in the second column and the file Williamsburg.jpg for the cell in the third column.

The inserted thumbnail images display in the table (Figure 5-78).

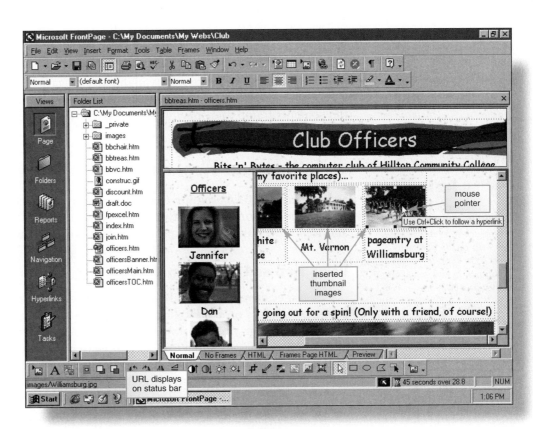

FIGURE 5-78

9 Click the Save button on the Standard toolbar. When the Save Embedded Files dialog box displays, point to the OK button.

The Save Embedded Files dialog box displays indicating Save in the Action column (Figure 5-79). The inserted thumbnail images automatically are named with _small appended to the original file name. The larger image files will not be overwritten.

10 Click the OK button.

The page and the embedded files are saved.

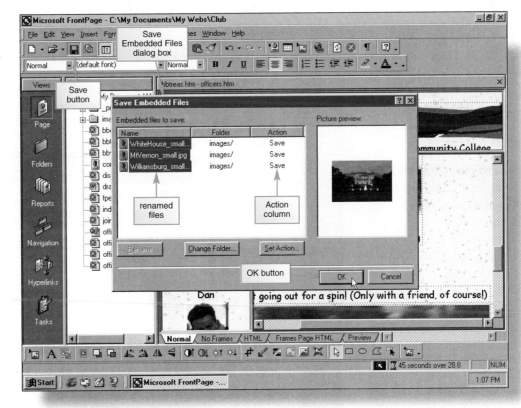

FIGURE 5-79

The thumbnail images are hyperlinks to their corresponding full-sized images. When a viewer clicks the thumbnail, the full-size image displays in the frame, much like a Web page would do. The browser is displaying an image file not a Web page, however, so hyperlinks are not available to navigate back to the previous page. The viewer will have to click the browser's Back button or click one of the hyperlinks in the contents frame to display another page in the frame.

Finding and Replacing Text in a Web

Sometimes due to last minute changes or discovered errors, you will have to replace text in one or more pages in the FrontPage web. FrontPage provides a global Find and Replace feature that makes this process more accurate and complete.

Using Find and Replace in a Web

In earlier projects for the Bits 'n' Bytes web, you inserted text and a hyperlink for an e-mail address on the Home page to direct e-mail to bbpres@hcc.edu, and you modified the form on the Join page to send e-mail to bbvp@hcc.edu. The Officers page refers to a Chair and Vice-Chair, however, as indicated in the draft charter document. With this in mind, it is appropriate to change the text and e-mail hyperlinks to bbchair@hcc.edu and bbvc@hcc.edu, respectively.

Although the text for the e-mail hyperlink is visible on the Home page, the actual URL and the URL in the form on the Join page are not visible directly. The Replace feature in FrontPage allows you to search either on the current page or in the HTML code for all pages. Perform the following steps to find and replace text in the HTML code for the Bits 'n' Bytes web.

Steps **To Find and Replace Text in HTML**

1 **Click Edit on the menu bar and then point to Replace.**

The Edit menu displays with the Replace command highlighted (Figure 5-80).

FIGURE 5-80

2 Click Replace. When the Replace dialog box displays, type bbpres@hcc.edu in the Find what text box. Type bbchair@hcc.edu in the Replace with text box. In the Search options area, click All pages below Find where. Click Find in HTML below Options. Point to the Find in Web button.

The Replace dialog box displays with the indicated changes (Figure 5-81).

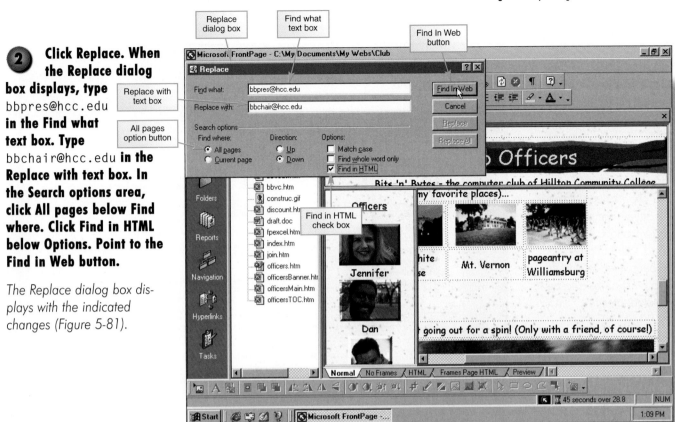

FIGURE 5-81

3 Click the Find in Web button. When the list box displays with a list of pages found, point to the found page in the text box.

A text box displays in the Replace dialog box with a list of pages, if any, where the indicated text was found (Figure 5-82). A count of the number of occurrences of the indicated text displays with each page.

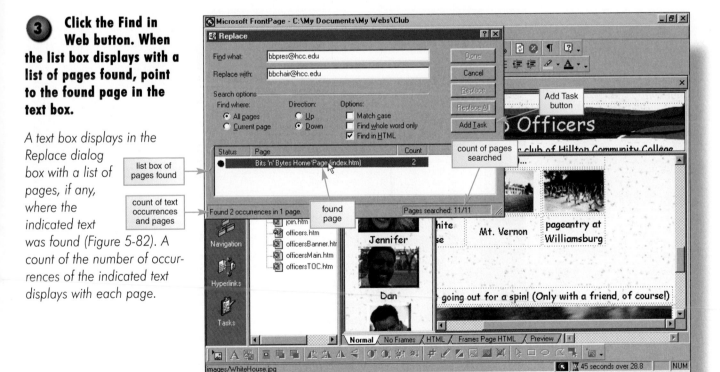

FIGURE 5-82

Double-click the page item in the text box list to perform the task of making the text replacement.

The selected page displays in HTML view with the search phrase highlighted (Figure 5-83). The Replace dialog box is still visible on top of the HTML page. Alternatively, the Add Task button could have been used to add the task to a list of tasks to be completed later.

FIGURE 5-83

5 **Click the Replace button.**

The selected HTML is replaced with the replacement text and the next occurrence, if any, displays (Figure 5-84).

FIGURE 5-84

6 Repeat Step 5 until the Finished checking documents dialog box displays. Verify that Save and close the current document is selected. Point to the OK button.

The Finished checking documents dialog box displays (Figure 5-85). This dialog box indicates that all occurrences of the specified text have been found on this Web page.

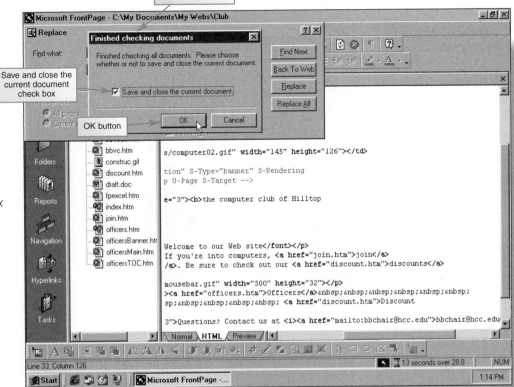

FIGURE 5-85

7 Click the OK button. Type bbvp@hcc.edu in the Find what text box. Type bbvc@hcc.edu in the Replace with text box. If necessary, click All pages and then click Find in HTML. Point to the Find in Web button.

The status of the previous find and replace task is changed to Edited and the Replace dialog box displays with the indicated changes (Figure 5-86).

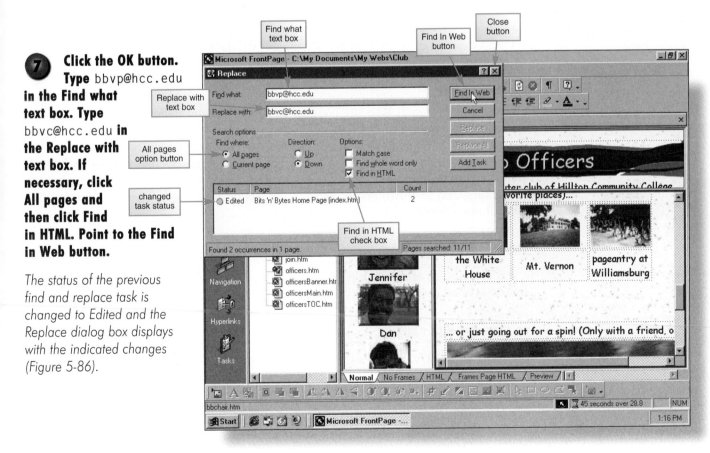

FIGURE 5-86

Repeat Steps 3 through 6 to find and replace the indicated text. Click the OK button in the Finished checking documents dialog box. Click the Close button to close the Replace dialog box.

The Web page displays in Normal view (Figure 5-87). The specified changes have been made throughout the entire Web.

Save button

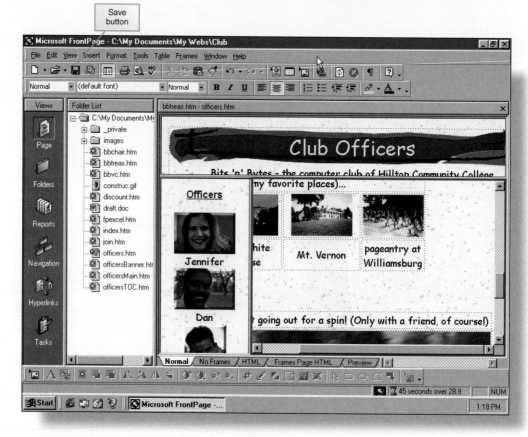

FIGURE 5-87

Other Ways

1. Press ALT+E, E
2. Press CTRL+H

Reporting on the Web Site

Even a relatively small Web site consists of many files and hyperlinks to possibly many more files, even on destinations outside of the Web site itself. Managing all of the pieces of a Web site can be a daunting task. FrontPage provides various reports to illustrate the status of the FrontPage web. FrontPage tracks many items in the Web such as the number of picture files, broken hyperlinks, slow pages, recently added files, and so forth. Before viewing reports or verifying hyperlinks, you should save all open pages.

Saving the Web Page

When editing of the Web page is complete, or prior to verifying hyperlinks, you should save all open pages on disk. The step below saves the Web pages.

TO SAVE THE WEB PAGE

 Click the Save button on the Standard toolbar.

The Web page is saved in the club folder on drive C (or the drive where you originally opened this web).

Other Ways

1. On File menu click Save
2. Press ALT+F, S
3. Press CTRL+S

Viewing Reports on the Web Site

One useful report provided by FrontPage shows all broken hyperlinks in the Web site. Determining which hyperlinks are broken can be a very slow and error-prone process when done by hand. Perform the following steps to view the FrontPage broken hyperlinks report.

To View the Broken Hyperlinks Report

1 **Click View on the menu bar and then point to Reports. Point to Broken Hyperlinks on the Reports submenu.**

The View menu and Reports submenu display (Figure 5-88). The recessed check mark to the left of the Site Summary command on the Reports submenu indicates the report that currently is visible when in Reports view.

FIGURE 5-88

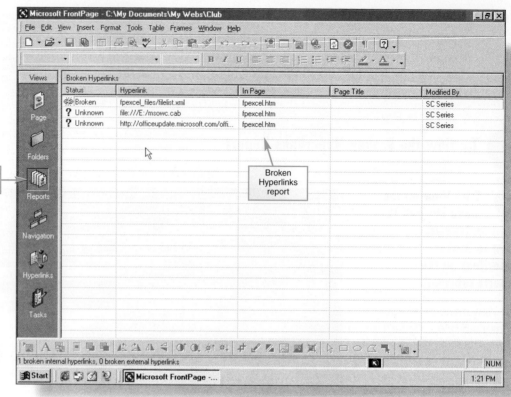

② Click Broken Hyperlinks.

The Broken Hyperlinks report for the Web displays (Figure 5-89). The recessed Reports icon on the Views bar indicates the page displays in Reports view. When a hyperlink needs to be repaired, you can double-click a line on the report to edit the hyperlink. If only the hyperlinks shown in Figure 5-89 display, no changes are necessary .

③ Click the Page icon on the Views bar to return to Page view.

FIGURE 5-89

 *Other Ways*

1. On View menu click Reports, click Broken Hyperlinks on Reports submenu
2. Press ALT+V, R, B
3. Click Report box arrow on Reporting toolbar, click Broken Hyperlinks
4. Click Verify Hyperlinks button on Reporting toolbar
5. Double-click Broken Hyperlinks on Site Summary report
6. Click Reports icon on Views bar, if necessary, double-click Broken Hyperlinks

Verifying Hyperlinks

Just verifying that all hyperlinks in a Web site are correct is a critical and possibly time-consuming task. FrontPage provides a means of verifying that the hyperlinks to external destinations (destinations that are outside of the web) are valid.

You need to be connected to the World Wide Web to verify external hyperlinks. Perform the following steps to use the Reporting toolbar to verify hyperlinks in the web.

More About 2000

Task History

When a task is completed, the task is hidden by default. To view completed tasks, if any, point to Task on the Edit menu when in Task view, and click Show History, if not already checked.

Steps To Use the Reporting Toolbar to Verify Hyperlinks in the Web

1 **Click View on the menu bar and then point to Toolbars. Point to Reporting on the Toolbars submenu.**

The View menu and Toolbars submenu display (Figure 5-90). The recessed check marks indicate the toolbars that currently are visible.

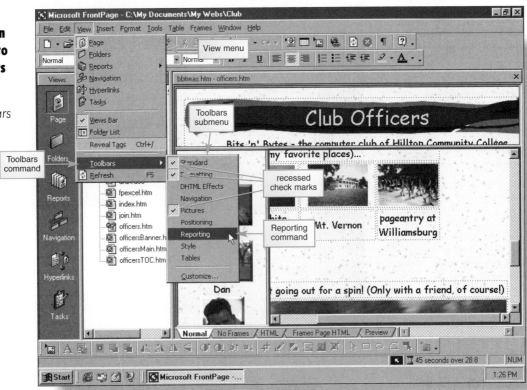

FIGURE 5-90

2 **Click Reporting. Point to the Verify Hyperlinks button on the Reporting toolbar.**

The Reporting toolbar displays (Figure 5-91).

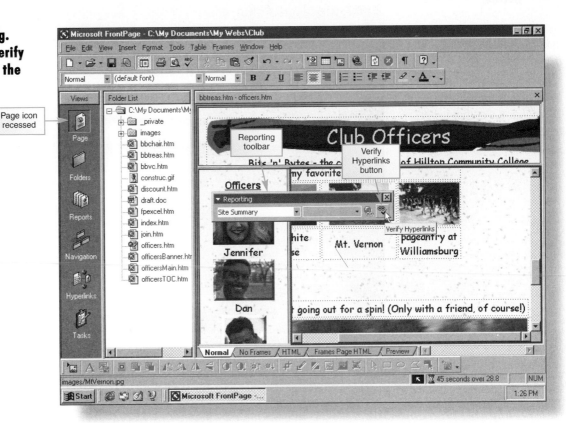

FIGURE 5-91

3 **Click the Verify Hyperlinks button. When the Verify Hyperlinks dialog box displays, if necessary, click Verify all hyperlinks. Point to the Start button.**

The FrontPage window changes to Reports view and the Verify Hyperlinks dialog box displays (Figure 5-92).

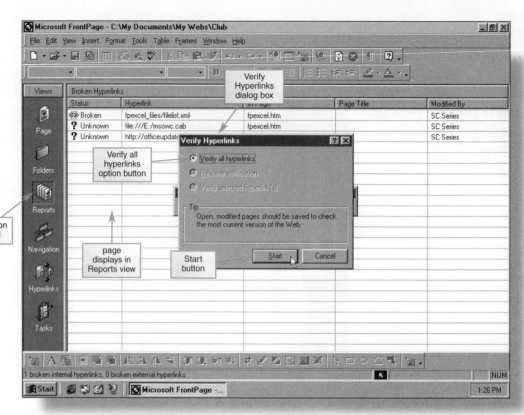

FIGURE 5-92

4 **Click the Start button.**

FrontPage verifies the hyperlinks and displays individual hyperlink results in the Broken Hyperlinks report (Figure 5-93). A count of broken internal and external hyperlinks is displayed on the status bar.

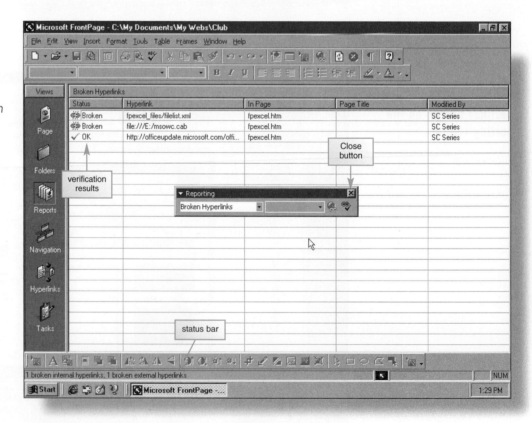

FIGURE 5-93

5 **Click the Close button on the Reporting toolbar. Click the Page icon on the Views bar. If you have any unsaved changes, click the Save button on the Standard toolbar.**

The web displays in Page view (Figure 5-94).

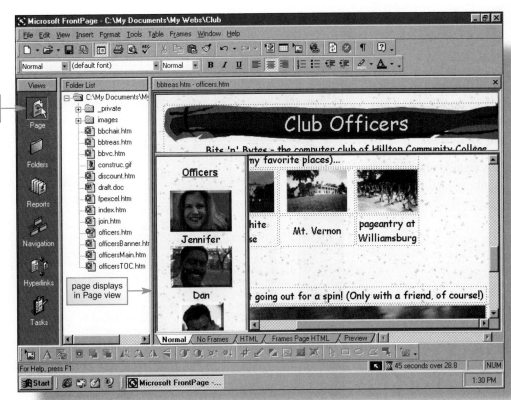

Page icon recessed

page displays in Page view

FIGURE 5-94

Other Ways

1. Press ALT+V, T, click Reporting on Toolbars submenu
2. Right-click a toolbar, click Reporting on shortcut menu

Printing Web Pages in Frames

Once all the pages in frames have been saved on disk, you can print them. You cannot print the entire frames Web page. You only can print each individual Web page in a frame. You do this by clicking the frame containing the desired Web page to make it the active frame, and then by printing that individual Web page.

To display the different Web pages in the right, or main, frame so you can print them, you need to click the hyperlinks in the contents frame. Perform the steps on the next page to print all the separate pages that make up the Officers frames page.

More About

Task View and Sort

FrontPage provides tools to help in managing the creation and maintenance of a Web site. Tasks can be named, assigned to individuals or groups, prioritized, and described. The status of each task is displayed. To view assigned tasks, if any, click the Tasks icon on the Views bar. The tasks shown may be sorted by the values in any column in the task list. Click a column label once to sort tasks, and double-click the column label to reverse the sorted order.

Steps **To Print the Web Pages in Frames**

1 **Ready the printer. Click the top frame. Click File on the menu bar and then click Print. Point to the OK button.**

The top frame becomes the active frame, and the Print dialog box displays (Figure 5-95).

FIGURE 5-95

2 **Click the OK button. Click the left frame to make it the current active frame. Click File on the menu bar and then click Print. Point to the OK button.**

The left frame becomes the active frame, and the Print dialog box displays (Figure 5-96).

FIGURE 5-96

3 **Click the OK button. Click the right frame to make it the current active frame. Click File on the menu bar and then click Print. Point to the OK button.**

The right frame becomes the active frame, and the Print dialog box displays (Figure 5-97). The personal information Web page for the club Treasurer currently displays in the right frame.

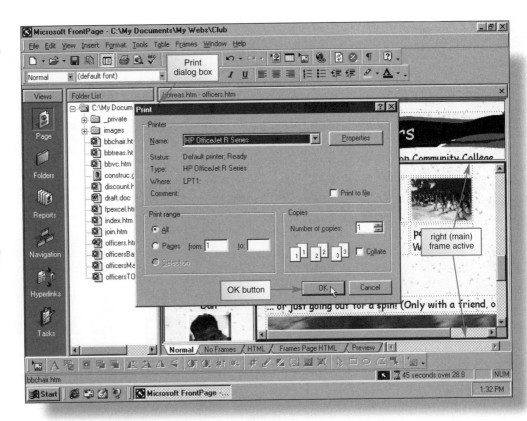

FIGURE 5-97

4 **Click the OK button. While holding down the CTRL key, click the bbchair.htm image hyperlink in the left frame. Release the CTRL key. If necessary, click the right frame to make it the active frame. Point to the Print button on the Standard toolbar.**

The personal information Web page for the club Chair displays in the right frame (Figure 5-98). The right frame becomes the active frame.

FIGURE 5-98

5 **Click the Print button. While holding down the CTRL key, click the bbvc.htm image hyperlink in the left frame. Release the CTRL key. If necessary, click the right frame to make it the active frame. Point to the Print button on the Standard toolbar.**

The personal information Web page for the club Vice-Chair displays in the right frame (Figure 5-99). The right frame becomes the active frame.

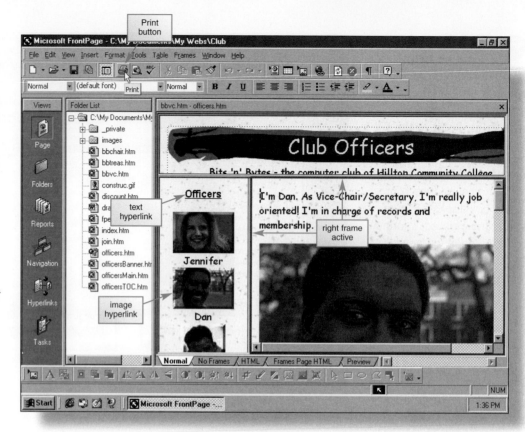

FIGURE 5-99

6 **Click the Print button. While holding down the CTRL key, click the Officers text hyperlink in the left frame. Release the CTRL key. Click the right frame to make it the active frame. Point to the Print button on the Standard toolbar.**

The Officers Web page displays in the right frame (Figure 5-100). The right frame becomes the active frame.

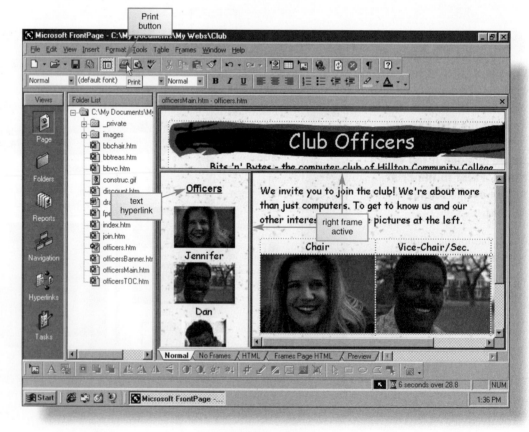

FIGURE 5-100

7 **Click the Print button on the Standard toolbar.**

When the printer stops, retrieve the printouts (Figure 5-101).

FIGURE 5-101

Recall from Project 1 that you may view and print the structure of a site in Navigation view. Perform the following steps to print the structure of the completed Web site.

 To Print the Web Site in Navigation View

 **Click the Navigation icon on the Views bar. Point to the Print button on the Standard toolbar.**

The Web site displays in Navigation view (Figure 5-102). Only pages previously added to the Navigation view are displayed.

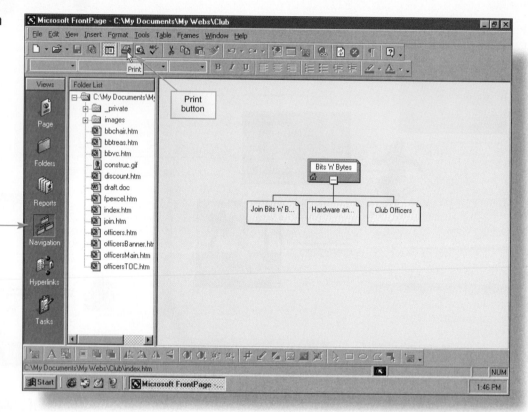

FIGURE 5-102

2 Click the Print button.

The Web page is printed in Navigation view (Figure 5-103).

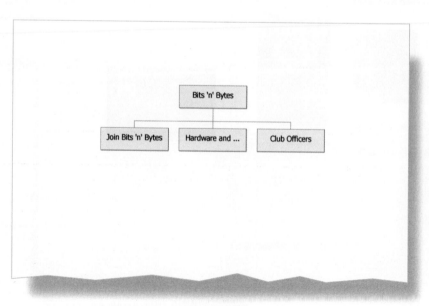

FIGURE 5-103

Publishing Changes to a FrontPage Web

You have added the frames Web page, the three initial Web pages, the three target Web pages, and the accompanying image files and Word document to the FrontPage web. For these new Web pages to be available on the World Wide Web, you must publish the Bits 'n' Bytes web again.

When you publish a FrontPage web that has been published before, FrontPage will install only those parts of the web that are new or have changed since the last time the web was published. This reduces the amount of data transfer that takes place, which is good for webs with many folders, Web pages, and files.

The following steps publish changes to a FrontPage web. Be sure to substitute your own URL or an error will occur. If you do not know what URL to use, ask your instructor.

TO PUBLISH CHANGES TO A FRONTPAGE WEB

1 Click the Publish Web button on the Standard toolbar.

2 When the Publish Web dialog box displays, type `ftp://www.hcc.edu/computer/club` in the Specify the location to publish your web to text box. If your Web server has the Microsoft FrontPage Server Extensions installed, you can publish using HTTP (hypertext transfer protocol). Otherwise, you must publish the web using FTP (file transfer protocol).

3 Click the Publish button.

4 Type your FTP user name and password. Click the OK button.

5 Click the Done button.

You now can view the Officers page by entering http://www.hcc.edu/computer/club/officers.htm in any browser and then pressing the ENTER key. Be sure to test the hyperlinks in the contents frame on the Officers page, as well as the hyperlinks to the Home, Join, and Discount pages, to the Draft Charter, and from the Home page to the Officers page.

Quitting FrontPage

When you have published the Bits 'n' Bytes web, you can quit Microsoft FrontPage. Perform the following step to quit FrontPage.

TO QUIT FRONTPAGE

1 Click the Close button on the FrontPage title bar.

The FrontPage window closes and the Windows desktop displays.

CASE PERSPECTIVE SUMMARY

The Web for the Bits 'n' Bytes computer club now is complete, and the officers are very satisfied with the result. They are impressed with the capabilities of FrontPage and want to gain more experience with it. They are pleased with your design and with what they have learned from you during the development of their Web site. They look forward to future development with you as their experience with their site grows.

Project Summary

Having completed Project 5, you now are ready to incorporate frames in your Web pages. In this project, you learned about frames and how you can use them. You imported Web pages and other Web resources into a FrontPage web. The project demonstrated how to use a frames template. You learned how to use an existing Web page as the initial Web page in a frame and how to adjust the size of a frame. You created a new initial Web page for a frame, and then you created hyperlinks to Web pages in frames and hyperlinks to whole pages. You learned how to modify properties of a frame and of a frames page and how to add thumbnail images to a page. You learned how to display and edit the No Frames HTML code and how to use Find and Replace across a Web site. Finally, you learned how to use FrontPage reporting features and how to verify hyperlinks.

What You Should Know

Having completed this project, you now should be able to perform the following tasks:

▶ Add a Thumbnail Image to a Web Page (*FP 5.53*)
▶ Adjust the Size of a Frame (*FP 5.23*)
▶ Create a Frames Page Using a Frames Template (*FP 5.13*)
▶ Create a Hyperlink to a Whole Page (*FP 5.48*)
▶ Create a New Page in the Main Frame (*FP 5.24*)
▶ Create Hyperlinks Targeting the Default Frame (*FP 5.43*)
▶ Create the Contents Frame Web Page (*FP 5.35*)
▶ Display the No Frames View (*FP 5.51*)
▶ Find and Replace Text in HTML (*FP 5.58*)
▶ Import Files into an Existing FrontPage Web (*FP 5.11*)
▶ Insert Pictures from a File into a Table (*FP 5.26*)
▶ Insert Text and a Table in the Main Frame Initial Page (*FP 5.25*)
▶ Modify Frame Properties (*FP 5.37*)
▶ Modify Frames Page Properties (*FP 5.39*)

▶ Modify Table Properties (*FP 5.28*)
▶ Move Image Files to the Images Web Folder (*FP 5.12*)
▶ Print the Web Pages in Frames (*FP 5.68*)
▶ Print the Web Site in Navigation View (*FP 5.72*)
▶ Publish Changes to a FrontPage Web (*FP 5.73*)
▶ Quit FrontPage (*FP 5.73*)
▶ Save Changes to the Frames Page (*FP 5.24*)
▶ Save the Frames Web Page (*FP 5.16*)
▶ Save the Initial Web Page (*FP 5.30*)
▶ Save the Web Page (*FP 5.62*)
▶ Start FrontPage and Open an Existing Web (*FP 5.10*)
▶ Use an Existing Web Page as the Initial Page in a Frame (*FP 5.20*)
▶ Use the Reporting Toolbar to Verify Hyperlinks in the Web (*FP 5.65*)
▶ View the Broken Hyperlinks Report (*FP 5.63*)

Apply Your Knowledge

Project Reinforcement at www.scsite.com/off2000/reinforce.htm

1 Making a New Frames Template

Instructions: Start FrontPage 2000 and perform the following steps with a computer.

1. Click File on the menu bar, point to New, and then click Page on the New submenu. When the New dialog box displays, click the Frame Pages tab. Click the Header, Footer, and Contents icon. Click the OK button.

2. A new frames page displays with four frames. If the top frame is not the currently selected frame, click in that frame to select it.

3. Click Frames on the menu bar and then click Delete Frame. The top frame is deleted and the outline is around the entire outer frame.

4. Click File on the menu bar and then click Save As. When the Save As dialog box displays, click the Save as type box arrow. Click FrontPage Template in the list. Type `footwtoc.tem` or a file name of your choosing in the File name text box. If necessary, change the directory. Click the Save button.

5. When the Save as Template dialog box displays, type `Footer and Contents` or another name of your choosing in the Title text box. This title will display when accessing the template to create a new page.

6. In the Description text box, type `Creates a Contents frame on the left containing hyperlinks that change the main page on the right. Hyperlinks in the Footer change the Contents frame.` This is a short description of what this frames template does. Click the OK button. Close the Web page.

7. Create a new Web page using the template you have just created. The new frames template should show as the Footer and Contents template in the Frames Pages sheet, as shown in Figure 5-104. The title you entered should show with a new frames page icon and the description you typed should show in the Description area. A preview of the frames page displays.

8. Test the new page to verify that hyperlinks in the contents frame target the contents of the main frame, and that links in the footer frame target the contents frame.

9. Save the Web page. Print the Web page, write your name on it, and hand it in to your instructor.

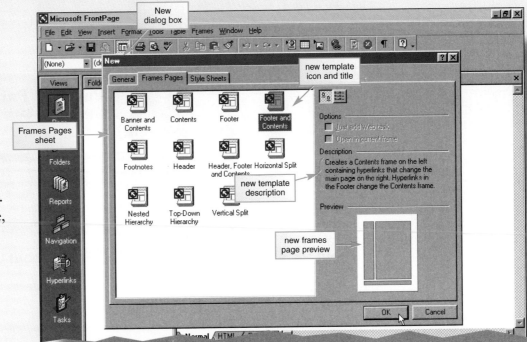

FIGURE 5-104

In the Lab

1 Modifying an Existing Web to Use Frames

Problem: You have decided to use a frames page to provide a table of contents for your Parts Web page created earlier for your automobile parts mail-order business. Because you do not want to make drastic changes to the pages already created, you decide simply to incorporate them, links and all, within frames.

Instructions: Perform the following activities to create the Parts 'n' Parcel frames page.

1. Start FrontPage and open the Parts 'n' Parcel web from Project 4. If you did not complete that assignment, see your instructor for a copy.

2. On the File menu, point to New, and then click Page on the New submenu. Click the Frames Pages tab and then click the Contents template. Click the OK button. Save the frames page as parts_frame.htm. Click the Set Initial Page button in the right (main) frame and then click index.htm. Click the New Page button in the left (contents) frame.

3. Insert a 4 by 1 table. Copy the three links from the home page into the first, third, and fourth rows, respectively, of the table. In the second row, copy and paste the category links from the parts page. Because these hyperlinks are relative to the parts page and now have been copied to a new page, they will reference locations in the new page. Modify these hyperlinks to refer to the original locations in the parts page. Select all of the category links and then click the Bullets button on the Formatting toolbar.

4. Right-click the left frame and then click Frame properties on the shortcut menu. Click Resizable In Browser to deselect the check box. Set Show scrollbar to Never. Click the Frames Page button. Click Show Borders to deselect the check box. Click the OK button in the Page Properties dialog box. Click the OK button in the Frame Properties dialog box. Save the frame as parts_TOC.htm.

5. Save and preview your page in a browser. Your page should resemble the one shown in Figure 5-105. Test the hyperlinks to verify the targets as correct.

6. Publish the Web page, if you have an available server. Print the Web page, write your name on it, and hand it in to your instructor.

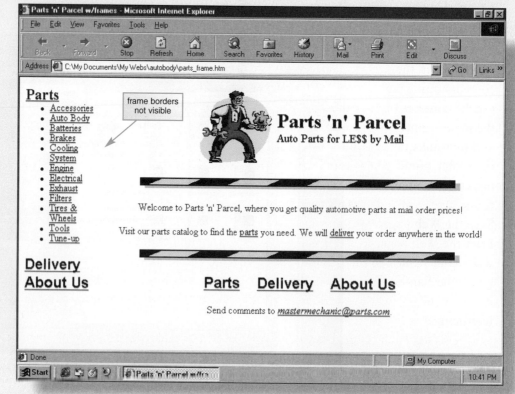

FIGURE 5-105

In the Lab

2 Using a Footer Frame to Control a Contents Frame

Problem: You have volunteered to design a Web site for The Pet Path, which is a nonprofit shelter for domesticated cats and dogs. The director of the shelter would like site visitors to see a main page with a banner frame, table of contents frame, and a footer frame. In the footer frame, the visitor would click his or her area of interest, either dogs or cats. Doing so would load a table of contents frame tailored for either dog or cat subjects. The tailored contents frame would in turn control the content of the main frame. Graphics used may be from the Clip Art Gallery, the Data Disk, or others sources of your choice.

Instructions: Start FrontPage 2000 and perform the following steps.

1. Create a new Web. Add a new Web page using the Header, Footer, and Contents frames template.
2. In the header frame, insert dog and kitten images as shown in Figure 5-106 on the next page. Between the graphics, using a style of Heading 2, type `The Pet Path` as the page name. Save the frames page as index.htm. Save the header page as Banner.htm.
3. In the contents frame, type `We specialize in Cats and Dogs!` Press the ENTER key. Type `Click the area below to indicate your interest.` In the properties for this frame, set Show scrollbars to Never. Click the Frames Page button and then click Show Borders to deselect the check box. Save the contents page as toc_pets.htm.
4. In the main frame, insert a 2 by 2 table. In the top leftmost cell, using a style of Heading 3, type `Where pets beat a path to our door!` Press the ENTER key. Type `Let us help you get on the right path to pet ownership!` Position the insertion point in the top rightmost cell.
5. In the top rightmost cell, insert a graphic that illustrates a path. Merge the two bottom cells and using the default style and font, type `Providing placement and provisions for displaced domestic pets.` Save the main page as main_pets.htm.
6. In the footer frame, insert the two pet graphics used earlier. Between the graphics, type `Kitten Kaboodle` and then press the SPACEBAR seven times. Type `Pet Path Home` and then press the SPACEBAR seven times. Type `Doggie Domain`. Save the footer page as bottom.htm.
7. Create a new contents page for cats. Type `Our feline friends:` and then press the ENTER key. Type `Adoptions` and make this a hyperlink to main_kittens.htm. Hold down the SHIFT key and then press the ENTER key. Type `Toys` and make this a hyperlink to cat_toys.htm. Hold down the SHIFT key and then press the ENTER key. Type `Beds` and make this a hyperlink to cat_beds.htm. Hold down the SHIFT key and then press the ENTER key. Type `Supplies` and make this a hyperlink to cat_supplies.htm. Save the page as toc_cats.htm and close the page.
8. Create a new contents page for dogs. Type `Our puppy pals:` and then press the ENTER key. Type `Adoptions` and make this a hyperlink to main_puppies.htm. Hold down the SHIFT key and then press the ENTER key. Type `Toys` and make this a hyperlink to dog_toys.htm. Hold down the SHIFT key and then press the ENTER key. Type `Beds` and make this a hyperlink to dog_beds.htm. Hold down the SHIFT key and then press the ENTER key. Type `Supplies` and make this a hyperlink to dog_supplies.htm. Save the page as toc_dogs.htm and then close the page.
9. On the footer frame page, bottom.htm, make Kitten Kaboodle a hyperlink to the toc_cats.htm page. Verify that it targets the contents frame, which should be the default. Make Doggie Domain a hyperlink to the toc_dogs.htm page. Verify that it targets the contents frame. Make Pet Path Home a hyperlink to index.htm and change its target to the Whole Page. Save the changes to the footer page.

(continued)

In the Lab

Using a Footer Frame to Control a Contents Frame *(continued)*

10. Be sure to save new embedded images, if any, in the images folder with unique names. Your pages should resemble those shown in Figure 5-106.

11. Print the Web pages, write your name on them, and hand in your work to your instructor.

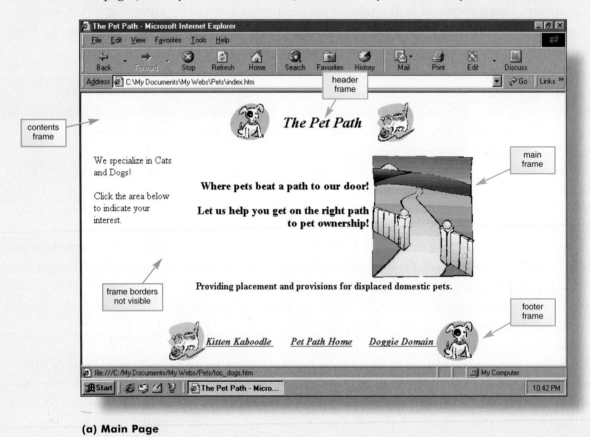

(a) Main Page

FIGURE 5-106

In the Lab

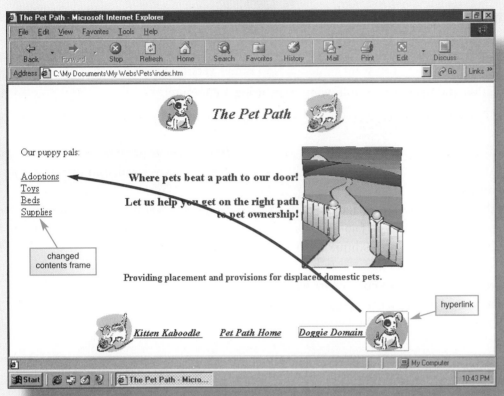

(b) Contents Page for Dogs

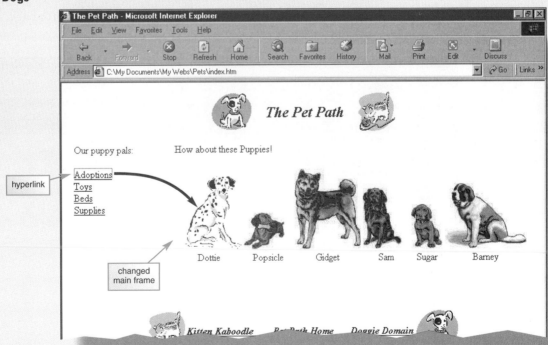

(c) Adoptions Page for Dogs

FIGURE 5-106 *(continued)*

In the Lab

3 Creating a No Frames Page

Problem: You like the frames used in Project 5, but believe that users should have a choice to not use frames, regardless of the capabilities of their browser. You want to add a No Frames version to the Bits 'n' Bytes Web site.

Instructions: Start FrontPage 2000 and perform the following steps using a computer.

1. Open the Bits 'n' Bytes web from Project 5. If you did not complete that assignment, see your instructor for a copy.

2. Open the Officers page, officers.htm. Click the No Frames tab. In the No Frames page, type Use the No Frames version to access the same content. Highlight the text, No Frames version, and then insert a hyperlink to officersNoFrames.htm.

3. Click the Normal tab. In the officersMain.htm page, position the insertion point below the hyperlinks to other pages. Use a font size of 1 (8 pt) and then type [no frames version]. Center the line. Highlight the inserted text and create a hyperlink to officersNoFrames.htm. Be sure to change the target frame to Whole Page. Save and close the page.

4. Double-click the file officersMain.htm in the Folder List pane. Save the file as officersNoFrames.htm before making any changes. In the text at the top of the page, highlight the text at the left. Type below as the replacement text. Modify the three pictures to be hyperlinks to the personal information pages of the respective officers.

5. Add the same banner and text to the top of this page as is in the top frame of the frames version. Save the page.

6. Test the no frames version by viewing the frames page in a browser and clicking the [no frames version] hyperlink. Your pages should resemble those shown in Figure 5-107.

7. Print the modified No Frames page and the newly created officersNoFrames.htm page. Write your name on them, and hand them in to your instructor.

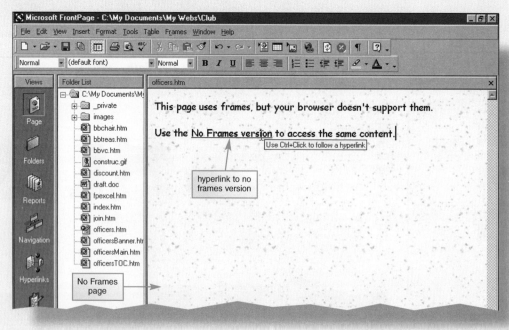

(a) No Frames Page

FIGURE 5-107

In the Lab

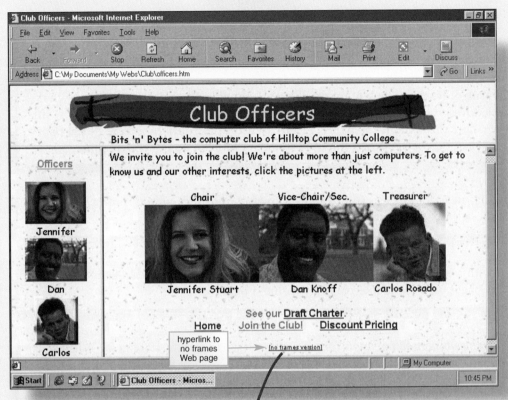

(b) Frames Version of Web Page

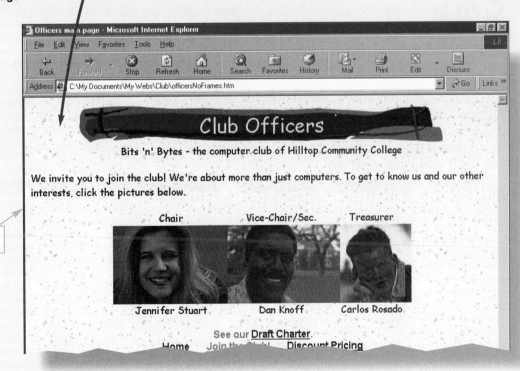

(c) No Frames Version of Web Page

FIGURE 5-107 *(continued)*

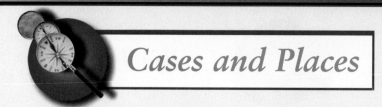

Cases and Places

The difficulty of these case studies varies:
▶ are the least difficult; ▶▶ are more difficult; and ▶▶▶ are the most difficult.

1 ▶ Develop a Web page using a frames template that will provide a table of contents for a paper that you have written or obtained from your instructor. Include hyperlinks in the table of contents to the title of the paper and to each heading throughout the paper. Ensure that the appropriate section of the paper displays in the main frame when the viewer clicks the corresponding table of contents hyperlink.

2 ▶ Develop a Web page that includes links to some of your favorite Web sites in one frame. When clicked, the main page of the selected Web site should display in a main frame.

3 ▶▶ Develop a Web page with a frames template for a table of contents. Include hyperlinks in the contents frame target complete pages, as well as relative links within a page.

4 ▶▶ Develop a Web page frames template having a footer frame with a copyright statement. Whenever you use the template, it should provide a footer frame with a fixed size already formatted with your copyright statement. Create a sample Web page using the template.

5 ▶▶▶ Modify the Web page from the previous project that allows students to provide evaluations for courses in a university system. Place a title and instructions in a fixed frame at the top of the page, with the form in a second, scrollable bottom frame.

6 ▶▶▶ Develop a frames template that will provide a table of contents on the left, an index on the right, and a main frame in the center. Banner and footer frames are optional. Use the right frame for hyperlinks to multiple documents, such as a paper or an online book. For each document selected, include a different table of contents in the left frame. Be sure the links in the contents frame will in turn display pages in the main frame.

Index

APPENDIX A
Microsoft FrontPage 2000 Help System

Using the FrontPage Help System

This appendix demonstrates how you to use the Microsoft FrontPage 2000 Help system to answer your questions. At any time while you are using FrontPage, you can interact with its Help system to display information on any FrontPage topic.

Help is available in Microsoft FrontPage in the form of the Microsoft Help window. As shown in Figure A-1, you access Help in Microsoft FrontPage by pressing the **F1 key**, clicking **Microsoft FrontPage Help** on the Help menu, or clicking the **Microsoft FrontPage Help button** on the Standard toolbar. FrontPage responds by displaying the Microsoft FrontPage Help window (lower half of Figure A-1)

Table A-1 on the next page summarizes the categories of Help available to you. Please review the rightmost column of Table A-1 for instructions on activating the desired category of Help.

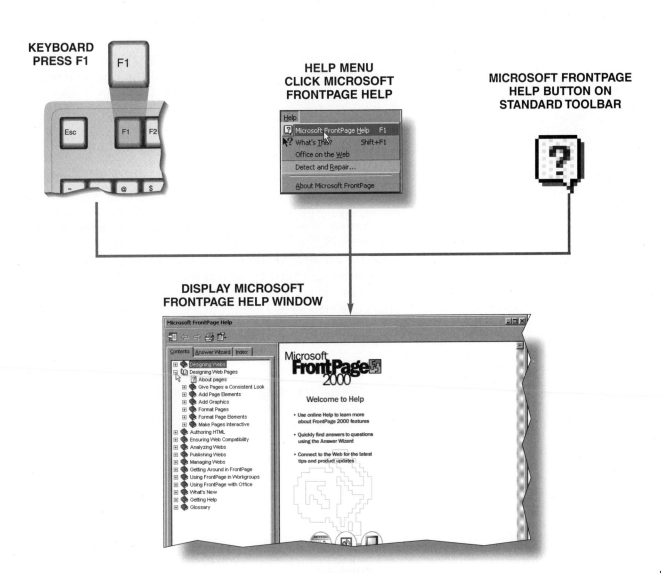

KEYBOARD PRESS F1

HELP MENU CLICK MICROSOFT FRONTPAGE HELP

MICROSOFT FRONTPAGE HELP BUTTON ON STANDARD TOOLBAR

DISPLAY MICROSOFT FRONTPAGE HELP WINDOW

FIGURE A-1

Table A-1   FrontPage Help System

TYPE	DESCRIPTION	HOW TO ACTIVATE
Answer Wizard sheet	Displays a list of topics that pertain to a natural language question or phrase that you type in the text box. From that point, you can select the topics that you want to display.	Click the Microsoft FrontPage Help button on the Standard toolbar. If necessary, maximize the Help window by double-clicking its title bar. Click the Answer Wizard tab.
Contents sheet	Groups Help topics by general categories. Use when you know only the general category of the topic in question.	Click the Microsoft FrontPage Help button on the Standard toolbar. If necessary, maximize the Help window by double-clicking its title bar. Click the Contents tab.
Detect and Repair command	Automatically finds and fixes errors in the application.	Click Detect and Repair on the Help menu.
Index sheet	Similar to an index in a book. Use when you know exactly what you want.	Click the Microsoft FrontPage Help button on the Standard toolbar. If necessary, maximize the Help window by double-clicking its title bar. Click the Index tab.
Office on the Web command	Use to access technical resources and download free product enhancements on the Web.	Click Office on the Web on the Help menu.
Question Mark button and What's This? command	Identify unfamiliar items on the screen.	In a dialog box, click the Question Mark button and then click an element in the dialog box. Click What's This? on the Help menu, and then click an item on the screen.

The best way to familiarize yourself with the FrontPage Help system is to use it. The next several pages show examples of how to use the Help system. Following the examples is a set of exercises titled Use Help that will sharpen your FrontPage Help system skills.

The Microsoft FrontPage Help Window

If you click the Microsoft FrontPage Help button on the Standard toolbar (Figure A-2), the **Microsoft FrontPage Help window** displays (Figure A-3). This window contains three tabs on the left side: Contents, Answer Wizard, and Index. Each tab displays a sheet with powerful look-up capabilities. Use the Contents sheet as you would a table of contents at the front of a book to look up Help. The Answer Wizard sheet answers your queries by responding with a list of topics that relate to the entry you make in the What would you like to do? text box. This entry can be in the form of a word, phrase, or written question. For example, if you want to learn more about saving a file, you can type, save, save a file, how do I save a file, or anything similar in the text box. The Answer Wizard responds by displaying a list of topics from which you can choose. Once you choose a topic, it displays the corresponding information. You use the Index sheet in the same manner as an index in a book. Click the tabs to move from sheet to sheet.

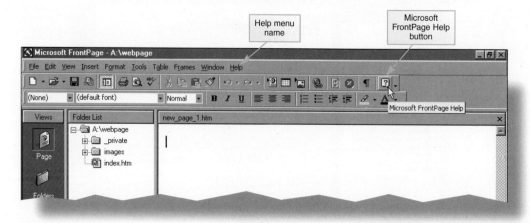

FIGURE A-2

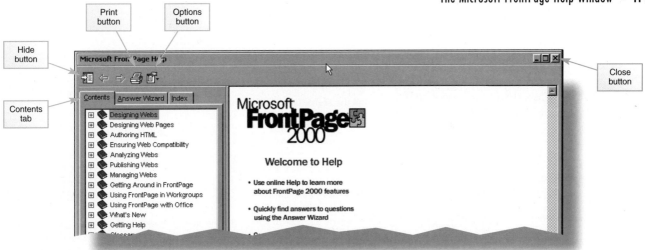

FIGURE A-3

Besides clicking the Microsoft FrontPage Help button on the Standard toolbar, you also can click the Microsoft FrontPage Help command on the Help menu or press the F1 key to display the Microsoft FrontPage Help window to gain access to the three sheets. When the Microsoft FrontPage Help window displays, you can choose to read it or print it. To print the information, click the Print button on the Microsoft FrontPage Help toolbar. The five buttons on the toolbar, Show or Hide, Back, Forward, Print, and Options are described in Table A-2. To close the Microsoft FrontPage Help window, click the Close button in the upper-right corner on the title bar.

Table A-2	Microsoft FrontPage Help Toolbar Buttons	
BUTTON	**NAME**	**FUNCTION**
⬅️ or ➡️	Show or Hide	Displays or hides the Contents, Answer Wizard, Index tabs
⬅	Back	Displays the previous Help topic
➡	Forward	Displays the next Help topic
🖨	Print	Prints the current Help topic
📋	Options	Displays a list of commands

Using the Contents Sheet

The **Contents sheet** is useful for displaying Help when you know the general category of the topic in question, but not the specifics. The following steps show how to use the Contents sheet to obtain information about Web folders.

TO OBTAIN HELP USING THE CONTENTS SHEET

1 Click the Microsoft FrontPage Help button on the Standard toolbar (Figure A-2).

2 When the Microsoft FrontPage Help window displays, double-click the title bar to maximize the window. If necessary, click the Show button to display the tabs.

3 Click the Contents tab.

4 Double-click the Designing Web Pages book on the left side of the window.

5 Double-click the Give Pages a Consistent Look book below the About pages subtopic.

6 Double-click the Themes book below the Give Pages a Consistent Look book.

7 Click the Change the styles used in a theme subtopic below the Themes book.

FrontPage displays Help on the subtopic, Change the styles used in a theme (Figure A-4 on the next page).

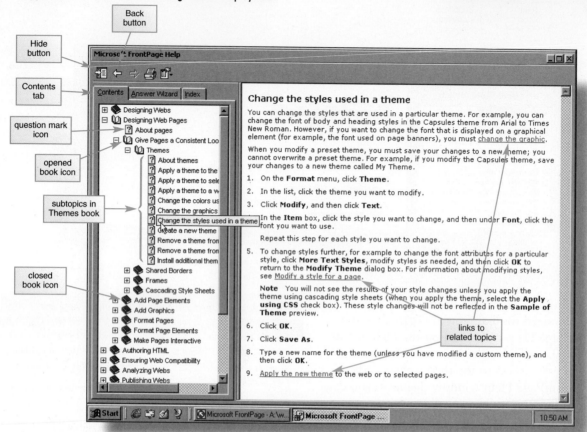

FIGURE A-4

Once the information on the subtopic displays, you can scroll through the window and read it or you can click the Print button to obtain a hard copy. If you decide to click another subtopic on the left or a link on the right, you can get back to the Help page shown in Figure A-3 on the previous page by clicking the Back button as many times as necessary.

Each topic in the Contents list is preceded by a book icon or question mark icon. A **book icon** indicates subtopics are available. A **question mark icon** means information on the topic will display if you double-click the title. The book icon opens when you double-click the book (or its title) or click the plus sign (+) to the left of the book icon.

Using the Answer Wizard Sheet

With the **Answer Wizard sheet,** you enter a word, phrase, or question and FrontPage responds with topics from which you can choose to display Help. The following steps show how to use the Answer Wizard sheet to obtain Help about themes in FrontPage.

TO OBTAIN HELP USING THE ANSWER WIZARD SHEET

1. Click the Microsoft FrontPage Help button on the Standard toolbar (Figure A-2 on page FP A.2).

2. When the Microsoft FrontPage Help window displays, double-click the title bar to maximize the window. If necessary, click the Show button to display the tabs.

3. Click the Answer Wizard tab. Type what are themes in the What would you like to do? text box on the left side of the window. Click the Search button.

4. When a list of topics displays in the Select topic to display list box, click About themes.

FrontPage displays Help about themes (Figure A-5).

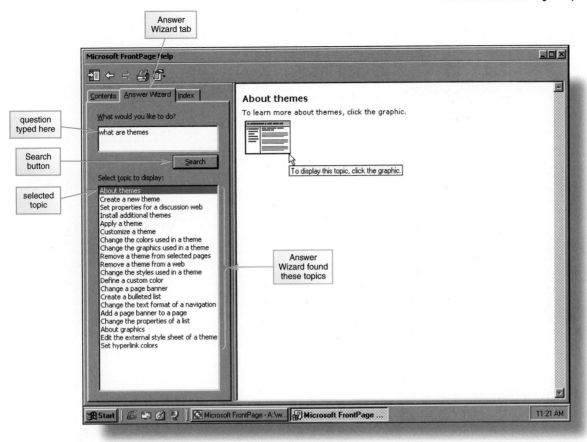

FIGURE A-5

If the topic, About themes, does not include the information you are searching for, click another topic in the list. Continue to click topics until you find the desired information.

Using the Index Sheet

The third sheet in the Microsoft FrontPage Help window is the Index sheet. Use the **Index sheet** to display Help when you know the keyword or the first few letters of the keyword you want to look up. The following steps show how to use the Index sheet to obtain Help on creating new themes.

TO OBTAIN HELP USING THE INDEX SHEET

1. Click the Microsoft FrontPage Help button on the Standard toolbar (Figure A-2 on page FP A.2).

2. When the Microsoft FrontPage Help window displays, double-click the title bar to maximize the window. If necessary, click the Show button to display the tabs.

3. Click the Index tab. Type create theme in the Type keywords text box on the left side of the window. Click the Search button.

FrontPage highlights the first topic (Create a new theme) on the left side of the window and displays information about creating a new theme on the right side of the window (Figure A-6 on the next page).

In the Choose a topic list box on the left side of the window, you can click another topic to display additional Help.

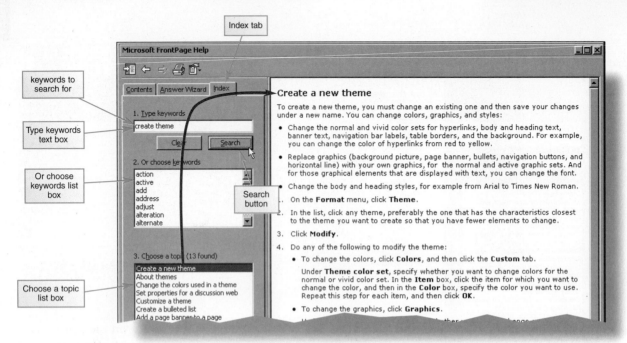

FIGURE A-6

An alternative to typing a keyword in the Type keywords text box is to scroll through the Or choose keywords list box (the middle list box on the left side of the window). When you locate the keyword you are searching for, double-click it to display Help on the topic. Also in the Or choose keywords list box, the FrontPage Help system displays other topics that relate to the new keyword. As you begin typing a new keyword in the Type keywords text box, FrontPage Help jumps to that point in the middle list box. To begin a new search, click the Clear button.

What's This? Command and Question Mark Button

Use the What's This command on the Help menu or the Question Mark button in a dialog box when you are not sure what an object on the screen is or what it does.

What's This? Command

You use the **What's This? command** on the Help menu to display a detailed ScreenTip. When you invoke this command, the mouse pointer changes to an arrow with a question mark. You then click any object on the screen, such as a button, to display the ScreenTip. For example, after you click the What's This? command on the Help menu and then click the Hyperlink button on the Standard toolbar, a description of the Hyperlink command displays (Figure A-7).

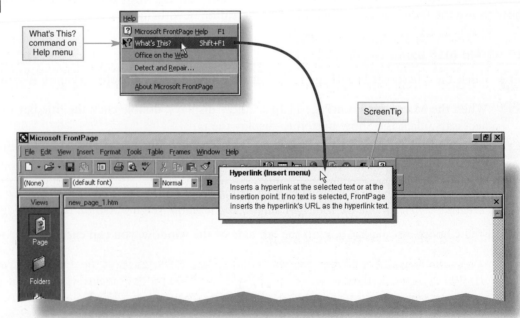

FIGURE A-7

You can print the ScreenTip by right-clicking it and then clicking Print Topic on the shortcut menu.

Question Mark Button

In a response similar to that of the What's This? command, the **Question Mark button** displays a ScreenTip. You use the Question Mark button with dialog boxes. It is located in the upper-right corner on the title bar of dialog boxes, next to the Close button. For example, in Figure A-8, the Print dialog box displays on the screen. If you click the Question Mark button, and then click the Print to file check box, an explanation of the Print to file check box displays in a ScreenTip. You can print the ScreenTip by right-clicking it and then clicking Print Topic on the shortcut menu.

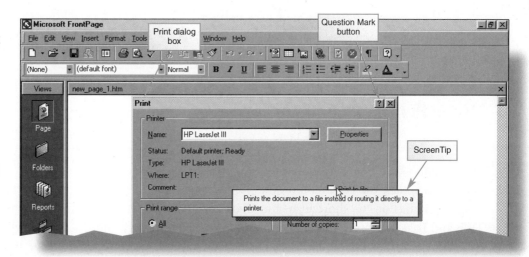

FIGURE A-8

If a dialog box does not include a Question Mark button, press the **SHIFT+ F1 keys**. This combination of keys will change the mouse pointer to an arrow with a question mark. You then can click any object in the dialog box to display the ScreenTip.

Office on the Web Command

The **Office on the Web command** on the Help menu displays a Microsoft Web page containing up-to-date information on a variety of Office-related topics. To use this command, you must be connected to the Internet. Once the page displays, you can click the FrontPage link, if necessary, on the left side of the window and then click the Assistance link. The FrontPage Assistance Web page contains several links such as Articles for Microsoft FrontPage 2000 and FrontPage User Groups.

Other Help Commands

Two additional commands available on the Help menu are Detect and Repair, and About Microsoft FrontPage. The Help menu of the other Office applications have similar commands that are beneficial when using each Office application.

Detect and Repair Command

Use the **Detect and Repair command** on the Help menu if FrontPage is not running properly or if it is generating errors. When you invoke this command, the Detect and Repair dialog box displays. Click the Start button in the dialog box to initiate the detect and repair process.

About Microsoft FrontPage Command

The **About Microsoft FrontPage command** on the Help menu displays the About Microsoft FrontPage dialog box. The dialog box lists the owner of the software and the product identification. You need to know the product identification if you call Microsoft for assistance. The three buttons below the OK button are the **System Info button,** it displays system information, including hardware resources, components, software environment, and applications; the **Tech Support button**, it displays technical assistance information; and the **Network Test button**, it launches a test that specifies technical information about your network configuration.

Use Help

1 Using the FrontPage Help System

Instructions: Perform the following tasks using the FrontPage Help system.

1. Start FrontPage.
2. If necessary, click the Page icon on the Views bar. Right-click the default page on the Normal tab. Click Page Properties on the shortcut menu. Click the Question Mark button and then display ScreenTips for Title and Base location in the upper area of the General sheet and Location in the Background sound area of the General sheet. Right-click the ScreenTips to print them. Close the Page Properties dialog box.
3. Press SHIFT+F1. Click Insert on the menu bar, point to Component, and then click Hit Counter. Right-click the ScreenTip to print it. Hand in the printout to your instructor.
4. Click Help on the menu bar and then click Microsoft FrontPage Help. Maximize the Microsoft FrontPage Help window. If the tabs are hidden on the left side, click the Show button. Click the Contents tab. Double-click the Designing Webs book. Double-click the Hyperlinks book. Click the subtopic, Add font effects to a hyperlink. Move the mouse pointer on the underlined link and note the response. Right-click the topic and print the information using the shortcut menu.
5. Close the Microsoft FrontPage Help window.

2 Expanding on the FrontPage Help System Basics

Instructions: Use the FrontPage Help system to understand the topics better and answer the questions listed below. Answer the questions on your own paper, or hand in the printed Help information to your instructor.

1. Click the Microsoft FrontPage Help button on the Standard toolbar. Maximize the Microsoft FrontPage Help window. If the tabs are hidden on the left side, click the Show button. Click the Index tab. Type reset in the Type keywords text box. Click the Search button. Click View or customize menus in the Choose a topic list. Print the information. Click the Hide button and then the Show button. Close the Microsoft FrontPage Help window. Hand in the printout to your instructor.
2. Press the F1 key. Maximize the Microsoft FrontPage Help window. Click the Answer Wizard tab. Type help in the What would you like to do? text box, and then click the Search button. Click Keyboard shortcuts. Click the Keys for menus and toolbars link. Read through the information that displays. Print the information.
3. Click the Contents tab. Click the plus sign (+) to the left of the Publishing Webs book. One at a time, click the three topics Check the publishing status of a web, Mark the pages to publish, and Hide a page from Web browsers. Read and print each one. Close the Microsoft FrontPage Help window. Hand in the printouts to your instructor.